NAFTA and the Politics of Labor Transnationalism

When the North American Free Trade Agreement (NAFTA) went into effect in 1994, many feared it would intensify animosity among North American unions, lead to the scapegoating of Mexican workers and immigrants, and eclipse any possibility for cross-border labor cooperation. But far from polarizing workers, NAFTA unexpectedly helped stimulate labor transnationalism among key North American unions and erode union policies and discourses rooted in racism. The emergence of labor transnationalism in North America presents compelling political and sociological puzzles: How did NAFTA, the concrete manifestation of globalization processes in North America, help deepen labor solidarity on the continent? And why did some unions more readily engage in transnational collaboration and embrace internationalism than others? In addition to making the provocative argument that global governance institutions can play a pivotal role in the development of transnational social movements, this book suggests that globalization need not undermine labor movements: collectively, unions can help shape how the rules governing the global economy are made.

Tamara Kay is Associate Professor of Sociology at Harvard University and Co-director of Harvard's Transnational Studies Initiative. Her work centers on the political and legal implications of regional economic integration, transnationalism, and global governance. She is interested in how organizations and social movements – particularly labor and environmental movements, nongovernmental organizations, and nonprofits – respond and adapt to processes of regional economic integration and globalization. Professor Kay has published in the *American Journal of Sociology* and the *American Sociological Review*. She has worked as a consultant to the International Labor Organization, the American Center for International Labor Solidarity, and the United Farmworkers of America. At Harvard, she has affiliations with the David Rockefeller Center for Latin American Studies, the Weatherhead Center for International Affairs, and the Hauser Center for Nonprofit Organizations.

Cambridge Studies in Contentious Politics

Editors

Mark Beissinger *Princeton University*
Jack A. Goldstone *George Mason University*
Michael Hanagan *Vassar College*
Doug McAdam *Stanford University and Center for Advanced Study in the Behavioral Sciences*
Suzanne Staggenborg *University of Pittsburgh*
Sidney Tarrow *Cornell University*
Charles Tilly (d. 2008) *Columbia University*
Elisabeth J. Wood *Yale University*
Deborah Yashar *Princeton University*

NAFTA and the Politics of Labor Transnationalism

TAMARA KAY
Harvard University

CAMBRIDGE
UNIVERSITY PRESS

CAMBRIDGE UNIVERSITY PRESS
Cambridge, New York, Melbourne, Madrid, Cape Town, Singapore,
São Paulo, Delhi, Dubai, Tokyo, Mexico City

Cambridge University Press
32 Avenue of the Americas, New York, NY 10013-2473, USA

www.cambridge.org
Information on this title: www.cambridge.org/9780521132954

First published 2011

Printed in the United States of America

A catalog record for this publication is available from the British Library.

Library of Congress Cataloging in Publication Data

Kay, Tamara, 1971–
NAFTA and the politics of labor transnationalism / Tamara Kay.
    p.   cm. – (Cambridge studies in contentious politics)
Includes bibliographical references and index.
ISBN 978-0-521-76287-8
1. Canada. Treaties, etc. 1992 Oct. 7.   2. Trade unions – North America.
3. Social movements – North America.   4. Transnationalism.   I. Title.   II. Series.
HF1746.K39   2010
331.88097 – dc22   2010011778

ISBN 978-0-521-76287-8 Hardback
ISBN 978-0-521-13295-4 Paperback

For my grandfather Michael Volpe, and
my husband, Harold Toro Tulla

Contents

Tables

Figures

Preface

Why NAFTA, why labor? Although this book is about the labor movement in North America, its central themes – how it is possible to build
social movements across borders and the effects of global governance
institutions on that process – resonate in an era in which most people understand the world through the prism of globalization. Whether
the poorest villagers fighting the construction of a dam or the wealth-
iest bureaucrats demanding banking regulation, all recognize that the
ubiquitous movement of capital, goods and services, and people across
the globe creates a web of both transparent and hidden connections. The
lessons learned from analyzing the case of NAFTA and labor transnationalism are therefore highly generalizable across issue areas; they speak to
international movements historically and currently, from those opposing
nuclear proliferation to those emerging to combat climate change. Even
as I write, the Greek economic collapse and an errant volcano threaten
the European Union, stirring debates about regulation and governance
while simultaneously highlighting our global interconnectedness.

NAFTA arrived at a moment in human history when many had begun
to contemplate their global connections. The end of the Cold War, which
had polarized the planet for decades, and the emergence of nascent democ-
racies around the world provided new opportunities to examine the links
among nations and activists. And there were many and varied links that
were reflected in the processes we now called globalization: the transfer
of new technologies, the explosion in communications, and the diffusion
of global political and cultural products (from national constitutions to
Sesame Street). At the same time, this moment laid bare the threats of
an expanding global economy. Economic expansion often benefited the

rich at the expense of the poor. Physical and intellectual property rights were privileged by and codified in the global economic order, but most social and human rights were not. The rules governing the global economy were made by elites generally behind closed doors, and when their policies failed or had disastrous unintended consequences, the majority of the world's citizens had little recourse. At the same time, the vast and dense network of economic ties among nations made each vulnerable to crises in others (which the U.S. economic meltdown in the fall of 2008 so aptly demonstrated as it rippled across the globe).

Most observers would not have guessed that a trade agreement would become the site of the first battle in the war against globalization and give birth to the antiglobalization movement that spread to Seattle, Quebec City, Mar del Plata, and beyond. One AFL-CIO official reflected on this improbability:

That you can really do grassroots work on a public policy issue, even one that is as arcane as a trade agreement, I mean who would have ever thought that a trade agreement was going to be the topic of dinner table conversation around the country? I mean it's a bizarre thing when you think about it, but in fact it was... for some people sort of revelatory. (Personal interview with Mark Anderson of the AFL-CIO, January 8, 2001)

In the early 1990s, however, trade captured all the tension and ambivalences about globalization, particularly for industrial workers who experienced its daily contradictions. Their jobs depended on trade but were vulnerable to its folly; factories closed at a moment's notice and reopened halfway around the world, imported products (whether cheaper or better) undercut sales of local ones, and entire industries were decimated because of fluctuations in stock prices, exchange and interest rates, and subsidies. Workers were at globalization's front line.

The effects of integration processes on North American unions and their responses to them provided the original question and the initial seed of an idea for this book. At Berkeley, I was in the right place at the right moment to contemplate it. In April 1998, Professor Harley Shaiken convened a gathering of labor activists from across the continent to discuss their experiences in NAFTA's wake. It quickly became clear that what was most compelling and unexpected was not what unions were doing to confront regional economic integration but *how* they were doing it – collectively. For two days, activists discussed building new transnational relationships and strategically using a complaint mechanism in NAFTA's side agreement to strengthen continent-wide labor rights campaigns. I was intrigued and decided to examine the origins, character, and limitations of labor transnationalism in North America.

I quickly realized that the same forces that congealed in the early 1990s to reveal globalization's limitations also exposed the proliferation of international laws, governance institutions, and nongovernmental organizations that could provide new arenas, tools, and opportunities for mobilization – including NAFTA. Although North American labor activists' opposition to NAFTA was expected, their decision to seize the new opportunities it provided and mobilize transnationally was not. Unions had never organized trinationally around a public policy issue in North America. Indeed, so many unions had stopped organizing domestically that some scholars no longer considered labor a social movement. Racism also constrained unions' abilities to build relationships across borders. It is this exceptionalism, however, that strengthens labor's value as a case; if the labor movement, stymied by racism, a parochial nationalism, and its bureaucratic iron cage, developed equitable transnational relationships, then movements without similar historical baggage should be even better equipped to do so.

Although the NAFTA story belongs to a particular time and place, the lessons from its analysis have significant implications beyond North America. It reveals the mechanisms and processes by which global governance institutions can help build social movements, demonstrating that even institutions with weak enforcement and policy outcomes can have strong movement outcomes. Almost no trade agreements, global governance institution instruments, or international human rights laws have strong enforcement mechanisms. Nation-states and corporations almost always oppose them. It is therefore important for scholars and movement actors to consider not only their architectures for enforcement but also those for movement building. Governance mechanisms can be structured to undermine or optimize movement outcomes. The NAFTA case is therefore relevant to the study of other movements and institutions, from climate change activists battling for international protocols to indigenous communities demanding World Bank protections, among many others. Engaging global governance institutions can help build transnational social movements.

Of course, the existence of global governance institutions does not guarantee movement building. NAFTA also serves as a useful case because unions responded differently to its effects, revealing the importance of leadership, strategy, and education to changing organizational cultures and illuminating how racism can be successfully challenged. Although racism was not completely eliminated among the continent's unions, it was significantly tempered, ultimately helping shift how unions deal with immigrant workers. As I write, labor unions in the United States are among the vanguard of the movement opposing Arizona's new draconian immigration law (SB 1070). Prior to NAFTA, that unions would lead the struggle for immigrant rights would have been unimaginable. The story of how NAFTA helped undermine racism is therefore one of the most important in the book, and it has largely been ignored in the historiography.

Ultimately the NAFTA story is about social change – how the North American labor movement changed our conception of trade in relationship to labor rights, how a toothless trade agreement changed the calculus by which labor activists evaluated the benefits of transnational activism, and how transnational collaboration changed the way activists saw each other and subsequently their international policies. These changes did not take root in every union; however, their permeation across the landscape of North American labor relations was transformative. In an era in which most people understand the world through the prism of globalization, the NAFTA case continues to resonate, allowing the seed of an idea to bear rich analytical fruit.

Acknowledgments

This book about solidarity was possible only because I benefited from so much of it. It takes a committed community to write a book, particularly one's first. Although mine changed and expanded as I moved into new phases of my life, it always provided the support I needed to meet new challenges and ultimately reach this final goal. This book began at Berkeley with mentors whose commitment to me both personally and professionally is unparalleled. Peter Evans, Neil Fligstein, Kim Voss, and Harley Shaiken's guidance and support enabled me to conceptualize this project, blossom intellectually, and maintain my vision. Their advice was invaluable and their dedication unwavering. Harley's indefatigable commitment to the labor movement ensured my access to key labor leaders and new events as they unfolded. Kim's early insistence on methodological rigor allowed me to explain variation in NAFTA's effect. Neil urged me to flesh out what NAFTA was a case of and root the analysis in broad sociological themes. Peter's mastery at identifying the inchoate ideas in the manuscript that would bloom with further development strengthened it immeasurably. His willingness to let me stumble at key moments – knowing that finding my own footing would allow me to develop confidence in my unique voice as a young scholar – was, and continues to be, his greatest gift to me.

I am particularly grateful to Peter, Neil, and Kim for remaining the pillars of my committed community even after I left the protective shadow of Barrows Hall. They continue to read and comment on my work, provide advice, and offer ceaseless encouragement. I am so grateful for their constant presence in my life.

I am also immensely fortunate that Peter recognized the importance of creating solidarity among his students, helping us form our own supportive community. Each week he welcomed us into his home, laid out a veritable feast of our favorite treats from Berkeley Bowl, and directed our discussions as we bonded and eagerly shared our work in the warmth of his living room. I am so thankful for those special evenings spent with him and Avri Beard, Malcolm Fairbrother, Christy Getz, Jason McNichol, Simone Pulver, Youyenn Teo, and particularly Angelina Godoy, who became my dissertation compañera. While in the field we encouraged and supported each other with email tomes of biblical proportions, and when in Berkeley we hunched over bottomless cups of coffee at Mocha Lisa to discuss our ideas, pore over chapter drafts, and debrief after months of challenging fieldwork. Lina's ability to persevere in the face of very difficult fieldwork (examining violence in Guatemala) and write a brilliant book was a constant source of inspiration for me.

This book is also the culmination of incredible support and intellectual insights from other friends and colleagues at Berkeley, and a few beyond Sather Gate, including David Bacon, Anthony Chen, Jennifer Chun, Barry Eidlin, Jacob Ely, Jill Esbenshade, Leslie Gates, Peter Olney, Sean O'Riain, Katie Quan, Robyn Rodriguez, Teresa Sharpe, Rachel Sherman, Kirsten Spalding, Eddy U, Paige Wyatt, and faculty and staff in the Department of Sociology, the Center for Labor Research and Education, and the Center for Latin American Studies. It was also made possible with financial support from the National Science Foundation and the Andrew W. Mellon Fellowship in Latin American Sociology, for which I am very grateful.

In September 2004, I left Berkeley for southern California. As a postdoctoral scholar at the Center for U.S.-Mexican Studies at the University of California, San Diego, I was welcomed into an incredible community of sociologists and an exciting interdisciplinary group of scholars at the Center who shared my love for Mexico. I am thankful for the mentorship of Chris Woodruff, Jeff Haydu, John Evans, Steve Epstein, Akos Rona-Tas, and Eric Van Young, and the support of Ruben Garcia and Jonathan Graubart. I am also fortunate to have the friendship and dedication of my book-writing group compañeros Tomás Jiménez and David Fitzgerald and the camaraderie of "las divas" – the female scholars of U.S.-Mex, who made sure that work was always balanced with fun, laughter, and great tequila.

My journey continued in 2006 when I left California for Cambridge. I arrived at Harvard and was quickly embraced into a new community that offered a tremendously rich intellectual environment. My colleagues in the Department of Sociology, the Weatherhead Center for International Affairs, the Hauser Center for Nonprofit Organizations, and the David Rockefeller Center for Latin American Studies have seen me through to the final stretch. Merilee Grindle, Jorge Domínguez, John Womack, and Steve Levitsky welcomed me into an engaged and exciting community of Latin American scholars and offered me ample opportunities to discuss and get feedback on my work. Elaine Bernard, Richard Freeman, and Paul Weiler nourished me and kept me well connected to the labor movement through my participation in the Harvard Trade Union Program. My colleagues at Harvard Law School, Martha Minow, Lani Guinier, and Ken Mack, included me in their community, engaging me in lively discussions of law and social movements. And my co-directors of the Transnational Studies Initiative, Sanjeev Khagram and Peggy Levitt, helped me hone my conception of transnationalism.

I am particularly appreciative to Beth Simmons and the Weatherhead Center for funding and organizing my book conference that brought Frank Dobbin, Malcolm Fairbrother, Andrew Schrank, Sidney Tarrow, and Chris Tilly together to discuss the manuscript. They each read it from cover to cover, provided pages of written comments, and devoted two days to discussing it and helping me sharpen my arguments. Words cannot express how grateful I am for their brilliant insights, sage suggestions, and unmeasured enthusiasm. Sid has continued to offer invaluable comments on updated drafts and shepherd the book toward publication, and to him I owe a big debt of gratitude. Lance Compa also read the full manuscript, offered tremendous feedback, and very generously and quickly answered technical legal questions at the final hour. Michèle Lamont and Peter Marsden also deserve special thanks for their encouragement and guidance through the publication process. For running technical reconnaissance on the final manuscript I thank the staff in the Department of Sociology, particularly Sonya Keller Driscoll, Laura Thomas, and Suzanne Washington, and graduate students Anmol Chaddha for examining union immigration policies, Oana Dan for analyzing NAAEC submission data, and Min Zhou for updating trade data. I also thank Jason Beckfield, Prudence Carter, Rowan Flad, Duana Fullwiley, Marshall Ganz, Filiz Garip, Neil Gross, In Paik, Rossana Rocha Reis, Mariano Siskind, and Jocelyn Viterna for their friendship and ceaseless encouragement.

Working with the editors and staff at Cambridge University Press has been an extraordinary experience. I am grateful for Lewis Bateman's clear and impeccable vision and generous stewardship, and so thankful for the inordinate amount of time that he, Professor Michael Hanagan and the editors of the *Cambridge Studies in Contentious Politics* series, and reviewers devoted to the manuscript. I am deeply appreciative of all Anne Lovering Rounds, Emily Spangler, and Helen Wheeler did to whip the manuscript into its final form. Some data from the book were originally published as "Labor Transnationalism and Global Governance: The Impact of NAFTA on Transnational Labor Relationships in North America" in the *American Journal of Sociology* (2005) and are reprinted by permission of the *AJS*. Other data from the book were originally published as "Legal Transnationalism: The Relationship Between Transnational Social Movement Building and International Law," *Law and Social Inquiry* (2011), copyright 2011 by the American Bar Foundation.

I thank the friends whose solidarity has sustained me for decades, cheering me on as the book took form and came to fruition: Nura Aly, Joshua Bloom, Angelina Godoy, Elliot Hinds, Sheila Holmes, Leah Johns, Gina Losito, Isaac Mankita, Isaac Martin, Dena Mottola, Mary Ann Mrugalski, Eréndira Rueda, Jason Spicer, Jennifer Utrata, and Travis Winfrey. But most of all I thank my family, whose undying commitment allowed me to cross the finish line. They include my parents, Karla and Michael Kay, and sister Rana Kay, and the Volpe and Toro families who form a steadfast circle of love and support. My mother deserves special thanks for her research assistance: photocopying union newspapers for days at Princeton, carrying my bags around Mexico City from interview to interview after I broke my shoulder and three ribs (well, after the horse did), and shuttling me to and from the airport at any and all hours.

My family also includes Rhonda Evans, Karriann Farrell Hinds, and Rebecca Milliken and their families. I am truly blessed by the years of love, laughter, and sisterhood-friendship they have given me. Their generosity is limitless, their wisdom boundless, their positivity infectious, and their devotion ceaseless. For them, my gratitude is profoundly beyond words. Above all else, I am thankful for my grandfather Michael Volpe (Bopie), with whom I shared a mutual devotion. Throughout his life he lavished me with words of encouragement and praise, reassured me in moments of difficulty and doubt, and reminded me that my true value would not be measured in the scholarship I produced but by the kindness and compassion I cultivated. He gave me resilience and strength, and his love sustains me still.

This book is about unintended consequences and the biggest for me is that writing it brought me to a person who is the most cherished and beloved in my life, Harold Toro Tulla. Our first years together in Berkeley were magical, spent salsa dancing in the Mission, running with the beloved pooch in Tilden, rummaging through Moe's and Rasputin's for rare copies of Durkheim and Mahler, and enjoying countless special moments with so many close and wonderful friends (when we weren't poring over our work, of course). Harold contributed so much to this project intellectually, but more importantly he contributed so much to the richness of my life, which enabled me to embrace and savor the hard work of completing this book. His encouragement and incomparable sense of humor bolstered me; his unwavering integrity, love, and limitless empathy strengthened me; and his insatiable intellectual and creative curiosity made every day exciting and still leave me always joyfully anticipating the next. It is to him – el amor de mi vida – and to my grandfather that I dedicate this book.

The most fulfilling part of writing this book was speaking with the labor activists who work so tirelessly for social justice in North America. I was riveted by their experiences and awed by their steadfastness and creative vision. I will forever cherish the memories of time spent traversing the continent; skating the serene frozen azure of the Rideau (not in a circle, but with a destination!), witnessing the outcome of the 2000 presidential elections in the bustling offices of the AFL-CIO, and marching across the zócalo in Mexico City with thousands of colorfully clad workers on May Day. I thank you all for helping me cultivate and appreciate my own North American identity.

San Juan, Puerto Rico

List of Abbreviations

ACILS	American Center for International Labor Solidarity
ACTPN	Advisory Committee on Trade Policy and Negotiations
ACTWU	Amalgamated Clothing and Textile Workers Union
AFL-CIO	American Federation of Labor-Congress of Industrial Organizations
AIFLD	American Institute for Free Labor Development
ANAD	National Association of Democratic Lawyers (Asociación Nacional de Abogados Democráticos)
CAW	Canadian Auto Workers
CEP	Communications, Energy, and Paperworkers Union
CETLAC	Education Center and Labor Workshop (Centro de Estudios y Taller Laboral A.C.)
CIA	Central Intelligence Agency
CILAS	Labor Research and Union Assistance Center (Centro de Investigación Laboral y Asesoría Sindical)
CJM	Coalition for Justice in the Maquiladoras
CLC	Canadian Labour Congress
CROC	Revolutionary Confederation of Workers and Peasants (Confederación Revolucionario de Obreros y Campesinos)
CROM	Regional Confederation of Mexican Workers (Confederación Regional de Obreros Mexicanos)
CT	Labor Congress (Congreso del Trabajo)

CTM	Confederation of Mexican Workers (Confederación de Trabajadores de México)
CUFTA	Canada-U.S. Free Trade Agreement
CUSWA	United Steelworkers in Canada
CWA	Communication Workers of America
CWC	Communication Workers of Canada
ECE	Evaluation Committee of Experts
FAT	Authentic Labor Front (Frente Auténtico del Trabajo)
FESEBES	Federation of Goods and Services Unions (Federación de Sindicatos de Bienes y Servicios)
FLACSO	Latin American Faculty of Social Sciences (Facultad Latinoamericana de Ciencias Sociales)
FTA	U.S.-Mexico Free Trade Agreement (before the inclusion of Canada)
FTAA	Free Trade Agreement of the Americas
GATT	General Agreement on Tariffs and Trade
GE	General Electric
GSP	Generalized System of Preferences
GU(F)	Global Union (Federation)
HERE	Hotel Employees and Restaurant Employees International Union
HSA	Hemispheric Social Alliance
IACHR	Inter-American Court of Human Rights
IAM	International Association of Machinists and Aerospace Workers
IBT	International Brotherhood of Teamsters
ICFTU	International Confederation of Free Trade Unions
ILGWU	International Ladies' Garment Workers' Union
ILO	International Labor Organization
IRCA	Immigration Reform and Control Act of 1986
ISI	import-substituting industrialization
ITS	International Trade Secretariat
IUE	International Union of Electronic, Electrical, Salaried, Machine and Furniture Workers
MAI	Multilateral Agreement on Investment
MERCOSUR	Southern Common Market (Mercado Común del Sur)
NAAEC	North American Agreement on Environmental Cooperation

NAALC	North American Agreement on Labor Cooperation
NAFTA	North American Free Trade Agreement
NAO	National Administrative Office
NDP	New Democratic Party
NGO	nongovernmental organization
OECD	Organisation for Economic Co-operation and Development
ORIT	Inter-American Regional Workers' Organization
PAN	National Action Party (Partido Acción Nacional)
PRD	Party of the Democratic Revolution (Partido de la Revolución Democrática)
PRI	Institutional Revolutionary Party (Partido Revolucionario Institucional)
PSI	Public Services International
PTTI	Postal, Telephone, and Telegraph International
RMALC	Mexican Action Network on Free Trade (Red Mexicana De Accion Frente Al Libre Comercio)
SEIU	Service Employees' International Union
SEMARNAP	Secretariat of the Environment, Natural Resources and Fisheries (Secretaría de Medio Ambiente y Recursos Naturales)
SITIAVW	Independent Union of Workers of the Volkswagen Automobile Industry (Sindicato Independiente de Trabajadores de la Industria Automotriz Volkswagen)
SME	Mexican Electrical Workers Union (Sindicato Mexicano de Electricistas)
SNTMMSRM	Mexican Miners and Metal Workers Union (Sindicato Nacional de Trabajadores Mineros, Metalúrgicos y Similares de la República Mexicana)
STIMAHCS	Union of Workers in the Metal, Iron, Steel, and Related and Similar Industries (Sindicato de Trabajadores de la Industria Metálica, Acero, Hierro, Conexos y Similares)
STRM	Mexican Telephone Workers' Union (Sindicato de Telefonistas de la República Mexicana)
UAW	United Automobile, Aerospace & Agricultural Implement Workers of America International Union

UE	The United Electrical, Radio and Machine Workers of America
UFW	The United Farmworkers of America
UNI	Union Network International
UNITE	The Union of Needletrades, Industrial and Textile Employees
UNT	National Union of Workers (Union Nacional de Trabajadores)
USAID	United States Agency for International Development
USTR	United States Trade Representative
USW	United Steelworkers of America
WTO	World Trade Organization

1

Introduction

NAFTA and Labor Transnationalism

Globalization arrived full force in North America in the form of a free trade agreement. While the economies of the United States, Canada, and Mexico had been integrating for decades, the process largely remained beneath the radar, inspiring little reaction from political pundits, the media, and the general public. Mexico's 1986 entry into the General Agreement on Tariffs and Trade (GATT) produced little public criticism, and resistance to the negotiation of the Canada-U.S. Free Trade Agreement (CUFTA) in the mid-1980s largely remained within Canadian borders. Talk that the George H.W. Bush Administration was considering an idea proffered by President Reagan in the 1980s to create a free trade zone extending across the Americas raised the hackles of free trade opponents.[1] But no one could have predicted the groundswell of grassroots opposition that occurred across the continent upon the North American Free Trade Agreement's (NAFTA) formal announcement in September 1990.

The public reaction to NAFTA was unprecedented. Politicians, presidential hopefuls, media personalities, and organizations representing interests as diverse as consumers and peasants entered the fray. The

---

[1] In his State of the Union Message delivered to Congress in January 1988, President Ronald Reagan proclaimed: "Next month I will be traveling to Mexico where trade matters will be of foremost concern. And, over the next several months, our Congress and the Canadian Parliament can make the start of such a North American accord a reality. Our goal must be a day when the free flow of trade – from the tip of Tierra del Fuego to the Arctic Circle – unites the people of the Western Hemisphere in a bond of mutually beneficial exchange; when all borders become what the U.S.-Canadian border so long has been – a meeting place, rather than a dividing line." *New York Times*, January 26, 1988.

overwhelming response led many observers to proclaim that NAFTA was responsible for repoliticizing trade politics and for ushering in an era of antiglobalization activism that would be felt from Seattle to Montreal, from Genoa to Mumbai.[2] NAFTA's most vocal critics warned of its potential effects on U.S. jobs and industries. Ross Perot memorably proclaimed that a "giant sucking sound" would be heard as jobs left the country. Many on the Left worried that by pitting workers against each other for jobs, the agreement would generate antagonism among North American unions and intensify economic nationalism.[3] They cautioned that NAFTA would undermine any possibility for cross-border cooperation among labor unions in the United States, Mexico, and Canada. Some suggested that the inevitable job losses north of the Rio Grande would generate a backlash against Mexican workers and immigrants. That in NAFTA's wake North American labor movements would be able to overcome geographic, linguistic, cultural, and ideological differences to create interests in common seemed improbable.

A Historic Shift

But, contrary to expectations, that is exactly what happened. Far from polarizing workers, this much hated neoliberal free trade agreement actually brought them together. NAFTA's effects on trinational coalition and relationship building were unprecedented. Labor unions' participation in anti-NAFTA coalitions that included organizations devoted to many different issues reflected a significant shift in the history of union relations in North America. For the first time, and practically overnight, North American labor unions engaged in an active struggle not only with environmental and other progressive organizations but also with their counterparts across the continent. And some unions even began to build formal relationships with their counterparts that transcended coalitional goals.

NAFTA – the concrete embodiment of globalization in North America – had the unanticipated consequence of catalyzing labor transnationalism, defined as ongoing cooperative and collaborative relationships among Mexican, U.S., and Canadian unions and union federations.[4] After years of struggle against free trade, North American labor unions, which for

---

[2] Evans (2002). See Rupert (1995) and O'Brien (1998).
[3] See Davis (1993), Neal (1993), and Farrell and Putzel (1993).
[4] Here I focus on labor unions and not other labor advocacy organizations such as NGOs, worker centers, etc.

decades had been isolated and estranged across national boundaries, emerged with new ties of cooperation and networks of protest. But NAFTA's effects went far beyond catalyzing labor transnationalism. The trade agreement also stimulated significant organizational changes within unions and union federations. Union leaders realized that in order to survive the vagaries of regional economic integration, they needed to create departments and positions to deal with trade, amend official policies to promote internationalism, and chip away at racist attitudes against Mexicans and immigrants that permeated their organizations. Thus, for many North American unions, NAFTA began to erode policies and discourses rooted in racism and economic nationalism.

The rarity of labor transnationalism makes its emergence extremely significant. Since the formation of the International Workingmen's Association (or First International) in 1864, workers and labor unions have articulated the need for a global working-class movement, yet the goal remains elusive. Labor scholars point to the multiple geographical, cultural, and political obstacles to labor transnationalism, while some economists insist that the interests of labor unions in developed and developing countries are antagonistic and therefore preclude cooperation (Bhagwati 2000). The Cold War exploits of the American Federation of Labor and Congress of Industrial Organizations (AFL-CIO) in Latin America created significant distrust and alienation among unions in North America.[5] And northern unions' tendency to discriminate against Mexicans and immigrants also did little to build trust with Mexican counterparts. For decades unions employed racialized rhetoric not only to respond to competition from immigrants at home but also to deal with competition from foreign factories and imports. Some U.S. and Canadian labor leaders responded to the threat of job loss by blaming foreign workers for "stealing" jobs and undercutting nonimmigrant workers by accepting lower wages. Racial scapegoating amounts to a racialized "foreign worker myth" that is often married to racist rhetoric about the abilities of foreign workers (e.g., foreign workers do not produce high-quality products and are not as skilled, productive, or capable as the workers from whom the work was "stolen"). Northern unions' international policies, dictated by Cold War politics, and their domestic policies, clouded by racism, combined to form a weak foundation for transnationalism. As a result, a lack of trust and permanence characterized contacts among North American unions prior

---

[5] See Cantor and Schor (1987), Spalding (1992), Morris (1967), and Herod (1997).

to NAFTA through various international and regional organizations.[6] Union interactions were not equitable, lacked long-term goals and programs, and rarely involved grassroots participation.[7]

The interactions that emerged in NAFTA's wake among North American unions stand in stark contrast to the sporadic and formal contacts that preceded them. Unions began to build and nurture relationships of a certain nature and quality. If the interactions in the pre-NAFTA era were like noncommittal dating, those after NAFTA were marriages. Most were written commitments to permanent, consistent interactions based on joint action and grassroots participation. But the most important characteristic of these nascent relationships was their unprecedented rootedness in equality and collective interest. And, although the process of chipping away at stereotypes was not uniform across the continent, divisive attitudes that blamed foreign workers and immigrants for potential NAFTA-related job loss north of the Rio Grande surfaced infrequently among labor leaders in the United States and Canada – and were frequently censured when articulated by the rank and file. The shift from Cold War era interactions was therefore quite striking.

The end of the Cold War, however, was not responsible for the emergence of transnational relationships among North American unions. There was a significant lag time between the end of the Cold War and the reconfiguration of the AFL-CIO's priorities and institutional structures. Although some changes did occur beginning in the early 1990s, more significant changes came after John Sweeney was elected president of the AFL-CIO in 1995. Sweeney reorganized the international department and eliminated the controversial American Institute for Free Labor Development (AIFLD) in 1997.[8] Many Cold War era staffers were replaced or left the federation, undermining its Cold War strategy. Thus the effects of the end of the Cold War within the AFL-CIO came years after initial transnational relationships were forged in the early 1990s.[9] According to

---

[6] Such as the World Federation of Trade Unions, the International Confederation of Free Trade Unions (ICFTU), and international trade secretariats (now called global unions, or global union federations, GUs and GUFs).

[7] For a discussion of the history and limitations of international labor organizations, see Stevis (1998) and Boswell and Stevis (1997). I characterize union relations in the pre-NAFTA era as similar to what Tarrow (1998) terms "contingent political alliances," which are based on ephemeral transnational "relays" or exchanges between social activists.

[8] Critics argue that AIFLD helped the U.S. government oust radical Left labor leaders, unions, and regimes, particularly in Latin America. For more on AIFLD, see Chapter 2.

[9] Some critics argue that the Cold War strategy has not died completely because a few influential Cold War era staffers remain, and the Solidarity Center continues to accept funds from the U.S. government.

Figure 1.1. North American Trade, 1950–2000. The trade data come from the "Direction of Trade" dataset compiled by the International Monetary Fund and have been adjusted by the U.S. Consumer Price Index (1982–1984=100) to correct for inflation. The following discussion is based on these data.

AFL-CIO officials, NAFTA actually helped to undermine the federation's Cold War priorities by forcing leaders to deal with the threats posed by regional economic integration. And, ironically, it was NAFTA itself that helped unions across the continent define and develop collective "North American" interests.

NAFTA as Catalyst? Alternative Economic Explanations

What, then, was unique about NAFTA? Some critics argue not much, and offer an economic explanation for the emergence of labor transnationalism in its wake: it was not NAFTA per se that catalyzed transnational relationships but rather the increased trade and market openings it stimulated. This explanation is problematic because although trade and investment have characterized the relationships between North American countries for decades, labor transnationalism has not. As Figure 1.1 shows, the long-term trend in North America is toward increased trade.

In 1950, U.S. exports to and imports from Canada were at parity; each figure hovered at just over $8 billion (all dollar figures in U.S. dollars). By 1980, U.S. exports to Canada reached almost $47 billion and U.S. imports from Canada reached approximately $50 billion. In

1950, Mexican exports to the United States were at $1.6 billion, and U.S. exports to Mexico were at $1.9 billion. In 1965, the Mexican government decided to boost the economy by introducing an export-oriented assembly industry program, which stimulated tremendous growth in trade. Mexico further solidified its commitment to export strategies in 1986 when it joined the General Agreement on Tariffs and Trade (GATT, which later became the World Trade Organization, WTO). Between 1970 and 1990, Mexican exports to the United States increased more than sevenfold from $2.6 billion to $19 billion, and U.S. exports to Mexico rose from $3.9 billion to more than $18 billion. Increasing trade has also characterized the relationship between Canada and Mexico. Between 1950 and 1990 Canadian exports to Mexico rose from $55.2 million to $336 million, and Mexican exports to Canada surged from $72.1 million to $653 million.[10]

If market openings alone are responsible for generating transnational relationships, we would expect to see a surge in transnationalism at critical historical moments of market expansion such as after Mexico implemented its export program or joined the GATT. But these openings did not generate transnational labor relationships, and neither did neoliberal state policies intended to stimulate trade and investment. As Table 1.1 shows, privatization and deregulation have proceeded at a gallop in North America since the 1980s, and although many unions opposed and fought these policies, they did not coordinate their opposition as a united transnational labor movement. Nor did they direct their ire against North American neoliberalism, which seemed to be sweeping the continent. Rather, they focused inward and tried to influence their respective states.[11]

NAFTA's Effects on Transnationalism

The emergence of labor transnationalism in North America therefore presents compelling sociological and political puzzles. First, how did

[10] Because these lines hover on the *x* axis, I do not include them in Figure 1.1.
[11] Moreover, many privatization and deregulation strategies were implemented in the mid-1990s, years after transnational labor relationships emerged. And, the majority of transnational relationships that emerged in the early 1990s occurred among unions that were not subjected to privatization or deregulation efforts. There is one exception, however. The breakup of the Bell system in 1984 forced the CWA to create ties with its Canadian counterpart in order to deal with increasingly recalcitrant management policies. The transnational relationship, however, did not include the Mexican telecommunications union (STRM) until NAFTA became a significant threat in the early 1990s.

Table 1.1. *Privatization and Deregulation in North America*

	United States	Canada	Mexico
Telecommunications	1984 (deregulation)	1998 (deregulation)	1989–1991 (privatization)
Airlines	1978–1986 (deregulation)	1988 (Air Canada)	1988 (Aeromexico) 1989 (Mexicana) (privatization)
Electric utilities	1992	varies by province; unions currently fighting efforts at deregulation and privatization	unions currently fighting efforts at privatization
Road transportation			1989 (trucking)
Rail industry	1976–1980 (deregulation)	1995 (privatization)	1997–2000 (privatization)
Banking	late 1970s, early 1980s (deregulation)		1989

NAFTA catalyze labor transnationalism? And, why did some unions more readily engage in transnational collaboration and embrace internationalism than others? Although the evidence supporting an economic explanation for NAFTA's effect is not terribly convincing, that for a political explanation is quite compelling. The answers to these questions about NAFTA's effect on labor transnationalism lie not simply in what NAFTA symbolized to North American labor activists – the concretization and institutionalization of neoliberal economic policies and the downward harmonization of wages and labor standards across the continent – but rather in what NAFTA *created*. NAFTA, an emergent "multilateral regime,"[12] a particular kind of global governance institution, catalyzed labor transnationalism by creating two new transnational institutional arenas through which North American labor activists could engage each other.[13] These new arenas were critical because they provided a space to mobilize collective action while constituting as transnational actors the very activists that would engage that space.

[12] For a discussion of multilateral regimes, see Krasner (1983) and Ruggie (1993).
[13] NAFTA is more accurately a regional governance institution, but for simplicity and consistency with the term used in the literature, I will refer to it as a global governance institution.

Here I refer to these new arenas as fields, defining a field as a "local social order"[14] of actors "who take one another into account as they carry out interrelated activities"[15] and *that is characterized by an orienting principle or goal* (Evans and Kay 2008).[16] The first new institutional field NAFTA created in 1990 was a transnational trade-negotiating field in which state officials and labor representatives in the United States, Mexico, and Canada hammered out the nature and scope of the substantive trade agreement and ultimately the labor side agreement. Although dominated by trade and business officials, the negotiating field also included labor representatives who participated directly through advisory committees and indirectly through allies in the U.S. Congress with access to negotiators. This new institutional field was critical to stimulating labor transnationalism during NAFTA's negotiation because it provided labor activists with a concrete target of engagement and protest that straddled the borders of North America. Labor unions in Canada, the United States, and Mexico, which for years had been isolated and estranged, could target not only nation-states and the general public but also a new and viable transnational institutional field.

During the prepassage contestation over NAFTA, activists' ongoing interactions in this field helped constitute them as transnational actors and enabled them to forge collective interests. NAFTA stimulated this process by serving as a collective threat to North American unions, which began to see their futures as linked, bringing them into contact and helping coalesce their interests, and compelling them to define and defend what they considered to be North American labor rights. During all stages of NAFTA's negotiation, unions worked in trinational coalitions lobbying their individual nation-states and mobilizing popular support to demand that the agreement have teeth.[17]

Debates over fast-track reauthorization provided an early opportunity for unions to mobilize politically, as well as for members of Congress to signal their demands to trade negotiators. Granted by Congress, fast-track privileges enable the president to negotiate trade agreements while restricting Congress's ability to amend them. Although fast-track extension was accepted in May 1991, labor activists working with sympathetic members of Congress forced President George H.W. Bush to develop an

---

[14] Fligstein (2001, p. 5).
[15] McAdam and Scott (2005, p. 10).
[16] See also DiMaggio and Powell (1991) and Fligstein (2001) for discussions of fields.
[17] As will be discussed, official Mexican unions such as the CTM, however, supported NAFTA.

action plan to deal with labor concerns.[18] When substantive negotiations concluded in August 1992, they were profoundly disappointed by the enormous 900-page document that included no labor rights protections and primarily reflected business interests. Both House Ways and Means Chair Dan Rostenkowski and House Majority Leader Richard Gephardt discussed the possibility of renegotiating the agreement because its passage appeared unlikely. The timing of the final negotiations catapulted the issue of free trade into the 1992 presidential election campaign and presented a problem for presidential candidate Bill Clinton. Whoever won the election could renegotiate the agreement, or would have the arduous task of garnering congressional support for it. But Clinton knew that labor and other anti-NAFTA activists would vigorously resist the agreement as negotiated by his predecessor and that without more stringent labor and environmental protections Congress probably would not ratify it.

Under intense pressure from labor and environmental activists, Clinton announced on the eve of the election his support for supplemental labor and environmental agreements. In November 1992, Clinton was elected president, and under his administration environmental and labor side agreements were negotiated to salvage NAFTA beginning in March 1993. Although they had pushed him to commit to stronger labor protections, many labor activists did not support a side agreement because they feared a political bait and switch; the administration could codify – before the outcome of supplemental negotiations would be determined – unacceptable policies in the primary agreement that would be difficult if not impossible to amend (Kay and Evans unpublished ms.)

Clinton, however, stirred unions' hopes that the labor side agreement would have teeth, proclaiming in a 1992 speech that a commission "should be established for worker standards and safety. It too should have extensive powers to educate, train, develop minimum standards and have similar dispute resolution powers and remedies. We have got to do this. This is a big deal."[19] Persuaded by administration officials who promised to address their concerns and heed their input, some unions – including the AFL-CIO and many of its affiliates – waited until side agreement negotiations had almost concluded to pass judgment. When the final agreement was unveiled in August 1993, they expressed their outrage over its inadequacy, and at their betrayal by a president they had helped elect.

---

[18] The action plan also addressed environmentalists' concerns. See Evans and Kay (2008).
[19] Clinton (1992).

Despite unions' efforts to kill the agreement, President Clinton cobbled together enough votes to secure its passage. An underlying distrust, however, characterized labor leaders' relationship with the president and the NAALC for the next eight years.

When NAFTA went into force on January 1, 1994, it created a second transnational institutional arena for activists to engage – a transnational legal field. This field consisted of nascent legal mechanisms, including the North American Agreement on Labor Cooperation (NAALC, NAFTA's labor side agreement), and National Administrative Offices (NAOs) in each of the three NAFTA countries. These new institutions were critical to stimulating new transnational relationships and nurturing existing ones because they enabled labor activists collectively to invoke and demand protection for newly defined North American labor rights claims. The NAALC created eleven North American labor principles or rights recognized by the three countries and established new rules, procedures, and venues to adjudicate complaints of labor rights violations in North America. But most significantly, by requiring submitters to file complaints outside of their home countries, the NAALC forced labor activists to seek assistance from counterparts in another NAFTA country and thereby catalyzed transnational relationships that had not previously existed.

The transnational institutional arenas NAFTA created were unprecedented, and so were their effects. But their potency lies in their constitutive functions: in the political mobilization period during NAFTA's negotiation, transnational interests and actors were created, and during the period of NAFTA's implementation, actors and rights claims were legitimized. The NAFTA story, then, is about how political-institutional fields serve as new transnational political opportunity structures for emergent transnational social movements. Faced with a trade agreement that could potentially undermine labor rights and standards in North America, labor unions entered these new political-institutional arenas to mobilize. Through their interactions, they began to develop not only a collective strategy and agenda for changing the rules of regional economic integration but also a sense of their collective interests as North American workers.

Variations in NAFTA's Effect

Despite the strength of NAFTA's effect, not all unions developed transnational relationships in its wake. The NAFTA story, then, has a sequel. The first part of the story centers on how NAFTA's institutional structures created new transnational opportunities for labor unions. The second part of the story focuses on how unions responded differently to those opportunities. As economic integration proceeded, North American unions and labor federations were differentially constituted as transnational actors. The majority of union leaders recognized that they shared some common interests with their counterparts across the continent, but the degree to which they embraced labor transnationalism varied significantly. Moreover, unions' adoption of strategies that furthered mutual interests through concrete action was not uniform. The obvious question then, is what explains the variation in the emergence of labor transnationalism in North America?

The most significant predictors of cross-border engagement are not economic but rather political; unions with progressive leadership that granted key players the authority to direct and nurture relationships were more likely to engage in transnationalism than unions in which NAFTA was simply perceived as a threat. Key actors in these unions – many of whom participated in the struggles around the Vietnam War and civil rights – altered the calculus of support for transnationalism by seeking out and nurturing relationships and educating and including the rank and file. Unions' cultural and organizational characteristics therefore had a tremendous effect on the emergence of labor transnationalism. The consistency of transnationalism with a progressive agenda helps explain its emergence among progressive unions. Ideologically left-of-center unions are more likely to value solidarity in theory and in practice, and to have key staff people that prioritize cooperation and manage relationship building. Moreover, unions that aggressively try to purge racism at home are less likely to tolerate it as part of their international policy.

In order to understand NAFTA's catalytic effect on North American unions, then, we must examine not only the nature of the transnational political opportunity structure it created but also the unique characteristics of unions poised to take advantage of it. It is important to emphasize that although I examine unions' central role and activities in the anti-NAFTA struggle – arguably the most significant social movement in North American history – much of my analysis centers on the emergence of trinational labor coalitions and campaigns, and relationships among unions. It would be too strong to claim the emergence of a coherent and well-defined North American labor movement in response to NAFTA. The process of coalition and relationship building it generated, however, richly informs and expands our understanding of transnational social movement emergence. Its analysis both benefits from and extends the theoretical tools employed in social movements scholarship. The remainder of this chapter will examine how studying NAFTA's effects on labor transnationalism helps us create better models to understand transnational social movements and governance institutions. Specifically, it will reconceptualize the dimensions of political opportunity structures and explore the constitutive effects of transnational institutional fields on social movements.

Transnational Institutional Fields: Connecting the Global and Local

A study of NAFTA offers a promising arena for developing a theory of political opportunity structure and mobilization that can link routine and contentious actions at both the domestic and transnational levels. In order for labor unions to build transnational relationships, however, they must begin to see their interests as mutual. Although it is possible for unions to do this outside the context of institutional fields, the NAFTA story shows that the creation of a new transnational field can be a quite powerful catalyst for labor transnationalism. The case therefore allows us to build theories about the emergence of transnational social movements in relationship to institutional fields.

Organizational scholars have focused on the creation of new fields, competing logics within fields, and the effect of outsiders on fields (see Armstrong 2002; Clemens 1993; Lounsbury 2007; Schneiberg and Soule 2005; McAdam and Scott 2005). Despite extensive scholarship on internal field dynamics, however, there has been little work on transnational fields and how they shape social movement activities and mobilization. And yet the institutional fields that NAFTA created cross national boundaries and serve as sites where social actors and their organizations frame issues, mobilize, build networks and coalitions, and contest or advocate particular policies or practices.

Theorizing the dynamics of transnational fields is critically important because they straddle transnational and national arenas. That is, actors are simultaneously rooted in a transnational context and their national context. This is particularly relevant for the labor movement, which, unlike other movements, has a unique institutional relationship with the state. In all three NAFTA countries, labor unions have obligations and responsibilities vis-à-vis the state, which in turn has obligations to unions, particularly in countries that have a corporatist structure, such as Mexico. Labor movements across the continent are therefore constrained by laws that dictate the strategies workers may use and the institutional mechanisms they must engage in their struggles against employers and the state.

Whereas other social movements are relatively autonomous from the state and can choose to eschew legal-institutional strategies altogether and focus primarily or solely on disruptive politics (as the environmental and antiglobalization movements can do), the labor movement must invoke legal-institutional mechanisms as part of its tactical repertoire. Failure to do so constitutes a violation of labor laws (e.g., if a U.S. union initiated a wildcat strike and refused to bargain in good faith). The ability of social movements to use disruptive noninstitutionalized tactics such as protests, strikes, boycotts, and the like can be critical to their success. It is hard to imagine that the U.S. civil rights movement would have been as effective without the bus boycott and the sit-in. Indeed, these strategies were crucial to the movement's success: they enabled activists to create openings in unfavorable political environments in which institutionalized grievance mechanisms were blocked. And yet effective strategies such as these are often denied to labor movements in all three NAFTA countries by legal restrictions and limitations. The relationship between the labor movement and the state is therefore contained within a prescribed and historically contingent national institutional field.

In many respects, labor movements are therefore quintessential *national* movements; they look to their states for protection and to redress what are usually local or national grievances. Because labor movements are primarily oriented toward their own nation-states, the emergence of labor transnationalism is unexpected and therefore quite compelling. Theorizing the dynamics of transnational fields illuminates the competing logics within them that emerge from their links to both domestic and transnational arenas. It also addresses a growing debate among scholars regarding the relevance of the nation-state in an era of globalization and, by extension, the efficacy of local versus global (or regional) social movement strategies.

The model of transnational fields I offer here suggests that constructing the local and global in opposition to each other is misguided. For labor unions with institutionalized relationships to the state, participating in a transnational labor movement that is completely autonomous from national arenas is not possible; when engaging transnationally, labor movements always straddle domestic *and* transnational arenas. Moreover, for unions to gain maximum leverage across fields that link domestic and international institutions, they must apply pressure locally (nationally) *and* internationally. Understanding transnational fields therefore helps reconcile the local–global dichotomy and social movement strategies that simultaneously target domestic and transnational institutions (such as nation-states and regional or global governance institutions).

Unions' rootedness in their national contexts also helps explain why not all unions exposed to NAFTA's institutional fields developed transnational relationships. Unions with less progressive leaders who constructed their interests nationally in relationship to the state were unable or unwilling to forge transnational ties. The strong pull of the national means that breaking out of its confines in order to build relationships transnationally can be extremely difficult. Transnational relationship building requires not simply economic incentives but an ideological vision and a strategic plan. Prior to NAFTA, North American labor unions framed their struggles primarily in nationalistic terms. But NAFTA's negotiation and passage helped constitute a core group of North American labor activists, who began to build a new understanding of their struggles not only as inextricably linked but also as shared. It was only when regional economic processes were infused with concrete political consequences that labor activists were moved to act trinationally. But it was only when NAFTA created new transnational institutional fields that they were able to mobilize effectively.

National and Transnational Political Opportunity Structures

The NAFTA story therefore shows that transnational institutional fields can serve as new transnational political opportunity structures, or openings for transnational movement building. The idea that transnational institutional fields span the domestic and the transnational helps ground a theory of transnational political opportunity structure in relationship to transnational social movement emergence. The concept of political opportunity, defined as "consistent – but not necessarily formal, permanent, or national – signals to social or political actors, which either encourage or discourage them to use their internal resources to form social movements," helps explain how political systems are challenged and how new political actors emerge.[20] Very little is actually known about the emergence of transnational social movements and the transnational political opportunity structures that affect them because political process theory developed almost exclusively in relationship to national

---

[20] Tarrow (1996, p. 54). For detailed discussions of political opportunity structures, see Tarrow (1994) and Kriesi et al. (1995).

social movements and nation-states. How well, then, does political process theory explain the emergence and strategic nuances of transnational
social movements? Specifically, can theories of national political opportunity structures simply be applied whole cloth to transnational political
opportunity structures, or do they need refinement to account for the
particularities of transnational social movements and their unique relationship to nation-states and global governance institutions?

Scholars are only beginning to tackle these questions. Whereas some
account for "multilayered" opportunity structures and "multilevel poli-
ties," others dismiss the idea of transnational political opportunity structures because they assume social movements target sites of institutionalized power leveraged through national, not transnational, arenas.[21] This
assumption is problematic, however, given the proliferation of global
governance institutions and social movements' frequent targeting of them
(such as the antiglobalization movement's targeting of the World Trade
Organization and International Monetary Fund). Keck and Sikkink's
(1998) work adds empirical weight to the idea that institutionalized
power is embodied in global governance institutions. The authors show
that activists use global governance institutions to leverage states and
provoke changes in state policies and practices. Although their analysis
illuminates the relationship between social movements and global governance institutions, it does not offer a clear articulation of a theory that
could be used to explain the *emergence* of transnational labor movements
in relationship to global governance institutions.[22]

The NAFTA story sheds light on this theoretical lacuna by showing how global governance institutions serve as transnational power
structures for emergent transnational social movements. But NAFTA's
stimulation of labor transnationalism also suggests that the model of
national political opportunity structures cannot simply be mapped onto
the transnational level because there are critical differences in the way
power is constituted at the transnational and national levels. The theoretical payoff of examining labor transnationalism is that it allows us
to refine the concept of political opportunity structure and explore its
efficacy at the transnational level.

Political process theorists generally highlight what McAdam identifies
as four primary "dimensions of political opportunity" at the national
level: (1) the relative openness or closure of the institutionalized political

---

[21] Khagram, Riker, and Sikkink (2002, p. 18). See also Tarrow (2005) for a discussion.
[22] Keck and Sikkink do not discuss labor movements among their cases.

system; (2) the stability or instability of elite political alignments; (3) the presence or absence of elite allies; and (4) the state's capacity and propensity for repression.[23] Although these variables allow for a rich analysis of national social movements, they lack explanatory power when applied to the transnational arena. Unlike nation-states, global governance institutions have neither democratic electoral accountability nor repressive capacity. A polity's relative accessibility is therefore largely irrelevant at the transnational level. Electoral politics, which Tilly (1984) cites as the primary engine behind national social movements' engagement with the nation-state, also lacks relevance in the transnational arena. Transnational elites are not elected, nor do they belong to transnational parties subject to voter sanction. At this stage of labor transnationalism in North America, the effect of transnational elites is therefore minimal.[24]

And, while power at the national level can be constituted through repression, global governance institutions lack repressive powers. NAFTA and the NAALC, for example, have no military power and little ability to impose severe sanctions. Moreover, all four dimensions of political opportunity structure at the national level presume the existence of one nation-state. But what if the political opportunity structure involves three nation-states (in North America) and one nascent global governance institution (NAFTA)?

I offer a new model of political opportunity structure at the *transnational* level to accommodate the uniqueness of how power is constituted in this realm. In this model, transnational institutional fields create transnational political opportunities by serving three constitutive functions: (1) constituting transnational actors and interests; (2) defining and recognizing transnational rights; and (3) adjudicating rights at the transnational level.[25] New opportunities therefore emerge from transnational institutional fields. The focus here is on mechanisms: what institutional fields *do* to create transnational political opportunities.

The first constitutive function of transnational institutional fields suggests that the constitution of regional actors with regional interests is critical to the emergence of transnational social movements. Political process theory assumes that, at the national level, the interests of movement activists emerge and coalesce prior to mobilization and are reinforced through ongoing interaction. Because transnational social movements

---

[23] McAdam (1996, p. 27) synthesizes key scholars' conceptualization of the term.

[24] National elites however, were critical to the passage and structure of NAFTA and the NAALC.

[25] This does not imply that there could not be more, only that these emerged from my data.

must overcome geographic and cultural barriers, their interests are frequently forged *through* mobilization. Global governance institutions can assist in this process. In North America, spurred by concerns about the havoc NAFTA would wreak in their own countries, labor unions began to mobilize against the agreement. Only after coming together to discuss their individual concerns did they begin to articulate North American interests and develop cooperative transnational networks and relationships to advance them. NAFTA actually facilitated the constitution of North American actors with North American interests (as opposed to national actors with national interests). This *does not* imply that social movement actors no longer retain national identities and interests but rather that these exist simultaneously and are compatible with their nascent transnational identities and interests.

Labor transnationalism is nearly impossible to cultivate unless racist attitudes and ethnocentrism are significantly undermined or eliminated. Efforts to build labor solidarity across national borders have been historically stymied by these attitudes; labor activists in different countries frequently see themselves as competitors for scarce jobs and construct their interests in opposition to each other. The elimination of racism and ethnocentrism is therefore critical to the process of establishing transnational actors and interests. NAFTA created not only a common market but also transnational institutional fields through which national unions in North America could temper racism and ethnocentrism and identify their common interests as *North American unions*.

The second constitutive function of transnational fields expands upon the first by emphasizing the importance of defining and recognizing transnational actors' and social movements' rights in the transnational arena. This dimension is similar to Tilly's (1984) assertion that national social movements target nation-states because they have the power to grant or deny legitimacy. In the transnational arena, global governance institutions have the same power. That is, they make and enforce rules that, however weak, establish transnational rights, standards, and norms (Kay 2005). By laying out eleven North American labor principles and recognizing transnational social movements' right of standing through the NAO submission process, the NAALC creates a set of North American labor rights to be protected in all three countries. Moreover, their violation allows for redress by any North American "citizen."[26] Thus the

---

[26] The NAALC actually allows any party, regardless of national origin, to file public submissions. As of this writing, no party outside North America has filed a public submission.

NAALC grants a legitimacy to North American labor unions and their grievances that did not exist prior to NAFTA's passage.

The third constitutive function of transnational institutional fields emphasizes the importance of adjudicating grievances at the transnational level. The NAALC, for example, not only defines and recognizes transnational rights but also adjudicates complaints of labor rights violations at the transnational level. And its procedural rules facilitate cooperation among North American labor unions in that adjudicative process. Whereas national political opportunity structures have both electoral and adjudicative dimensions, transnational political opportunity structures lack the former. At the transnational level, political opportunity structures are embedded in rules and bureaucratic processes rather than electoral processes. This is another reason for the minimal role of the polity and elite alignments at the transnational level.

Developing Collective Interests: The Constitutive Effects of International Law

The emergence of labor transnationalism in North America not only demonstrates that cooperation among unions in different countries is possible but also raises compelling questions about how unions can overcome seemingly opposing interests.[27] The first function of transnational institutional fields – the constitution of transnational actors and interests – is therefore the foundation for the two others. Scholars have not fully fleshed out the *process* by which workers in different countries recognize and develop mutual interests and how new legal structures and mechanisms facilitate their creation. While they have been concerned with the development of working-class consciousness and solidarity (Voss 1993; Katznelson 1985; Hattam 1992; Aminzade 1979), the importance of cohesive collective identities for social movements (Melucci 1985), and the creation of cultures of solidarity among workers (Fantasia 1988),

---

[27] The burgeoning literature on labor transnationalism tends not to focus on this question but rather on the history of labor transnationalism (Sikkink and Smith 2002; Herod 1997; Stevis 1998; Howard 1995) and the causes of success and failure of particular transnational campaigns that are possible once interests coalesce (see Armbruster 1995, 1998; Cohen and Early 1998; Jessup and Gordon 2002; Zinn 2002; Anner 2002; Wilson 2002). Although scholars suggest that NAFTA's labor side agreement facilitates labor transnationalism, they have not fully fleshed out the process by which this occurs (see Alexander 1999; Carr 1999; Damgaard 1999a, 1999b; de Buen 1999; Compa 1999; Cook 1997; Kidder 2002; Thorup 1993; Luján 1999).

we know very little about how collective identities are developed across borders and how the obstacles to their formation are overcome.

This dearth of knowledge is surprising given the importance Karl Marx and his successors ascribed to the development of an international proletariat. Marx's suggestion that serial crises in capitalist accumulation would catalyze international solidarity as the bourgeoisie searched out new markets for its products has obviously not come to pass. Economic crisis does not necessarily generate collective interests. The emergence of labor transnationalism in North America suggests that reconfigurations in governance structures among nations can facilitate interest-building processes. That is, international laws and legal mechanisms can have constitutive effects on transnational social movements by imbuing transnational actors with collective interests.[28]

Sociolegal scholars have devoted significant attention to how the law constitutes legal actors and interests at the national level. In contrast to more traditional approaches that construct law as formal sets of rules that people conform to, a constitutive approach highlights the law's dynamism and plasticity in shaping how individuals view themselves in relation to the law and to each other. It conceptualizes law as "a complex repertoire of discursive strategies and symbolic frameworks that structure ongoing social intercourse and meaning-making activity among citizens."[29] A constitutive approach illuminates the law's effects on social movement building – particularly how the law promotes and constrains collective interests and action. Some of the earliest efforts focused on the labor movement and its relationship to labor law. Scholars linked the bureaucratization of the labor movement to labor legislation, which tempered class struggle by privileging collective bargaining rights (see Klare 1978; Stone 1981; Rogers 1990). As Klare explains, labor legislation resulted in the "creation of the rudiments of what later became an increasingly formalized and regulated institutional structure for the state administration of the class struggle" (Klare 1978, pp. 268–69). The law, then, helped "contain" the U.S. labor movement by limiting the nature and scope of labor struggles and constituting activists as bureaucratic actors with particular roles and obligations.

---

[28] I use the terms international and transnational law interchangeably. Although NAFTA applies to only three countries, political scientists would use the term international law. See the distinctions in Tarrow (2005).

[29] McCann (1994, p. 282). See also Merry (1990), Ewick and Silbey (1998), Silbey (1992), Sarat (1990), and Minow (1990).

Although the law can undermine collective action, it can also have the opposite effect by constituting social movement actors in ways that build social movements. As studies of the civil rights, women's rights, pay equity, gay rights, and other movements have shown, the law can help catalyze movements, recruit members, promote rights consciousness, and nurture solidarity among movement activists (McCann 1994; Schneider 1986; Andersen 2005). According to McCann, the law helps constitute social movement actors in particular ways. It can help nascent movements "name" and frame their grievances in relationship to particular rights violations they experience and seek to redress. Even unsuccessful attempts at legal mobilization can galvanize activists by highlighting the need for political or legal reform (McCann 1998). The law and the rights claims it articulates can therefore provide a concrete mechanism that helps form cohesive collective identities and interests that are so crucial for social movement development.

Sociolegal scholarship on the law's constitutive effects reveals much about how legal consciousness develops within social movements. But, like political process theory, it is limited by a focus on these processes at the national level. Although the emergence of labor transnationalism is surprising, particularly given labor activists' derision of the NAALC itself, its analysis opens a theoretical window onto the processes and mechanisms by which social movement building occurs at the *transnational* level in relationship to the law. Here I suggest that, at the transnational level, legal rules and mechanisms help constitute transnational actors with collective interests. Legal rules then legitimize transnational actors and their interests by granting them rights and grievance mechanisms at the transnational level. NAFTA provides us with an interesting case to examine the law's constitutive effects at the transnational level. The introduction and negotiation of a legally binding trade agreement allowed labor unions to recognize the common threat to wages and health, safety, and environmental standards. It enabled them to build common agendas and proposals for dealing with the threat. During the initial political mobilization period, transnational activists developed their collective interests by working together to try to kill the agreement. After NAFTA's implementation, the NAALC defined and legitimized their rights in the transnational arena.

The NAFTA story shows, however, that the strength of the NAALC's adjudicatory mechanisms is critically important for unions' long-term participation in the legal field. Although many unions were willing to come to the new legal mechanisms the NAALC built, they were not always willing to stay. During the first seven years of its existence, the NAALC process was one of the key arenas of cross-border labor cooperation and a significant indicator of its persistence. Unions' inability to get meaningful redress, coupled with the election of the more conservative antilabor Bush administration, eroded unions' confidence in the NAALC's efficacy. During the second seven years under NAFTA, unions used the process less frequently. Whereas unions and labor organizations filed fourteen submissions with the U.S. NAO during the first seven years, they filed half that number during the second seven. To the extent that the NAALC fails to provide meaningful redress on core issues such as freedom of association, its ability to serve as a mechanism to build labor transnationalism is compromised.

To summarize my argument, transnational political opportunity structures emerge from transnational institutional fields that create spaces where activists come together, mobilize, and develop their interests and identities in relationship to each other. In order for fields to be catalysts, they must promote or facilitate the constitution of transnational actors and interests and the definition, recognition, and adjudication of transnational rights. The two fields NAFTA created not only helped constitute new transnational actors and interests but also propelled key unions through the process of developing relationships (as will be discussed later in the book). In the course of mobilizing and adjudicating collectively in these fields, activists built trust and began to chip away at racism and ethnocentrism. Their collective activities in the transnational trade-negotiating field helped ensure that labor protections and free trade would be linked. These protections were ultimately embodied in the NAALC itself. Collective action in the transnational legal field helped build networks and support broader labor rights campaigns.

Figure 1.2 provides a visual illustration of how NAFTA helped catalyze labor transnationalism by creating nascent transnational fields that constituted an emergent transnational political opportunity structure.

As Figure 1.2 suggests, transnational institutional fields are the sites through which political opportunities are manifested and exploited.

The constitutive power of transnational institutional fields, however, is not absolute. NAFTA's institutional structures created new transnational opportunities for labor unions, but unions responded differently to them. Thus, whereas the first part of the NAFTA story is about structure, the second part is about agency. Only progressive leaders who constructed their interests to embrace transnationalism developed cross-border

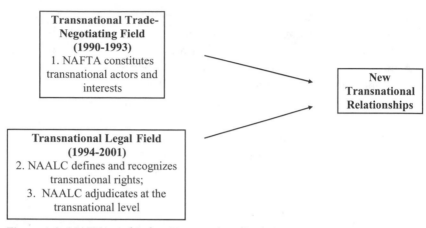

Figure 1.2. NAFTA and Labor Transnationalism

relationships and nurtured a culture within their unions to support them. Individual union leaders therefore had significant effects on transnationalism outcomes.

NAFTA and Governance

Although globalization has generated intense public and scholarly debate, we know little about the web of institutions and policies that advance and regulate it.[30] And we know even less about how these institutions and policies operate and interface with state and nonstate institutions, and the social movement actors that try to influence them.[31] The relationship between NAFTA and labor transnationalism reveals much about the processes and mechanisms by which power is constituted and contested at the transnational level. And it suggests that all governance institutions and structures are not created equal – equally useful to social movements, that is.

---

[30] Here I use Tarrow's definition of globalization, influenced by Keohane (2002): "increasing volume and speed of flows of capital and goods, information and ideas, people and forces that connect actors between countries" (Tarrow 2005, p. 5). Tarrow sees globalization and internationalization as two parallel processes that, in part, overlap. Distinguishing between the two is quite useful because it allows us to draw distinctions between institutions and treaties that advance and regulate globalization. Tarrow defines internationalism as "a dense, triangular structure of relations among states, nonstate actors, and international institutions, and the opportunities this produces for actors to engage in collective action at different levels of this system" (Tarrow 2005, p. 25).

[31] For exceptions, see Tarrow (2005), Keck and Sikkink (1998), O'Brien et al. (2000), and Smith and Reese (2008).

Governance institutions that have concrete mechanisms to engage and enable nonstate actors to participate, the NAFTA story shows, are much more efficacious for transnational movement building. For example, popular resistance to World Trade Organization, International Monetary Fund, and World Bank policies is usually manifested in large transnational demonstrations precisely because these institutions have no public adjudicative processes that activists can engage. Activists cannot file complaints of labor rights violations with the World Trade Organization or World Bank, and they fervently criticize these institutions for their lack of adjudicatory mechanisms, transparency, and democratic participatory processes. By providing some of these mechanisms in North America, NAFTA galvanizes resistance to globalization processes in different ways than global governance institutions that lack these functions. The *kind* of governance mechanisms a particular global or regional governance institution provides is therefore critical to social movements' ability to resist policies that undermine rights.

But the nature of these mechanisms is also critical to processes of movement building. As NAFTA shows, legal mechanisms that require transnational contact and collaboration through procedural rules can be essential to the stimulation of transnationalism. Governance institutions that lack rules to promote collaborative filing of complaints generally have not fomented transnational relationships among North American unions. The procedural rules of the International Labor Organization (ILO) and the Inter-American Court of Human Rights (of the Organization of American States) (IACHR) require central filing of complaints, do not encourage complainants to file jointly, and do not permit public hearings.

Like the NAALC, the ILO and IACHR procedures lack enforcement mechanisms. And instead of encouraging North American unions to file complaints together, the labor clause of the Generalized System of Preferences (GSP) actually pits them against each other; U.S. unions file complaints unilaterally against other governments, requesting the United States to withdraw trade preferences from nations that do not comply with their labor laws. This unilateral mechanism did little to build collective power among North American unions.[32] Although unions utilized the ILO, IACHR, and GSP mechanisms prior to NAFTA's passage, they

---

[32] Schrank and Murillo (2005) and Piore and Schrank (2008) suggest that some countries improved labor rights under the threat of losing trade preferences. NAFTA eliminated the use of GSP preferences for and complaints against Mexico.

generally did not use them collectively or as part of larger transnational campaigns for North American workers' rights.[33] Most important for the analysis here, unions' use of these transnational mechanisms did not help catalyze transnational relationships.

A comparison of the NAALC to NAFTA's environmental side agreement, the North American Agreement on Environmental Cooperation (NAAEC), highlights the importance of institutional structure on transnational social movement building. Unlike the NAALC, the NAAEC does not have NAOs or their equivalents in each country, and submitters *are not* required to file in a country other than the one in which the violation occurred. Rather, submitters file complaints of environmental law violations with one entity, the Secretariat of the Commission for Environmental Cooperation (located in Canada).

Although environmental activists filed more than twice the number of NAAEC submissions than labor activists filed through the NAALC, they rarely did so jointly. Of the sixty-five NAAEC submissions filed between 1994 and 2008, only two were filed by submitters from all three NAFTA countries. Thirty-three submissions were filed by Mexican environmental organizations and/or individuals alone, and eleven were filed jointly by U.S. and Canadian organizations. In addition, very few of the submissions emerged from or developed into large trinational environmental campaigns with grassroots involvement. And, of most relevance to the analysis here, there is little evidence that any strong permanent transnational relationships among environmental organizations emerged and developed in response to the NAAEC.[34] According to Jonathan Graubart, who analyzed the NAAEC submissions and interviewed environmental activists across North America: "No one was talking about the importance of collaboration."[35] Research suggests that the most significant results of the NAFTA struggle and the NAAEC process have been the stimulation of environmental activism and the creation of new environmental NGOs and organizations within Mexico.[36] The very different

---

[33] A few U.S. unions however, worked with their counterparts in other Latin American countries on GSP petitions to deal with extreme violations of labor and human rights (e.g., under dictatorships).

[34] Although I did not conduct interviews with environmentalists as I did with labor activists. A few organizations, such as Greenpeace, have Mexican affiliates or chapters.

[35] Personal communication with Jonathan Graubart on September 24, 2009. See Graubart (2008) for an analysis of the efficacy of the NAALC and NAAEC submissions.

[36] Of course, these are very significant outcomes in their own right but remain understudied and undertheorized.

outcomes of the two NAFTA side agreements suggest that the construction of transnational governance institutions has effects on transnational
movement building. The NAALC, which requires collective adjudication,
has helped stimulate it.

My argument is *not* that North American labor activists should app-
laud the passage of NAFTA or that the NAALC improved labor conditions across the continent. NAFTA undermined labor's bargaining power,
stimulated capital flight in North America (see Campbell et al. 2001;
Bronfrenbrenner 1997), and has done little to improve labor standards
and conditions. Rather, I argue that despite the negative effects of free
trade and the NAALC's many flaws and inadequacies, NAFTA helped
generate labor transnationalism. NAFTA shows that even institutions
with weak enforcement and policy outcomes can have strong movement
outcomes. For scholars and activists who view the NAALC as useless,
my suggestion that NAFTA had unintended positive consequences – by
helping undermine racism and forging transnational solidarity – could
be disconcerting. Illuminating reasons for optimism, however, is not
a blind endorsement of free trade agreements. Rather, it is a warning
that how governance institutions are structured *matters* for activists and
their ability to maneuver in ever-changing regional and global economies.
Moreover, to dismiss NAFTA on its face because its outcomes are not
optimal prevents the telling of a very important historical story about
how North American workers not only resisted free trade collectively
but also fought to change the internal dynamics of labor unions that had
prevented transnational cooperation in the past.

The NAFTA story also suggests the importance of transnational institutions and institution building for transnational social movement *emergence*. I probe this link by examining NAFTA as a case of a global
governance institution that spurred unions to collaborate across North
American borders. In the process of examining NAFTA's concrete effects
on labor transnationalism, we can develop a better understanding of
the relationship between global governance institutions, the emergence
of labor transnationalism, and the development and idiosyncrasies of
transnational institutional fields. If the development of national social
movements requires nation-states (Tilly 1984), the case of NAFTA implies
that statelike entities in the international arena can play a pivotal role
in the development of transnational social movements. Thus, the creation of new global governance institutions that provide mechanisms for
social movement engagement and participation should help stimulate the
growth of transnational social movements. Once NAFTA's institutional

mechanisms were built, a critical number of labor activists came to engage them. NAFTA therefore provides a heuristic lens through which to examine how international laws and governance institutions constrain and expand transnational social movements.

Of course, it is important to underscore that I am not arguing that trade agreements are necessary conditions for stimulating transnationalism or providing a general explanation for how all cases of labor transnationalism emerge. There are many examples of labor transnationalism emerging at different historical moments and in different parts of the world that are unrelated to free trade agreements in general, much less NAFTA. My analysis focuses on why and how labor transnationalism emerged in North America in the early 1990s. However, my institutional argument about how new fields can generate transnationalism has implications for a wide range of governance institutions and social movements. The book shows how a new institutional structure – in this case, a transnational system for adjudicating labor conflicts – can create an arena that helps stimulate transnational movement building. My analysis of this case should alert analysts and activists to the potential effects of other new international governance structures emerging in other contexts on different kinds of social movements, from environmental movements seeking climate change regulation to investors lobbying for corporate governance reform.

Research Focus, Strategy, and Book Organization

This book examines a particular historical case of labor transnationalism: the emergence of *trinational* labor cooperation in North America in the early 1990s. Because it analyzes *what caused the initial shift* toward transnationalism, the book focuses on the decade after the emergence of the first transnational relationships – from the end of 1990 to 2001 – and devotes less attention to transnational relationships after 2001. The analysis I present here allows us to understand the processes by which labor transnationalism emerged and developed from the pre-NAFTA period (1950–1989) into the post-NAFTA period (1990–2001),[37] distinguish between different types of labor interactions, and mark the trajectory of particular relationships. Examining negative cases (i.e., unions that did

---

[37] I define the post-NAFTA period as between 1990 and 2001 because although it was not passed until 1993, NAFTA posed a threat that stimulated union mobilization across the continent, beginning when negotiations were announced in September 1990.

not develop transnational relationships) enables us to isolate the factors that stymie these processes.

NAFTA created a sea change – a big institutional shift for unions – because of the new institutional fields it created. Although the political environment changed after 2000 with the election of conservative pro-business presidents in the United States and Mexico and the events of 9/11, the new institutional equilibrium created by NAFTA remained in place. Since 2001, labor transnationalism has stagnated; the relationships that were established during NAFTA continue, but few new relationships have emerged. Post-2001 events, however, do not affect my argument about *what caused the initial shift* toward transnationalism. As a point of comparison, the decline of the civil rights movement in the early 1970s does not undermine the history of how and why it emerged in the mid-1960s. North American labor transnationalism will continue to ebb and flow and develop – as does civil rights activism – as time progresses and political environments change. But careful analysis of the roots of its initial emergence remains crucial.

The NAFTA case suggests that labor transnationalism is a *process* of relationship and institution building. Using the transnational relationship as a unit of analysis illuminates labor transnationalism not only as an outcome but also as a process of creating a transnational union culture based on cooperative complementary identities – defined as shared recognition of mutual interest coupled with a commitment to joint action. I measure the quality and intensity of unions' relationships by distinguishing between three types. Relationships that involve periodic interactions based on mutual interest, trust, and equality are identified as moderately developed. Those that involve ongoing interaction based on mutual interest, trust, and equality *and* are semiformalized and/or institutionalized are identified as partially developed. Relationships that involve ongoing interaction based on mutual interest, trust, and equality, are fully formalized and/or institutionalized (e.g., through joint programs and permanent staff positions), *and* achieve cooperative complementary identification among counterparts are recognized as fully developed. A transnational relationship is quite distinct from what I refer to as a transnational contact. Transnational contacts are not necessarily based on mutual interest, trust, and equality and tend to be short-term and one-sided. Contacts are similar to what Tarrow (1998) terms "contingent political alliances," which are based on ephemeral transnational "relays" or exchanges between social activists.

A fully developed transnational relationship can be defined as such even if participants are not able to fully exercise the potential of their relationship and achieve its maximum capacity. For example, two unions may have a good working relationship and commitment to mutual support but lack a transnational organizing campaign. The full capacity of their relationship is therefore not realized. Similarly, fully developed transnational relationships cannot be defined by traditional notions of success such as winning campaigns and contracts. It is excruciatingly difficult to overcome the state and employer opposition that unions face in all three countries. Relationships must therefore be measured by their strength and potential rather than by their results. I do not make grand claims about extraordinary successes among North American labor unions. Rather, I illuminate the development of labor transnationalism as a process of relationship and institution building that has the potential for success (in the traditional sense) in the future.

Broadly speaking, this book focuses on processes of labor transnationalism among union federations and the largest unions in the communications, electronics manufacturing, auto, trucking, steel, and garment/apparel industries in North America (not the history of how U.S. and Canadian internationals formed[38] or binational campaigns between U.S. and Mexican unions). I selected the largest industrial unions across North America as cases because they were in key industries most likely to be affected by trade and were more likely to embrace nationalistic protectionist strategies and eschew transnationalism (as had been the case historically up until NAFTA). Examining service and agricultural unions, whose workers are less susceptible to being replaced overseas, would reveal much less about processes of transnational relationship building than studying unions faced with imminent job loss. Moreover, agricultural and service unions were marginally involved in the anti-NAFTA struggle – precisely because they had little stake in the outcome. Also, much of the transnational cooperation among these unions involves unionizing immigrant workers in the United States (or those in Mexico seeking to enter the United States).

Table 1.2 lays out both the positive cases (i.e., union triads that participate in transnational relationships; see rows one through seven) and the negative cases (i.e., unions that do not have transnational relationships;

---

[38] In the United States, "international unions" generally refer to U.S. unions, usually with Canadian affiliates.

see rows eight through thirteen) among the sample of eighteen unions and union federations.[39]

Because the study measures a shift in the nature of the relationships among unions, it required a qualitative and comparative approach. I conducted in-depth interviews with key informants in each union.[40] In-depth interviews were essential because archival materials are incomplete. The AFL-CIO, for example, has not released or made public documentation of its involvement in Latin American union politics (despite numerous calls from scholars and activists to do so). Moreover, because more equitable relationships were not a priority in the pre-NAFTA era, there are few written records, and key individuals in each union usually manage international relations. I was able to collect more substantive documentation of transnational relationships after 1990 as priorities began to change.

Because of the lack of recordkeeping on this issue, a survey would have generated innumerable blank responses. Memories needed to be gently prodded, and documents locked away in files needed to be consulted to verify dates and places. Determining the key players was not difficult – they were inevitably labor leaders or union elites. Between 1999 and 2001, I conducted over 140 interviews with Mexican, Canadian, and U.S. labor leaders and union staff, government officials, NAALC officials, labor activists in NGOs, and labor lawyers representing over fifty-three individual labor federations, unions, and labor advocacy organizations across North America.[41] The timing of the initial interviews and data collection is a strength of the analysis because they were proximate to the process of creating the institutional shift that generated transnational relationships.

In 2009 and 2010, I conducted a small set of follow-up interviews with key labor leaders to gauge whether the landscape of labor transnationalism had changed significantly since my initial interviews. They revealed that it has not: industrial unions that developed relationships during the NAFTA struggle maintain them, and with the exception of the USW,

---

[39] Rows nine through thirteen represent hypothetical cases, or triads among U.S. and Canadian unions and a hypothetical CTM counterpart in the same industry.

[40] See the bibliography for a list of interview respondents. For confidentiality, I list respondents in the text as anonymous when they request or when, by my own judgment, I deem material to be sensitive.

[41] This number is larger than the number of unions in the sample because it includes union affiliates and locals, NGOs, law firms, and other entities.

Table 1.2. *Unions, Industries, and Transnational Relationship Outcomes*

Unions	Industry	Transnational Relationship
1 **UE, CUSWA, FAT** United Steelworkers in Canada (CUSWA)[a] United Electrical, Radio and Machine Workers of America (United States) Authentic Labor Front (FAT, Mexico)	Electrical manufacturing	Yes: fully
2 **CWA, CEP, STRM** Communications, Energy, and Paperworkers Union (Canada Communication Workers of America (United States) Mexican Telephone Workers' Union (STRM)	Telecommunications	Yes: partially
3 **AFL-CIO, CLC, UNT** Canadian Labour Congress American Federation of Labor and Congress of Industrial Organizations National Union of Workers (Mexico)	Labor federations	Yes: partially
4 **AFL-CIO, CLC, FAT**	Labor federations	Yes: partially
5 **UAW, CAW, STIMAHCS** National Automobile, Aerospace, Transportation and General Workers Union of Canada (CAW) United Automobile, Aerospace & Agricultural Implement Workers of America International Union (UAW, United States) Union of Workers in the Metal, Iron, Steel, and Related and Similar Industries (STIMAHCS, Mexico)	Auto	Yes: moderately

#	Union	Industry	Contacts
6	**UNITE, UNITE (Canada), FAT** Union of Needletrades, Industrial and Textile Employees (UNITE, United States and Canada)[b] FAT (Mexico)	Garment/apparel	Yes: moderately
7	**IBT, IBT (Canada), FAT** International Brotherhood of Teamsters (IBT, United States and Canada) FAT (Mexico)	Trucking	Yes: moderately
8	**AFL-CIO, CLC, CTM** Confederation of Mexican Workers (Mexico)	Labor federations	No: contacts
9	**UAW, CAW, CTM**	Auto	No: contacts
10	**UNITE, UNITE (Canada), CTM**	Garment/apparel	No: contacts
11	**IBT, IBT (Canada), CTM**	Trucking	No: contacts
12	**UE, CUSWA, CTM**	Electrical manufacturing	No: contacts
13	**USW, CUSWA, CTM** United Steelworkers of America (USW, United States)	Steel	No: contacts

Notes: Rows nine through thirteen represent hypothetical cases, or triads among U.S. and Canadian unions and a hypothetical CTM counterpart in the same industry. There are no national auto, garment/apparel, or trucking unions in Mexico. The FAT presents an interesting case because it is a union federation but also resembles and acts like a national union would in the United States or Canada. That is, as one of the only independent Mexican labor federations prior to 1997, the FAT had unions in key industries such as auto, garment/apparel, and electronics. Each of these unions acted as a national independent union in its respective industry.

[a] The United Steelworkers in Canada does not use the acronym CUSWA. I employ it to distinguish between the United Steelworkers in Canada and the United Steelworkers in the United States, both of which belong to the USW.

[b] In 2004, UNITE and the Hotel Employees and Restaurant Employees International Union (HERE) merged to form UNITE HERE.

which developed a new and quite strong relationship with a Mexican mining union (as discussed in Chapter 4), industrial unions that did not prioritize transnationalism have not developed new relationships. Labor leaders also reaffirmed their position that the NAALC is a weak and insufficient mechanism for redressing labor rights violations across the continent, confirmed that under the Bush administration its enforcement deteriorated, and revealed that they planned to test new NAO submissions under the Obama administration.

The NAFTA story unfolds in two distinct parts divided into eight chapters. Part One explores the *emergence* of labor transnationalism in relationship to NAFTA. Part Two examines *variations* in unions' engagement in transnational activities in response to NAFTA. The first half of the book therefore focuses on the overarching shift to transnationalism, whereas the second half focuses on variations in that shift among different unions. Chapter 2 explores the history of labor transnationalism prior to NAFTA – a history of diplomatic "relations" among unions. It examines the political-economic context in which these relations occurred, particularly the effects of the Cold War. It also briefly describes North American unions' pre-NAFTA policies on a variety of issues, including trade and immigration.

The next three chapters explore NAFTA's catalytic effects on labor transnationalism: the processes by which NAFTA constituted transnational actors and interests, created a North American labor rights regime, and stimulated transnational relationships and shifts in union ideologies and internal structures to facilitate relationship building. Chapter 3 details how anti-NAFTA coalitions and nascent transnational relationships emerged in the transnational trade-negotiating field and began to develop collective North American interests and identities. Chapter 4 focuses on how the NAALC stimulated and strengthened labor transnationalism by establishing new transnational labor rights standards and legal mechanisms to adjudicate complaints of labor rights violations. It discusses the NAALC process, various NAO submissions, and collaborative activities related to NAO submissions. Chapter 5 explores unions that took advantage of the transnational political opportunities NAFTA created to nurture relationships after its negotiation.

Part Two examines *variations* in unions' engagement in transnational activities in response to NAFTA. Chapter 6 focuses on unions that missed the opportunities NAFTA provided and did not develop relationships after NAFTA's passage. Chapter 7 illuminates the relevant variables to explain the variation in NAFTA's effect on unions. Although all unions were exposed to NAFTA as a potential catalyst of labor transnationalism, NAFTA did not generate relationships among all unions. That is, it only generated transnational relationships among those that had certain ideological and organizational characteristics. This raises compelling questions about the necessary and sufficient conditions for the development of labor transnationalism, and its limitations. This chapter reveals how some unions and labor federations were differentially constituted as transnational actors during NAFTA's negotiation and in its wake.

The conclusion, Chapter 8, suggests how the book's theoretical and empirical findings can inform our understanding of transnational political opportunity structures and institutional fields more generally, and teases out the implications of this study for future research on transnational social movements and global governance institutions. The dimensions of transnational institutional fields, political opportunity structures, and global governance institutions I identify as being the most salient to labor transnationalism provide a useful yardstick by which to measure other global governance institutions and their potential to serve as catalysts for various types of transnational social movements. Although it is too early to predict the impact of labor transnationalism on unions' power, influence, and success, it is probable that the role of transnational social movements poised to contest inequalities wrought by processes of globalization will only become more important as these processes proceed across the globe.

PART ONE

THE EMERGENCE OF TRANSNATIONALISM

2

Labor Nationalism

Diplomacy and Distance among Unions
Prior to NAFTA

The union relationships that developed during NAFTA's negotiation are
so momentous because they stand in stark contrast to the interactions that
preceded them. How did North American unions interact prior to 1990,
and what influenced their interactions? This chapter describes the nature
of labor transnationalism during the pre-NAFTA era between 1950 and
1989, when the structure of union relations was national and not very
integrated across borders. Although some U.S. union "internationals"
included Canadian affiliates with formal ties, the focus here is on the
history of relations between U.S. and Canadian industrial unions and
their Mexican counterparts. It explores the history of diplomatic "relations" among unions and examines these relations against the backdrop
of the political and economic forces that shaped them. During this first
time period, U.S. and Canadian unions engaged Mexican unions sporadi-
cally, their interactions usually consisting of vacuous letters of support,
elaborate dinners, and staged photo-op handshakes. There were some
crisis-driven collaborations, but in general labor relationships were not
institutionalized, permanent, or programmatic. An analysis of this first
time period is critical because it illuminates the dramatic nature of the
shift toward transnationalism in the second period after NAFTA from
1990 to 2001.

The story of North American unionism between 1950 and 1989 is
one of diplomacy and distance. Many union leaders saw their interests as aligned with national governments and industries engaged in a
struggle to promote capitalism across the globe. They believed that their
efforts would result in jobs and strong economies. Unions therefore fell
into lockstep with governments and corporations in the march against

communism. As Cold War politics reverberated across North America, unions were not immune from its effects.

The Cold War: Labor Fighting Communism

The threat of communism generated a common ideological front among North American unions. The AFL-CIO, as the representative of the majority of unionized U.S. workers, led the charge. Prior to 1989, the AFL-CIO's international program devoted significant resources to promoting U.S. business interests and combating global communism. In the 1960s, the AFL-CIO created four international institutes to promote these goals abroad. The American Institute for Free Labor Development (AIFLD), founded in 1962, focused on Latin America.[1] AIFLD was funded largely with U.S. government money from the U.S. Agency for International Development (USAID) and beginning in 1985 the National Endowment for Democracy, which is funded by both USAID and the U.S. Information Agency. The AFL-CIO's willingness to accept government money for its international work drew fire from progressives in the U.S. labor movement, who warned that the federation would become handmaidens of the government and its rabid anticommunist policies.

Some scholars claim that critics' fears were prescient. Despite the institutes' goal to promote democracy and labor rights around the world, evidence suggests that the organization supported anticommunist, conservative, government-controlled unions, destabilized independent (and often communist) unions, and participated in military coups in Latin America. AIFLD's most strident critics contend that it was little more than a front for the U.S. government, particularly the U.S. State Department and Central Intelligence Agency (CIA).[2] As one critic described the institutes: "Their mission was to promote foreign unions' cooperation with U.S. government policies and business interests. Where they encountered resistance, such as in Nicaragua, Honduras, and Russia, AFL-CIO operatives set up dual unions to compete with (or replace) existing ones" (Kelber 2001). According to a former executive director of the International Labor Rights Fund:

[William, Jr.] Doherty oversaw AIFLD's operations and was best known for finding allies in the countries of the Americas and providing them with funds to

---

[1] The African-American Labor Center focused on Africa, the Free Trade Union Institute on Europe, and the Asian-American Free Labor Institute on Asia.

[2] See Cantor and Schor (1987), Spalding (1992), Morris (1967), and Herod (1997).

create and sustain national trade union organizations aligned with the respective country's right wing political party. The long lasting effect of Doherty's reign at AIFLD was to force the labor movement in most countries of the Americas to divide along ideological lines, siding either with the leftist parties or the right wing union created and sustained by AIFLD.... To this day, the effects of this divisiveness are still apparent.[3]

Although the extent of the AFL-CIO's activities during the Cold War remains a mystery (because it refuses to make relevant documents public), the federation earned a reputation as a puppet for the U.S. government. Labor activists in all three countries and within the AFL-CIO itself reflected during interviews on its unseemly (yet perhaps well-deserved) moniker during this period: the "AFL-CIA."

The AFL-CIO and CLC

Although less strident and active in its anticommunist agenda, the Canadian Labour Congress (CLC) followed the AFL-CIO's anticommunist line. The two federations primarily worked as a united front to bolster their governments' foreign relations policies. According to one CLC official, the activities of the international department caused some contention within the organization:

[The CLC] had the international department and there were always rumors that a couple of the guys who'd headed it up were in fact old spies. You know, one guy was in Chile at the time of the coup. I can't think of what the other guy's credentials were but there was enough so that every time the international report came to the floor at the CLC convention up until maybe five or six years ago, the left would always get out there and attack it. It was always seen as extremely right wing. Yeah, so it was pretty much the same at the CLC [as at the AFL-CIO].[4]

Although some Canadian labor activists actively struggled against the CLC's adoption of AFL-CIO policies, especially collusion between the AFL-CIO and the U.S. government in Latin America, their efforts did not bear much fruit. The AFL-CIO's ability to sway the CLC was rooted in the history of international unionism between the two countries. Beginning in the 1930s, a number of U.S. industrial unions organized Canadian workers and incorporated Canadian sections into U.S. union structures. Because some CLC affiliates also belonged to the AFL-CIO, the latter's influence was substantial. In many other respects, the relationship

---

[3] Dubro (2001).
[4] Personal interview with CLC official, 2001.

between the two federations was – as the CLC's former executive vice president characterized it – "in [a] deep freeze." He explained how relations between the AFL-CIO and CLC were strained in the years before NAFTA's negotiation: "Well the historical relationship between the AFL and the CLC was not a very good one.... The CLC didn't really have much interaction with them and vice versa, we didn't care."[5]

The symbiotic relationship between the federations was replicated among U.S. international unions and their Canadian affiliates. During the Cold War, a significant number of U.S. industrial unions had Canadian affiliates, including in the auto, electrical, garment/apparel, communications, trucking, and steel industries. The nature of the interactions among U.S. and Canadian affiliates varied. Some, like the Canadian Steelworkers, remained relatively autonomous. Others, such as the Canadian section of UNITE, were quite integrated into the international union and dependent on it for support.

Historically, however, this "international unionism" did not guarantee a strong and fruitful relationship. Indeed, internationals rarely took full advantage of their ability to leverage two governments and put pressure on companies in both countries. Few internationals actually bargained contracts or organized campaigns binationally. The institutional ties among many Canadian affiliates and their U.S.-based internationals were relatively weak. The international often treated the Canadian affiliate with benevolent neglect, and the affiliate resented its treatment as poor stepchild. Beginning in the 1970s, these weak ties ultimately led some Canadian affiliates to separate from internationals and form their own autonomous Canadian-based unions.

Mexico: Anticommunist Ally

U.S. and Canadian unions' interest in Mexico was inextricably linked to the anticommunist struggle. Mexico was one of the few Latin American countries considered an ally by the AFL-CIO and CLC in their struggle against communist regimes. Despite a bloody revolution that began in 1910 and lasted over a decade, Mexico remained committed to capitalism. Its leaders promoted industry and extolled the virtues of democracy while maintaining a stranglehold on the state, populace, and unions for over half a century. The government's control over Mexican unions emerged from

[5] Personal interview with Hassan Yussuff of the CLC, February 28, 2001.

the need to garner support for its economic development strategies. As Middlebrook (1995) points out, the ability of Mexican elites "to pursue policies that promoted rapid industrialization and capital accumulation at the expense of some workers' welfare depended on effective political control over labor mobilization."[6] Control was achieved in the form of a social pact between the ruling government party, the Institutional Revolutionary Party (PRI), and Mexico's leading labor federation, the Confederation of Mexican Workers (CTM). In exchange for government protections such as price controls, increased wages, and social benefits, the CTM supported the government's economic development project and maintained labor peace (Middlebrook 1995).

The Mexican government's control over the CTM did not undermine its worthiness as a potential ally in the eyes of AFL-CIO and CLC leaders. All that mattered was that the CTM officially opposed communism and committed the organization to its eradication within Mexico and across Latin America. Of course, the CTM's anticommunist stance increased and solidified its power at the national level. Independent unions (those not controlled by the government or ruling party), the majority of which were left-leaning, found it nearly impossible to build power in Mexico. The Authentic Labor Front (FAT), for example, had never been able to organize successfully in the maquiladoras or in key industries such as autos. The government, often collaborating with the CTM or other official unions, crushed the FAT and other independent unions' organizing efforts. Progressive and/or dissident labor leaders were frequently killed, disappeared, or were thrown in jail. To be an independent unionist in Mexico could result in physical harm, but it always resulted in marginalization.

In the pre-NAFTA era, the AFL-CIO and CLC reinforced this marginalization by privileging their relations with the CTM. The strength of the AFL-CIO's ideological and political commitment to the CTM was so strong that it had a policy of exclusivity with the federation: the AFL-CIO worked only with the CTM, thereby preventing any relationships with independent Mexican unions. Of course, the exclusive arrangement with the CTM amounted to little more than ideological posturing; rather than spark a thriving relationship, it created one of convenience.

Relationships between the northern federations and independent Mexican unions were therefore nonexistent. Bertha Luján, formerly a FAT

---

[6] Middlebrook (1995, p. 217).

national coordinator, explained: "The old leaders were not interested in us and we were also not interested in them. It was a very conservative leadership, anticommunist, that promoted a discriminatory unionism. And with very little interest in Latin America."[7] An AFL-CIO official confirmed Luján's conception of the federation's decision not to engage the FAT or other independent Mexican unions: "The AFL-CIO knew about FAT during the Kirkland-Donahue years. And there were people like Bill Doherty saying the FAT's a bunch of communists, don't want anything to do with them, and they don't represent anybody."[8] As a result of the AFL-CIO's neglect, and its anticommunist activities in Latin America, independent Mexican unions promulgated a rhetoric that portrayed U.S. unions as "yanquis," a derogatory term that conjured up images of the self-interested, protectionist, and manipulative gringo. To many independent unions, U.S. unions were agents of the U.S. government, and the CTM puppets of the AFL-CIO.

The AFL-CIO, CLC, and CTM solidified their exclusive arrangement by participating in various international labor institutions such as the ILO, the International Confederation of Free Trade Unions (ICFTU), and the latter's regional subsidiary, the Inter-American Regional Workers' Organization (ORIT). The ILO permits only certain unions (in practice, usually with the informal approval of national governments) to formally participate in its policy and adjudicative functions. Not surprisingly, the CTM was the union federation granted standing with the ILO. Because the ICFTU and ORIT focused on fighting communism in the 1960s, progressive unions in the Americas did not join. Independent unions such as the FAT joined the Christian-aligned and socialist-sympathetic World Confederation of Labor and its regional arm in Latin America, the Latin American Workers Central.

Although the CTM garnered political clout and financial support through its exclusive relationship with its U.S. and Canadian counterparts, many within the CTM were deeply suspicious of the AFL-CIO's motives and clandestine activities in Latin American politics. Official Mexican unions often appeased the AFL-CIO by not actively and openly courting communist or radical unions in other countries, but CTM leaders worried about maintaining their autonomy and the sovereignty of their organization and that of the Mexican government.

---

[7] Personal interview with Bertha Luján of the FAT, August 29, 2000.
[8] Personal interview with AFL-CIO official, 2001.

Because suspicion and coercion characterized the relations among North America's major labor federations during this period, they never moved beyond declarative or signatory contacts. An AFL-CIO official described the nature of relations with the CTM: "The relationship at the international level was basically with the CTM, but not even much of a relationship with the CTM."[9] A CLC official echoed the same comments: "Well, before the NAFTA period the relationship between the Canadian and Mexican unions was really very, very distant. It was essentially friendly but [we had] very little to do with each other. You know, we knew the leadership of the CTM and the CTM would know the leadership here, but that was about the extent of it."[10]

Although they came together in the context of various international organizations and meetings each year, the federations did very little collaborative work. There were few discussions within the AFL-CIO and CLC about engaging Mexican unions in meaningful ways, and even fewer efforts to cooperate on joint projects. When asked about the AFL-CIO's involvement in transnationalism prior to NAFTA, a leader in the federation's international department explained:

Basically there was nothing, or very little before NAFTA. The AFL was involved with the CTM and worked mostly through the International Labor Organization on issues not related to the U.S. or Mexico, but on other Latin American countries and problems... The transnational activities that existed prior to 1990 were not really linked to national unions, but rather were carried out by progressive locals, or dissident northern movements, and did not involve long-term relationships usually.[11]

The relations among individual North American industrial unions mirrored those of the federations. Many came into contact through participation in International Trade Secretariats (ITSs), organizations that brought together unions from around the world with members in particular industries.[12] UAW officials, for example, attended regular meetings of the International Metalworkers Federation, where they interacted with CTM auto union leaders. Although the ITS system enabled unions to share information and have semiregular contact, it did not foster permanent strategic relationships.

[9] Personal interview with Mark Anderson of the AFL-CIO, January 8, 2001.
[10] Personal interview with Richard Martin of the CLC, February 26, 2001.
[11] Personal interview with AFL-CIO official, 2000.
[12] International Trade Secretariats are now referred to as Global Unions or Global Union Federations.

The structure of Mexican unions often frustrated attempts to build stronger bonds across the continent. Mexico does not have *national* auto, garment/apparel, or trucking unions. Unlike U.S. and Canadian unions that affiliate by industry or as locals of a larger national union, Mexican unions are generally organized by plant and affiliated to a labor federation such as the CTM. A national counterpart to the UAW, CAW, UNITE, or IBT therefore does not exist. In an effort to build more contact and collaboration among auto unions, UAW President Walter Reuther met with CTM leaders in 1966 to discuss the creation of a national Mexican auto union. Although they seemed to support the idea, it never materialized.

Union relations during the pre-NAFTA era can therefore be characterized as sporadic contacts intended primarily to serve as ideological ballast against communism in the Americas. These interactions did not rise to the level of transnational relationships because they were not equitable, did not create and nurture long-term programs based on mutual interests, and usually only involved union leaders and elites.[13] Critics even claim they amounted to little more than expensive union tourism. The intermittent letters of solidarity, the joint anticommunist proclamations, the meetings held at posh hotels, and other union activities in the pre-NAFTA period accomplished relatively little to propel labor unions toward collaborative cooperative relationships.

In addition, the threat of communism provided a relatively weak foundation for building a sense of collective interest among unions. The associate director of the AFL-CIO's International Affairs Department asserted that their focus on anticommunism "made for a really very superficial relationship . . . between the AFL-CIO and the CTM. It was almost a kind of ceremonial relationship."[14] Although unions accepted a common ideological position, their joint activities to thwart communism were relatively nonexistent. The Cold War politics of this period did not constitute North American labor unions as regional actors with regional interests because the intangible threat of international communism paled in comparison with the real and concrete national threats workers increasingly faced: job loss, wage decreases, benefit reductions, and a growing corporate antiunionism. Concerns about import competition, factory relocation, and cheap immigrant labor (in the U.S. and Canada) and lack of capital investment (in Mexico) only reinforced workers' sense of their

---

[13] For a discussion of the history and limitations of international labor organizations, see Stevis (1998) and Boswell and Stevis (1997).

[14] Personal interview with Stan Gacek of the AFL-CIO, August 23, 2009.

national interests. It would be virtually impossible to develop a sense of the collective good among North American unions if workers viewed their interests as being in opposition to each other.

While the cold warriors of North American labor unions jetted across the Americas, workers at home became increasingly preoccupied with forces that were changing the nature of their work – forces we now refer to as globalization. Workers attributed their job insecurity to a triple threat made possible by the ability of people, capital, and goods and services to traverse national boundaries with greater ease: competition with low-wage workers (usually immigrants), the movement of jobs and plants overseas, and foreign imports. How union leaders and workers evaluated and managed the threat was not value-neutral. Because they perceived it through racial lenses, they engaged in complex processes of "othering" immigrant and foreign workers in ways that undermined meaningful cross-border collaboration for decades.

Constructing the "Other" in North American Labor Movements

Historically the earliest threat U.S. workers collectively responded to came from the south – the movement of people from Mexico. Immigrant laborers and unions have a conflictual history in the United States and, to a lesser extent, in Canada.[15] Unionized workers often fear that immigrant and migrant workers – whether they are freed slaves, national migrants from poor areas, or foreign nationals – will accept lower wages and lesser working conditions, depressing the former and diminishing the latter. Union leaders also frequently argue that immigrants undermine unions; they are either unwilling or unable to organize.

For the AFL-CIO and other U.S. unions, Mexico has historically presented a dilemma because of its proximity to and shared border with the United States and the large number of Mexicans who legally and illegally enter the country. Union policies on immigrant and migrant labor have been relatively consistent over time. Most U.S. unions supported the enforcement of immigration laws that prevented Mexican immigrants from entering the U.S. labor market. In some cases they opposed legislation such as guest worker plans that allowed Mexicans to work in the United States legally. The United Farm Workers of America (UFW) vehemently opposed the bracero program because it created a labor surplus, providing employers with little incentive to raise wages and sign union

---

[15] Similar dynamics prevail in Mexico in response to Central American immigrants.

contracts. The union also criticized the program for enabling employers to flagrantly violate workers' rights. Cesar Chavez famously referred to the bracero program as indentured servitude. Despite their concern for foreign workers' welfare, UFW leaders were primarily concerned with those they believed to be potential union members. Although not anti-immigrant, at times they advocated that the border patrol be used against Mexican immigrant strikebreakers.[16]

A 1968 report of the AFL-CIO Executive Council on U.S.-Mexican Border Problems demonstrates unions' tendency to blame, in part, foreign workers – even when they enter the country legally – for undermining U.S. labor. The report states:

One issue is the use of Mexicans holding permanent resident alien status, but living in Mexico, to undermine U.S. working conditions across the border. These Mexicans – so-called "green carders" – by living in Mexico and working in the U.S. are largely beyond the reach of the trade union movement. Because of the differences in national living standards and costs, they have little motivation to participate in the struggle of their fellow workers in the U.S., most of them also of Mexican origin, to raise their living standards through collective bargaining. While employment rates are at depressed levels and per capita income is below poverty levels along the U.S. side of the border, commuters have been exploited on occasion to undermine organizing drives and to break legitimate strikes. This reflects seriously on U.S. immigration policy. We strongly urge the Immigration Department to take the administrative steps necessary and possible to prevent exploitation of Mexican commuters to undermine U.S. standards.[17]

The report also reflected the AFL-CIO's limited analysis of the underlying economic and social problems that stimulate immigration.

The treatment of Mexican immigrants by the U.S. government and unions did not go unnoticed in Mexico. Independent unions were particularly vocal about the fair treatment of Mexican workers north of the Rio Grande. Upon President Jimmy Carter's visit to Mexico in 1979, the FAT called for a national alliance to denounce "the aggression and exploitation that workers of Mexican descent or nationality are subjected to in the United States."[18] The union federation urged an alliance to push

[16] Frank Bardacke, "Cesar's Ghost: Decline and Fall of the U.F.W." *Nation*, July 26, 1993, p. 132.
[17] "Report of the Subcommittee of Executive Council on U.S.-Mexican Border Problems," AFL-CIO, 5 August 1968, RG1-038, Office of the President-George Meany Files, 1940–1980, The George Meany Memorial Archives.
[18] "En el D.F. Se organizan los trabajadores para recibir a Carter." *Resistencia Obrera*, Number 13, January 1979, p. 5.

a national agenda that included the "absolute respect for the rights of Mexican workers in the U.S."[19]

Unions' primary concern when it comes to immigration is maintaining control over work. But union policies on legal and undocumented immigrants are not ideologically neutral. They reflect larger conceptions of the "other" worker. As such, they are laced with implicit and sometimes explicit racism, nativism, and/or ethnocentrism. In the 1920s, U.S. union officials often used racist rhetoric to argue for restrictive immigration legislation, and even gained the support of nativist legislators and civic groups by linking immigration to the demise of white political power. The Arizona State Federation of Labor warned that the Mexican immigrant was "a positive threat to our most cherished industrial, political and social institutions."[20] At a meeting of the Senate Immigration Committee in 1928, the vice president of the California State Federation of Labor queried senators:

We have a great virgin country, and if we do not remain on guard it is not going to be our country; it is going to be somebody else's country. This country is going to be as densely populated as Italy someday, and it remains only to be seen what kind they are going to be. Do you want the kind of people that sit in this Capitol . . . or do you want a mongrel population consisting largely of Mexicans and Orientals?[21]

Another labor official told a senator: "We are doing our best and always count on you as one of our most valued friends to preserve our country as a heritage to the white race."[22] U.S. unions' rhetoric proved so compelling to the Knights of the Ku Klux Klan and the Daughters of the American Revolution that they joined their struggle to restrict Mexican immigration.

Exclusion clauses also gave teeth to the historic racism against Mexican Americans in many unions. Like African American workers, Mexican American workers were often prevented from joining U.S. unions by clauses that excluded them based on race and/or ethnicity. A UAW local in Dallas that had its charter revoked by the international in 1952 for excluding Mexican American workers responded by joining the International

---

[19] "En el D.F. Se organizan los trabajadores para recibir a Carter." *Resistencia Obrera,* Number 13, January 1979, p. 5.
[20] Reisler (1976, p. 173).
[21] Ibid.
[22] Ibid.

Association of Machinists, which allowed it to retain its exclusion clause (Hill 1985).

Economic Nationalism and the "Foreign Worker" Myth

Unions historically employed racialized rhetoric not only to respond to competition from immigrants at home but also to deal with competition from work in other countries in the form of foreign factories and imports. In order to generate union concessions or ensure relative labor peace, multinational companies often threaten to send work to locations where the costs of labor and production are cheaper (see Bronfenbrenner 1997). This strategy of "whipsawing" creates actual or threatened competition among workers; it pits workers from different countries against each other. It can also stop an organizing drive dead in its tracks.

Some U.S. and Canadian labor leaders responded to whipsawing by identifying the problem, in whole or in part, as the foreign or "other" worker. In so doing, they made manifest the perceived or actual threat of competition with foreign workers through racial scapegoating (e.g., blaming foreign workers for "stealing" jobs, undercutting workers in developed countries by accepting lower wages and a lower standard of living). Racial scapegoating amounts to a racialized "foreign worker myth" that is often married to racist rhetoric about the abilities of foreign workers (e.g., foreign workers do not produce high-quality products and are not as skilled, productive, or capable as the workers from whom the work was "stolen"). For workers in developing countries, the racial scapegoating has a different spin with a similar intention – to obtain or retain jobs. They often brand workers in developed countries who attempt to keep jobs as greedy and protectionist. Racialized rhetoric is therefore inextricably linked to issues of international trade and capital mobility.

Prior to NAFTA's negotiation, however, trade within North America did not pose a large threat to workers. As discussed previously, trade between the United States and Canada has historically been quite robust. The potentially harmful effects of trade between U.S. and Canadian workers, however, were mitigated because many belonged to the same international unions, some of which lobbied for and often won special trade and tariff agreements between the two nations.[23] Signed in 1965, the Canada-United States Automotive Products Agreement, for example,

---

[23] In my sample of unions in the auto, electronics, communications, garment/apparel, steel, and trucking industries – all at one time had been part of an international union with U.S. and Canadian membership.

eliminated trade tariffs on auto parts. It stated that one car had to be built in Canada for every car sold in Canada, and that the former had to be produced with sixty percent Canadian parts and labor content.[24] The agreement ensured that jobs would be allocated fairly between the two countries.

Beginning in the 1970s, however, ideological, financial, and strategic differences led some Canadian affiliates to leave U.S.-based internationals to form their own unions. In 1972, Canadian telecommunications workers broke from the CWA to create the Communications Workers of Canada (CWC), which became the CEP in 1992. From the 1930s until 1985, Canadian auto workers belonged to the UAW. But as processes of economic globalization expanded and market factors changed, the Canadians began to realize that UAW strategies, particularly the tendency to accept company concessions, harmed them. In 1984, a majority of Canadian auto workers voted to leave the UAW, and in 1985 they established the CAW.[25]

Despite the growing movement for sovereign Canadian unionism, U.S. and Canadian unions continued to see themselves as allies in trade struggles, particularly against the onslaught of Asian imports. But in the mid-1980s, when the United States and Canada announced their intention to negotiate a free trade agreement, the reaction varied drastically between unions in the two countries. Whereas U.S. unions viewed the threat as minimal and largely ignored it, Canadian unions launched an all-out assault in opposition to it. The CLC warned that free trade with the United States would undermine Canada's sovereignty and social protections and Canadians' way of life. A December 1986 edition of the CLC newspaper *Canadian Labour* dedicated a full page to the anti–free trade campaign. Although the article warned of job loss, it focused on Canadian sovereignty:

Under free trade, the Americans would want what they call a "level playing field." That means they'd want to do away with things like our health care system. Our system of government pensions. Our unemployment insurance system. Why? American business says these things give Canadian companies an advantage. Free trade means making our way of life the same as the American way. It means deregulating our industries and selling off our public assets and services to private interests.[26]

---

[24] Tariffs would apply if these conditions were not met. NAFTA undermined the Auto Pact, and in February 2001 it was cancelled after the World Trade Organization deemed it an "unfair" trade practice.

[25] Canadian UE District 5 joined the CAW in 1991.

[26] *Canadian Labour*, December 1986.

On January 1, 1989, the Canada-U.S. Free Trade Agreement (CUFTA) became law. By 1993, the year before NAFTA went into effect, U.S. exports to Canada had reached almost $65 billion, and U.S. imports from Canada reached almost $79 billion.[27]

Trade between Mexico and its northern neighbors did not present a great concern for workers in any of the three countries until only a few years before NAFTA's negotiation. In fact, Mexico did very little importing prior to the 1970s, when it followed an economic development strategy of import-substituting industrialization (ISI), producing manufactured durable goods for domestic use.[28] The goal of ISI was to promote rapid industrialization and capital accumulation, and for years it succeeded. Between 1940 and 1965, Mexico's gross domestic product rose by an average of 6.3 percent per year in real terms; the "Mexican miracle" was heralded as a model for other developing Latin American countries.[29]

In 1965, the Mexican government decided to boost the economy by introducing an export-oriented assembly industry program. The plan allowed U.S. companies to build assembly plants (known as maquiladoras) in staggering numbers along the U.S.-Mexico border. Items 806 and 807 of the Tariff Schedule of the United States allowed goods assembled in Mexico with U.S. components to be imported into the United States with duty paid only on the value added (Sklair 1993). The plan resulted in increased trade and integrated production. Total U.S. imports saw a tenfold increase between 1970 and 1987, surging from $40 billion to $400 billion, while imports under 806/807 "increased more than thirty-fold, from about $2 billion to over $68 billion" (Sklair 1993, p. 11). Many high-tech manufacturing plants in Mexico proved to be as productive and therefore as competitive as their U.S. and Japanese counterparts (Shaiken 1990, 1994), providing an additional incentive for companies to take advantage of 806/807.

The miracle of ISI, even with the maquiladora program, was ephemeral. In 1982, the Mexican government's heavy borrowing from international creditors led to indebtedness and financial collapse. In response to this crisis, Mexico embarked on a new strategy of export-led industrialization characterized by the increased privatization of state-owned

---

[27] The trade data come from the "Direction of Trade" dataset compiled by the International Monetary Fund and have been adjusted by the U.S. Consumer Price Index (1982–1984=100) to correct for inflation.

[28] Middlebrook (1995, p. 208).

[29] Ibid.

industries, a reduction of government production and consumption subsidies, a reduction of tariff barriers on imports of capital goods, and the facilitation of direct foreign investment.[30] By 1982, U.S. imports from Mexico totaled over $14 billion.[31] Mexico solidified its commitment to export strategies in 1986 when it joined the General Agreement on Tariffs and Trade (GATT, which later became the World Trade Organization, WTO).

While trade within North America generated relatively little concern from the continent's unions until the mid-1980s, North American unions worried little about trade and foreign imports from *any* nation until the mid-1970s. In fact, the AFL-CIO, CLC, and their affiliates strongly supported trade liberalization, believing it benefited North American workers by opening foreign markets to their goods. As the U.S. economy weakened in the mid-1970s and foreign companies took advantage of its liberal trade environment and competed effectively, however, U.S. industries and workers felt the threat.

In a dramatic shift from their previous support for trade liberalization, U.S. unions and their congressional allies demanded changes in government policy. Businesses hurt by imports also joined the trade protection chorus. Import dumping and foreign subsidies, they claimed, placed them at an unfair disadvantage (Evans 2002). Although a movement against imports was not new in North America – indeed it can be traced back to the colonial period and protests over imported British tea – the AFL-CIO's change in policy was quite significant.[32] It was not simply a discursive shift but one that launched the federation on a new strategic course. In the 1970s and 1980s, the AFL-CIO's strategy to combat increasing imports combined legislative action and public participation. As Evans (2002) notes, when the NAFTA struggle emerged "labor had occupied the role of the primary oppositional actor in the U.S. trade system for more than a decade."[33]

On the legislative side, the federation sought legislation to stem the flow of imports. A 1985 announcement in *AFL-CIO News*, "America's Voices Are Saying: Stop Job-Killing Imports – Pass Trade Laws That Curb Unfair Trade Practices!" urged workers to send a message to Congress

---

[30] Middlebrook (1995, pp. 254–255).
[31] The trade data come from the "Direction of Trade" dataset compiled by the International Monetary Fund and have been adjusted by the U.S. Consumer Price Index (1982–1984=100) to correct for inflation.
[32] See Dana Frank's (1999) excellent historical analysis of economic nationalism.
[33] Evans (2002, p. 48).

demanding passage of protective legislation.[34] In addition to a variety of trade- and import-related bills, the AFL-CIO advocated the denial of trade preferences under the Generalized System of Preferences (GSP) to countries that violated workers' rights. At the time, Mexico *was not* listed among the violating countries.

A surfeit of articles and commentary about the import peril appeared in the AFL-CIO's newspaper from the mid-1980s to the early 1990s. A 1985 article assailed President Reagan's veto of import curbs on various products as an assault on "import-ravaged industries."[35] Free trade opponents warned in the newspaper that "unfair" trade practices by foreign countries would only depress wages in the United States and undercut U.S. producers. The ILGWU research director warned that wages could not be reduced "without creating a shameful Third World of our own."[36]

On the consumer side, the AFL-CIO and CLC endorsed strategies of economic nationalism by spearheading "Buy American" campaigns to convince consumers to buy American-made products. At the time, the federations did not consider Mexico as part of America. Unions, with the support of companies that also stood to lose if their products could not compete with cheaper foreign imports, labeled products with special tags identifying them as American-made. In a 1985 *AFL-CIO News* article titled "Who says imports cost less?" the writer quotes then president of the ILGWU Sol C. Chaikin: "American consumers, who are also workers, know now that they get no bargain in buying imports. All that they do is to place their own jobs in jeopardy when they buy foreign-made goods."[37]

In general, "Buy American" campaigns did little to thwart the consumer scramble for cheaper or better-made foreign goods. The campaigns, however, were extremely popular rhetorically, particularly in the halls of Congress. A 1987 *AFL-CIO News* article praised members of the U.S. House of Representatives for tossing out foreign-made flatware in favor of U.S.-made flatware in a very public Capitol Hill ceremony:

"Made in the U.S.A." became the motto of the House of Representatives, as Speaker of the House Jim Wright junked foreign-made stainless steel forks, knives

---

[34] *AFL-CIO News*, August 31, 1985, p. 8.

[35] *AFL-CIO News*, Vol. 30, No. 51, December 21, 1985, p. 1.

[36] "Failed Trade Policy Hit for Raising Risk of More Job Losses." *AFL-CIO News*, Vol. 30, No. 47, November 23, 1985, p. 1.

[37] "Who Says Imports Cost Less?" *AFL-CIO News*, Vol. 30, No. 47, November 23, 1985, p. 1.

and spoons used in the members' dining room and replaced it with American-made products.... As several hundred congressmen, union members, and industry officials looked on, waiters gathered up the imports and replaced them with new flatware donated by the [United Steelworkers of America] and the specialty steel industry. "I bent mine a bit before I threw it in the box," said Rep. Austin Murphy (D-Pa.).[38]

U.S. labor leaders appealed to union members to lead the "Buy American" movement. The *AFL-CIO News* reported: "Sec.-Treas. John Mara [of the AFL-CIO Union Label and Service Trades Department] pointed out that "there is a groundswell of interest in this country emphasizing a movement of 'Buy American.'" He urged trade unionists to help correct the foreign trade balance by choosing high-quality union-made and American-made products and services."[39]

In order to reinforce its anti-import campaign, the AFL-CIO regularly linked foreign imports to lost "American" jobs. One article quoted an ACTWU labor activist who likened the flight of industry to "economic capital punishment."[40] The idea that better-paying industrial jobs belonged to Americans, and that Americans were entitled to retain them, is explicit in the federation's rhetoric. A 1986 editorial argued: "What [our trading partners] get to keep are the jobs – not just union jobs, but American jobs – jobs that built the American middle class and raised the American standard of living."[41]

"Buy American" campaigns and opposition to foreign imports are not necessarily a reflection of or motivated by racism. Indeed, labor activists in all three countries argued that unions would be neglecting their responsibility if they did not defend the "right" of workers to keep and attract jobs. But "Buy American" and other anti-import campaigns can cross the line into racism and xenophobia when they combine nationalistic rhetoric with racial stereotypes. The UAW's campaign against Japanese cars was rife with nationalistic rhetoric. Historian Dana Frank details a 1978 cartoon circulated in a Detroit auto plant that read "We Have to beat the Japs" and featured "caricatured Japanese workers with slanty eyes and

[38] "House Junks Import Flatware." *AFL-CIO News*, Vol. 32, No. 5, January 31, 1987, p. 1.
[39] "Label Week." *AFL-CIO News*, August 30, 1986.
[40] Gene Zack, "Reagan Job-Export Scheme Draws Fire: Runaways Spell Misery for American and Mexican Workers." *AFL-CIO News*, Vol. 31, No. 48, November 29, 1986, pp. 1–2.
[41] "Economic Realities." *AFL-CIO News*, Vol. 31, No. 24, June 14, 1986, p. 7.

tricky smiles."[42] She also quotes a leaflet distributed by one UAW shop committee in 1991 after General Motors announced the imminent closure of twenty-one plants:

A call to arms for all Americans to declare war on Japanese products and all non American made products! When Japan bombed Pearl Harbor – we went to war!... And when Japan threatens the security of American jobs we must go to war again – with a complete boycott of all products not made in America![43]

Because U.S. and Canadian unionists did not perceive Mexican imports (and the workers in Mexico who made them) to be a considerable threat to northern jobs and industries prior to the mid-1980s, they did not cast them as villains in the trade war (although in the immigration war they took center stage). "Buy American" campaigns focused primarily on Asian imports.

But unions' almost myopic focus on Asian products shifted in 1986 when the AFL-CIO turned its attention to a very specific problem related to international trade to which it had previously given little attention – Mexican maquiladoras. Although Mexico began its maquiladora program in 1965 and the import peril was regularly discussed in the pages of *AFL-CIO News*, articles about the threat of Mexican imports or the relocation of U.S. jobs to Mexico were rare. One AFL-CIO official confirmed the federation's relative lack of interest in the maquiladoras during that period: "We started looking at the maquila program and [problem] with any degree of seriousness in the late eighties, in a less serious way [probably] in the mid-eighties, focusing on U.S. legislation."[44]

By 1986, however, the explosion of border factories, and more importantly their success, forced the U.S. labor movement to take notice. The new Mexican threat materialized in the pages of *AFL-CIO News*. One article scathingly criticized runaway plants to Mexico and the economic woe engendered by capital flight. The article accused the Reagan administration of supporting "the extension of American assembly lines across the U.S.-Mexican border," which "contributed to a problem with growing social and economic consequences for workers in both countries."[45] In 1987, the AFL-CIO's economist, Mark Anderson, reported massive U.S. job losses when he testified before the U.S. International Trade

---

[42] Frank (1999, p. 163).
[43] Quoted in Frank (1999, p. 163).
[44] Personal interview with Mark Anderson of the AFL-CIO, January 8, 2001.
[45] Gene Zack, "Runaways to Mexico Spread Economic Woe." *AFL-CIO News*, Vol. 31, No. 47, November 22, 1986, p. 1.

Commission, urging repeal of tariff provisions that "encourage these runaway firms." The *AFL-CIO News* recorded Anderson's testimony: "In 1970, ... there were 120 companies employing 19,000 workers in the Mexican border program. Today it has grown to more than 800 maquiladoras employing more than 300,000 workers, and the value of their exports to this country has skyrocketed from $145 million in 1969 to $5.5 billion in 1985." Anderson quipped: "It is an understatement to say that our worst fears have been realized."[46]

The high productivity of maquiladoras presented a bigger problem to U.S. labor unions than their sheer volume. By the 1980s, many Mexican high-tech manufacturing plants, particularly in the auto industry, were as productive and competitive as their counterparts in the developed world (Shaiken 1990). And U.S. labor activists were well aware that Mexican facilities often rivaled their own. As the UAW's assistant director of governmental and international affairs explained: "The case then as now is that often the actual production facilities are more modern than the ones in the U.S. that the companies are leaving."[47]

Whereas historically the foreign worker myth often emphasized the inferiority of foreign workers and their products, by the mid-1980s the claim lost its primacy. An *AFL-CIO News* article reflects this change in rhetoric. Its author quoted a member of the International Union of Electronic, Electrical, Salaried, Machine and Furniture Workers (IUE): "The people in Mexico will enjoy our jobs while we are at home starving. We need the work just like everybody else. We can do it just as good as they can, or better."[48] The assumption that Mexican workers are unproductive and incapable of producing quality products is absent. In fact, the rhetorical posturing is reversed; it is constructed not as an affirmation of foreign workers' inadequacy but rather as a defense of U.S. workers' abilities in the face of unquestioned Mexican capacity and productivity. This rhetorical shift reflects not only a change in attitude but also a change in reality; to claim that Mexican workers lacked skill and abilities and produced low quality prodcuts would have contradicted the facts as known and accepted by U.S. labor leaders.

---

[46] Gene Zack, "Huge Tariff Breaks Aid Runaway Firms: Growth of U.S.-Owned Plants in Mexico Jeopardizes Economy." *AFL-CIO News*, Vol. 32, No. 35, August 29, 1987, p. 1.

[47] Personal interview with Steve Beckman of the UAW, December 19, 2000.

[48] Gene Zack, "Runaways to Mexico Spread Economic Woe." *AFL-CIO News*, Vol. 31, No. 47, November 22, 1986, p. 6. (Headline changes to "Mexican Connection: Exploiting Abused Workers" on page 6.)

If U.S. trade policy could not be assailed for sending work to unproductive workers, it could be criticized for sending illegal workers to the United States. Constructing the maquiladora "problem" in relationship to illegal immigration was a new rhetorical turn on the foreign worker myth. A 1987 *AFL-CIO News* article criticized the maquiladora program for employing young women and queried about the fate of Mexican men: "Some of them are idle, others have taken temporary employment, but the vast majority have slipped across the border as undocumented workers that American agribusiness attracted over the years."[49] The AFL-CIO's suggestion that "illegal" Mexicans had "slipped across" the border was surely not meant to inspire confidence in and support for U.S. trade policies. On the contrary, the rhetoric played on fears that free trade would lead not only to runaway factories but also to the replacement of American workers on American soil by "illegal" immigrants.

Economic nationalism and the foreign worker myth were the U.S. labor movement's unsophisticated interpretation of and response to complex processes of capital mobility, economic uncertainty, international trade, and the machinations of multinational companies. In this mythology, foreign imports and competition with foreign workers were the real problems. The real solution for U.S. unions was to promulgate protectionist policies that maintained "American" jobs on U.S. soil and to keep immigrants out of the United States. The content of *AFL-CIO News* suggests that from the mid-1980s until NAFTA's passage, U.S. labor activists viewed Mexican workers as "other." American apparel workers, one article quipped, "are fed up with being the casualties of other nations' economic problems. They don't understand why their government is more interested in protecting the interests of foreigners than the interests of our own citizens."[50]

From "Other" to Ally

Prior to NAFTA, many North American labor leaders managed market threats and shocks in part by invoking explicitly racist or implicitly racialized rhetoric that constructed foreign workers or the products they

[49] "Poverty and Profiteers Fuel Maquiladora System: Jobs of American Workers Wiped Out as Multinational Firms Search for Lowest Wages." *AFL-CIO News*, December 19, 1987.

[50] Gene Zack, "Huge Tariff Breaks Aid Runaway Firms: Growth of U.S.-Owned Plants in Mexico Jeopardizes Economy." (Headline changes to "Tariff Concessions Lure U.S. Plants to Mexico" on page 5. *AFL-CIO News*, Vol. 32, No. 35, August 29, 1987, p. 5.

made as the enemies of American workers. And American, as they saw it, did not include anyone south of the Rio Grande. The possibility of building a continental solidarity that could effectively combat the power of corporate interests in North America appeared impossible at worst and implausible at best. But at the time it was not apparent that North American unions would need to collectively respond to the threats of an ever-expanding regional economy. Indeed, AFL-CIO economist Mark Anderson could not have predicted in 1987 when he sat in front of the U.S. International Trade Commission to discuss maquiladoras that only three years later even greater fears would be realized with the threat of a free trade pact between the U.S. and Mexico, and ultimately Canada.

Nor could most observers and critics have guessed that key labor unions and federations in all three countries would manage that threat collectively through cooperation rather than divisiveness, developing a sense of their collective interests as North American workers. Although there are exceptions (which will be discussed in the chapters that follow), North American unionists began to chip away at the foreign worker myth and reconceptualize themselves in new collaborative ways in relationship to "other" workers in North America. They began to reject not only the racism but also the isolationism of the past. This rejection marks a historic shift toward labor transnationalism in North America that begs analysis and explanation.

3

NAFTA as Catalyst

Constituting Transnational Actors and Interests

By the mid-1980s, the growth of the maquiladoras, Mexico's entrance into the GATT, and the three North American governments' willingness to relax trade rules signaled that the regional economic integration tsunami was unlikely to recede. North American unions, however, were unprepared to respond *collectively* to the possible economic devastation they faced. Forty years of Cold War politicking and divisiveness left them with a weak institutional foundation from which to organize trinationally. And then came NAFTA. It was widely believed the agreement would generate national responses by labor unions in each of the three countries, but little transnational contestation. This assumption was plausible given past behavior – the underwhelming response of U.S. unions to NAFTA's precursor, the Canada-U.S. Free Trade Agreement (CUFTA). Whereas the agreement catalyzed the most significant political struggle in decades among Canadian unions (and civil society organizations), it generated little reaction from unions south of their border, despite joint membership in many of the same internationals. The former secretary-treasurer of the CLC revealed that this caused some resentment among Canadian activists:

There were a number of discussions between the leadership of the AFL-CIO and the CLC . . . and the AFL-CIO simply just didn't think it was a big issue that they were prepared to put all their resources into as opposed to NAFTA. . . . And it angered us somewhat, saying you know, oh yeah, they mouth all the right words but they're doing diddly squat about it.[1]

The assumption that labor contestation against free trade would remain national could not have been more wrong when it came to

---

[1] Personal interview with Richard Martin of the CLC, February 26, 2001.

NAFTA, however. The trinational struggle against NAFTA became the largest campaign to influence a regional socioeconomic policy in North American history. It stimulated relationships among unions that fought together against its passage, many of which survived long after the agreement went into force. This unexpected result begs the obvious question: Why and how did NAFTA generate labor transnationalism among key unions? The evidence reveals that NAFTA catalyzed labor transnationalism not simply by generating a threat but by creating two new transnational institutional fields – trade-negotiating and legal fields – through which labor activists could mobilize. In these emergent fields, North American labor activists found ways to overcome the geographical, cultural, economic, and political obstacles to their sustained collaboration. Moreover, many began to redefine their interests as mutual and to see themselves not as competitors for jobs but as allies in the struggle to prevent downward harmonization across the continent. Labor leaders realized they would not succeed in killing the trade agreement if they acted as individual national labor movements; the forces supporting NAFTA were too powerful. The struggle against NAFTA would have to be a collaborative one, a uniquely North American one.

Part of the process of constituting regional actors and interests involved undermining racialized and ethnocentric stereotypes about foreign and immigrant workers. The labor unions and federations discussed here were able to engage in labor transnationalism because they either developed prior to NAFTA or constructed because of NAFTA antiracist and antiethnocentric policies and discourses regarding foreign and immigrant workers and trade policy. U.S. and Canadian unions that developed transnational relationships in NAFTA's wake had leaders and key staff – many of whom had participated in the civil rights, farmworker, and anti–Vietnam War struggles – who actively tried to undermine the "foreign worker" myth. That is, they attempted to frame their concerns about NAFTA and processes of regional economic integration in nonracist, nonethnocentric terms. As the IBT's Matt Witt explained: "People from the sixties coming to positions of influence in the labor movement – whether it was influence near the top or just influence at the local level –... brought a whole different idea about the relationship between us and people in other countries, borne of the Vietnam war."[2]

Mexican unions that engaged their northern counterparts shed their own version of the foreign worker myth – which dictated that workers

---

[2] Personal interview with Matt Witt of IBT, January 17, 2001.

north of the Rio Grande were all imperialists and/or protectionists – and began to view U.S. and Canadian unionists as potential allies. I do not make grand claims that NAFTA undermined racism in North American labor movements, but rather that NAFTA compelled key labor leaders to reevaluate and re-create the racial ideologies and discourses promulgated by their unions or members in the past.[3] Newly constituted as regional actors with regional interests, they emphasized how NAFTA would undermine the living and working conditions of *all* North Americans. Thus, NAFTA participated in the rupture of stereotypes about the "other" worker (i.e., the foreign worker) and helped chip away at various obstacles to transnational cooperation and collaboration.

It is important to note that the use of the term racism was not imposed on union leaders; the term spontaneously and unexpectedly arose time and again in interviews and documents to describe policies and practices that involved marginalizing Mexican workers and immigrants or blaming them for job losses.[4] It is clear that many union leaders employed a broad conception of race that approximates Nobles's definition as "a complex and often internally contradictory set of ideas about human similarity and difference" (Nobles 2000, p. xi). They therefore frequently conflated racism with ethnocentrism, xenophobia, and even protectionism and economic nationalism. To accurately capture this understanding, I use the term racism to include prejudicial "othering" based on ethnicity or ethnic origin and race.

U.S. and Canadian labor leaders' willingness to discuss and acknowledge anti-Mexican racism within their unions lends weight to a history for which there exists precious little documentation. Whereas a substantial literature chronicles racism directed at African Americans in U.S. unions, there is no equivalent record of the history of racism against Mexican Americans, Mexican immigrants, or foreign Mexican workers.[5] But leaders' often unprompted descriptions of a history of racist policies and strategies not only illuminated a past from which they wished to distance themselves but also revealed how NAFTA helped shape their choice of a future direction less sullied by racism.

This chapter explores why and how North American labor unions mobilized collectively in response to NAFTA. Here I focus on the two

---

[3] Here I discuss approaches by the leaders of national unions. I do not examine these phenomena among local unions or their membership.

[4] My interview questionnaire included a question about racism, protectionism, and xenophobia. Respondents frequently mentioned these issues before I asked the question.

[5] For exceptions, see Reisler (1976) and Kiser and Kiser (1979).

forms their response took: involvement in large trinational anti-NAFTA coalitions that included labor and other civil society organizations (e.g., environmental, consumer, and farmers' groups, among others), and participation in nascent transnational relationships with union counterparts. For the latter, my analysis centers on three sets of North American unions and federations that formed transnational relationships after 1989 in response to NAFTA. The first set consists of unions with workers in electronics manufacturing industries. This trio includes the Authentic Labor Front (Frente Auténtico del Trabajo, FAT), the United Electrical, Radio and Machine Workers of America (UE), and the United Steelworkers in Canada (CUSWA). The second set comprises unions in telecommunications industries and includes the Communication Workers of America (CWA), the Communications, Energy, and Paperworkers Union (CEP, formerly the Communications Workers of Canada, CWC), and the Mexican Telephone Workers' Union (STRM). The final set are labor federations (AFL-CIO, CLC, and FAT). Prior to NAFTA, none of these unions or federations had trinational relationships.

Initial Contacts: Mexico-U.S. Dialogos

The story of North American unions' collective response to NAFTA begins in the late 1980s in the modest Washington, D.C., office of the progressive Mexican daily newspaper *La Jornada*. There, David Brooks, the paper's U.S. correspondent, hatched a plan to bring together civil society organizations in the United States and Mexico (and later Canada) to discuss North American economic integration. Brooks, like other concerned activists in the wake of the CUFTA struggle, believed that it was only a matter of time before a threat great enough to provoke a response from slumbering U.S. activists would appear and that it would likely come from the south. Brooks's brainchild, dubbed Mexico-U.S. Dialogos (Dialogos), was the earliest trinational group to deal with the perils of regional economic integration.

In meetings convened annually beginning in 1988, Brooks brought together representatives from various social sectors directly affected by economic integration processes in each of the three countries. As he explained: " ... the idea was that these people ... would have an ability to find each other, to engage with each other and to discuss what the consequences of that were."[6] With the help of a core group of conveners that

---

[6] Personal interview with David Brooks of Mexico-U.S. Dialogos, January 4, 2001.

usually included officials from the UAW and ACTWU, Brooks organized meetings, known as "exchanges." Exchanges did not have formal agendas, but usually included plenary sessions to discuss "national/domestic priorities of social constituencies in Mexico, Canada and the United States and an analysis of what the governments are doing in each country."[7] Participation varied, but generally averaged between fifty and seventy-five activists. Brooks organized seven general exchanges between 1988 and 1996 (see Appendix Table A.2). He also facilitated several trinational "sectoral/organizational initiatives" that emerged from the general meetings, including a women's trinational meeting held in Mexico City, a telephone/communications workers alliance, the Americas summit of textile workers, and a trinational agricultural exchange.

It was during Dialogos exchanges that many union activists from the United States, Mexico, and Canada came into contact for the first time. According to an AFL-CIO leader, AFL-CIO representatives *unofficially* attended Dialogos exchanges, beginning with the first in September 1988. The AFL-CIO's then director of international economic affairs confirmed his participation:

I'd started to have some relations with various social actors including trade union people in Mexico through the auspices of a good friend of mine named David Brooks who's the U.S. correspondent to *La Jornada* . . . So I got to know a number of people from various parts of the Mexican labor movement including the FAT, some more quote "progressive" elements of the CTM, teachers, at that time just the telephone workers, Hernández Juárez [STRM's General Secretary].[8]

Because the AFL-CIO maintained its exclusivity with the CTM at the time, the federation did not publicly reveal its participation. Brooks verified that CWA, STRM, and FAT officials also attended Dialogos meetings:

It was one of the first places where communication workers from both countries met, the STRM and the CWA people met. Who came to these things was very uneven. From Mexico it was usually Hernández Juárez, always someone from the CTM, the FAT. These are people who would never get together in Mexico and never allow a photograph of them together but they would meet here.[9]

As Brooks suggested, Mexico-U.S. Dialogos was a safe forum for North American labor activists. It not only provided a venue for union leaders

---

[7] "Proposed Draft Agenda for Trinational Exchange, Mexico 1996." Memo written by David Brooks to "Trinational Conveners." April 16, 1992.

[8] Personal interview with Mark Anderson of the AFL-CIO, January 8, 2001.

[9] Personal interview with David Brooks of Mexico-U.S. Dialogos, January 4, 2001. Participation confirmed by archived lists of attendees.

at opposite poles of the political spectrum within Mexico to meet but also served as a trinational arena for cross-border dialogue. Although it would take NAFTA to move these and other activists beyond contacts toward transnational relationships, until NAFTA was announced Dialogos was the only arena available to them.

Mexico-U.S. Dialogos was two years old when a free trade agreement between the United States and Mexico (the initial agreement did not include Canada) was first announced on September 25, 1990. The announcement caught labor participants off guard. Behind closed doors, administration officials told labor leaders it would never happen. The AFL-CIO's director of international economic affairs at the time remembered:

Well NAFTA was quite frankly a surprise. I mean I remember in the building across the street having a meeting of my quote "Labor Advisory Committee on Trade Policy" with Carla Hills [U.S. Trade Representative under President George H. W. Bush]. [I] had met with her two months before, [and she] said, "no no no, never never never never." Two months later she sits in the AFL and says, "Oh sorry, we changed our mind."[10]

President Bush's announcement of NAFTA's impending negotiation therefore sent shockwaves through North America's labor unions.

NAFTA's Threat

Although CTM and other "official" Mexican unions remained in the minority during the NAFTA battle, the vast majority of North American unions not only opposed the agreement but also tried desperately to stop it. The forces of regional economic integration had proceeded at a gallop across North America for decades with little collective response from North America's labor unions; NAFTA, however, embodied these processes in concrete and transparent ways. As the UE's Bob Kingsley explained: "In the consciousness of America's workers and to some extent the consciousness of America's labor movement the translation of globalization into most understandable terms is NAFTA."[11]

The agreement presented a significant threat to North American unions charged with protecting workers' rights. It represented the institutionalization of policies that labor activists believed would result in downward harmonization across the continent. U.S. and Canadian labor leaders

---

[10] Personal interview with Mark Anderson of the AFL-CIO, January 8, 2001.
[11] Personal interview with Bob Kingsley of the UE, January 23, 2001.

worried that NAFTA would result in job loss, undermine working conditions, and send wages spiraling downward. According to the UE's director of international affairs: "The truth of the matter is that I think NAFTA was the icing on the neoliberal cake ... it was far from the beginning of the transformation of the international economy. It was really a step along the way. But it became sort of a touchstone or a rallying cry."[12]

NAFTA's introduction also created a sense of urgency among independent Mexican unionists who feared Mexican workers would suffer by not being able to compete with modernized U.S. and Canadian industries, and that neoliberal policies and economic austerity programs would be forced down their throats as a prerequisite to NAFTA's passage. They worried that NAFTA's effects would also indirectly hamper the growth of an independent labor movement as the Mexican government attempted to woo foreign investment by offering Mexico as a haven for labor stability and low wages. Given the potential havoc NAFTA could wreak, Mexican activists decided they needed to seek out northern allies with whom they could fight against the free trade agreement. As one Mexican labor activist explained: "The circumstances were a natural development of the relations that were growing out of the struggle against free trade, against NAFTA. It was creating the conditions that made organizations in both countries upset and receptive."[13] Independent Mexican unionists were not alone. Joining them in a chorus of opposition were indigenous activists who, in 1994, would launch their own worldwide struggle against the government's neoliberal policies from the jungles of Chiapas.

NAFTA embodied the site of real and symbolic contestation over hegemonic globalization. Labor leaders and other civil society actors bristled at what they considered to be an unfair and undemocratic process of trade policy negotiation and implementation in North America. They worried that multilateral economic institutions like NAFTA that set goals and policy standards without the participation of regional "citizens" would wreak social and economic havoc across the continent. These agreements, they argued, would only reinforce the power of multinational corporations and economic elites.

Canadian unionists spoke from experience. Although they had long accepted their country's dependence on trade, most opposed CUFTA when it was unveiled in 1984. Enraged that the negotiations lacked transparency and democratic participation, the CLC promulgated a rhetoric

---

[12] Personal interview with Robin Alexander of the UE, December 21, 2000.
[13] Personal interview with Alejandro Quiroz Soriano of SEMARNAP, July 6, 2000.

that posed the United States and Canada as polar opposites, and warned that the agreement would undermine Canada's sovereignty and could eliminate social protections such as government health insurance. CLC leaders argued that Canadians' culture and way of life would be jeopardized. More historic than their rhetorical stance was how unions organized against it. They helped create broad cross-sectoral coalitions representing labor, farmers, women, native peoples, environmental, consumer, and human rights organizations that came together to create the Pro-Canada Network (which later became the Action Canada Network) and the Council of Canadians (see Ayres 1998).

These cross-sectoral coalitions were the first to emerge in response to free trade anywhere in the world.[14] And they were instrumental in setting the tone and agenda for the struggle and the terms of the public debate. Sam Gindin of the CAW explained the leading role Canadian labor unions took in the anti-CUFTA campaign: "In Canada it was the unions that were really leading this fight, and within the unions we were a leading force. And this was a national issue in Canada, it was a main issue in an election. It was *the* issue. And the political party wasn't even leading, it was being led by a coalition that we were heading."[15] Although the coalitions did not defeat CUFTA, they became the model for how to mobilize cross-sectorally at the national level against processes of regional economic integration (Evans 2002).

When the Canadian government placed NAFTA on the table, Canadian unions wasted no time resuscitating this rhetoric and national cross-sectoral coalitions. Explained David Mackenzie of the Canadian Steelworkers:

We weren't about to agree to trade deals that would remove Canada's own capacity to act on its behalf whether it was for reasons of industrial policy or economic planning, or equalization or social programs or what have you. We wanted those things protected. And all of the assurances in the world that they would be protected had proven to be virtually meaningless.[16]

Put succinctly by the AFL-CIO's director of international economic affairs, North American unions mobilized in order to influence how the rules governing the regional economy were made: "And the question here is simply not a free trade agreement but the fact that we're making new rules for the North American market and for us the question is what are

---

[14] For an excellent discussion, see Ayres (1998).
[15] Personal interview with Sam Gindin of the CAW, February 14, 2001.
[16] Personal interview with David Mackenzie of CUSWA, February 16, 2001.

the rules. I mean that was the basic thing for us, what were the rules?"[17] NAFTA's threat forced North American labor activists to draw a line in the sand and decide what they were willing to struggle against and the direction that struggle would take.

The introduction of NAFTA presented a "shock" to the landscape of North American labor movement relations. It was not inevitable, however, that labor activists would interpret and construct NAFTA's threat as a shared one that would not simply hurt workers in each country but would harm them *collectively* as North Americans. Nor was it predictable that unions would respond to the threat collectively by reevaluating previous strategies of isolationism and protectionism and embracing transnational cooperation. Institutional scholars have long recognized that severe shocks to stable organizational fields in the form of legal or policy shifts can force organizations to change their own policies and strategies (see Fligstein 1985, 1991). Shocks also impact organizational transformations within labor unions (Voss and Sherman 2000). But changing how unions in the three countries had related to each other since the Cold War would take more than a threat, however great. Although social movements often emerge in response to threats (Berejikian 1992; Goldstone and Tilly 2001; Jenkins, Jacobs, and Agnone 2003), the NAFTA story suggests that transnational movement emergence also requires an organizational infrastructure to build new cultures and identities and to direct and facilitate mobilization.[18]

Constituting Transnational Actors and Interests

As labor activists began to recognize the threat of regional economic integration, it was NAFTA itself that provided a new institutional arena – a transnational trade policy arena – in which they could mobilize *and* develop mutual interests and goals. The transnational trade-negotiating field was an amalgam of different state and nonstate actors and organizations, including the office of the U.S. Trade Representative (USTR), members of official advisory committees, and negotiators from various government offices and agencies, including the U.S. Treasury and the Departments of State, Labor, and Agriculture, and counterparts in Mexico and Canada that began to coalesce when the agreement was announced in

---

[17] Personal interview with Mark Anderson of the AFL-CIO, January 8, 2001.
[18] Although their origins vary, threats and political opportunities often generate similar responses. Both can force social movement actors to decide what is worth fighting for and to mobilize.

1990 (Evans and Kay 2008). The field itself was unique among U.S. government policy arenas because it institutionalized labor participation. While the USTR negotiates on behalf of the president, congressional mandate requires a three-tier corporatist advisory system that includes labor union leaders and business representatives. During NAFTA negotiations, two labor leaders contributed at the first level on the Advisory Committee on Trade Policy and Negotiations (ACTPN).[19] Approximately eighty union members from different industries also participated on a Labor Advisory Committee. Although U.S. labor officials had direct access to negotiators and an official seat at the table, Bush administration officials and business leaders dominated the table itself; over forty-five companies participated on the ACTPN.

To compensate for their relative weakness on the committees, labor unions expanded the trade-negotiating field outside the official realm. Trinational union coalitions, individual unions, and labor NGOs organized as "outsiders" to try to affect the negotiating process. By rallying support for their anti–free trade message among rank-and-file union members and the general public, labor activists attempted to sway members of Congress who had final ratification authority and who could also wield influence among committee members. Their actions, including protests, popular education, and advocacy, sent decision makers a strong message that they would face a groundswell of opposition if labor rights protections were not included in the final proposal.

Labor activists' collective engagement in the transnational trade negotiating field helped initiate a process of constituting transnational actors and interests among key North American unions in various industries. As interactions progressed, however, many labor activists came to recognize that they actually shared interests in common. As they became constituted as regional actors, they emphasized how NAFTA would undermine the living and working conditions of *all* North Americans.

The FAT's Bertha Luján explained how the trade agreement helped change the consciousness of Mexican activists, particularly the way they viewed their northern neighbors and the process of economic integration:

NAFTA permitted us to understand that we were all a part of the same strategy and process of economic integration. It helped us to see that we face the same challenges and problems. Globalization has provoked the fall of labor standards and salaries in the three countries. The consequences have been for us to realize that the same labor and economic policies that cause the fall in labor standards

[19] ACTPN includes presidentially appointed leaders in economic sectors affected by trade.

and salaries apply in the three countries, and that we're therefore facing the same enemies.[20]

Luján's colleague, Benedicto Martínez, echoed her comments, capturing the nature of the shift toward labor transnationalism in North America:

I would say that one of the great benefits of NAFTA is that it obligates us – unions and organizations – to seek out relations and strengthen them, and to create alliances. Now relations do not result from mere circumstance, but from a recognition of mutual interests. I think that before NAFTA there was not an understanding of the reality and the phenomenon of globalization.[21]

The STRM's Rafael Marino Roche expressed similar opinions about NAFTA's role in generating North American interests:

In reality NAFTA was what accelerated a lot the possibility of international relations. In reality in Mexico for a long time U.S. unions were seen as a means for imperialism. We also thought this here, and we had no relation with the AFL-CIO. I think this changed with NAFTA, because it changed the old conceptions of the Cold War that existed among Mexican unions. That ideology decreased and people began to talk about common interests. And the U.S., principally the AFL-CIO, abandoned many of its conceptions.[22]

Canadian and U.S. labor leaders articulated the same revelation. According to Thea Lee, the AFL-CIO's assistant director for international economics, the struggle against NAFTA was instrumental "in cementing the idea that there were common interests between Mexican and American workers." She added: "And I think it's something that we always believe and we always say that the battle against NAFTA was not a battle against Mexican workers but against U.S. corporations or other multinational corporations that were abusing the rights of Mexican and American and Canadian workers."[23] Canadian labor leader Fred Pomeroy concurred: "Well in my view we just wanted to try and involve unions from each of the countries because we were all going to get hurt somehow. The employers didn't raise the standards for people in Mexico, as they tried to push it down in the U.S. and Canada. They squashed heads at all

[20] Personal interview with Bertha Luján of the FAT, August 3, 1999.
[21] Personal interview with Benedicto Martínez Orozco of the FAT, July 27, 1999.
[22] Personal interview with Rafael Marino Roche of the STRM, May 15, 2000.
[23] Personal interview with Thea Lee of the AFL-CIO, December 8, 2000.

ends."[24] The UE's Robin Alexander described how the developing sense of collective interest helped undermine the foreign worker myth:

Because I think at that time – much more than now . . . there was a currency to the "Mexican workers are stealing U.S. jobs", and what we were doing was showing the example that not only wasn't that the case, but there was a different kind of explanation. And that the solution was international solidarity. And I think that was very exciting to people. And so in that sense I think that NAFTA . . . sort of was an impetus towards moving people to seeing the world somewhat differently.[25]

Mexico-U.S. Dialogos founder David Brooks explained that as U.S. labor activists reeled from NAFTA, a new concept of protectionism began to emerge:

And then there was this sort of emerging, sort of what I would call a more progressive line, which was understanding protectionism within the dynamic of what was happening with economic integration. And that protectionism had to do with the concept of not only protecting your own communities, workers, or your own constituency, but that you couldn't do that without also fighting to protect the interests of constituencies on the other side of your equation.[26]

Brooks suggests that some labor activists began to realize that protecting the interests of their Mexican counterparts was essential to their own economic security. Labor activists across the continent articulated a consistent definition of solidarity as finding common interests. As the former director of the Solidarity Center's Mexico program explained:

I have never thought that solidarity was charity. And it's not noblesse oblige. Solidarity is seeking common interests across borders. And that means your interest is involved; it always is involved. And if you don't put it on the table, people are going to be suspicious of your motives, and they're right to be suspicious. So the best way to engage in solidarity is to say yeah, I have an interest here, and here's my interest. If your wages are so low and continue to remain so low, I'm going to lose all the jobs I've got. So it's in my interest that your wages increase. What's your interest? Well, your interest is in increasing your wages. So guess what, we have a common interest. That's the only solid basis for solidarity, common interest . . . [and in the human rights sense] I can't have the right to organize and bargain collectively as long as you don't.[27]

[24] Personal interview with Fred Pomeroy of the CEP, February 28, 2001.
[25] Personal interview with Robin Alexander of the UE, December 21, 2000.
[26] Evans (2002), p. 306.
[27] Personal interview with Jeff Hermanson of the AFL-CIO's Solidarity Center, August 24, 2000.

A Mexican labor lawyer concurred:

Today we have a new age of organizing across borders, a new international attitude and activities. In the face of globalization unions need to organize internationally and NAFTA is part of that process. . . . Today cooperation is not about charity but seeing for the first time the common interests between each other. This is an innovation since the late 1980s.[28]

It quickly became clear to anti–free trade activists that NAFTA would be won or lost in the United States because its passage depended primarily on U.S. congressional votes. Whereas in both Mexico and Canada the president or prime minister has free rein over trade policy content and ultimate passage of trade agreements, in the United States the executive branch negotiates content and the legislature has final ratification authority. With the PRI-controlled unions such as the CTM fully behind a determined Mexican President Carlos Salinas de Gortari, NAFTA opponents in Mexico could do little to alter the outcome. And, in Canada, even a lack of support for the agreement among voters could not derail the neoliberal project of Prime Minister Brian Mulroney and his conservative party. Although anti–free trade coalitions emerged in Mexico and were resurrected in Canada, the majority of *trinational* efforts to kill the agreement targeted the transnational trade-negotiating field and were centered in the United States.

The first hurdle to NAFTA's codification was congressional permission for the president to negotiate the agreement. Therefore, the first challenge faced by labor activists – many of whom had participated in Mexico-U.S. Dialogos – was to defeat a fast-track reauthorization vote in Congress. Fast-track authority would allow President Bush to negotiate a free trade agreement that Congress could vote for or against but could not amend. Congress would have sixty legislative days to extend fast-track authorization for the agreement after President Bush officially requested fast-track extension (which occurred on March 1, 1991).

Although in the fall of 1990 it was unclear when President Bush would request extension, anti–free trade activists shifted into high gear in preparation for the announcement and the subsequent congressional vote. Canadians, reeling from their lost CUFTA battle and determined to stop the free trade onslaught, reactivated their anti–free trade coalitions and sent representatives to the United States and Mexico to warn of the effects

---

[28] Personal interview with José Alfonso Bouzas Ortíz of the National Autonomous University of Mexico, February 29, 2000.

of free trade even though their government was not party to the agreement at the time (Evans 2002). In October 1990, sixty Mexican social organizations and thirty-six Canadian organizations met and reached an agreement to work against free trade in North America. In November, Canadian activists met with U.S. labor and environmental groups and hammered out a plan to work against free trade as a trinational coalition (Evans 2002).[29] Coalition members included the AFL-CIO, CLC, and FAT.

An (Unofficial) Break with the CTM

Conspicuously missing from the trinational coalition was Mexico's largest labor federation. Whereas the AFL-CIO and CLC vigorously opposed NAFTA, the CTM fell into lockstep with the PRI government to actively endorse and pave the way to its passage. The CTM's decision to support NAFTA helped land a blow to the exclusive arrangement between the three federations; it proved to be a considerable source of contention among them. As former Executive Vice President of the CLC Richard Martin explained:

But after the... proposal and then the introduction of NAFTA, the relationship... became much worse.... Essentially the CTM was very much for NAFTA, and that was in keeping with their relationship with PRI.... And our position, of course, was opposed to the way NAFTA had been negotiated and implemented, so there was bound to be some very headstrong arguments on both sides with respect to NAFTA. And it overflowed into the Inter-American Regional Workers' Organization Executive also, because it became a very major thing. Basically with ourselves and the AFL-CIO lined up against the negotiated agreement, and the CTM inside of the negotiated agreement.[30]

CTM leaders' policy on NAFTA was consistent with their support of maquiladoras; they believed both would bring jobs to Mexico and ensure foreign investment. In 1990, before NAFTA was officially introduced, the AFL-CIO requested to meet with Fidel Velázquez to discuss a possible free trade agreement. The iconic leader refused to meet, and an AFL-CIO official explained that his refusal was the first step in severing the exclusivity of the AFL-CIO–CTM relationship. The initial break in exclusivity, however, was neither official nor public. The AFL-CIO

---

[29] The coalition also included groups dedicated to human rights, women's rights, farmers' advocacy, consumer advocacy, and indigenous rights.

[30] Personal interview with Richard Martin of the CLC, February 26, 2001.

maintained its relations with the CTM, but AFL-CIO leaders did not reveal to CTM officials that they were talking with other Mexican unions. Instead, AFL-CIO officials continued to pursue common areas of concern. Mark Anderson, who led the AFL-CIO Task Force on Trade during the NAFTA struggle, explained that during NAFTA's negotiation, he pushed various labor rights proposals, hoping to find common ground with the CTM. However, his efforts did not bear fruit. He described a meeting in Tijuana that further strained the relationship between the federations and their leaders: AFL-CIO President Lane Kirkland and his Mexican counterpart, Fidel Velázquez (usually referred to respectfully as don Fidel):

We did a couple of joint efforts with the CTM in the early 1990s. We had two joint meetings, one in Matamoros and another one in Tijuana, and don Fidel was at both, as Kirkland was at both. And it was at the Tijuana meeting where we were talking about the maquilas and the need to improve labor rights and whatnot where the CTM were telling us that they don't want to be party to anything that would increase wages in the maquilas because it would detract, they thought, from investment. Whereupon Kirkland told me, he said to me, "That's it, I don't want to have anything to do with the CTM ever again. If you have to deal with them you deal with them, but not me," and walked out of the room and flew home. He just said screw 'em, I'm not dealing with these people, which then actually gave me more space in a sense to try to deal with other stuff.[31]

The AFL-CIO and CLC's relationship with the FAT developed slowly and clandestinely. And it was quite contentious within the AFL-CIO itself. The UE's Chris Townsend described how the federation initially responded to his union's work in Mexico with the FAT:

Ten years ago when we went to Mexico and started dealing with the FAT the leadership of the AFL-CIO not only frowned on it; [they] would violently oppose such a thing. I mean it was... for them... an outrage – how dare this union go down there and actually hook up with another bunch of goddamn leftists to stir up trouble? And of course they were the big AFL-CIO.... They had official relations with the CTM.[32]

The AFL-CIO's Mark Anderson explained his experience on the inside; while maintaining a cordial relation with the official Mexican federation, he secretly began to court independent Mexican union leaders:

I mean I think I was the first person from the AFL ever to talk to anybody from the FAT, I was the first person to meet Hernández Juárez [of the STRM]. This is

---

[31] Personal interview with Mark Anderson of the AFL-CIO, January 8, 2001.
[32] Personal interview with Chris Townsend of the UE, December 18, 2000.

stupid, or I thought it was stupid, I mean it made no sense to me at all. I remember I first met Bertha [Luján of the FAT] at a David [Brooks Dialogos] meeting.... It raised problems.

[TK: What kind?]

You know what the hell's Anderson doing meeting with these people, we have a relationship with the CTM, they're very jealous of their prerogatives in Mexico. And who the hell are these guys anyway, a bunch of left wing rabble to begin with.... Clearly they were uncomfortable about it, they being the international affairs people.... I used to fight with them all the time about this.... And essentially we got to the point where we expanded our relationship [with independent unions]... which is not to say we shouldn't have a relationship with the CTM. You know they're there, they're an actor, don't misunderstand me, but they aren't the only actor.[33]

AFL-CIO leaders' lack of honesty and openness with CTM officials about their dalliances with independent unions reflects the tenuousness and lack of trust that characterized the relations between the federations. According to more than one AFL-CIO official, however, it was clear the CTM was aware of the infidelity.

The CTM's stance on NAFTA, however, did not have to undermine its relations with its counterparts. As will be discussed in the next section, the STRM's participation in the transnational trade-negotiating field allowed it to build a relationship with the CWA and CEP despite its support of NAFTA. This suggests that engagement in the field was more critical for generating a transnational relationship than a union's position on NAFTA. Although the CTM's refusal to participate in NAFTA's transnational trade-negotiating field constrained its relationship with northern federations, the FAT's willingness to engage the field helped facilitate its relationship with the AFL-CIO and CLC. The field brought the three federations into contact and served as an arena in which to develop collective goals with other members of the anti-NAFTA coalition. Although the FAT is relatively small, it was able to magnify its significance beyond its size because of the unique role it plays as a multisectoral independent and progressive union federation in the field. NAFTA thus facilitated the relationship among the FAT, AFL-CIO, and CLC in two ways: by undermining northern federations' exclusive arrangement with the CTM and by creating a new transnational field in which to mobilize and develop collective goals and interests.

---

[33] Personal interview with Mark Anderson of the AFL-CIO, January 8, 2001.

The Emergence of Transnational Coalitions during
Fast-Track Reauthorization

The anti-NAFTA coalition's first action was to organize a trinational public forum titled "Opening Up the Debate" on January 15, 1991. The forum's goal was to counter Bush administration officials who vehemently opposed the incorporation of labor and environmental issues into the agreement and actively solicited congressional support for this position. Organizers hoped to preempt the administration with an open and well-publicized discussion of the effects uncontrolled economic integration could have on workers, the environment, farmers, consumers, and a range of other groups across the continent (Evans and Kay 2008).[34] Speakers and workshop leaders came from all three North American countries, and labor participants included the AFL-CIO, FAT, UE, and UAW.

The event was extremely successful. Although the House Ways and Means Committee was the target audience of the forum, over four hundred "Washington insiders" showed up for the event (Evans 2002).[35] Subsequently, several members of Congress signaled their support for including social protections in the agreement, which sent a strong message to players in the transnational trade-negotiating field that excluding protections could result in a failed fast-track reauthorization vote (Evans and Kay 2008). As USTR Hills warned: "Opposition groups [are] forming even as we speak. . . . There are those who would be quite happy to take away our fast-track authority and in so doing cripple us."[36] On February 5, President Bush announced that Canada would enter into continent-wide free trade negotiations. The coalition's pressure and the congressional support it garnered backed the USTR into a corner. Finally, after a House Ways and Means Committee hearing on February 20, 1991, USTR Hills conceded; the administration would address the labor and environmental concerns of the groups that threatened to derail the agreement (Evans and Kay 2008).[37]

The forum and press conference achieved success not only by compelling the USTR to amend its negotiating priorities but also by strengthening the ties among activists in the trinational coalition (Evans 2002). The success also confirmed the efficacy of a trinational strategy to fight

[34] Maggs (1991). See also McQueen (1991) and Auerbach (1991). *Inside U.S. Trade* (January 11, 1991).
[35] See Brecher and Costello (1994).
[36] Dunne (1991, p. 4).
[37] *Inside U.S. Trade* (February 22, 1991).

NAFTA, which ultimately brought more organizations into the fold and proved that transnational cooperation was possible. April 1991 proved to be a momentous month for transnational organizing. Two key organizations modeled after the Canadian national coalition Common Frontiers were created to build trinational bridges in the nascent transnational trade-negotiating field. Led by the FAT, Mexican social organizations formed the Mexican Action Network on Free Trade (RMALC). U.S. activists, many of whom had organized the forum, created the Alliance for Responsible Trade, whose earlier incarnation had been the Mobilization on Development, Trade, Labor and the Environment.

Also in April, the Quebec Coalition, part of the Action Canada Network, released a declaration describing and criticizing the effects of two years of free trade between the United States and Canada. At the end of the month, a trinational coalition of Canadian, U.S., and Mexican labor unions held a meeting to discuss the impending North American free trade agreement, and participants released another scathing criticism of regional integration. On the eve of the congressional vote on fast-track reauthorization, a variety of labor unions and organizations with labor union participants were directly engaged in the transnational trade-negotiating field and indirectly engaged in the legislative arena.

On May 23, 1991, cross-sectoral coalitions lost the battle over fast-track reauthorization when Congress gave the president authority to negotiate NAFTA. Instead of forcing them to surrender, the defeat only strengthened the resolve of labor unions and other concerned groups; they continued to mobilize during the formal negotiations of the agreement and the labor side agreement (as Chapter 4 details). Although union cooperation began in trinational coalitions, some labor union interactions quickly extended beyond the constraints of anti-NAFTA coalitions and networks to include more formal transnational relationships. As negotiators moved forward with substantive negotiations, key unions began to solidify their positions against free trade and look across their borders for allies with whom they could work more closely.

From Wetback to Compañero and Yanqui to Estadounidense: Labor Federations Counter Racism

Developing transnational interests and goals in the face of NAFTA presented labor leaders in all three countries with a plethora of challenges. One of the most significant was the need to build trust and respect against the backdrop of a history that had undermined both. This was particularly true for the AFL-CIO and CLC. The AFL-CIO's nefarious reputation in Latin America, affiliates' campaigns against Mexican immigrants, and affiliates' use of racist and ethnocentric stereotypes about foreign and immigrant workers (and the CLC's relative acquiescence) did little to engender good will among Mexican unions and workers. It would be incredibly difficult to build transnational coalitions and individual union relationships if racialized stereotypes and discourses were not undermined.

Naysayers said that it could not be done. By pitting workers against each other for jobs, they argued, NAFTA would only intensify antagonism among North American unions and generate a backlash against Mexican workers and immigrants.[38] The emergence of a bevy of anti–free trade pundits who employed the rhetoric of the "foreign worker" myth to rail against NAFTA confirmed the naysayers' fears. Leading the charge were Pat Buchanan and Ross Perot, who argued that NAFTA would obliterate U.S. jobs and industries. The meaning behind Perot's famous declaration that a "giant sucking sound" would be heard as U.S. jobs moved to Mexico was not lost on Mexican labor activists. Explained one STRM official: "I know about Ross Perot and the great sucking sound. The idea that Mexicans are going to rob Americans of jobs. Since the beginning of humanity people have looked for scapegoats, usually foreigners, to blame, and this has happened in the United States."[39]

For years, federation leaders did relatively little to construct a different message for their constituents and often turned a blind eye and a deaf ear to the racist strategies and rhetoric of individual union leaders and rank-and-file workers. When NAFTA became a concrete reality, labor leaders had two choices: they could resurrect the foreign worker myth or replace it with an analysis of regional economic integration centered on the decisions corporations and nation-states make that result in job loss and downward harmonization. Many leaders chose the latter.

For some, the decision reflected instrumental concerns that mobilizing the foreign worker myth would alienate the public and potential allies. But for others, many of whom had participated in the civil rights movement, the farm workers' struggle, and various Latin American solidarity movements, the decision reflected moral concerns that its use fomented racism and xenophobia and contradicted the supposed values of an international

---

[38] See Davis (1993), Neal (1993), and Farrell and Putzel (1993).
[39] Personal interview with Alicia Sepúlveda Núñez of the STRM, June 24, 1999.

labor movement. By 1990, many of these civil rights–trained leaders had assumed positions of power within unions, replacing cold warriors or mitigating their influence (Voss and Sherman 2000). Their impact on undermining the foreign worker myth during the NAFTA struggle was therefore quite significant.

The strongest and most united voice against a racist response to NAFTA came from the Canadian labor movement. From the moment of NAFTA's introduction, Canadian labor leaders made a conscious decision to stay away from racist discourse and attack it whenever it reared its head during the free trade debates. The evidence appears in a 1990 letter Robert White (then president of the CAW) wrote to Shirley Carr (then president of the CLC) expressing his opinion about how the CLC should publicly frame issues related to the extension of CUFTA to include Mexico. He emphasized: "We have to not just avoid, but *counter any racist tendencies.* The enemy is not Mexican workers. It is corporations trying to escape obligations, and governments trying to guarantee these corporations a 'favourable' environment by attacking trade union, human and political rights."[40] In 1991, Mexican President Carlos Salinas de Gortari visited Canada to push NAFTA. Shirley Carr met with him for thirty minutes, and the meeting was reported in *CLC Today*:

Carr told Salinas that the CLC opposition to the proposed three-way trade deal had nothing to do with animosity toward Mexican workers. "This debate is not about Canadian workers opposed to Mexican workers, this is about multinational corporations not caring about workers.... We oppose the idea of Mexican workers being played off against Canadian workers while corporations reap the profits." Carr told Salinas that she had sympathy with the Mexican trade union movement and their interest in increased foreign investment but at the same time understood that corporations were not interested in Mexican families, social conditions or the environment.[41]

The CLC's leadership did not ignore Robert White's suggestions for how to frame the federation's anti-NAFTA rhetoric. The former executive vice president of the CLC explained the federation's position on racism and how the issue was dealt with internally when NAFTA appeared on the political horizon:

When the trade agreements came in, we were very conscious to make sure that we weren't going to use Mexicans or southern U.S. Americans or any ethnic group as

---

[40] Letter from CAW President Robert White to CLC President Shirley Carr, September 4, 1990 (CAW archives). Emphasis in original as underline.

[41] "The Trade Deal Stand-Off." *CLC Today*, May 1991, p. 6.

a whipping boy. We were going to stick right to the policies of the government and the strategy of multinational corporations and such. When you're in leadership sometimes there's a bit of a cocoon that develops around you and you have to be careful. But generally speaking I did not hear very many racist remarks or xenophobia about the U.S. or Mexico. I'm proud to say I think we kept it on a pretty high plane, and not only coming from the President and myself and other officers of the CLC, but it was basically leadership of affiliated unions that tried to make sure that we didn't go there, that the last thing we wanted to do was inject any type of racism into the whole thing. So we stuck to policies and programs.... And I said aside from it being morally wrong, it's strategically stupid if we put forward that we don't want to have jobs go to the wetbacks or something like that. Now I'm not saying to you it was loudly discussed, but it was a conscious thing and there was a discussion to make sure this ... does not end up into that type of thing.[42]

The CLC directed its ire not against foreign workers but against the Canadian and U.S. governments and transnational corporations. Indeed, a 1990 *CLC Today*[43] article titled "Trade Vultures Gather for Easy Pickings" read:

Bragging about their "finely honed" services, the consultants refer to Mexican workers with a callousness that might be more appropriate in reference to beef cattle.... While thousands of Canadian jobs have already been lost in the Mexican shuffle, the groundwork has already been laid for an even greater loss: The Mexican economy is crying out for an influx of investment capital, jobs in Mexico – even at 60 cents an hour – are at a premium, and perhaps worst of all for Canadian workers, the business vultures and the consultants are smiling.[44]

Former CAW leader Sam Gindin explained how the Canadian version of economic nationalism differed from that of its southern neighbor and how it informed the debate in Canada against free trade:

You know, if your ideology is fighting companies, you have an ideology that's anti-racist too. It's solidarity against corporations. If your ideology is nationalist and corporatist, then who's the enemy? ... Who speaks for protectionism in the States? It's Perot and Buchanan. And in Canada it's been the left, and ... protectionism in Canada, our nationalism is – as in the third world a lot of nationalism is – anti-imperialist. Ours is anti-corporate. It's about trying to find the space against the corporations. It's about trying to regulate them. And we consciously did, though, we really tried to say, this isn't ... it isn't even anti-American, which was easy in Canada.[45]

---

[42] Personal interview with Richard Martin of the CLC, February 26, 2001.
[43] *Canadian Labour* ended its run in 1989 and the CLC's new publication was named *CLC Today*.
[44] "Trade Vultures Gather for Easy Pickings." *CLC Today*, October 1990.
[45] Personal interview with Sam Gindin of the CAW, February 14, 2001.

The CLC executive vice president revealed how the CLC attempted to build consensus for a nonracist public discourse by censuring and educating leaders:

But it was also good [that] in the organizational setting there was reinforcement constantly. We would take those things on when we had our big meetings with our leadership and somebody would get up and say something stupid. The leadership would just say no excuse me, this is not about the Mexican workers and calling them names and blaming them for our problems, it's about something else and let's put it back in the context. Again, our leadership learned that they couldn't say those things even if they were thinking it. They couldn't say it in the context of our public discourse, and [in] our private discourse we were having educational seminars. And it was very good because people were starting to develop a different framework and trying to put the agreement in real context rather than seeing it as something else.[46]

To educate rank-and-file workers about the situation of Mexican workers, Canadian unions began to send rank-and-file workers to Mexico on trinational exchanges and delegations. In October 1990, CWC members participated in a weeklong conference called Common Frontiers in Juárez, Mexico. A few months later, an article titled "There Is No Use Getting Mad at Mexican Workers" appeared in the CWC's newspaper *Connections*. It opened by quoting a CWC member: "Words simply cannot describe what I saw and how I felt." The article explained, from the member's perspective, the dire economic situation in Juárez and the lack of labor rights, concluding:

"There is no use Canadians getting mad at Mexican workers," he added, "How can we blame them for just trying to survive?" The answer, he said, lies in helping Mexicans to overcome what amounts to economic and political repression. The first step will be a joint Declaration to be issued in the near future, stemming from the Common Frontiers Conference. That declaration can then be used as an education tool in Canada to gain support for Mexican workers.[47]

Like the CWC, many Canadian unions reported on exchanges with Mexican workers in their newspapers to educate them about the realities in Mexico, reinforce their antiracist message, and garner support for an internationalist approach to the impending trade agreement.

Many labor leaders in Canada went beyond avoidance of racist economic nationalism and articulated the need to be proactively engaged in

---

[46] Personal interview with Hassan Yussuff of the CLC, February 28, 2001.
[47] Communications Workers of Canada, "Words Simply Cannot Describe What I Saw and How I Felt." *Connections*, Winter 1991, pp. 4–5.

trinational mobilization. Robert White, in his 1990 letter to Shirley Carr, urged her to work with Mexican anti–free trade groups:

> We should develop ties with *opposition groups in Mexico*. We should not underes-
> timate the potential of our experience with the [CU]FTA to impact on their debate:
> how, at first, it seemed like it would breeze through and how we forced a public
> debate, how we almost won, its impact on jobs and sovereignty, and the broader
> link between the narrowness of such a business-market-competitiveness agenda
> and the disintegration of Canadian society.... We should consider a *conference*
> on the corporate agenda for North America which includes not just American
> representatives but Mexican involvement.[48]

White's framing of the problem as rooted in corporate greed across the continent, and his insistence that combating it required trinational organizing, shows how NAFTA's threat began a process of constituting regional actors and interests.

NAFTA's constitutive process similarly affected AFL-CIO leaders, who began to see the connection between their struggles and those of their northern and southern counterparts. As one labor lawyer who works closely with the AFL-CIO explained:

> So I think that on . . . some of the rhetorical stuff, there is this consciousness that
> we're in this together with the Mexicans and with the Canadians to some extent,
> and so we've got to figure out how to deal with that, and I think that on balance
> that's a good thing because that's the truth, we are in this together.[49]

Many AFL-CIO leaders actively struggled to combat the racialized arguments against free trade promulgated by Ross Perot, Pat Buchanan, and leaders of some local affiliates. Indeed, the AFL-CIO and CLC tried to draw a sharp distinction between their message and popular reactionary discourse. AFL-CIO officials recognized that racialized rhetoric alien-ated potential allies. This lesson was hammered home in the late 1980s when the AFL-CIO tried to elicit support and partners for the creation of a cross-border organization dedicated to education and advocacy on behalf of maquiladora workers, which became the Coalition for Justice in the Maquiladoras (CJM). Many progressive Mexican organizations were wary of joining because of the AFL-CIO's history of anticommunist activi-ties and economic nationalism. One Mexican union leader described the position of some Mexican labor activists: "The work with maquiladoras

---

[48] Letter from CAW President Robert White to CLC President Shirley Carr, September 4, 1990. Emphasis in original as underline.
[49] Personal interview with Lance Compa, December 19, 2000.

was difficult because many people didn't want to work with American coalitions."[50]

The AFL-CIO's poor track record in Latin America also left some progressive U.S. organizations and NGOs cautious of entering into relationships with the federation. According to Browne and Sims (1993), at least one "U.S. group turned down the Coalition's invitation to join for fear of damaging its working relations with Mexican counterparts."[51] An AFL-CIO official instrumental in creating CJM explained how confronting the AFL-CIO's difficult past head-on and articulating a commitment to change helped him win over potential allies:

I played a major role in building the Coalition and going out and meeting with organizations and encourag[ing them] to join this Coalition in 1989, '90, '91. But when I would go and talk to groups, I would say look . . . I realize the AFL-CIO has a terrible history of what I think is certainly bordering on a racist attitude towards Mexican workers and we have this tremendous history in terms of our international involvement in Latin America, which is deplorable. And there is a commitment to developing a program which is a departure from the past and that we need to develop a program that educates our members about the need to work with brothers and sisters, workers in Mexico, in order to fight a common enemy. And that's how people were willing to join a coalition in which the AFL-CIO played a major role. . . . I saw a need that in order to do this work it was necessary to be self-critical of the AFL-CIO, and in order to build this work that that was necessary. And it happened. So I think . . . that's the position that ultimately the AFL-CIO took, in support of that kind of approach.[52]

When NAFTA was proposed six months after work on CJM began, the route the AFL-CIO needed to take was clear for many of the federation's leaders and key staff. Regarding the decision not to engage the rhetoric of the foreign worker myth, one AFL-CIO official explained: "I think it was a conscious decision. It was based on our experience with the maquilas prior to NAFTA. I'm sure there were people who preferred the Buchanan approach or Perot. I mean that's one thing I would never do, I wouldn't talk to [Perot or Buchanan]."[53] Echoing these comments, the AFL-CIO's assistant director for international economics stated:

I think the leadership was very clear that it's just morally wrong to argue this on a racist basis and not only morally wrong but it's stupid, so I think leadership did the best it could to try to drag the arguments away from the Mexican bashing towards

---

[50] Personal interview with Alicia Sepúlveda Nuñez of the STRM, August 27, 2000.
[51] See Browne and Sims (1993).
[52] Personal interview with AFL-CIO official, 2001.
[53] Ibid.

the gee, why are corporations taking advantage of workers who lack basic human rights, and why is the Mexican government repressing its own people? It's always like I said an ongoing issue, ongoing struggle. . . . Every once in a while I'll do like a radio talk show and somebody will call in and say, 'yeah but it's the Mexicans' fault.' Basically it's always out there, there's some element that we have to not be Pollyanna-ish about.[54]

A UAW official explained how his union viewed the problems of trade and attempted to control the rhetoric that came out of its locals:

Well if you go back and look at the stuff we did on maquiladoras, none of that was [to] bring the plants home. It was all [to] improve conditions for workers at the plants. . . . It forced us to confront some of our members saying bring back the work or screw the Mexican workers, we need the jobs. And we tried to make those arguments in the manner in which we had been making them all along and to state that we were not going to fall into traps. That didn't prevent some of our local leaders from making statements that were not consistent with that decision. . . . Because more people got interested in the issue, familiar with the issue, and read a lot about it, read what we and other people wrote, they ended up looking at it from the perspective of the importance of these international relationships and improving conditions for workers everywhere rather than seeing trade and economic integration in entirely insular terms and looking out for our domestic interests and the hell with everybody else. That's not a viable strategy.[55]

AFL-CIO leaders realized that the rhetoric of economic nationalism did not resonate with the American public. As one explained:

At this point protectionist is a bad word, to be labeled protectionist, and I think that's probably the view of the majority of people in the U.S. I think polls have shown that to be the case. So you can't embark on a chauvinist-protectionist project. No one wants to be called a protectionist anymore. The whole Buy American thing fell flat on its face, it didn't work. People didn't stop buying Toyotas simply because the unions didn't want them to, and in fact saw it as a sort of reactionary position, saw through it, I think.[56]

The struggle against NAFTA also brought many workers across the continent into contact with each other for the first time, which helped undermine the foreign worker myth among the rank and file. Mexico was a

---

[54] Personal interview with Thea Lee of the AFL-CIO, December 8, 2000.

[55] Personal interview with Steve Beckman of the UAW, December 19, 2000.

[56] Personal interview with Jeff Hermanson of the AFL-CIO's Solidarity Center, August 24, 2000.

short flight or bus ride away, and many U.S. workers, like Canadian
workers, participated in union tours and exchanges and learned the facts
about their supposed enemies. As Steve Beckman, the UAW's assistant
director of governmental and international affairs, explained:

It's not that hard to get to the border, and you could see exactly what people were
going through. And it was awful, and it was obviously awful. It's no complexity
when you see people in the maquiladoras, who work for American companies
that are making money hand over fist, who are paid next to nothing and who live
in just awful conditions with no running water, with no electricity, with sewage
running in the streams right next to their houses, in close proximity to these fancy
new plants. It was just absolutely clear to people what was going on.[57]

Unions that embraced nonracialized rhetoric attempted to enforce its
use in the transnational trade-negotiating field. Unions that invoked
racialized rhetoric often faced censure from other field participants,
including progressive labor activists across the continent, foreign workers
and their unions, and immigrants in the United States. The reflections of
a U.S. labor activist illuminate the effects of unions' engagement in these
new transnational fields:

The increased communication and contact with union activists from Mexico
meant that whatever instinct people might have had to go in that direction ran
up against the real coalition work people were doing based on the traditional
union principle that you either raise and maintain standards together or you face
a race to the bottom. And I also think the fact that we were working so closely
in coalition with environmental and women's groups and others who would not
have taken kindly to that approach probably kept some people from thinking in
that direction.[58]

As he suggests, many unions did not want to antagonize new friends
and potential allies. It therefore became increasingly difficult for unions
engaged in NAFTA's transnational fields to rely on tactics that grew out
of isolationist perspectives and experiences.

Although there was general consensus among labor leaders to manage
the threat of NAFTA by eschewing racist rhetoric, that did not completely
eliminate its use during the struggle against the free trade agreement.
Labor leaders were frank about the racist attitudes they confronted among
their colleagues and rank-and-file members. Some even revealed their own

[57] Personal interview with Steve Beckman of the UAW, December 19, 2000.
[58] Personal communication with Matt Witt of the IBT.

invocations of the foreign worker myth. An AFL-CIO official expressed
deep regret for a simple t-shirt he sent to affiliates:

Sometimes people say stuff and then regret it. I mean to me I regret one of the –
one of many – but one of the sayings that we used during the NAFTA fight
was "Don't send my child to Mexico." And in retrospect that was a mistake. I
shouldn't have done that.
  [TK: Why not?]
  Because it was a shorthand.... It wasn't even what we were telling members.
I mean when I think back on it it was so odd. All that stuff that we wrote, we
sent out, it was more detailed. It was, "Listen, let's not get mistaken about what's
at stake here. The Mexican worker isn't stealing your job. GM is moving your
job, so let's understand who's the enemy here." And then for some reason I came
up with this stupid slogan about don't send my child to Mexico. [To] which my
friend in El Paso said, "Don't send any of those damn t-shirts down here." I said
okay.[59]

The use of a slogan that was shorthand for a racist idea about the unde-
sirability of living and working in Mexico was not new in the U.S. labor
movement. But experiencing sanctions by a colleague for its use was
quite remarkable. In this case, the colleague, head of the El Paso Central
Labor Council of the AFL-CIO, sent a strong message that he would not
tolerate the invocation of a message with racist overtones. The inten-
sive interaction among unions in the transnational trade-negotiating field
facilitated censure for incantations of the foreign worker myth. These
sanctions were quite effective and powerful because they were *collective*.
The transnational trade-negotiating field therefore provided an arena in
which participating unions could, in Durkheimian fashion, reinforce the
antiracist values of the group and deliver a collective reprimand to unions
that undermined those values.

   As northern labor leaders pushed more sophisticated analyses of international markets and trade, and began a process of critical self-evaluation,
the foreign worker myth began to collapse under its own anachronistic
weight. The shift would be apparent three years later in the pages of the
AFL-CIO's newspaper. A 1994 *AFL-CIO News* article reads: "Implicit
in labor's call for bilateral trade negotiations between the United States
and Chile is opposition to extension of the flawed North American Free
Trade Agreement, which protects financial investors in Mexico while
leaving workers on both sides of the border vulnerable to exploitation
and job loss."[60] Instead of drawing a distinction between us and them,

---

[59] Personal interview with AFL-CIO official, 2001.
[60] "Worker Rights Link to Trade Gains Supporters." *AFL-CIO News*, July 11, 1994.

the AFL-CIO's rhetoric began to focus on "we." A 1994 photograph that appeared in *AFL-CIO News* provides further evidence of the change. The photo (see front book cover) depicts U.S. workers gathered outside Sony Corporation headquarters in New York to protest election fraud at a Mexican facility. One protester holds a sign that reads: "Restoring employee rights is good for America. And Mexico."[61] It appears the protester wrote in the last two words with magic marker.

The efforts of U.S. and Canadian labor leaders to make real and lasting changes in their strategies and rhetoric regarding Mexican workers and immigrants did not go unnoticed south of the Rio Grande. Perhaps the most accurate measure of the shift away from racist rhetoric among U.S. and Canadian unions is Mexicans' recognition of that shift. An examination of the FAT's union newspaper from the 1970s to 2000 reveals a significant change in the way independent Mexican unions view U.S. unions. Gone from current issues is the more derogatory "yanqui," replaced with the Spanish equivalents of (U.S.) American: norteamericano and estadounidense.[62] And recent issues do not focus on American imperialism and protectionism as they once did. On the contrary, issues are filled with reports on exchanges with U.S. and Canadian unions, acts of solidarity, and international meetings. As one Mexican labor scholar proclaimed: "What I celebrate is the AFL abandoned its racist attitudes against Mexicans."[63] AFL-CIO officials recognized the change in perception among independent Mexican unions. As the former director of the Solidarity Center's Mexico program explained: "I think where NAFTA had its biggest effect was on the attitude of Mexican unions. They began to think about... no longer see U.S. unions involved here as necessarily only an assault on their sovereignty, or autonomy [but] maybe something that was necessary or welcome."[64] This change in attitude is reflected in a statement made by the FAT-sponsored Mexican Action Network on Free Trade (RMALC):

The best way to defend jobs in the United States is to work together to elevate the level of salaries and workplace and environmental conditions in Mexico, so that

[61] The photo appeared in *AFL-CIO News*, May 16, 1994, p. 5.
[62] Because all citizens of North and South America are "American" and Mexicans are also "North American," I use the adjective "U.S." throughout the book. Because in English there exists no noun except "American" to describe U.S. citizens, I use it only when necessary.
[63] Personal interview with Graciela Bensusán of FLACSO, June 26, 2000.
[64] Personal interview with Jeff Hermanson of the AFL-CIO's Solidarity Center, August 24, 2000.

our misery stops being the way we compete with our fellow workers to the north. We Mexican workers are not enemies but strategic allies for workers north of the Rio Grande.[65]

The AFL-CIO and CLC's antiracist stance helped facilitate relationships with independent Mexican unions, particularly the FAT. FAT activists noted the change in the AFL-CIO's strategies, and a decrease in leaders' racist posturing. RMALC leader and former Mexican Congressman Alejandro Villamar elaborated:

I think there is a tendency to abandon the racist position and the discriminatory position, and above all the position based on fear that occurs when one doesn't know the other and that produces fear. And this is on both sides, not only on one side. Our vision, based on our anti-imperialist history, considered all Americans imperialists. This is beginning to change in the mentality of Mexican unionists. But it is not easy. We have found U.S. unionists with excellent and clear positions and class and social consciousness. But I can't say that all U.S. unionism has this position. U.S. unionism is very complex.[66]

As Villamar suggests, in the eyes of independent Mexican unionists, NAFTA helped forge a new antiracist discourse that did not flame fears of U.S. interventionism and racist protectionism but rather began to chip away at them. The comments of independent Mexican labor activists suggest the ability of U.S. and Canadian labor leaders to reject the foreign worker myth undermined decades of mistrust among U.S., Canadian, and Mexican unions.

Electronics Industry Unions: UE, FAT, and CUSWA

Whereas the AFL-CIO, CLC, and FAT had to overcome years of mutual disregard in order to build a relationship, the FAT did not have a contentious history with the UE and CUSWA; it simply had no relationship with them at all. And yet the unions share much in common. Although the core membership of the unions is diverse, each represents some workers employed in electronics manufacturing industries. All three unions are also quite independent and progressive. The Canadian Steelworkers formed in 1942. Although part of the United Steelworkers of America (USW), it remains extremely independent and autonomous. In 2000, CUSWA had 190,000 members. The FAT was formed in 1960 as an

---

[65] Hathaway (2000, p. 176).
[66] Personal interview with Alejandro Villamar, February 29, 2000.

independent federation of Mexican labor unions, worker-owned coop-
eratives, and community and farmworker organizations, and claimed
30,000 members in 2000. It is a left-leaning organization, promulgating
gender equity and democratic values in each of its affiliates. The UE was
born in 1936 and was the first union chartered by the CIO. In 1949,
it broke with the CIO to protest red baiting and suffered raids by other
unions, which undermined its strength and numbers. Despite its small size
(in 2000 the union had 35,000 members), it has maintained its focus on
democratic unionism and remains unaffiliated with the AFL-CIO. Like
the FAT, it is a political outsider. Of course, both unions view their independent status – and their concomitant distance from Cold War era union
politics – as a source of pride and distinction.

Despite all they had in common for decades before NAFTA, however,
the UE and FAT did not have a relationship prior to 1991. As the UE's
Bob Kingsley explained:

We have both a left history and an otherwise critical analysis of the AFL-CIA and
its approach to trade union solidarity. That wasn't unique to the period of the
eighties and the nineties; it follows the entire history of our union. But we felt that
we might also be guilty of what we found much of the rest of the labor movement
to be guilty of, which is what I would describe as a paper form of solidarity.
We'd find somebody that agreed with us politically in another country and issue
perhaps a joint proclamation condemning those bastard bosses and what they
were doing to us but the work between the unions didn't ever go beyond that.
That was nice, it was nice we had people with whom we could be in common
cause, but we didn't really to our mind find ourselves in a common fight because
we were not fighting alongside one another in any real and concrete way.[67]

An analysis of the coincidence of NAFTA with the relationship's emergence illuminates how critical the trade-negotiating field was to its stimulation. Although it is possible that their paths crossed at a Dialogos
meeting, UE and FAT leaders' memories of their first contact were in the
context of NAFTA negotiations. Less than a year after the anti-NAFTA
coalition organized the "Opening Up the Debate" forum, its members
arrived in Zacatecas, Mexico, to oppose free trade once again. It was
there, in October 1991, that the trade ministers of the three North American countries met to negotiate the substantive free trade agreement. The
trinational group convened a forum in the same city, which they dubbed
"Public Opinion and the NAFTA Negotiations: Citizen Alternatives."

[67] Personal interview with Bob Kingsley of the UE, January 23, 2001.

The UE's director of organization, Bob Kingsley, explained that in the months leading up to the forum UE leaders worried that a free trade agreement would intensify the flight of UE jobs to Mexico. In order to deal with the loss of UE jobs, which had been decreasing since the 1980s, the UE hoped to begin a dialogue with the FAT, which vigorously opposed the agreement. The UE viewed the Zacatecas forum as an opportunity to create more solidary relationships with Mexican unions. It was through participation in this forum that FAT and UE representatives first met. NAFTA therefore provided the political impetus for labor activists to begin to mobilize transnationally. As the UE's Bob Kingsley explained:

I had come down [to Zacatecas] after discussions with the leadership of our union to try to figure out what else we could do to try to make a link to the FAT that would be more than just the cordial distant relationship that existed at that time. We knew of them, we had perhaps corresponded with them, but we hadn't done much with them. So during the course of it I was able to get together with Bertha Luján and a couple of other leaders of the FAT . . . to sit down and talk about what is possible in terms of a relationship between the UE and FAT that takes our unions forward, that takes international solidarity work forward.[68]

Kingsley explained the unique circumstances of his first meeting with the FAT, which took place on a lawn outside a local university:

Here's a piece of story that not many people know. I get into Zacatecas and the meeting is to be held in some auditorium downtown, and [we] are expecting a good number of people, you know hundreds of people are coming to this meeting. But the meeting and its agenda are not exactly in line with the government's program. So the day before the meeting is supposed to take place the government sends in federal troops to remove the seats from the auditorium in which we were going to meet. They literally went in and screwed them and pulled them out, so that the facility was no longer available or useful for us to have the meeting in. . . . And what [organizers] did was there was a university on the outskirts of town and they were able to get the main lecture hall at the university and cram all the people in there.[69]

One of the FAT's three national coordinators confirmed this account of how the FAT-UE relationship began:

Before NAFTA certain unions in the U.S. suggested we start to work together in the face of the negotiations that were going on over NAFTA. The UE was one of them. So we started to create alliances and solidary mechanisms with the idea of creating them by sector. So through events in both countries, support for

[68] Personal interview with Bob Kingsley of the UE, January 23, 2001.
[69] Ibid.

our organizations, we have developed relationships that are more tight and solid, beginning with our compañeros from the UE.[70]

According to the FAT's Bertha Luján: "In reality the majority of relationships with unions in the United States began with NAFTA, and our activities against NAFTA."[71]

The Canadian Steelworkers also had their first significant interactions with the FAT in the context of the struggle against NAFTA. In 1985, the Canadian Steelworkers created a Humanity Fund to raise money for humanitarian aid during the famine in Ethiopia. CUSWA members support the Fund by contributing one penny for every hour worked, as bargained through their collective contracts.[72] In the 1990s, in response to NAFTA, the fund began to devote more attention to labor solidarity work. One of the founders of the Humanity Fund described how regional economic integration made relationships with Mexican unions more relevant and how CUSWA leaders identified the FAT as a partner in this new context:

I mean . . . a number of the people who were working in the Humanity Fund had long histories in solidarity work and it was because of that that we were aware of the FAT. . . . And as we thought our way through the question of involvement in Mexico, and Mexico was increasingly relevant particularly with the arrival of NAFTA, it seemed to us that – I mean you talk about tricky labor terrains in which to work; Mexico was a classic example of that – . . . we needed I think a kind of relatively secure sort of anteroom to the world of labor and labor politics in Mexico. . . . And the FAT was an obvious candidate for that; they were solid, they had survived, they were thoughtful, they had careful analysis, they believed a lot in solidarity, so it was just sort of a no-brainer for us.[73]

He elaborated and explained how NAFTA provided North American unions an opportunity to solidify their positions and push common agendas:

Someone once said about NAFTA that one of its best by-products was the sort of solidarity platform it created for social movement actors and trade unionists,

---

[70] Personal interview with Alfredo Domínguez of the FAT, April 3, 2000.
[71] Personal interview with Bertha Luján of the FAT, August 29, 2000.
[72] As of 2010, according to CUSWA's Website, "the Humanity Fund has been bargained into about 530 Steelworker agreements, representing close to 80,000 members. Those one-penny-per-hour contributions, plus matching funds from the Canadian International Development Agency (CIDA), mean that Steelworker members are generating close to $1.5 million annually for the work of the Fund." (http://www.usw.ca/program/content/1288.php).
[73] Personal interview with Gerry Barr of CUSWA, March 1, 2001.

and I think there is some truth in that. And one of the important pieces of that theory is that the FAT is a great believer in it; they themselves think that.[74]

As CUSWA's David Mackenzie explained:

In the early 1990s there was an important meeting in Mexico. . . . It was a meeting of NGOs and some of the Labor Funds with organizations in Mexico to talk about the next wave of solidarity work; again it was more of an emphasis on labor development. That's when we started building our relationship with the FAT. This was [in the] early nineties.[75]

The opportunity NAFTA provided was concrete: a transnational trade-negotiating field enabled labor activists to develop common agendas and try to influence the outcome of negotiations.

The three unions' commitment to antiracism policies and discourses regarding foreign and immigrant workers and trade policy helped them build transnational relationships. The UE came to the NAFTA struggle with a history of fighting racism through progressive policies and rank-and-file education, and with a progressive agenda on trade issues. The union rejected scapegoating foreign workers for the policies of multinational corporations. Historian Dana Frank quotes a resolution passed by delegates at the UE's convention in 1990:

While it is understandable that many U.S. workers advocate a 'Buy America' policy, it will not succeed in ending oppression of foreign workers or protecting our jobs. By viewing foreign workers as an enemy to be beaten in a dog-eat-dog competition, U.S. workers will only be playing into the hands of the multinationals that seek to drive wages and working conditions down to the lowest common denominator.[76]

In opposition to the "Buy American" slogan popular in the mainstream labor movement, the UE offered its own unique alternative: "Foreign Competition: Made in the U.S.A." (Frank 1999, p. 186). UE leaders explained that they focused their free trade message on its effects on all workers, and consciously undermined racist and racially charged protectionist arguments through discussion and education. According to the UE's Bob Kingsley:

Do we have some members who think that "Buy American" is an answer? [H]ave we had [them]? Yeah, and have we had to have some hard discussions occasionally about why we don't think that that's the answer? Yeah, we have. . . . We were, through serious educational efforts and regular discussion within the forums of

---

[74] Personal interview with Gerry Barr of CUSWA, March 1, 2001.
[75] Personal interview with David Mackenzie of CUSWA, February 16, 2001.
[76] Frank (1999, p. 185).

the union, able to win the point here on the recommended form of international solidarity [with our members] pretty easily, even though some of our members would at the same time cling to "Buy Americanism" because of its nationalistic appeal in part.... It wasn't difficult for us once we went to people with the facts. I mean you don't just go to people and say this is the way it is, you go with an analysis of what's happened to industrial workers in the United States over the last couple of decades, how many jobs have been lost to Mexico, what's happening to the people down there. You bring into that real-life members of the union who have been down there and observed this and bring back their stories and take the time at district council meetings and local meetings to explain to people what they've found.[77]

In 2009, Robin Alexander recounted a moment when she realized how strong the culture of solidarity had become in her union. She described what transpired between an artist – commissioned by the UE and FAT to paint a mural in the union hall of a UE local – and members of the local's executive board:

She was asking various questions and people were talking about how that local has been decimated.... So people were talking about how this line was moved out or that line was moved out, so finally, she said, "Well, so what are you doing?" People said, "Oh, well, we're working with the FAT in Mexico." Most of those lines that had moved had moved to Mexico – so it was such a powerful moment because it easily could have been something really different. It could have been Mexicans are stealing our jobs. It could have been anti-immigrant. It could have been any number of things, but it wasn't. It was our union is working in solidarity with workers in Mexico.[78]

The UE's progressive message was not lost on the FAT. One FAT leader explained that the UE distinguished itself from other North American unions during the NAFTA struggle by not promulgating a nationalistic, protectionist rhetoric: "Originally, during the initial fight over NAFTA negotiations, the attitude of American and Canadian unions was protectionistic. They wanted to engage in actions with unions like ours to prevent companies from leaving the U.S. and coming to Mexico. We wanted to create real collaboration and solidarity and strong relationships based on exchange and understanding of our cultures, and they had an idea that was a bit protectionistic. The UE was an exception."[79]

The UE's stance on NAFTA, then, facilitated its relationship with the FAT. Its view that NAFTA was a threat to North American unions, not

---

[77] Personal interview with Bob Kingsley of the UE, January 23, 2001.
[78] Personal interview with Robin Alexander of the UE, August 21, 2009.
[79] Personal interview with Benedicto Martínez Orozco of the FAT, July 27, 1999.

simply U.S. unions, helped build a common agenda and trust with the FAT. So committed is the UE to eliminating the "foreign worker" myth that it is one of its primary goals, through international solidarity work. As the union proclaims on its Web site: "We include as a basic objective working to under-cut racist stereotypes."[80]

Like the UE, the Canadian Steelworkers created an anti-NAFTA message that did not tap into racist stereotypes. CUSWA's Gerry Barr explained that this was a conscious decision and reflected broader efforts within his union to combat racism:

There's a lot of concern and worry about racism and a lot of proactive work in the union domestically and a lot of very thoughtful stuff going on. And good and progressive stuff going on in that area. And internationally I think it always was the view, of our progressive leadership within the Steelworkers for example, that the way forward was a solidarity route and . . . the protectionist thing was just never going to work. It wasn't fated to work, it wouldn't work in the long run, and probably wouldn't work in the short run. There really only was one way to get at this from the point of view of workers and it was through solidarity ties, [a] sort of common struggle and that sort of thing. No matter how unlovely the consequences might be . . . there just was no practical or morally sound protectionist defense. On the other hand, there was a practical and morally sound strategy in the other direction. And so – I think I can say fairly – it just seemed always a more attractive option.[81]

The UE and CUSWA's commitment to antiracism education among their memberships, and international strategies and discussions that undermined the foreign worker myth, provided a strong foundation upon which to build their solidarity work with the FAT.

North American Telecommunications Unions

Whereas the relationship between the FAT and its northern counterparts emerged with relative ease, that between North America's communications unions required work to overcome years of distrust that had developed during the Cold War. Prior to 1972, Canadian telecommunications workers belonged to CWA District 10. In 1972, because of various ideological conflicts and a desire for autonomy, they broke from the CWA and created the Communications Workers of Canada (CWC), which became the CEP in 1992.[82] Until the late 1980s, activities between the CWC and

---

[80] http://www.ueinternational.org/SolidarityWork/fat.html.

[81] Personal interview with Gerry Barr of CUSWA, March 1, 2001.

[82] The CEP was formed in 1992 from a merger of the CWC, Canadian Paperworkers Union, and Energy and Chemical Workers Union Gas Workers Federal Union No.1.

CWA were few and far between, and consisted largely of the odd letter of support and solidarity and joint attendance at meetings of the Postal, Telephone, and Telegraph International (PTTI), an international coalition of postal and telecommunications unions in more than one hundred countries.[83]

A relationship between the CWA and CWC began to develop in 1989 when CWA Local 1109 in New York launched a five-week strike against Northern Telecom (Nortel), based in Canada. Before negotiations, the CWA organized support with the CWC and the CAW, two of Nortel's major unions in Canada. The presidents of both unions sent letters of protest to Nortel's CEO, and the letters were distributed among the unions' rank and file. A grassroots campaign ensued when locals distributed leaflets in CAW and CWC workplaces detailing Nortel's antiunion activities in the United States.

The leaflets also connected Nortel's antiunion activities to the export of jobs to the United States. Local 1109 strikers met with Nortel workers in Canada to educate them about the struggle. The CWC's president, Fred Pomeroy, attended negotiations in New York and vowed that "Northern Telecom has to understand that it cannot pretend to be a good corporate citizen in Canada while it denies basic rights to its employees in other parts of the world. We intend to do all in our power to help Northern Telecom workers – wherever they live in the world – improve their working conditions."[84] CWA activists attribute the successful resolution of the dispute to a transnational strategy.[85] Fred Pomeroy explained the effect he believed his presence had:

But I think what scared them most was we basically between us and CWA laid it on that maybe we couldn't hurt them a lot in the U.S., but we could hurt them elsewhere in the world. At that time there were still a huge number of major telephone companies that were state owned. And we could go to places like Germany and a lot of other places in the world and say, look, this is an antiunion rogue company and you ought not be buying equipment from them, and start making a lot of racket and have some political influence. You know in the States, if we went and told AT&T you shouldn't do something they'd say well yeah, get lost. But in a place where it's government owned, you can have some influence. So I think they kind of backed off.[86]

---

[83] The PTTI was an International Trade Secretariat or Global Union Federation (as they are now called). In 1997, it became the Communications International and in January 2000 the Union Network International (UNI Global Union).

[84] Cohen and Early (1998, p. 151).

[85] Ibid.

[86] Personal interview with Fred Pomeroy of the CEP, February 28, 2001.

Although the Nortel strike triggered cross-border support between the CWA and CWC, these pre-NAFTA activities did not include Mexican unions. Before 1976, the STRM was affiliated with the CTM and participated in PTTI. In 1976, Francisco Hernández Juárez and his cadre of university-trained intellectuals took control of the union and severed its relationship with the CTM, forming an independent union. Leftist STRM leaders were highly suspicious of the AFL-CIO and its anticommunist activities in Latin America. Alicia Sepúlveda Nuñez, the STRM's former Foreign and Recording Secretary, explained that leaders feared the union would be co-opted and controlled by its northern neighbors: "And the times were such that the AFL-CIO here in Mexico was considered the AFL-CIA."[87] The STRM severed its ties with the PTTI, a move that eliminated all contact between the STRM and northern telecommunications unions.

The CWA's former national director for international affairs explained how the STRM's break with the CTM and PTTI placed the CWA in a precarious position with Hernández Juárez's new regime: "In 1980, when I became the CWA National Director for International Affairs, I set it in my mind that I was going to try to bring the Mexicans back in. . . . I never met Francisco, these people were totally unreachable, unapproachable, because as I said they came from the hard left of Mexico."[88] The CWA would not have the opportunity to realize this goal for over a decade.

In 1990, the CWA and CWC responded to NAFTA's announcement with unequivocal opposition. The STRM, however, supported the agreement. Alicia Sepúlveda Nuñez explained her union's position:

I don't think that we [the Mexican labor movement] had a very strong position against NAFTA. Most of the unions didn't really have a critical position at all, or the only thing that they demanded was that their rights were safeguarded and they didn't much care about the contents of the NAFTA agreement. . . . The STRM supported the NAFTA agreement. They said it was going to create jobs in Mexico, that it was going to open up opportunities for other industries to grow here in Mexico, that workers would benefit and that it would be all for the good of the country.[89]

Although a bitter feud over NAFTA eventually severed ties of exclusivity among the continent's largest labor federations, the STRM's support of NAFTA did not undermine the possibility of creating a fledgling

[87] Personal interview with Alicia Sepúlveda Nuñez of the STRM, June 24, 1999.
[88] Personal interview with CWA official, 2001.
[89] Personal interview with Alicia Sepúlveda Nuñez of the STRM, August 27, 2000.

relationship with the CWA and CWC. CWA President Larry Cohen explained that these problems were not insurmountable: "No, you can't have that as a litmus test.... [E]very national context is different, and the situation in the U.S. is pretty complicated in terms of the future of worker organizations, but in a different way it's complicated in Mexico as well."[90]

Indeed, the STRM's decision to support NAFTA, while working to mitigate any negative effects it might have on the union, led it to look for relationships with other North American telecommunications unions. According to the STRM's Eduardo Torres Arroyo: "After 1976 we had no transnational relations with unions.... But NAFTA gave us the greatest incentive to make the definite decision to move toward international unionism."[91] The STRM's Alicia Sepúlveda Nuñez elaborated on NAFTA's effect: "During the NAFTA negotiations relations were established to share information and come up with a common strategy of action. We wanted to have a plan of action to confront the opening in the market that was going to hit us in all three countries as part of the telecommunications industry."[92] The STRM's Mateo Lejarza, assistant to Hernández Juárez and member of the STRM's Executive Committee, agreed that NAFTA was a catalyst for the STRM's relationship with its northern counterparts:

We also have an alliance with CEP and CWA that we have had since 1991. It was initiated for two fundamental reasons. One was because of NAFTA. We had different positions: They were against, we were in favor. But we recognized that we had common labor issues. The more obvious reason was we are in the same sector.... It is a cooperative alliance to improve our collective contracts and support our struggles over contract revisions, and local struggles, and to share experiences.[93]

CWA President Larry Cohen told a similar story: "Well NAFTA and World Bank initiatives led to the opening and the investment of Southwestern Bell Corporation into Telmex [the Mexican telephone company]. I mean that wouldn't have happened otherwise. And that's definitely what triggered the relationship between the CWA and STRM of any depth."[94]

Although NAFTA provided the STRM with an incentive to work with its northern counterparts, the union was hesitant and initial interactions

[90] Personal interview with Larry Cohen of the CWA, March 28, 2001. At the time of the interview, Mr. Cohen was the CWA's executive vice president.
[91] Personal interview with Eduardo Torres Arroyo of the STRM, July 12, 1999.
[92] Personal interview with Alicia Sepúlveda Nuñez of the STRM, June 24, 1999.
[93] Personal interview with Mateo Lejarza of the STRM, May 9, 2000.
[94] Personal interview with Larry Cohen of the CWA, March 28, 2001.

proceeded slowly. Former CWC President Fred Pomeroy explained the STRM's initial trepidation, and its leaders' reasons for preferring a trinational relationship: "Frankly in the initial contacts we had with the STRM they kind of wanted to deal with . . . have us in the loop and make it a three-way dance, because they really felt at some peril getting involved with just the U.S. unions by themselves. And we were sort of a comfort cushion."[95]

CWA leaders ultimately convinced the STRM leadership to meet with them in Washington in 1991. The initiation of a dialogue between the STRM and CWA began to undermine stereotypes that had made deeper relationships impossible prior to NAFTA. A CWA official confirmed that the AFL-CIO's past presented obstacles to labor transnationalism:

And at the beginning they were very very skeptical. . . . So I went there [to Mexico City at the STRM's request] and I spoke to them again, I let them rip me apart, ask whatever questions. They had a lot of misconceptions; they thought that there was an orchestrated thing that we had and that we were tied with the CIA and all of these different things . . . you know rumors that had gone on. So I was able to dispel a lot of that.[96]

CWA leaders ultimately convinced STRM leaders that they were trustworthy. As Mateo Lejarza described: "Before they were interested in political and ideological things, anti-communism, now they want to talk about labor problems, jobs, globalization, now there is a discussion. But this all started with NAFTA. From them to us. And now we have plans and propositions."[97]

The first trinational meeting among CWA, CWC, and STRM leaders and key staff occurred at the CWA's annual convention in July 1991. In February 1992, the three unions signed a formal agreement solidifying their alliance to "defend union and workers' rights" through "joint mobilization" of members in each of the countries. This agreement provided the first step toward labor transnationalism among North American telecommunications unions. A CWA official described the content of the agreement and how the three unions began to put its principles into practice:

I prepared something very simple, basic principles, respect for one another, the regularity at which we would meet, a subcommittee that would be composed of myself and someone that each one of the other principles would nominate. . . . And

---

[95] Personal interview with Fred Pomeroy of the CEP, February 28, 2001.
[96] Personal interview with CWA official, 2001.
[97] Personal interview with Mateo Lejarza of the STRM, May 9, 2000.

it worked, it worked. We started to have regular meetings. We would meet one time in Canada, another time in Mexico, another time here. You know, we'd change, we'd meet every six months by the arrangements that we'd made.[98]

The trust the three unions developed during NAFTA's negotiation enabled them to jointly define the problem of regional economic integration as a threat to workers' rights in all three NAFTA countries.

North America's telecommunications unions had to counteract the effects of years of mistrust the Cold War had generated. A CWA official explained how the relationship the three unions embarked on prior to NAFTA's passage actually helped undermine the foreign worker myth:

So by the time the free trade agreement came out, there was no doubt in their mind.... [W]hile the rest of the unions in Mexico were criticizing their counterparts in the U.S. saying that the AFL-CIO was opposing... the free trade agreement because they didn't want to help the Mexicans, and all these different things that went on, our counterparts did not have that problem because they knew us already and we knew them.[99]

The STRM's Eduardo Arroyo argued that the contact NAFTA stimulated among leaders helped undermine racial stereotypes:

Before NAFTA I think there was racism and xenophobia. After NAFTA, it has been modified. We went to a meeting in the U.S. and the U.S. unionists said they had previously thought Mexican unions were corrupt, tied to the government, and vertical, and worthless. Now their opinion is totally different. The experiences of the telephone workers in the U.S. and in Mexico have been very beneficial for the three regions... And they've seen that we have an advanced relationship with our telephone company. Now the Americans don't consider us dependent and backward as they once did before NAFTA.[100]

Arroyo suggests that as ideas flowed north across the border, northern labor leaders came to see their Mexican counterparts not as "other" but as ally. This shift in attitude helped Mexican labor leaders see their counterparts as allies as well. The STRM's Sepúlveda Nuñez added that rank-and-file worker exchanges helped to further erode racist stereotypes of Mexican workers:

The interchanges have allowed us to break many of those stereotypes because when unionists come to our country and begin to see for themselves the real working conditions, for example in the maquilas, their conceptions begin to

---

[98] Personal interview with CWA official, 2001.
[99] Ibid.
[100] Personal interview with Eduardo Torres Arroyo of the STRM, July 12, 1999.

change. I think this is a positive outcome. And the changes in the attitude of the leaders is reflected in the attitude of the workers because they no longer use the pretext of Mexican workers to justify bad things that are happening in the United States. They don't do it. Now the guilty ones are the transnational companies and global finance and not the workers who are suffering the same effects of global capitalism. Racism has always affected cooperation because who is going to collaborate with someone who's inferior to me, an enemy? When these conceptions are broken and when we view each other as allies we can support each other.[101]

As will be discussed in subsequent chapters, the efforts of these unions to undermine the foreign worker myth within their ranks provided a solid foundation on which to build relationships based on mutual interest and equality.

A Historic Shift

The analysis in this chapter demonstrates that the transnational relationships that emerged out of the struggle to defeat NAFTA differed significantly from the labor relations that preceded them. Prior to NAFTA, North American unions saw their struggles as isolated and particular to their own nations. After NAFTA, ephemeral and weak contacts among key unions were replaced by permanent commitments to cooperate and collaborate across national borders for the mutual benefit of all workers. The emergence of labor transnationalism in North America presents compelling sociological and political puzzles: What enabled these relationships to emerge, and how did the process unfold?

The evidence reveals that NAFTA presented a significant threat to the North American unions charged with protecting workers' rights across the continent. The rules of regional economic integration were being negotiated with little consideration for their potential impact on living and working conditions. Moreover, the process lacked democratic participation and transparency. Whereas the economy of North America had become more integrated in the decades prior to NAFTA's negotiation through increased trade and investment, North America's labor unions had not. It was only when these economic processes were infused with concrete political consequences – and opportunities – that labor activists were moved to act trinationally.

Those opportunities emerged in the form of transnational fields that brought labor activists into contact with each other, helped coalesce their

---

[101] Personal interview with Alicia Sepúlveda Nuñez of the STRM, June 24, 1999.

interests as North American unions, and generated intense trinational political mobilization. NAFTA's effects on trinational coalition building were unprecedented. For the first time, North American labor unions engaged in active struggles not only with environmental and other progressive organizations but also with their counterparts across the continent. And some unions even began to build formal relationships with their counterparts that transcended coalitional goals. NAFTA, then, catalyzed a new kind of North American labor struggle by constituting transnational actors whose complementary interests transcended physical and cultural borders.

At the same time, NAFTA led some unions to reevaluate the rhetoric of economic nationalism that had posed significant obstacles to labor transnationalism in the past. Despite fears that North American unions would join the coterie that used racist rhetoric to push their anti–free trade agenda, most did not. Indeed, quite unexpectedly, the opposite occurred; leaders of key unions made conscious decisions to frame the anti-NAFTA struggle in nonracist terms. Some went further by censuring rogue local leaders and affiliates who invoked the foreign worker myth. As a result, divisive incantations that blamed foreign workers and immigrants for potential NAFTA-related job losses north of the Rio Grande were not promulgated among the upper echelons of the AFL-CIO, CLC, UE, CUSWA, CWA, and CWC/CEP. Unions' engagement in the transnational trade-negotiating field helped temper racist rhetoric; participants who employed racist rhetoric faced collective sanctions from more progressive members who would not tolerate its use.

Contrary to what naysayers predicted, NAFTA did much more to create ties among labor unions than to polarize them. In the aftermath of the fast-track defeat, North American labor unions could have allowed their trinational coalitions to atrophy and discarded their antiracist message. Their decision to continue to confront NAFTA collectively speaks volumes not only about their belief in the efficacy of transnational strategies but also in the ability of newly emerging transnational fields to strengthen transnational ties and provide a forum in which new discourses could be developed and defended. As unions moved into the next phase of the NAFTA struggle, their commitment to antiracist strategies would allow new transnational relationships to emerge and others to deepen. And their collective influence on the negotiation of the labor side agreement would be possible in part because in chipping away at the foreign worker myth they came to recognize their mutual interests and view each other not as enemies but as compañeros.

4

Constituting Transnational Labor Rights

The struggle over fast-track began a process of constituting transnational actors and interests as labor activists came together in the transnational trade-negotiating field. The process intensified as they mobilized to demand stronger labor protections in the side agreement. In an ironic twist, however, activists' ceaseless efforts to link free trade to labor protections directly resulted in the negotiation and passage of a historic labor side agreement, the North American Agreement on Labor Cooperation (NAALC), which they then vigorously denounced. And in another unintended twist, whereas labor leaders in all three NAFTA countries predicted it would do little to promote labor rights in North America, the NAALC did have one unexpected outcome – it stimulated and facilitated relationships among unions that then organized to collectively demand stronger labor rights protections in North America (including strengthening the NAALC itself).

This chapter explores how, by creating a new transnational legal field, the NAALC helped generate labor transnationalism in two ways. First, it defined and codified transnational labor rights by establishing eleven North American labor principles and recognizing labor unions' right of standing through a complaint submission process.[1] In so doing, the NAALC created a North American labor rights regime based on

---

[1] As will be discussed, these eleven labor principles do not comprise a supranational labor law. Rather, the NAALC obligates the three countries to maintain high labor standards in domestic law and enforce labor laws related to the eleven labor principles. In practice, labor activists view these principles as a set of North American labor rights, in the same way they view ILO principles as a set of international labor rights – despite problems of enforcement.

a set of rights that all three NAFTA nations agreed to protect.[2] The creation of this regime provided a foundation for labor transnationalism; by granting legitimacy to North American labor unions and their grievances and enabling them to see their grievances as inextricably linked, it helped constitute them as transnational actors with transnational interests.

Second, the NAALC established new legal mechanisms and adjudicatory venues for filing complaints of labor violations that allowed labor activists to collaborate in concrete and meaningful ways. National Administrative Offices (NAOs) in each of the three NAFTA countries were established to handle complaints of labor rights violations (called public submissions or communications) at the transnational level. Quite unexpectedly, by requiring cooperation and collaboration through its procedural rules, which require that a submission be filed in a country *other* than the one in which the alleged labor law violation occurred, the NAALC strengthened existing transnational relationships and catalyzed new ones. This chapter also reveals how unions that participated in the transnational trade-negotiating field during NAFTA's negotiation were more likely to engage the NAALC process and recruit other unions to join them in filing submissions.

The emergence of labor transnationalism in response to new transnational legal institutions and mechanisms is surprising, particularly given activists' derision of the NAALC itself and the lack of NAO submissions that resulted in trade sanctions. Theoretically, its analysis opens a window onto the processes and mechanisms by which social movement building occurs at the *transnational* level in relationship to the law. Scholarship on the law's effects on movement building developed almost exclusively in relationship to social movements and laws at the *national* level. We therefore know very little about how collective interests and identities (which can facilitate collective mobilization and action) form and develop across borders. The *process* by which workers in different countries recognize and develop mutual interests, and how new legal structures and mechanisms facilitate their creation, remains unexamined.

The law contributes to movement building at the national level in two key ways: by influencing collective identity formation (constitutive effects)

---

[2] According to Krasner, regimes are " . . . sets of implicit or explicit principles, norms, rules, and decision-making procedures around which actors' expectations converge in a given area of international relations" (Krasner 1983, p. 2).

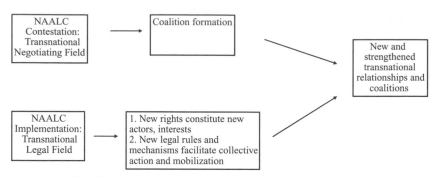

Figure 4.1. NAALC and Labor Transnationalism: Contestation and Implementation Phases

and by shaping political opportunity structures (opportunity effects).[3] Many analyses of the law's constitutive and opportunity effects on movement building capture them at either one of two moments: prior to a law's passage (prepassage contestation) or when a law is already in force (implementation). NAFTA provides an interesting and unique case to evaluate transnational social movement building in relationship to the law – both before *and* after a law's passage. The data reveal that initial constitutive processes began in the transnational trade-negotiating field during the contestation phase as labor activists formed coalitions through which they tried to shape the nature and content of the NAALC. Only after coming together to discuss their individual concerns did they begin to articulate North American interests and develop cooperative transnational networks and relationships to advance them.

Constitutive processes continued in the transnational legal field once the NAALC went into force; new legal rules and mechanisms helped forge collective interests and legitimized them through adjudication. These rules and mechanisms – particularly the procedural rule requiring foreign filing of NAO submissions – also served as transnational opportunity structures, facilitating activists' cooperation and collaboration. Figure 4.1 builds on Figure 1.2 by providing a more detailed visual illustration of how the NAALC helped catalyze labor transnationalism during its contestation and implementation phases.

The remainder of this chapter provides an in-depth analysis of the NAALC's constitutive and opportunity effects on transnational relationship building during its contestation and implementation periods,

---

[3] See McCann (1998).

illuminating the processes by which labor transnationalism emerged and developed in relationship to a new transnational legal institution.

Prepassage Contestation: Building Coalitions to Strengthen the NAALC (1992–1994)

When NAFTA negotiations concluded on August 12, 1992, labor activists and other members of the anti-NAFTA coalition geared up for the next stage in the NAFTA battle: supplemental negotiations.[4] To suggest that labor unions were dismayed by the negotiated agreement would be an understatement; they were livid. The enormous 900-page document included no labor rights protections and primarily reflected business interests. At the Watergate Hotel, where the final meetings took place, labor and other activists involved with the Citizen Trade Watch Campaign, dressed as Presidents Nixon and Bush, gave toilet plungers labeled "Where's a plumber when you need one? Stop the Secrecy!" and "I survived the NAFTA ministerial" to negotiators and the press (Evans 2002). And participants in the anti-NAFTA coalitions released a trinational declaration condemning the secrecy of the negotiations.

The public contestation over NAFTA pushed the trade agreement to the center of the 1992 presidential election. If elected, Bill Clinton could either accept the agreement as negotiated by President Bush, renegotiate it, or negotiate separate side agreements. Clinton knew that without more stringent labor and environmental protections, NAFTA would be unacceptable to labor and other activists, and many members of Congress. British Columbia's trade minister pointed out how U.S. activists were uniquely situated to influence the outcome: "Now that the NAFTA has been initialed, only special interests in the U.S. stand a chance of changing the text by lobbying Congress. Canadians have no such opportunity."[5] Of course, the minister failed to grasp how the transnational trade-negotiating field could attract and facilitate trinational collaboration.

In September, over fifty organizations opposed to NAFTA organized a "Trade Conference for the 21st Century" to sway the position of Clinton and the other presidential candidates. They demanded that the candidates

---

[4] Between May 1991 and August 1992, anti-NAFTA activists continued their struggle to influence the negotiation of the substantive free trade agreement and key unions nurtured nascent transnational relationships with their counterparts.

[5] Evans and Kay (2008, p. 983).

either significantly change or reject the agreement. Ninety-six House democrats echoed this view in a letter to Clinton urging him to renegotiate the agreement to address workers' rights, environmental protection, and health and safety standards (Evans 2002). Finally, on the eve of the election, Clinton announced that he would support supplemental labor and environmental agreements. In a speech at North Carolina State University in October 1992, he emphasized the importance of enforcement mechanisms:

> Perhaps the toughest issue of all is how to obtain better enforcement of laws already on the books on the environment and worker standards. It's interesting that the agreement negotiated by the Bush team goes a long way to do this in protecting intellectual property rights and the right to invest in Mexico, but is silent with respect to labor laws and the environment. I want to remedy that. I'm interested in the impact of this agreement on the rest of the people, not just those investing in Mexico, but the rest of the people in this country and the rest of the people in their country. So we need a supplemental agreement which would require each country to enforce its own environmental and worker standards. Each agreement should contain a wide variety of procedural safeguards and remedies that we take for granted here in our country, such as easy access to the courts, public hearings, the right to present evidence, streamlined procedures and effective remedies.[6]

Although Clinton's commitment to negotiate strong side agreements reassured some labor activists, others were not convinced. As a UNITE official said: "When NAFTA was put together, the worker rights stuff was an afterthought. It was just like this political bone Clinton threw us."[7] Activists worried that supplemental negotiations would not rectify the deficiencies of the substantive agreement that would then be difficult to amend before the outcome of supplemental negotiations was complete (Evans 2002). Mark Anderson, at the time head of the AFL-CIO's Task Force on Trade, explained how federation leaders failed to convince Clinton to renegotiate NAFTA but were hopeful he would improve it:

> We were involved in this very much when Clinton was running. There was a big debate going on in his staff essentially about two options, the "no but" and "yes and" options. The "no" being we don't like the Bush NAFTA but we love Mexico, elect me and we'll negotiate a new agreement. The "yes and" option was well, we'll take that agreement and try to add some new stuff onto them which

---

[6] Clinton (1992).

[7] Personal interview with Alan Howard of UNITE, December 15, 2000.

then came to be the labor side agreement, environmental side agreement and the little known import surge agreement. We were pushing real real hard for the no option. I think I had a $500 phone bill to Little Rock during that period. We didn't win, obviously. He gave a speech in North Carolina where he said we're going to fix these things.[8]

After Clinton's election in November, administration officials promised to address unions' concerns and solicit their input about the labor side agreement.

Developing a Transnational Labor Rights Agenda

The process of constituting transnational actors and interests intensified in March 1993 as negotiators began to hammer out the structure and content of the NAALC. Labor unions involved in the trinational coalitions solidified their positions and pushed common agendas in the face of a labor side agreement that could stimulate a race to the bottom across the continent. Gerry Barr of the Canadian Steelworkers explained how the space created by the NAALC's negotiation allowed unions to contemplate North American labor rights policies: "[B]ecause of the context created by NAFTA there were lots of opportunities for relevant discussions and sort of common policy discussions and so on."[9] Mexican labor lawyer Arturo Alcalde echoed Barr's point: "These are important relationships, and they basically were created through working on NAFTA and the labor side agreement in defense of a common agenda for democracy and to improve working conditions."[10] The transnational trade-negotiating field provided labor activists in all three countries the opportunity to try to influence the outcome of supplemental negotiations.

But the dialogue among unions that began in the transnational trade-negotiating field during fast track simultaneously helped lay the groundwork for a transnational legal field centered on labor rights and enforcement mechanisms. Labor unions across the continent came together to ensure that the side agreement would be as strong as possible. Through their efforts to influence the transnational trade-negotiating field, these new actors began to define a body of North American or transnational rights. As the AFL-CIO's Thea Lee explained, the process was

---

[8] Personal interview with Mark Anderson of the AFL-CIO, January 8, 2001.
[9] Personal interview with Gerry Barr of the Canadian Steelworkers, March 1, 2001.
[10] Personal interview with Arturo Alcalde Justiniani of the FAT, March 29, 2000.

not always easy, but it was extremely important for building collective interests:

> I learned a lot from those meetings. I remember one in Toronto. . . . [W]e had different reasons for not liking the agreement and we'd try to put together language that would lay out an alternative and we'd come against some pretty serious obstacles. . . . And so it was a really important educational process . . . sitting down with the three countries and from different sectors.[11]

Labor activists built consensus around a position that they would not endorse the NAALC if it did not provide significant enforcement mechanisms for key labor rights, including freedom of association and the right to strike and bargain collectively.

The NAALC negotiations put the AFL-CIO in a difficult position. The federation was under extreme pressure to back the Democratic president they helped elect. Administration officials met privately with labor leaders in an effort to persuade them not to publicly oppose supplemental negotiations, signaling that they would be active participants in the process. The AFL-CIO complied because they did not want to antagonize potential allies in other policy battles and because the administration led them to believe their participation could influence the outcome. AFL-CIO leaders therefore worked with the USTR to attempt to improve the labor side agreement while trying to publicly minimize opposition to the president (Evans 2002). As the AFL-CIO's Mark Anderson explained:

> We opposed the Bush NAFTA because it had . . . nothing. . . . [T]hen Clinton comes in with our support and says "I'm going to negotiate some other stuff, give me a chance, hold off." That's when we started the "Not this NAFTA." Before it was no, the Bush NAFTA sucks. So it was only after Clinton came in and we worked with the administration from January until August of that year trying to see if we could fashion a labor side agreement that we could then talk to the affiliates to see whether or not this is good enough for them to swallow.[12]

Despite their adoption of a "wait and see" position, the AFL-CIO demanded strong labor protections from the administration: a North American set of worker rights and minimum labor standards based on International Labor Organization (ILO) standards, and unions' ability to file complaints of labor violations against governments *and* corporations in any North American country (Evans 2002). These demands were consistent with those made by Canadian unions, and independent Mexican unions.

---

[11] Personal interview with Thea Lee of the AFL-CIO, December 8, 2000.
[12] Personal interview with Mark Anderson of the AFL-CIO, January 8, 2001.

In an effort to expand the coalition of unions fighting to improve the side agreement, the AFL-CIO again tried to pursue common areas of concern with the CTM. Mark Anderson explained that during the NAALC's negotiation he pushed various labor rights proposals, hoping to find common ground with the federation:

Well I was working the CTM to see if irrespective of what our ultimate position was going to be on the agreement, whether or not as two labor movements perhaps we could reach an agreement on labor rights and standards. If we had differences about the other part, put that aside, but can we coalesce around this. And through [that] winter [and into] spring '93, while we were still negotiating the labor side agreement I might add, [I] went to Mexico. I'd been communicating in writing and in various different ways and I was given to believe that there was a possibility we could reach an agreement on that narrow issue. And I viewed that to be important both substantively and tactically given the timing of it and whatnot. And so I agreed to go to Mexico City to meet at a staff level to see if we could work out a draft staff-approved document that we could then present to our leaders.[13]

Anderson's hopes for building a united front were dashed, however, after the ill-fated 1993 meeting in Mexico City. He explained what transpired:

[I] get to the headquarters, ushered into the executive board room, if you will, of the CTM, whereupon don Fidel had assembled the entire executive board. So there's little Mark and don Fidel.... And they presented me with a proposal on labor rights that was totally bull.... I probably have it somewhere. It didn't address collective bargaining, free association, right to organize, it had no enforcement mechanism, said maybe talk about things later, workers of the world unite, it was that kind of thing. And so I just sit there and tell don Fidel no. I did take a few deep breaths, and they worked us over pretty good. And at the close of the meeting they had alerted every newspaper in Mexico City. I was on the front page of a half dozen Mexico City dailies the next day. I mean they set us up quite frankly, leading me to believe that there was a possibility of some real progress surrounding an agreement but then figuring okay we'll get them down there and we'll trap them with this other proposal and alert the press about it.[14]

The CTM's actions provide further evidence that its relationship with the AFL-CIO was severely lacking in mutual respect and trust. But for many in the AFL-CIO, the CTM's tactics justified the decision to explore relationships with independent Mexican unions whose position on the NAALC was consistent with their own.

By the summer of 1993, it was clear to AFL-CIO leaders that the supplemental labor agreement was not going to be sufficient to warrant their

[13] Personal interview with Mark Anderson of the AFL-CIO, January 8, 2001.
[14] Ibid.

support (Evans and Kay 2008). Writing to USTR Mickey Kantor, AFL-CIO Secretary-Treasurer Tom Donahue made the federation's position clear: "The administration's proposal fails to identify even minimal labor rights and standards to be enforced, establishes an oversight process so vague, discretionary, and protracted that a timely resolution of a dispute would be virtually impossible, makes individual violations of even national law non-actionable, and provides at the end of the process no effective remedies."[15] The AFL-CIO leadership decided their best strategy was to kill the entire deal and finally began to gear up for a grassroots campaign (Evans and Kay 2008). In addition to holding press conferences, town meetings, and plant gate demonstrations and lobbying local government representatives, the federation's Task Force on Trade organized mail-in campaigns and displayed 60 billboards across the country. The AFL-CIO also became more active participants in the anti-NAFTA coalition, coordinating with member organizations and contributing money to its efforts (Evans 2002).

The AFL-CIO's decision to launch an unprecedented grassroots anti-NAFTA campaign and to garner support for votes against NAFTA among legislators meant that it turned its focus away from the bargaining table (Evans and Kay 2008). As Mark Anderson suggested, the shift in the AFL-CIO's decision likely came too late:

And when they finally came out with these agreements in August 1993, that's when we said these agreements suck; no, we're going to try to take it down. Now that may have been a tactical mistake on our part ... because that gave us a very short window to try to mobilize and get stuff up; it was mid to end of August. And so then the vote was when, in November? So at most you're talking about a three month window.[16]

But the decision proved to be significant for the outcomes of both side agreements. Without AFL-CIO pressure, pro-labor U.S. negotiators had little power to leverage their Canadian and Mexican counterparts. As Steve Herzenberg, the assistant to the chief negotiator of the labor side agreement to NAFTA, explained:

The U.S. labor movement was pretty ineffectual. All they – the AFL-CIO Task Force on Trade – would tell the U.S. negotiators is that we would never support this thing, and if you strengthen it it will be a little less of a [war] by the U.S. labor movement. So there was nobody on the outside putting any pressure on the U.S. negotiators which would lead them to make a pragmatic calculation to make the

---

[15] Donahue (June 17, 1993).
[16] Personal interview with Mark Anderson of the AFL-CIO, January 8, 2001.

agreement stronger.... I think the U.S. labor movement could have put pressure and that could have led to a different agreement.[17]

The AFL-CIO's move thus enabled Mexican negotiators – who were under tremendous pressure to accept trade sanctions – to concede to more stringent environmental oversights in order to demand weaker labor regulations. U.S. House majority leader Gephardt and Senator Max Baucus informed USTR Kantor at the beginning of August that the threat of trade sanctions was crucial to ensure that national laws were enforced.[18] On August 6, after agreement could not be reached on international legal standards and sanctions, the lead Mexican negotiator met with Gephardt, who emphasized that sanctions were essential for U.S. legislative passage of the agreement.[19] As a result, Mexican negotiators agreed to accept sanctions for both agreements in exchange for a narrower labor scope that excluded violations of collective bargaining and freedom of association rights from trade sanctions.[20] Environmental law remained broadly defined. *Inside U.S. Trade* reported at the time:

Informed sources said that it may have been easier for Mexico to agree to trade sanctions in the environmental accord after the U.S. bowed to Mexican demands for a weak labor side accord. Mexico insisted that any provisions to encourage autonomous unions be kept out of the list of issues that could come under the scrutiny of ministers, including the right of collective bargaining and freedom of association.[21]

North American unions engaged in the transnational trade-negotiating field expressed their unanimous disdain when the NAALC was unveiled on August 13, 1993, and vowed to collectively fight its passage. At the end of September, anti-NAFTA coalition groups met trinationally for the

---

[17] Personal interview with Steve Herzenberg, U.S. Department of Labor, September 27, 2002.

[18] *Inside U.S. Trade* (August 13, 1993, p. 10).

[19] The U.S. wanted the agreement to create a higher standard, while the two other countries wanted the agreement to be based on each nation's existing laws. Canada was faced with the problem that most of its environmental laws were under provincial jurisdiction, while Mexico did not want to alter its system of corporatist bargaining. The compromise was that "mutually recognized" laws rather than international standards were used (cited in Cameron and Tomlin 2000, p. 196).

[20] Mexican negotiators' preference for weaker labor oversight is not surprising given that the government and the CTM opposed core labor standards with enforcement mechanisms. Mexico's labor secretary was especially concerned about maintaining Mexico's corporatist system of labor relations, and the CTM supported this negotiating position (Cameron and Tomlin 2000).

[21] *Inside U.S. Trade* (August 13, 1993, p. 18).

fifth time since NAFTA's announcement. They created a document titled "A Just and Sustainable Trade and Development Initiative for North America" that not only detailed the problems of the NAALC but also outlined the fundamental characteristics of an acceptable trade agreement (Evans 2002). They agreed as a trinational coalition that equitable regional economic integration should be transparent and democratic, incorporate trinational standards, and promote corporate accountability. And more specifically, they demanded an agreement that protected basic labor rights, including the rights to organize, collectively bargain, and strike.

Despite their tremendous collective effort, anti-NAFTA organizations lost the NAFTA battle when President Clinton stitched together enough votes to ensure its passage in September 1993.[22] But labor activists' achievements were quite significant; they had helped ensure labor rights protections in a trade agreement that only months earlier included none. The NAALC – unprecedented for linking trade and labor rights for the first time in a free trade agreement – would not have existed at all were it not for labor activists' constant pressure. Labor leaders across the continent, however, almost universally viewed its passage as a crushing defeat.[23] They bemoaned its lack of teeth and predicted it would do little to advance labor rights in North America when it went into force on January 1, 1994.

What labor activists could not predict was that, despite its many weaknesses, the agreement they despised would actually help solidify their nascent transnational relationships. The NAALC indirectly advanced labor rights across the continent by compelling labor activists to collectively demand them. The key to the process by which the NAALC helped generate labor transnationalism lies in how the agreement articulated transnational labor rights and provided a venue for their adjudication. I turn now to a brief discussion of the NAALC's structure, jurisdiction, principles, and adjudicatory mechanisms, and then to a more detailed examination of its procedures and key NAO cases in order to illuminate the *process* by which the NAALC's new institutional arena helped stimulate transnational collaboration.

---

[22] Clinton opted for individual trade and nontrade side payments to unaligned members of Congress in a final effort to secure sufficient votes for NAFTA's passage (Evans 2002). Estimates of the costs of the deals ranged from $300 million to $4.4 billion (Wines 1993; Lewis 1993; Citizens Trade Campaign, November 12, 1993).

[23] The majority of official Mexican unions were the exception.

The NAALC and Transnational Rights

The final agreement, embodied in the NAALC, committed each of the three signatory countries to *"protect*, enhance and enforce basic workers' rights,"[24] while advancing regional market integration, enhancing the competitiveness of North American firms, and creating new employment opportunities. But the NAALC emphatically states that the goals of protecting workers' rights and promoting improved working conditions will *not* be achieved by creating a supranational labor law. Article 42 specifically states that one party (i.e., signatory nation) may not enforce labor laws in another's territory.

The NAALC is a supplemental labor side agreement entered into by three autonomous nation-states. It attempts to maintain each nation's sovereignty and autonomy by basing labor rights on national labor legislation rather than a supranational labor code. Under the NAALC, each nation must enforce its own domestic labor laws. This stipulation was created in order to deal with concerns over national sovereignty. Mexican officials worried that the U.S. government would dominate and dictate legal proceedings to their country's detriment. Whereas the Canadian federal government signed the NAALC, each province decided whether or not to sign onto the labor side agreement. Workers under the jurisdiction of the federal government (approximately ten percent of the workforce)[25] and those in the four provinces that have ratified it – Alberta, Quebec, Prince Edward Island, and Manitoba – are covered by the NAALC. Workers in Canada's other provinces are not.[26] The NAALC also allows each nation discretion as to how its labor laws should be interpreted, enforced, and adjudicated. Thus, nation-states remain critical to the NAALC process and to the development of a transnational legal field on labor rights in North America.

The NAALC established eleven "guiding principles" each signatory agreed to promote: (1) freedom of association and protection of the right to organize, (2) the right to bargain collectively, (3) the right to strike, (4) prohibition of forced labor, (5) labor protections for children and young persons, (6) minimum employment standards, (7) elimination of

[24] "North American Agreement on Labor Cooperation." September 14, 1993.
[25] Commission for Labor Cooperation (2000, p. 33).
[26] Ontario and Quebec are Canada's most populous provinces, together accounting for over 60 percent of the nation's population in 2009 (Statistics Canada at: www.statcan.gc.ca).

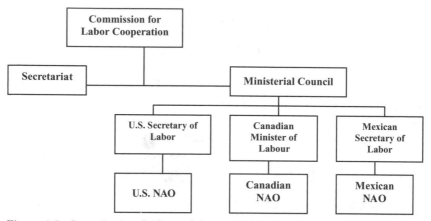

Figure 4.2. Organizational Chart of the Commission for Labor Cooperation

employment discrimination, (8) equal pay for women and men, (9) prevention of occupational injuries and illnesses, (10) compensation in cases of occupational injuries and illnesses, and (11) protection of migrant workers. Complaints of labor rights violations are filed against a NAFTA country for failing to enforce its labor laws. They cannot be filed against an employer, company, or individual. The NAALC process can begin even if domestic remedies have not been initiated or exhausted.

The NAALC created new adjudicatory venues and procedures for filing complaints alleging a signatory country failed to effectively enforce its labor laws related to one or more of the eleven labor principles. The Commission for Labor Cooperation (CLC) is composed of a Secretariat and a Ministerial Council. The latter serves as the governing body of the Commission and has ties to each party's federal government, specifically the labor department (or its equivalent),[27] which maintains a National Administrative Office (NAO) to receive and respond to complaints of labor rights violations. The organizational chart in Figure 4.2 illustrates the structure of the Commission for Labor Cooperation.

Each country established its own complaint-filing procedures, which are relatively straightforward. A submission should explain the nature of the alleged violations (i.e., what labor principles were violated) and provide the facts of the case. Submissions can range from fewer than ten to hundreds of pages and can include affidavits of witnesses and other

---

[27] The U.S. Department of Labor; Human Resources and Skills Development Canada; and the Ministry of Labor and Social Welfare (Secretaría del Trabajo y Previsión Social).

supplemental materials and evidence (photographs, leaflets, pay stubs, company documents, etc.). Once a submission is filed, the NAO can solicit information about it from businesses, government entities, etc. If a company is named in a submission, it usually provides public comments on the case. The process of filing submissions, though uncomplicated, can be quite expensive; unions with attorneys on staff must allocate significant time to prepare, and those without attorneys must hire private firms to handle the cases. Travel and lodging expenses for legal teams and witnesses who must travel outside their home country can add up quickly.

The NAALC process has one particularly strict procedural requirement: that a submission be filed in a country other than the one in which the alleged labor law violation occurred. For example, a citizen or group in any country may file a submission with the U.S. NAO. The only requirement is that the submission address labor law violations by Mexico or Canada. The agreement also permits submissions to more than one NAO. A U.S. submitter, for example, may file a complaint with the Mexican and Canadian NAO offices. In addition, a submitter need not be party to a particular case. As an NAALC publication clarifies, "Individuals, unions, employers, non-governmental organizations or other private parties may file submissions seeking NAO reviews."[28]

Other procedures for accepting and adjudicating submissions among the countries are comparable but vary. For example, the U.S. NAO guidelines allow for a public hearing if a submission is accepted, whereas the guidelines of Canada and Mexico do not (although in practice Canada holds them and Mexico has held them). The U.S. guidelines state that the NAO has sixty days from the date a submission is filed to determine whether to accept it for review and 120 days from its acceptance date to complete the review and issue a public report (a sixty-day extension can also be provided at the NAO's discretion). Canadian guidelines are similar, but the Mexican NAO does not have strict deadlines for review or release of a public report.

There are three primary levels in the adjudicative process. Not all types of complaints, however, can reach the highest level in the institutional hierarchy. Ministerial Consultations can be initiated based on an alleged failure to enforce labor laws associated with any of the eleven labor principles. An Evaluation Committee of Experts (ECE) can be convened if the alleged violation pertains to eight labor principles (excluding freedom of association and the rights to bargain and strike). And, finally, an

28 www.naalc.org/english/info/broch_7.htm.

Table 4.1. *NAALC Labor Principles and Levels of Treatment*

Ministerial Consultations	Evaluation Committee of Experts	Arbitral Panel
Freedom of association and the right to organize		
The right to bargain collectively		
The right to strike		
Prohibition of forced labor	Prohibition of forced labor	
Labor protections for children and young persons	Labor protections for children and young persons	Labor protections for children and young persons
Minimum employment standards	Minimum employment standards	Minimum employment standards
Elimination of employment discrimination	Elimination of employment discrimination	
Equal pay for women and men	Equal pay for women and men	
Prevention of occupational injuries and illnesses	Prevention of occupational injuries and illnesses	Prevention of occupational injuries and illnesses
Compensation in cases of occupational injuries and illnesses	Compensation in cases of occupational injuries and illnesses	
Protection of migrant workers	Protection of migrant workers	

Arbitral Panel can be invoked if the submission deals with labor protections for children and young persons, minimum wages, and/or prevention of occupational injuries or illnesses. Trade sanctions can be levied only at this level. In order for an ECE or an Arbitral Panel to be established, the matter must be both trade related and covered by mutually recognized labor laws. Table 4.1 details the eleven principles and their different levels of treatment in the NAALC process.

Nation-States and Transnationalism

Although the role of the three nation-states is important to the adjudication of NAO submissions, the three levels of treatment involve trinational adjudication. The primary power each NAO has in the public

Table 4.2. *NAO Submission Statistics (1994–2008)*

Public Submission Summary	Number of Submissions
Total cases filed	37
Total cases filed with at least one union participant	35
Cases filed in Canada	6
Cases filed in Mexico	9
Cases filed in the United States	22
Cases against Canada	2
Cases against Mexico	23
Cases against the United States	12
Ministerial consultations convened	16
ECEs convened	0
Arbitral Panels convened	0
Cases withdrawn or declined for review	11

Note: Statistics provided by the Commission on Labor Cooperation.

submission process is whether or not to accept a public submission and whether it merits Ministerial Consultations. There is a high rate in both the acceptance of submissions and Ministerial Consultations (although both declined during the Bush administration). As Tables 4.2 and 4.3 reveal of the thirty-five submissions filed with union participation between 1994 and 2008, sixteen resulted in Ministerial Consultations. As of this writing, no submissions have reached the ECE or Arbitral Panel stages.

Once a submission is accepted and goes to Ministerial Consultations, the adjudicatory process becomes trinational. Ministerial Consultations involve deliberations by the U.S. and Mexican secretaries of labor and the Canadian minister of labour. ECE and Arbitral Panels include experts chosen by consensus by the three countries. Moreover, an Arbitral Panel must include experts from each country involved in a dispute. Although the submission process is not independent of North American nation-states, it would more accurately be described as embedded in a trinational process dependent on the collective and consensual will of three nations. Because the NAO process depends on the collective action of U.S., Canadian, and Mexican representatives, it is not subject to the individual whim of a single nation. Thus, the politics of a particular country would have little effect on unions' choice of where to file an NAO submission. That decision would be driven primarily by the NAALC's procedural rules that prohibit the filing of submissions in the country in which the alleged violation occurred. The ability to file multiple submissions provides unions with additional protection from political or other factors that could bias the adjudicatory process. Indeed, interview data reveal that unions' preference for filing submissions is primarily driven by transnational factors, in particular the existence of a viable counterpart in the "foreign" country to assist in the submission process.

Although the NAALC did not create a supranational labor law in North America, in practice its eleven core labor principles formed a body of recognized continent-wide labor rights, granting a new legitimacy to labor activists who tried to invoke them. Prior to the NAALC, labor activists could only file claims of labor rights violations with their national governments or through various international institutions (ILO, IACHR) whose jurisdiction was not limited to North America but whose procedures, like the NAALC, lack enforcement mechanisms. These new rights also provided a new platform around which activists continued to solidify their collective interests. As the associate director of the AFL-CIO's international department explained:

[The NAALC process] has created a paradigm. It has created a mind-set. It's created a frame of reference in which we understand ourselves in the labor movement to work on a trinational basis. And there is a need for that. And that, I think, has tremendous benefits in the point of view of labor solidarity. So that aspect, I think, is very critical.[29]

According to the former secretary of international relations for the STRM: "The side agreement provides a platform to discuss what is needed to improve the lives of workers in the three countries. It allows us to make the agenda more profound and analyze the problems. So it is an advance."[30] In describing her participation in one of the first NAO cases, the director of international labor affairs for the UE explained how an international platform to address labor rights violations was crucial for labor activists: "But at the point where we first filed the NAO cases, there was no official platform that independent lawyers or trade unionists could use to talk about what was going on."[31] Once the NAALC created a platform, constructing problems as violations of North American labor rights became possible.

The NAALC also helped constitute transnational interests by expanding the conception of labor rights to the whole continent. For the first time, labor activists in each country saw their rights, and remedies for rights

---

[29] Personal interview with Stan Gacek of the AFL-CIO, August 23, 2009.
[30] Personal interview with Alicia Sepúlveda Nuñez of the STRM, August 27, 2000.
[31] Personal interview with Robin Alexander of the UE, December 21, 2000.

violations, as inextricably linked to those of their compañeros beyond their own borders. A FAT activist explained:

I think NAFTA opened relationships between unions in the three countries. . . . Through NAFTA, relationships have been pushed a lot more than they were before. . . . Before unions were worried about their national problems, what happened in their own homes. Now they are worried about what happens outside because what happens there has repercussions here because we are under the same treaty. So this has improved relations. You have to care about what happens there, you have to have allies there to improve problems. And to know that what affects them there will affect us here. So there has been a growth of relations.[32]

A Mexican labor lawyer concurred: "But the NAALC process gives more pressure because it is regional, between two or three countries. So between these countries they are looking at the violations because it is in their interest, and there is a public audience, and because of this it creates links between unions in the three countries. And this gives workers a new perspective."[33]

According to Bertha Luján, former national coordinator of the FAT, this new perspective, coupled with the NAALC's nascent mechanisms, enables unions to develop collective goals across the continent: "It's allowed us to construct an agenda in common. Through the submissions, for example, labor freedom has become a unifying goal among unions in the three countries. We realize that the only way to rectify violations of union liberty which occur in the three countries is through unity. The side agreements have helped us strengthen our efforts toward this goal."[34]

This new perspective is reflected in how lawyers actually put together their NAO cases and use the NAALC process to foreground collective conditions and goals. A U.S. lawyer explained the significance of having U.S. and Mexican workers testify together at one particular NAO hearing:

And then when we were preparing for the hearing in Mexico City with the Mexico NAO, the question arose whether we should have Anglo workers also be part of the group. . . . The American side was disposed to not do that because we figured . . . look it's the Mexican NAO, we'll go down there, it's Mexican workers that are the main workers having the problems, and we'll be able to work in Spanish the whole time. And the Mexicans said no, no, it's important to show that both Mexican workers and American Anglo workers are affected by these conditions, and it's important to us to have [them there]. So that actually

---

[32] Personal interview with Ruben Ruiz Rubio of the FAT, April 13, 2000.
[33] Personal interview with Oscar Rubio González of ANAD, May 3, 2000.
[34] Personal interview with Bertha Luján of the FAT, August 3, 1999.

turned out to be a great kind of symbolic thing that you had Mexicans working in the U.S. side-by-side with a woman, fifty years old, a large blonde-haired woman, [who] didn't speak a word of Spanish but she'd worked in the warehouses all her life . . . so that was all very good.[35]

Although this decision was strategic, it also reflected a developing sense that workers' interests across the continent are quite similar.

Facilitating Collective Action and Mobilization

The NAALC's effects on constituting transnational actors and interests did not end once transnational rights were established. In addition to helping constitute transnational actors and interests, the NAALC also helped generate collective action. Indeed, one of the NAALC's most significant effects was to create a new legal institutional context for transnational cooperation and collaboration. Specifically, the NAALC established new legal mechanisms and adjudicatory venues that facilitate transnational mobilization by allowing labor activists to collaborate in concrete and meaningful ways. One of the primary ways the NAALC catalyzes transnationalism is through its procedural rule that requires a submission be filed outside the country in which a violation occurred.

This procedural rule not only makes it extremely difficult for a union to file with a "foreign" NAO without the assistance of a "foreign" union but also provides an incentive for unions to collaborate on submissions across borders. Although the NAALC does not *require* that a submitter seek out a foreign counterpart to assist with the submission, that is exactly how the NAO procedure evolved. As Mexican labor lawyer Arturo Alcalde explained, the evolution of the agreement in practice reflects the difficulty of filing submissions without the assistance of counterparts in other countries:

I think the side agreement facilitates relations among unions; there is an intimate relation between these submissions and international relations. In our experience one of the most important sources of relations has precisely been this type of submission because above all else you must present them in another country. If you don't have contacts you can't submit complaints.[36]

Many unions filing submissions develop more than contacts with their foreign counterparts, however. A U.S. labor lawyer explained how

---

[35] Personal interview with Lance Compa, U.S. labor lawyer, December 19, 2000.
[36] Personal interview with Arturo Alcalde Justiniani of the FAT, March 29, 2000.

working on submissions helped build relationships among unions:

I'd be on the phone with . . . a couple people at the Teamsters in Washington, D.C., and a couple people in Mexico, planning. . . . We talked about the complaint, we talked about how to get ready for the hearing, and everything . . . and just that experience of working together on a very concrete thing. It's very different when you're working on a case, where you've got to prepare witnesses, you've got to draft a complaint, you've got to put together a media strategy. That's a lot different than writing a resolution, you know, or agreeing to make some denunciatory statement and that's the end of it. And that had been, by and large, the mode of cross-border labor collaboration before this instrument became available. They'd be high-level meetings at the Inter-American Regional Workers' Organization or something and top union officials would go to meetings, they don't speak the language, they would just adopt resolutions that the staff wrote and that would be the end of it. . . . And what the NAALC has created is this kind of framework for a lot of rich interaction between union activists in the countries.[37]

By enabling newly constituted transnational labor activists to collaborate in concrete and meaningful ways, the NAALC unexpectedly helped generate cross-border collaboration.

Perhaps even more significantly, unions almost always request assistance to file submissions against *their own* governments – not against foreign governments. An analysis of the thirty-five submissions filed with union participation between 1994 and 2008 reveals that thirty-four were filed by, or at the request of, unions against their own governments.[38] Unlike other transnational legal mechanisms that encourage U.S. unions to file complaints unilaterally against other governments, the NAALC mechanism helps build collective power among North American unions by facilitating the joint filing of submissions. A Mexican labor leader revealed her preference to use the process against her own government, and explained how doing so infused her union's leadership with new ideas that emerged from interaction with U.S. and Canadian unions:

First of all the side agreements which are very weak and have no teeth . . . have one, I think, good part to them: that I could not go against the Mexican government without the intervention of either an American or a Canadian or American and Canadian unions. So if I wanted to launch a complaint against my government, I would have to find a partner in either country or both. So that helped, because I had to start looking around and say look I need somebody to sign this complaint

---

[37] Personal interview with Lance Compa, U.S. labor lawyer, December 19, 2000.
[38] The one exception is the Decoster Egg (9803) submission filed by the CTM against the U.S. government for failing to protect the rights of Mexican migrant workers in the United States.

for me, who can that be? So it promoted looking for partners on both sides or all sides of the border, even the Canadian border.... Also in some cases we saw what could be done with political mobilization. We saw what American unions did, what Canadian unions did, and it started sort of creating an attraction from some of us towards those unions and trying to find people to talk to, or to talk to within those unions.[39]

An AFL-CIO representative also preferred using the NAALC process against his own government:

I used to say this to the Mexicans and the South Americans in other contexts: that the reason that I'm interested in getting really strong labor rights language in a trade agreement, particularly on the right to organize and bargain, is not so I can complain about you. I want it so you can help me by complaining against the U.S. And that's why I wanted an agreement: it's a lever for us here domestically.[40]

Steve Herzenberg, assistant to the U.S. chief negotiator of the labor side agreement to NAFTA, explained that while some labor negotiators realized the procedural rule might stimulate cross-border collaboration among unions, that was not the intention of the business and government representatives:

The side agreement contributed to that increase [in international solidarity] because it created new venues through which you could act in solidarity and support one another and.... we were aware of that when the side agreement was crafted.... The Canadians were the first ones who came up with this notion of a dispute resolution procedure which would include the possibility of filing complaints against another country in another country, and that ultimately [sets] up some kind of a trilateral dialogue. And at some point... the U.S. negotiators or at least some of us began to sort of recognize that... this in some ways is actually better than starting trinational. And one of the reasons is because in fact it would require coordination between labor folks from at least two of the countries. And so... if you had a problem in your country and you actually wanted to use this agreement to get leverage, you had to go to somebody in the other country, you couldn't file it yourself.[41]

Herzenberg explained that the pro-business contingent did not foresee this possibility and described their reaction four years after its implementation:

The conventional wisdom view – the stories one hears come from people like Jaime Serra[42] – ... was that this labor agreement that they'd let be created was

---

[39] Personal interview with Alicia Sepúlveda Nuñez of the STRM, August 27, 2000.
[40] Personal interview with Mark Anderson, AFL-CIO, January 8, 2001.
[41] Personal interview with Steve Herzenberg, U.S. Department of Labor, September 27, 2002.
[42] Jaime Serra was one of Mexico's NAFTA negotiators.

totally useless, and the dispute settlement in particular was sort of the subject of great merriment.... If you look at ... the four-year review ... one of the reviews was done by a three-person committee ... from the Mexican expert you get a little bit of this flavor of we've been had. That we didn't know it was going to do this and it's not fair. So that reinforces your interpretation that it was certainly not intended on their part.[43]

Indeed, dissension emerged among the NAALC four-year review committee of experts. The majority opinion – largely influenced by U.S. and Canadian members Clyde Summers and Pierre Verge, respectively – quite favorably evaluated the work of the secretariat and NAO. Luis Medina, the Mexican expert on the committee, disagreed so strongly with the tone of the majority opinion that he insisted on writing a separate dissenting opinion. Medina's dissent focused on what he believed was the politicization of the NAALC process, including a critique of its stimulation of labor transnationalism:

The political designs of the independent trade unions have found a certain echo and indeed reply in the protectionist dispositions of United States trade unionism. This factor has led to agreements such as the Alliance for Strategic Organization, concluded between [the UE] and the [FAT] for the consolidation of joint action in the in-bond industries situated along the northern Mexican border. Other United States trade unions have initiated similar projects with independent Mexican organizations, especially those functioning in the areas of clothing and textile manufacture, telecommunications, foodstuffs and transportation. While the convergence of this type of interest and form of action may be clearly perceived in the submission procedures so far initiated, the fact that conflict [i.e., unions collectively denouncing employers and the governments of the three countries] is stressed over and above cooperation would also seem to indicate a desire to imbue the NAALC with a character that it simply does not possess.[44]

As Medina observed, the NAALC's procedural rules that require transnational contact and collaboration are incredibly useful for generating transnational relationships. The failure of other international labor rights mechanisms to stimulate the kinds of labor relationships the NAALC did may be explained, at least in part, by their lack of similar rules. The ILO has two labor complaint mechanisms, the Committee of Experts on the Application of Conventions and Recommendations (CEACR) and the Committee on Freedom of Association (CFA). The

---

[43] Personal interview with Steve Herzenberg, U.S. Department of Labor, September 27, 2002.
[44] See Medina (1998).

CEACR allows governments, trade unions, and employers to file complaints for violation of an ILO convention against a country that has ratified that convention. Created in 1951, the CFA handles complaints that a country has violated ILO Conventions 87 and 98 on freedom of association, the right to organize, and the right to collective bargaining whether that country ratified either convention or not. Complainants file documentary evidence directly with the committees, neither of which conducts trials or holds hearings. And although the committees issue reports and recommendations, they lack enforcement mechanisms.

The procedural rules of the IACHR also require central filing of complaints to the Inter-American Commission on Human Rights alleging labor violations by OAS member states (whether or not they have ratified its human rights convention). The Commission reviews complaints and makes recommendations, but can only bring cases to the Inter-American Court against countries that have ratified the convention (neither the U.S. nor Canada has). The Court can issue nonbinding "advisory opinions" against nonratifying countries.

Beginning in 1984, U.S. unions could file a petition with the Office of the U.S. Trade Representative to request that a country's preferential GSP status be reviewed and suspended if it violates labor rights.[45] The mechanism encouraged U.S. unions to file petitions unilaterally against other nations without the consent or participation of foreign unions. Moreover, because suspending a country's GSP status undermined trade and therefore jobs, many foreign unions believed the mechanism did more harm than good. An analysis of the NAALC's scope and structure compared with other international legal mechanisms therefore suggests that all international laws are not equally useful for transnational movement building. I now turn to a discussion of key NAO cases in order to illuminate the *process* by which the NAALC's legal-institutional arena helped stimulate transnational mobilization.

Testing the NAALC under the Clinton Administration (1994–2001)

During the Clinton presidency, unions involved in the transnational legal field tested and pushed the nascent NAALC mechanism and publicly

---

[45] Some research suggests some countries passed stronger labor legislation and devoted more resources to enforcing labor laws under the threat of losing trade preferences (Schrank and Murillo 2005; Piore and Schrank 2008). NAFTA eliminated the use of GSP preferences for and complaints against Mexico.

voiced their concerns when the administration failed to demand its strong enforcement. Indeed, the NAALC process was one of the key sites of labor contestation during the administration. Unions filed fourteen submissions with the U.S. NAO, which accepted all but two for review, and recommended Ministerial Consultations for eight submissions. The unions' strategy of garnering publicity for the submissions, and the larger campaigns of which they were a part, was quite successful even though the NAALC process did not provide meaningful redress. Indeed, many national newspapers, including the *New York Times*, regularly reported on events associated with key submissions such as Han Young and Echlin. The press attention helped keep labor rights issues on the national agenda.

Unions' general frustration with the NAALC process, however, reflected a broader disenchantment with the Clinton administration and its labor policies. In the eyes of many U.S. labor activists, the administration was difficult to pressure and target: Clinton consistently signaled his support for labor, but never followed through with labor policies that met activists' expectations. As one UE official wryly quipped: "[The U.S. labor movement did a] better job defending our interests under Reagan/Bush than pushing our agenda under Clinton."[46] And although President Clinton appointed officials supportive of labor issues, he never gave them enough power to make meaningful changes. Labor activists believed Secretary of Labor Robert Reich and the team he put in place at the U.S. NAO and Secretariat (including Lance Compa, the Secretariat's director for labor law and economic research) were supportive of labor. Compa affirmed that perception:

They have this Secretariat . . . and they had to decide who's going to be the senior U.S. position there and Bob Reich, who was a classmate from law school, was the Secretary of Labor . . . And they wanted to be sympathetic to the labor movement and they knew that I was a labor guy and would kind of bring that perspective to the organization. So they offered me the post and I had quite a bit of discussion with my gang, you know, Pharis [Harvey] and John Cavanagh and friends from the unions and so on. You know, do you think I ought to do this? And I decided that it's worth going in there and trying to make something good out of it compared with standing on the outside and throwing bombs . . . at somebody who wouldn't do as good a job at it. So I sort of took it as . . . somewhat of a personal challenge.[47]

---

[46] Personal interview with Chris Townsend of the UE, December 18, 2000.
[47] Personal interview with Lance Compa, U.S. labor lawyer, December 19, 2000.

Labor activists remained skeptical, however, of what pro-labor appointees could accomplish given the NAALC's lack of enforcement mechanisms. As the UAW's Steve Beckman explained: "Well we knew there were problems from the beginning because the Clinton administration's commitment to [NAFTA] was a political commitment; it was not made with any understanding of what was really needed, or what could be done or would be done."[48] Despite their lack of confidence in the NAALC, many union leaders decided to utilize it to see if it could help them get what workers needed. They decided to push the process as far as they could while highlighting its inadequacies and the need for its renegotiation.

Building Transnational Relationships Through NAO Submissions

North American labor activists began to test the waters of the new transnational legal field the NAALC established as soon as it went into force in January 1994. As Table 4.3 shows, however, their first steps were tentative; only three unions – the UE, FAT, and IBT – filed submissions during the NAALC's first year.

All three had been key players in the transnational trade-negotiating field. Table 4.3 reveals that this was not an anomaly; the majority of unions that spearheaded submissions from 1994 to 2001 had also participated in the field prior to NAFTA's passage. Unions that engaged the transnational trade-negotiating field were more likely to utilize the NAALC process because they had knowledge and interest in it after fighting the agreement's passage, had contact with unions in their home countries that participated in submissions and shared their expertise, and/or had initiated relations with counterparts in the other NAFTA countries who could help them submit complaints.

The first NAO submissions (Honeywell and General Electric) were actually filed to complement and reinforce union organizing campaigns under way prior to the NAALC's signing. Ultimately, the process of filing complaints not only strengthened transnational relationships but also helped shape a strategic plan to promote labor rights across the continent. The Teamsters filed the first submission (known as Honeywell) in February 1994, approximately one month after the NAALC went into effect.[49]

---

[48] Personal interview with Steve Beckman of the UAW, December 19, 2000.

[49] Each submission is assigned an identifying number by an NAO, but within the labor rights community the submissions are generally referred to informally by the name of the company accused of violating labor rights.

Table 4.3. *Union Participation in NAO Cases Filed during the Clinton Administration (1994–January 2001)*

	Year	NAO	Submission	Issue/Principle	About	Outcome	Unions
1	1994	U.S.	Honeywell (940001)	1	Mexico	Ministerial consultations not recommended	IBT (FAT, UE)
2	1994	U.S.	General Electric (940002)	1	Mexico	Ministerial consultations not recommended	UE (FAT, IBT)
3	1994	U.S.	Sony (930003)	1	Mexico	Ministerial consultations recommended	ANAD (FAT, AFL-CIO)
4	1994	U.S.	General Electric (940004)	1	Mexico	Accepted for review, then withdrawn	UE (FAT)
5	1995	Mexico	Sprint (9501)	1	United States	Ministerial Consultations consultations recommended	STRM (CWA, CEP)
6	1996	U.S.	SEMARNAP[a] (9601)	1	Mexico	Ministerial Consultations recommended	FAT (IBT, UE)
7	1996	U.S.	Maxi-Switch (9602)	1	Mexico	Accepted for review, then withdrawn	CWA, STRM (CEP, FAT)
8	1997	U.S.	Gender Discrimination (9701)	7	Mexico	Ministerial Consultations recommended	FAT
9	1997	U.S.	Han Young (9702)	1, 9	Mexico	Ministerial Consultations recommended	STIMAHCS (UE, FAT, CUSWA, UAW, CAW and five other organizations)
10	1997	U.S.	Echlin[b] (9703)	1, 2, 9	Mexico	Ministerial Consultations recommended	UE, FAT, CUSWA, STRM, AFL-CIO, CLC, UAW, CAW, UNITE, IBT, USW and over forty other unions and organizations
11	1998	Canada	Echlin (98–1)	1, 9	Mexico	Ministerial Consultations consultations recommended	UE, FAT, CUSWA, STRM, AFL-CIO, CLC, UAW, CAW, UNITE, IBT, USW and over forty other unions and organizations

(continued)

Table 4.3 (continued)

	Year	NAO	Submission	Issue/Principle	About	Outcome	Unions
12	1998	Canada	Yale/INS (98–2)	6, 11	United States	Declined for review	UNITE and over eighteen other unions and organizations
13	1998	Mexico	Solec (9801)	1, 2, 6, 7, 9, 10	United States	Ministerial Consultations recommended	
14	1998	Mexico	Apple Growers (9802)	1, 2, 6, 9, 11	United States	Ministerial Consultations recommended	FAT, IBT, UNT
15	1998	Mexico	Decoster Egg (9803)	6, 7, 9, 10, 11	United States	Ministerial Consultations recommended	CTM
16	1998	Mexico	Yale/INS (9804)	6, 11	United States	Ministerial Consultations recommended	UNITE
17	1998	U.S.	Flight Attendants (9801)	3	Mexico	Declined for review	
18	1998	U.S.	McDonald's (9803)	1, 2	Canada	Accepted for review	IBT
19	1998	U.S.	Rural Mail Couriers (9804)	1, 2, 7, 9, 10	Canada	Declined for review	CUSWA, CWA, CEP, CLC, IBT and over sixteen other unions and organizations
20	1999	U.S.	TAESA (9901)	1, 2, 6, 9	Mexico	Ministerial Consultations recommended	FAT, AFL-CIO, UAW
21	2000	U.S.	Auto Trim/Custom Trim (2000–01)	9, 10	Mexico	Ministerial Consultations recommended	USW and over twenty-three other unions and organizations

Note: Two additional submissions were filed by companies: Tomato/Child Labor (U.S. NAO 9802) and EFCO (Canada NAO 99–1). The final column only includes unions/federations in my sample. Those in parentheses participated without officially signing as submitters (e.g., by donating funds, supporting the campaign, offering strategic advice, publicity, etc.). Data in columns 1–6 provided by the Commission on Labor Cooperation.

[a] Also referred to as SUTSP.

[b] Also referred to as ITAPSA (in the U.S. and Canada submissions).

The NAO submission grew out of a broader anti-NAFTA campaign the Teamsters launched while the agreement was being negotiated. Although the FAT did not officially sign on as petitioners, FAT attorneys participated with the Teamsters informally.

Matt Witt, then Teamsters communications director, explained how the IBT and FAT expanded their work together by developing a general campaign against Honeywell: "This was a whole campaign that we did – twenty workers who were fired at a FAT organizing drive at Honeywell – and the Teamsters represented the Honeywell workers in Minnesota at the main operation of Honeywell in the U.S. And so over a period of time we did a whole campaign about this. And eventually it turned into the [NAO] complaint."[50] The Honeywell submission alleged that the Mexican government failed to enforce its labor laws guaranteeing freedom of association and the right to organize after Honeywell fired activists leading a struggle to organize.

The second NAO case (General Electric) followed the same pattern as the first. Filed by the UE with the FAT's participation, the complaint grew out of an extensive organizing campaign carried out by the two unions at General Electric (GE) plants in Mexico. The submission asserted that GE violated health and safety laws, failed to pay overtime, and undermined workers' rights to organize and associate freely. Bob Kingsley, the UE's director of organization, explained how the unions decided to file the submission after the company and the Mexican government undermined the campaign:

Now we sat down and said all right, so one possibility would be to pursue legal action in Mexico which would probably carry forward well into the next century to absolutely no avail, and another option might be to pursue a complaint under the NAO. But if we do so we cannot expect that we will get any kind of a real remedy. So we were tempted to reject it as an option, but our conclusion instead became let's use this case – there were a couple of other cases going on at the same time like Honeywell – we'll use this case to expose sort of the fraudulent nature of the side agreements in a very public way. Let's work through, get some good publicity for the efforts undertaken by our union and our allies in Mexico, get some bad publicity for the Clinton Administration and for the NAO and for what that's about as a way of informing future ongoing debate in discussion on trade issues.[51]

During the submission process, the UE and FAT worked closely to develop a strategy, gather the facts of the case, and prepare the submission. UE

---

[50] Personal interview with Matt Witt of the Teamsters, January 17, 2001.
[51] Personal interview with Bob Kingsley of the UE, January 23, 2001.

General President John H. Hovis, Jr., who signed the GE submission, also penned the cover letter to the Acting Secretary of the U.S. NAO. In closing, he queried whether the NAO's review would fulfill the NAALC's promise:

NAFTA and its labor side accord are put to the test by this submission. Will the United States government treat seriously the issues raised here and go forward with a review and a public hearing, and, if needed, with the further steps contained in the NAALC? Or will the United States government brush off this submission, exposing the labor side accord as an empty promise? UE calls on the NAO to initiate a review of the matters in this submission and give meaning to the promise of an effective North American Agreement on Labor Cooperation.[52]

After submitting the complaint, the unions also organized publicity around the submission. The UE and Teamsters covered a significant portion of the expenses for the first NAO cases, and even brought two Mexican workers to the United States for ten days to visit different unions and talk about the submission and labor conditions in Mexico. Mexican workers fired from Honeywell in Chihuahua met with IBT Honeywell workers in Minnesota and spoke at the national Teamsters Women's Conference. UE leaders' doubts about the NAALC's efficacy appeared to be confirmed, however, when the U.S. NAO ruled on the Honeywell and GE submissions. Although it found that "the timing of the dismissals appears to coincide with organizing drives by independent unions in the two plants," it did not recommend Ministerial Consultations.[53] To many labor leaders across the continent, the decision proved that the NAALC they had tried so desperately to defeat was worthless. Unions vociferously denounced the NAO's decisions. Amy Newell, UE's general secretary-treasurer, lambasted it, as reported in the *UE News*:

"The NAO report confirms what labor has maintained all along, that the NAFTA side agreements were toothless and ineffective.... " ... Companies like GE and Honeywell are free to trample on workers' rights," she said, "protected by the lack of any action on the part of the U.S. government." Newell said UE is calling on Congress to replace the side agreements "with a viable alternative that serves to defend labor rights in the U.S, Canada and Mexico.... The NAO was given little real power by the Clinton Administration but could have requested that U.S. and Mexican officials consult about GE and Honeywell's violations of Mexican workers' rights. The NAO refused to take even that modest step.[54]

---

[52] Letter to Jorge F. Perez-Lopez, acting secretary, United States National Administrative Office, from John H. Hovis, Jr. In re: General Electric Company. February 10, 1994.
[53] Atleson et al. (2008, p. 287).
[54] *UE News*, November 18, 1994, p. 5.

IBT General President Ron Carey's response was no less scathing: "The Clinton Administration promised working people that NAFTA would protect workers' rights on both sides of the border, but they clearly have no intention of keeping that promise."[55]

Despite their adjudicatory loss, the unions' engagement in the process of filing the submissions furthered the collective labor rights struggle in North America. At the procedural level, the U.S. NAO adopted a broad procedural approach for reviewing the first submissions advocated by the filing unions. Honeywell, GE, and the United States Council for International Business argued that the submission should not be accepted because workers had not invoked or exhausted remedies in Mexico, their dismissals occurred before the NAALC went into effect, their allegations did not involve a "pattern of practice" of violations under the agreement, and the submission focused not on the Mexican government's failure to enforce its labor laws but rather on the corporations (Atleson et al. 2008). The U.S. NAO, however, agreed with the union attorneys, who collectively pushed for a broad procedural approach in their construction of the first submissions.[56] Although the NAALC's general language justified the NAO's decision, it likely also reflected the intense pressure labor activists brought to bear during the first months the NAALC was in force (Atleson et al. 2008). Not accepting the submissions for review would have sent a resounding message to labor that the agreement was indeed a sham.

The political fallout from the NAO's decision also generated outcomes favorable to labor. The NAO's failure to recommend Ministerial Consultations put Secretary of Labor Robert Reich – one of the three members of the NAALC's Ministerial Council – in a difficult position. On the morning the *New York Times* broke the story of the NAO decision with the headline "Reich Supports Mexico on Union Organizing, Vexing Labor," Reich was scheduled to give a speech at the UAW convention. Reporter Allen R. Myerson wrote that the labor secretary "refused to pursue complaints that Mexico had failed to enforce union organizing rights. . . . Reich sided with corporations and Mexican officials."[57] Reich was reportedly furious, demanding that the U.S. NAO never compromise him again (Atleson et al. 2008). In almost all accepted submissions that followed during the Clinton administration, the U.S. NAO recommended

---

[55] *UE News*, November 18, 1994, p. 5.
[56] For a more detailed discussion of the procedural issues in the first NAO cases, see Atleson et al. (2008).
[57] Atleson et al. (2008, p. 287).

Ministerial Consultations, and the Mexican and Canadian NAOs followed suit; Ministerial Consultations therefore "became an expected state in the NAALC complaint process."[58]

The quasi-institutionalization of Ministerial Consultations also benefits North American unions by creating a public forum in which they can expose corporate and government labor rights abuses. It is clear that corporations are keenly aware of, and do not appreciate, the bad publicity of the NAALC's "sunshine effect." Although the NAO assigns each case an official identification number, unions, labor activists, and the press routinely refer to submissions by the name of the corporation or entity implicated in the case. Submissions 940001 and 940002 therefore became the Honeywell and GE submissions in popular parlance.

Two Mexican business representatives bemoaned this nomenclature in the NAALC four-year review:

As representatives of industry it worries us that the obligations contained in the agreement are wrongly applied to companies and not to the governments that function as "Parties" under the agreement. Because the lack of proper application of labor legislation is the point of discussion in public submissions, we ask that they not be referred to by the name of the company (General Electric, Han Young, Sony, etc.).[59]

Iconic GE CEO Jack Welch also disliked the shorthand, reportedly telling his top executives: "I never want to see a so-called 'GE case' under the NAALC in the papers again."[60] The bad publicity surrounding the GE submission and the concomitant pressure applied by unions on both sides of the border had an impact: senior GE management in the U.S. told Mexican executives in their plants across the border not to fire workers who organized, to rehire workers that had been fired for doing so, and to offer "enhanced severance pay" to those who were fired but decided not to accept their jobs back.[61]

Although UE and FAT activists overwhelmingly viewed the GE submission as a failure despite these gains, the value of having an institutional arena (however weak) in which to engage cannot be ignored. This new and viable arena provided the UE and FAT recourse after their organizing efforts were thwarted, legitimized their claims, and, perhaps most significantly, allowed them to strengthen their relationship.

---

[58] Atleson et al. (2008, p. 287).
[59] Annex 5: Public Comments in *Review of the North American Agreement on Labor Cooperation 1994–1997*.
[60] Atleson et al. (2008, p. 290).
[61] Atleson et al. (2008, pp. 287–288).

The NAALC process also served as a vehicle to strengthen the relationship between the Communication Workers of America (CWA), the Communications, Energy, and Paperworkers Union (CEP) in Canada, and the Mexican Telephone Workers' Union (STRM). In 1995, STRM became the first Mexican union to file a complaint against the U.S. government under the NAALC. The case involved Sprint's closure of its La Conexion Familiar subsidiary in San Francisco (geared toward the Latino market) when workers began an organizing drive to join the CWA. A former CWA official explained that a trinational strategy had been planned from the very beginning:

> The reason we became involved with it is because that was a mutual promise of solidarity between the two [Mexican and Canadian] groups. When we had the Sprint problem in San Francisco, we had the Canadians and we had the Mexicans, they came down. Francisco [Hernández Juárez, secretary general of the STRM] himself came. And Fred [Pomeroy, president of the CEP] came to a meeting that we had in San Francisco with the press to try to expose the situation.[62]

As Cohen and Early (1998) explain, the STRM's move attracted a lot of attention because "It had previously been assumed that NAALC's complaint procedures – a sop to NAFTA foes in the United States – would mainly be used by American unions complaining about workers' rights violations in Mexico that help keep unions weak, wages low, and working conditions poor in the runaway shops of U.S. multinationals."[63] STRM officials realized, however, that Sprint's desire to enter Mexico's long-distance market through a joint venture with the Mexican telephone company Telmex could mean that Mexican labor rights would similarly be jeopardized. STRM Secretary General Francisco Hernández Juárez declared: "We don't want the mass firings of workers to happen here."[64]

In its NAO complaint, the STRM demanded that Sprint be barred from doing business in Mexico until it reinstated the fired U.S. workers at La Conexion Familiar and agreed to recognize unions in either country chosen by a majority of workers. In September 1995, Hernández Juárez invited CWA President Morton Bahr to speak at the STRM's national convention in Mexico City. Bahr declared to the delegates: "We are using NAFTA to provide a forum to air the problems of U.S. workers,

---

[62] Personal interview with CWA official, 2001.
[63] Cohen and Early (1998, p. 156).
[64] Ibid.

particularly immigrant workers, and Mexican workers.... Your participation is vital to our efforts."[65]

The CEP also participated in the Sprint case. Former President Fred
Pomeroy described joint actions associated with it: "We created a racket
over that. The PTTI [Postal, Telephone, and Telegraph International, an
international trade secretariat] was having their World Congress here
so we had a big demonstration with delegates from about eighty-nine
countries in Montreal and we hired a lawyer to get involved in that
one."[66] Although the NAO complaint did not result in victory for the
Sprint workers, STRM officials pointed out the benefits of using the
NAALC process. Eduardo Torres Arroyo explained:

I think the submission process stimulates and facilitates transnational collaboration and cooperation. NAFTA has been incredibly important for us in our
solidarity between unions. I would say fundamental. I think it makes a difference
and it is beneficial to have international alliances because in the face of globalization we think international unionism is fundamental.... But NAFTA has assisted
this process. In the case of Sprint we recognized that Sprint is one of the most
anti-union companies, and we protested by creating an alliance with American
workers. And when an American multinational comes to Mexico, U.S. unions
recommend that they create an alliance with us. The problem is an American
multinational doesn't come here to deal with a strong union, it comes to deal
with a union like the CTM, pay low wages, etc., for a financial paradise. We have
a different idea, that they should pay decent wages, and of course should be able
to compete. And workers should benefit from high productivity and quality. And
therefore we need to create alliances with American and Canadian unions in the
area of NAFTA.[67]

In 1996, another opportunity to build unity around an NAO submission emerged. This time, northern unions supported their Mexican
counterpart. The CWA and CEP assisted the STRM by filing an NAO
submission to contest the treatment of Mexican workers at Maxi-Switch,
a manufacturer of high-technology keyboards in Cananea, Mexico. Maxi-
Switch also maintains a distribution center in Tucson, Arizona – 160 miles
from the Cananea plant. Maxi-Switch workers who attempted to organize an independent union through the Federation of Goods and Services
Unions (FESEBES, of which the STRM was an affiliate) were denied the
right to organize. The STRM organized a cross-border meeting in Her-
mosillo, and CWA Local 7026 in Tucson attended and pledged support.
The NAO submission grew out of this initial meeting.

[65] Cusick (1995, p. 10).
[66] Personal interview with Fred Pomeroy of the CEP, February 28, 2001.
[67] Personal interview with Eduardo Torres Arroyo of the STRM, July 12, 1999.

An STRM lawyer described the strategic decisions behind the case: "We chose Maxi-Switch because it was a transnational. It also had establishments in the United States; that was another reason. CWA was the principal union to help us, then the AFL-CIO. It was a decision in common; we already had a close relationship with the CWA."[68] The submission is considered one of the most successful because four days before the April 1997 scheduled public hearing on the case, the Mexican government issued a legal registration to the independent union. This was the first instance in which a "participant in a NAFTA labor side agreement proceeding has capitulated and agreed to follow its own laws" (Cohen and Early 1998, p. 159).

The Teamsters' most significant NAO case not only strengthened its relationship with the FAT but also helped counter the negative image of the union generated by its efforts to oppose NAFTA's Chapter 12, which permits the free movement of surface transportation carriers across all borders in North America. The Teamsters vigorously opposed Chapter 12 and organized a cross-border trucking campaign to try to prevent its implementation. Although Teamsters officials contend that the union privileged internationalism and made a conscious effort not to scapegoat Mexican workers, many labor activists across the continent assailed key aspects of the campaign as racist (as will be discussed in Chapter 6). These same critics, however, applauded the Teamsters' efforts to protect Mexican migrant workers by working collaboratively through the NAALC process on the Apple submission.

Filed in May 1998 with the Mexican NAO, the submission accused the Washington State apple industry of labor violations (particularly against migrant workers), including freedom of association, health and safety, and employment discrimination, among others. The Teamsters worked on the case with the United Farmworkers of America, FAT, the UNT, STIMAHCS, and the Democratic Farm Workers Front. Andy Banks, who at the time was the Teamsters' international representative of the president assigned to work out of the office of strategic campaigns, described how the case emerged:

[U]p to that point... I think [most] of the NAO complaints had been about Mexico not applying its labor law. And my feeling and my work relationships with Mexican trade unionists – even ones who hated the system, hated the PRI there – said that Mexicans get tired of hearing yankees tell them how inadequate they are. You guys aren't perfect. And so I figured well, that's a really good thing to tap into, and it's true, too. So what about American labor law not being

---

[68] Personal interview with Hector Barba García of the STRM, May 8, 2000.

applied, or health and safety law and migrant rights sort of things? And so we looked. I contacted Lance [Compa], who had just left the [Commission for Labor Cooperation]. We talked about this strategy of finding out if we could get a group of Mexicans interested in filing charges against us.[69]

The FAT's Bertha Luján explained how the FAT became involved in the submission:

They invited us to work as part of the organization with Latino workers in this area. And we presented a complaint with the NAO office.... about the working conditions in this industry in this state, showing that workers' universal rights had been violated, and they were discriminated against. And we did this to support the work of the Teamsters.[70]

The Apple NAO case was significant because the Teamsters prioritized gaining the trust and support of Mexican unionists and organizations. They worked closely with a local community in Mexico and focused their submission on the violations of Mexican migrant workers' rights. Andy Banks explained:

[The submission] was enthusiastically embraced. And especially once we went to Mexico we found out like, for example, that in Chihuahua there was a thriving apple industry that had totally been devastated by the dumping of these apples in the Mexican market... and that they were very upset. And that the union there, the Chihuahua apple workers, were upset because it meant unemployment problems. So there was a lot of sympathy.... And here we were saying, wait a second, part of our job as Teamsters is to protect the rights of migrant workers in America. That's a great thing for a North American union to say to Mexican workers. They couldn't believe we were saying that.[71]

According to Banks, the Teamsters' strategy helped build trust among the unions and laid the foundation for a relationship based on mutual respect and support. It also presented another side to the union that helped temper criticism of its cross-border trucking campaign:

This was a very different message, that our members here all have stories that are horrible stories about how they're treated in this country. And that everybody in Mexico knows somebody who's gone to America and been abused. And so we're going to file charges against a very big case of that abuse. And part of it was to try to convince the AFL-CIO to send a group of organizers – workers from the Chihuahua union and some other people from FAT

[69] Personal interview with Andy Banks of the Teamsters, January 10, 2001.
[70] Personal interview with Bertha Luján of the FAT, August 29, 2000.
[71] Personal interview with Andy Banks of the Teamsters, January 10, 2001.

and some other unions – up to investigate, or to look, to educate themselves on what was going on. And they came two weeks before the election and they were able to report back – when they went back to Mexico – unbelievable violations like the INS [Immigration and Naturalization Service] visiting people's homes and threatening them, and all these types of very important things. And we got an enthusiastic response.... But just from a total observer point of view this is a fascinating story, it's a really fascinating story... it's a very different model than the trucking model which was... totally different, top-down, based on our political relationship with the White House, that type of stuff.[72]

As Banks suggested, the Washington apple campaign was the antithesis of the cross-border trucking campaign in both tactics and results. The Teamsters worked with their counterparts, gained their respect and support, and saw a very different outcome.

Building a Continent-Wide Campaign

U.S. and Canadian participants in the Han Young struggle, like the Teamsters, tried to build trust with their Mexican counterparts and support a campaign that reflected the real needs and interests of Mexican workers. The Han Young campaign was a watershed event for North American labor organizing; it was the largest trinational campaign focused on Mexican workers' rights in the continent's history, and the largest campaign to include an NAO submission as part of its strategic repertoire up to that point. For three years, activists from across the continent engaged in a variety of transnational actions to demand that Mexican workers' rights be protected at a Tijuana factory that produced truck chassis and shipping containers for Hyundai. Beginning in April 1997, workers at the Han Young factory attempted to organize an independent union to deal with the myriad health and safety and economic issues at the plant. They supported STIMAHCS, an independent union affiliated with the FAT, and demanded an election to vote out the PRI-backed Revolutionary Confederation of Workers and Peasants (CROC), which enjoyed a "protection contract" with Han Young.[73]

Han Young workers actively sought out support for their struggle from transnational allies. Using a classic "boomerang strategy" (Keck and Sikkink 1998) that rallied international pressure and criticism to force the Mexican state to respond, Han Young activists gained initial support from

---

[72] Personal interview with Andy Banks of the Teamsters, January 10, 2001.
[73] David Bacon via email.

the FAT and the Support Committee for Maquiladora Workers (a San Diego–based NGO). These organizations provided a plethora of union and NGO ties across North America that rallied the public and media at key moments during the campaign. After the company attempted to repress and intimidate workers for almost four months, for example, the Tijuana labor board met to set a date for a union election, but suspended proceedings when the CROC announced that the CTM also wanted to file for union recognition. Four hours after U.S. supporters called the board to demand an election date (which coincided with a Han Young worker protest), it finally set a date. On October 6, 1997, Han Young workers became the first to elect an independent union in any of Mexico's 3,000 maquiladoras.

International pressure was used again in conjunction with local worker agitation after Han Young – in defiance of the election results – fired four more workers and announced it would fire all union supporters and hire new workers from Veracruz. On October 22, allies began a U.S. consumer boycott of Hyundai, and eight days later filed a submission with the U.S. NAO detailing the Mexican government's failure to enforce its labor laws.[74] On November 10, the Tijuana labor board announced that it would not certify the election. Four fired Han Young workers began a hunger strike, and workers organized a series of work stoppages. North American allies conducted a one-day fast in solidarity with the hunger strikers, organized candlelight vigils, and sent letters to the labor board, the governor of Baja California, Mexican President Zedillo, U.S. President Clinton, and Hyundai. The Mexican government ultimately forced the Tijuana labor board to certify the election. Han Young, however, failed to bargain with the union. In March, the union announced that it would launch a strike against Han Young if negotiations were not conducted in good faith, and in May the FAT began the first legal strike of a maquiladora by an independent union.

The Han Young struggle continued for almost two more years. During that time, workers faced intimidation by management, official union supporters, and police. The government issued arrest warrants for a union organizer and the FAT's attorney. Government officials assailed the involvement of transnational allies and used nationalist rhetoric to discredit the FAT and other independent unions. According to Baja

---

[74] The original submission was filed by the Support Committee for Maquiladora Workers, the International Labor Rights Fund, the National Association of Democratic Lawyers (ANAD), and STIMAHCS.

California's director of labor and social services, the strike was "provoked by foreign unions" in an attempt to undermine investment in Mexico.[75] The Han Young plant manager offered a similar opinion: "This conflict is being used by U.S. unions and political parties in Mexico who don't want us here. They [the independent unions] aren't sincere."[76] One company posted a sign in its factory that read "The FAT is a foreign union."

Transnational allies maintained their support despite the attacks. In February 1998, the United Steelworkers of America, the UAW, the CAW, and two NGOs filed an addendum to the NAO submission on health and safety issues.[77] Activists declared February 7 a day of local action in solidarity with Han Young workers. The Support Committee for Maquiladora Workers issued an alert that announced "The boycott of Hyundai Motors will continue until the Han Young workers have justice" and requested that delegations of clergy and human rights groups visit Han Young workers in Tijuana. Activists in over twenty-five cities across the United States demonstrated at Hyundai car dealerships, car shows, Mexican consulates, and U.S. government buildings. Various unions and community groups hosted visits by Han Young workers, who shared their stories and asked for solidarity. Local activists and unions often gave it. At the Port of Portland, for example, labor activists picketed a ship waiting to be unloaded at Hyundai's dock that International Longshore and Warehouse Union members then refused to unload, resulting in significant financial losses for Hyundai (Williams 2003).

Utilizing the NAALC process enabled the FAT to embarrass and pressure the Mexican government by exposing labor abuses and threatening its trade relationship under NAFTA. Representative David Bonior and fourteen other members of Congress wrote a letter to President Clinton urging him to discuss the Han Young situation with President Zedillo. The Clinton administration sent signals to labor activists that the president supported the NAO submission process when Vice President Al Gore raised the Han Young issue with President Zedillo personally. A sample letter to Mexican President Zedillo crafted by campaign supporters pointed out that "The outcome of events at Han Young/Hyundai could affect future trade relations between the United States and Mexico."

---

[75] David Bacon via email.
[76] Ibid.
[77] The NGOs were the Maquiladora Health and Safety Support Network and Worksafe! Southern California.

There is evidence that the struggle influenced members of Congress as they contemplated renewing the president's fast-track authority in 1997. As David Bacon reported:

Opponents of fast track used the Han Young election as a symbol of NAFTA's failure to protect workers' rights. As the administration sought to line up support, Democratic representatives David Bonior and Richard Gephardt buttonholed Congress members, telling them about Han Young. It worked well. In the end, even with substantial Republican support, President Clinton couldn't come up with the necessary votes and pulled fast track off the floor.[78]

The U.S. NAO ruled in late April 1998 that the Mexican government had failed to enforce its own labor laws. NAO Secretary Irasema Garza blamed the Tijuana labor board: "We have found that the workers at Han Young encountered a number of obstacles in attempting to form an independent union. Although the Mexican Constitution and the federal labor law guarantee freedom of association and the right to form independent unions, there appear to be inconsistencies in the application and enforcement of the law." Despite the NAO's findings and the efforts of Han Young workers and their transnational allies, the struggle did not result in a victory for workers. In the fall of 1999, Han Young, in a flagrant violation of Mexican labor law, closed the factory and opened another in eastern Tijuana. The struggle ultimately lost momentum and dissipated.

Although many activists and scholars quite legitimately read it as a terrible defeat for the Han Young workers and the NAALC process,[79] the Han Young struggle did have quite positive outcomes for strengthening the transnational legal field. It proved it was possible to galvanize support for a continent-wide labor rights struggle that captured the public's imagination and triggered international diplomacy. The response of the Mexican federal government and Hyundai to transnational pressure at various points during the Han Young struggle reflects the potential impact of boomerang strategies. Other workers in Mexico's maquila factories had tried and failed to organize independent unions and strikes. It is unlikely that Han Young workers would have been able to achieve these goals if the campaign had not brought international pressure to bear on the Mexican government.

---

[78] Bacon (1998).
[79] See Heather L. Williams's (2003) compelling account.

The campaign was also significant because it centered on the needs and interests that Mexican workers articulated; the focus and strategies were not dictated or imposed by northern counterparts. This built trust among participants. As Williams (2003) explains:

The fact that the mass media in the United States and Mexico focused on the issues of worker autonomy and union democracy rather than simply sweatshop conditions or worker poverty indicates, first, a significant maturation of cross-border networks. Such maturation had much to do with the impact of sustained contact between groups on both sides of the U.S.-Mexico border. Whereas in the early 1990s many labor unionists in the United States and Canada portrayed their counterpart workers in Mexico as victims – or perhaps unwitting dupes in runaway factories that had left Americans and Canadians unemployed – solidarity partners now focused on the Han Young struggle as an issue of worker democracy.[80]

As this chapter shows, the NAALC was in part responsible for the sustained contact among North American labor unions that catalyzed the issue shift across labor rights networks. Moreover, the NAALC's articulation and legitimation of freedom of association and collective bargaining rights at the transnational level helped shape and bolster activists' claims; there was now a right to invoke, not simply a sweatshop to condemn. U.S. and Canadian activists could therefore more clearly see that they faced problems similar to those of workers in Mexico. An alert the Campaign for Labor Rights sent supporters revealed that some northern activists saw parallels between their own history and that of their Mexican counterparts: "Some U.S. supporters pushing for federal intervention [by the Mexican government] likened the situation to the scene in the 1950s when the governor of Arkansas stood in the doorway blocking black children from entering the [school] after the Brown vs. Board of Education decision by the Supreme Court and the U.S. government had to send in the military to oppose the state governor."[81] By focusing on rights, the NAALC process helped reinforce workers' shared experiences and collective interests.

The NAALC Process as Catalyst

While the NAALC strengthened ongoing campaigns and existing relationships among key North American unions, it also stimulated new

---

[80] Williams (2003, p. 532).
[81] Campaign for Labor Rights, March 6, 1998.

transnational relationships among others. One of the most important relationships the NAALC process facilitated was between the FAT and the AFL-CIO. As will be discussed later, FAT leaders viewed building relationships with U.S. and Canadian unions through the NAALC process as a way to increase their visibility, influence, and power within the Mexican labor movement and with the Mexican government.[82] They therefore actively sought allies with whom to file NAO submissions. In 1994, the AFL-CIO began to "unofficially" support NAO submissions in which the FAT participated. Robin Alexander, a UE lawyer, revealed that AFL-CIO officials arranged a meeting with the unions that participated in the first submissions: the UE, Teamsters, and FAT. The meeting, she explained, was held in secret: "Because of that case, or at the time we filed that case, the AFL-CIO hosted a lunch for us at their offices. Now that was before the change in AFL policy, so it was not an official lunch. But, it was a way in which various people got to meet."[83]

Until 1997, when the AFL-CIO officially signed onto its first NAO submission, it frequently worked behind the scenes to support other unions engaged in the NAALC process. During the Han Young struggle, for example, the AFL-CIO rallied congressional support for the workers.[84] The federation was careful, however, not to publicly condemn the CTM. In the 1996 Maxi-Switch submission, the CWA alleged CTM collusion in setting up a ghost union to thwart workers' efforts to organize an independent union, stating: "It offers evidence of how Maxi-Switch, in collusion with government officials and representatives of the CTM and the Conciliation and Arbitration Board of the State of Sonora, have consistently violated the law to prevent Maxi-Switch workers from joining a union of their own choosing."[85] In a 1996 letter to the U.S. NAO, the AFL-CIO requested to "associate itself" with the Maxi-Switch submission. In contrast to its affiliate, however, the federation did not raise the issue of union collusion or mention the CTM by name, and emphasized its impartiality with regard to Mexican workers' choice of union representative. The following excerpt captures the letter's framing of the

[82] They did not view it as the only way to build relationships, however, and actively participated in other kinds of transnational conferences, campaigns, and activities.

[83] Personal interview with Robin Alexander of the UE, December 21, 2000.

[84] Campaign for Labor Rights "Hyundai Boycott – Q&A Update" dated October 28, 1997.

[85] CWA press release "Communications Workers of America Files NAFTA Complaint Charging Failure by Mexico to Enforce Labor Laws" dated October 11, 1996.

government and companies as the true culprits in workers' rights abuses
in Mexico:

In urging these actions, the AFL-CIO in no way intends to suggest any preference
between different Mexican federations or confederations. We believe such choices
should be left entirely up to Mexican workers. Our concern is that in the case
of Maxi Switch and many others like it, government agencies and company
management are intervening to impose the choice of unions and contracts on
workers without their knowledge or consent. It is this violation of the NAALC
that prompts our support of this case.[86]

By emphasizing its neutrality, the AFL-CIO attempted to deflect what
would be seen as a direct attack on its ally. Fourteen months later, however, the federation signaled the official demise of its exclusive relationship
with the CTM and its willingness to publicly criticize it by signing on as
co-petitioner to the Echlin NAO submission, which directly implicated
the CTM in collusion activities.

The Echlin case is significant not only because it was the first official
NAO submission for the AFL-CIO but also because it stimulated a trinational relationship among the UE, FAT, and the Canadian Steelworkers
as they worked to protect unions' mutual interests. The transnational
activity surrounding the Echlin case epitomizes how the NAALC process
stimulated new transnational relationships by creating a concrete mechanism to engage and articulating collective interests. The NAO submission
served as a key focal point around which unions developed and extended
their campaign. In 1997, seven unions in the United States, Canada, and
Mexico created the Echlin Workers Alliance to support workers across
the continent employed by the Echlin Corporation, a U.S.-based transnational auto parts manufacturer.[87] One of the primary objectives of the
Echlin Alliance was to support Mexican workers in their struggle to
improve the working conditions in Echlin plants. A statement adopted
at its founding meeting read: "We will make a special effort to support
Echlin workers in Mexico who suffer the lowest wages and worst conditions and who face the worst repression when they stand up for their
rights" (Hathaway 2000, p. 191). The Echlin Alliance, then, was created
because the unions viewed protecting workers' rights in plants in all three
NAFTA countries as their common interest and goal.

---

[86] Letter to Irasema Garza, secretary of the U.S. NAO, from AFL-CIO President John J.
Sweeney, October 21, 1996.
[87] Echlin later became the Dana Corporation.

The alliance was called to action soon after its founding when STIMAHCS, a FAT-affiliated independent metal workers union, began an organizing drive at ITAPSA, a plant in Mexico City affiliated with Echlin.[88] The company and the Mexican government attempted to quash the campaign, and STIMAHCS asked the alliance for assistance. Bob Kingsley, director of organization for the UE, described the alliance's response:

Before very long even though the initial organizational vision was sort of a broader one about how we were going to go out and cooperatively by comparing notes and joining forces in Canada, Mexico, and the U.S. attempt organization throughout this chain, the thing became focused on ITAPSA because the Mexicans were first out of the gate. They went to the factory and they tried to organize it and faced horrible repression. Of course this new organization then closed ranks behind the workers involved in that struggle and made that the prime piece of our work. And that work took a number of forms, from activities we tried to organize in the various organized shops to protest the company's actions, our first instinct being to involve the rank-and-file Echlin workers to take on this company. And we were able to undertake activities in Canada [and] in the United States, in support of what was going on at ITAPSA in Mexico.[89]

Faced with a recalcitrant company, the alliance filed a public submission with the U.S. NAO in December 1997 that accused the corporation, the CTM, and two CTM locals of labor rights violations and demanded that the Mexican government enforce its labor laws. The submission was historic for a variety of reasons; in addition to the alliance unions, over fifty organizations from all three NAFTA countries – the largest number to date – signed the submission. The submission also marked the AFL-CIO's first public condemnation and legal action against the CTM since brokering an alliance with the federation during the Cold War. The UE's Bob Kingsley explained its significance:

[The Echlin submission] eventually drew the official support of the AFL, which shocked us out of our shoes. We considered this a major step at the time in the way the AFL-CIO was conducting its international union relations. For them to side with us knowing that the primary Mexican representatives were from an independent union that was not the CTM and to publicly declare themselves in support of this complaint and testimony and activities that were taking place around it seemed to me to be a watershed moment.[90]

---

[88] The submission is generally known by the name Echlin, although some refer to ITAPSA and others Dana because Echlin was eventually sold to the Dana Corporation.

[89] Personal interview with Bob Kingsley of the UE, January 23, 2001.

[90] Ibid.

Finally, the Echlin alliance built a larger campaign around the submission; participating unions protested in plants across the continent, held demonstrations in front of the company's headquarters, and took action at its shareholders meeting. At the shareholder's meeting, the alliance demanded that the company sign a code of conduct that would apply in Echlin's plants in Mexico, the United States, and Canada. The UE's director of organization described the action at the shareholders meeting this way:

And it was just right, it was the scene that ought to be. Here's their corporate headquarters, this palatial setup overlooking this beautiful lake, [this] comfortable location used by these overpaid executives that run this outfit. And here we are, a nasty bunch of skunks attending their garden party and bust[ing] up this meeting by raising the Echlin issue and demanding that they respond to us on this topic, that they contemplate adopting a corporate code of conduct, that justice be done for these people who've been done wrong. And it was a good day for us ... when we were able to do that.[91]

Despite the alliance's efforts, the U.S. NAO submission and joint actions failed to remedy the problem at ITAPSA. Thus, a year later, the alliance filed a second public submission with the Canadian NAO. The Canadian Steelworkers participated in the alliance, and they agreed to spearhead the case. CUSWA's Gerry Barr described how, through their engagement in the transnational legal field, the three unions' relationship began to coalesce trinationally:

So the FAT was keenly interested in and valued the international tie. And as a result of that interest as well ... I think that moved us forward to a much more mature kind of level of participation with each other's work. And then of course there were – simultaneously and preceding our sort of formal connection with the FAT – ... other ties of course that the FAT had created with unions in the United States. ... And one of the most obvious points of connection is their relationship with the small but very valiant United Electrical Workers. And so they had created a very high-quality point of contact and very thoughtful, very careful, very long-term, and naturally we became involved in three-way discussions between ... Canada – the Steelworkers in Canada – the UE and the FAT.[92]

It was through the NAO process, however, with the FAT as an intermediary, that the Canadian Steelworkers developed a relationship with the UE. The UE offered significant support as the CUSWA prepared the

---

[91] Personal interview with Bob Kingsley of the UE, January 23, 2001.
[92] Personal interview with Gerry Barr of the CUSWA, March 1, 2001.

submission. When asked to describe the benefits of the NAO case, Robin Alexander, the UE's director of international affairs, responded: "I think that one benefit for us is we really did get to know the Canadian Steelworkers much better as a result of all of this."[93] Alexander's comments suggest that the NAALC process helped build a relationship between the unions by providing a concrete mechanism to engage:

There had been no NAO cases filed in Canada. And so the [Canadian] Steelworkers agreed to really be the point people on that case, because of their relationship with the FAT, and the FAT had through the Echlin Workers Alliance asked for assistance, and so a decision was made to file cases both here and in Canada and so the Canadian Steelworkers agreed to really coordinate that work.... I wound up working very very closely with people in their Humanity Fund and with their lawyers and got to know them.[94]

Gerry Barr's comments reveal that another quite important result of the NAO submission was to help stimulate and reinforce collective interests. He explained that although the Canadian Steelworkers were reluctant to utilize the NAALC process, his union decided to participate in the case in order to support the FAT:

In Canada this turned out to be the first time that a union aimed at using the side agreement; the view with respect to the NAFTA side agreement had been very very harshly negative and we thought and to some extent still think that this is a procedure designed to not work and designed to be inaccessible and designed for inefficacy not efficacy, and to some extent we still think that, but it does remain true that it was a venue, right? It was a place to engage and so because the FAT was interested in that we became interested in it. And because they valued it we suspended some of the critique with respect to the non-utility of the platform and were prepared to accompany them, ... and to sort of give some weight to their interest in having it aired in Canada, and we became the lead agency as it were.[95]

The Canadian Steelworkers' decision to participate in the process was significant. The submission required a large amount of time and money and yet did not directly involve the violation of Canadian workers' rights. The union made the decision because, as Barr suggests, it came to see its interests as linked to those of the FAT. The Echlin NAO case thus helps illuminate the *processes* through which the NAALC helped galvanize collective interests by establishing new transnational rights and adjudicatory

---

[93] Personal interview with Robin Alexander of the UE, December 21, 2000.
[94] Ibid.
[95] Personal interview with Gerry Barr of the Canadian Steelworkers, March 1, 2001.

mechanisms, and helped stimulate new relationships by providing a transnational institutional arena to engage in tangible and solidary ways.

Building a Transnational Labor Rights Network

The strength of the NAALC's effects on labor transnationalism is reflected by the number of unions and labor rights organizations that filed NAO submissions jointly during the Clinton administration from 1994 to January 2001 (see Table 4.3). Of the twenty-one submissions filed with at least one labor union participant during that time period, seven had ten or more co-petitioners.[96] Although the first few cases were submitted by single unions or a U.S. and a Mexican union working together, the number of unions and NGOs participating in cases jointly began to increase as the process evolved. Nine petitioners signed onto the 1997 Han Young submission. And, as discussed above, over fifty organizations from all three NAFTA countries participated in the Echlin NAO submissions.

An archaeology of NAO submissions reveals that the majority included as petitioners unions that had actively engaged in the transnational trade-negotiating field prior to NAFTA's signing. Of the twenty-one submissions mentioned previously, eighteen included at least one co-petitioner that had participated in the field. This suggests that the nascent transnational labor rights network that emerged during NAFTA's negotiation facilitated the joint filing of NAO submissions. Many unions that had actively challenged the labor side agreement worked together in this emergent transnational arena, built fledgling relationships, and then tested the waters of its new transnational adjudicatory mechanism together. It was easier for these unions to utilize the NAALC process because they already had come into contact with and previously worked with their transnational counterparts. It was therefore also easier for them to introduce new unions to the process.

Table 4.3 reveals that a core group of labor activists and lawyers with particular interest and expertise in the NAO process initiated and participated in a majority of NAO submissions. It also shows that a majority of submissions involved the direct or indirect participation of three key unions: the UE, FAT, and Teamsters. These unions had lawyers who developed an expertise in the process and utilized their networks to

---

[96] NAO submissions that did not include labor union participation include EFCO Corporation (Canadian NAO 99–1) and Florida Tomato Exchange (U.S. NAO 9802). Neither was accepted for review.

contribute to a process of "legal strategic osmosis" as more unions sought advice and assistance with their own submissions. It is quite common for two unions to come into contact in the context of a particular NAO case brokered by a person or third party with previous relationships with both. For example, Arturo Alcalde, a labor lawyer with the FAT, participated in the SEMARNAP submission for the National Association of Democratic Lawyers (ANAD).[97] Alcalde had a relationship with the Teamsters and the UE from previous work with the FAT. He facilitated the first contacts between these unions and SEMARNAP, and although they did not sign on as petitioners, the Teamsters and UE supported the NAO submission. SEMARNAP's Alejandro Quiroz Soriano described the Teamsters' support:

When we had direct contact with the Teamsters was when we had our conflict with SEMARNAP. They gave us a lot of support with our NAO submission. They were one of the union groups that were most active in supporting our submission and giving us legal support so that it would have a positive impact. We still get political support from the Teamsters, more than economic support. And this is a positive thing.[98]

In 1998, the AFL-CIO and CLC strengthened their fledgling relationship with the FAT and solidified the informal network of labor rights activists by organizing a trinational conference in Mexico City to evaluate the NAALC process and the effects of NAFTA in each of its three signatory countries. The meeting, which included the participation of over 115 labor law activists, or "laboralistas" as they became known, formalized the growing transnational network of labor lawyers and activists who had trailblazed the use of the NAALC process in each of their three countries. During the two-day conference, jointly organized with Mexican labor scholars, the laboralistas shared their experiences and developed international labor rights strategies. U.S. labor lawyer and attendee Lance Compa described the historic alliance:

In an extraordinary meeting in Mexico in early December 1998, labour lawyers from Canada, Mexico, and the United States who have been involved in NAALC cases formulated a common strategy for working together in new NAALC cases challenging the three governments to live up to the 11 labour principles they adopted. Elements of their strategy include: case selection that targets systematic

---

[97] SEMARNAP involved the union representing workers in Mexico's Ministry of the Environment, similar to the U.S. Environmental Protection Agency. It is now called Secretaria de Medio Ambiente y Recursos Naturales (SEMARNAT).
[98] Personal interview with Alejandro Quiroz Soriano of SEMARNAP, July 6, 2000.

Table 4.4. *Submissions by Labor Principle (1994–2008)*

Labor Principle	Number of Public Submissions
Freedom of association	27
Right to bargain collectively	16
Right to strike	4
Forced labor	2
Child labor	2
Minimum employment standards	14
Employment discrimination	9
Equal pay	3
Health and safety	19
Compensation for injuries	10
Protection of migrant workers	6

problems, not just single-workplace incidents; more use of simultaneous complaint filings with 2 or 3 NAOs on the same topic; more consultation among advocates from all three countries prior to filing a complaint.[99]

A key aspect of the laboralistas' strategy was to include rank-and-file workers in campaigns associated with these submissions. The AFL-CIO and FAT, along with two leading Mexican universities, published a book the following year titled *Memories: Trinational Meeting of Democratic Labor Law Activists*, which included a description of the event and essays written by participants. The laboralistas worked on NAO submissions, held various meetings to discuss strategies (trinational meetings were held in Mexico City in 2000 and Toronto in February 2001), convened a trinational conference focused on North American labor rights, and created a Web site to share information.

Labor lawyers from all three countries also agreed on a strategy to push the NAALC process to its limits while drawing attention to its deficiencies. They privileged NAO submissions that alleged freedom of association violations because if workers could organize, they could fight for all other rights themselves through their unions. It is therefore not a coincidence that the violation most often cited in submissions is one that cannot reach the highest level in the NAALC process. And by filing submissions based on health and safety violations, they hoped to succeed in reaching the highest level in the NAALC process and obtain sanctions. Table 4.4 provides data on the types of submissions filed between 1994 and May 2001.

[99] Compa (1999, p. 210).

As the table shows, of the 29 submissions, 20 involved violations of freedom of association and 13 alleged health and safety violations. This seemingly odd occurrence resulted from a conscious and joint strategic decision to maximize and leverage the NAALC's mechanisms. Discussions in laboralista meetings revealed a shared commitment to push for the highest labor standards across the continent. For example, a U.S. lawyer at the 2001 Toronto meeting warned the group that hosting a forum to expose U.S. laws that allowed striker replacement could harm Canadian and Mexican workers if their governments adopted similar legislation. The warning also suggested that participants now saw themselves as transnational actors whose actions should promote the collective good for the continent's workers.

The NAALC process, then, did not simply generate a flurry of legal paperwork. As with the Han Young and Echlin cases, many unions involved in NAO submissions used them to complement campaigns, joint projects, or other actions and thereby to promote and demand labor rights across the continent. This suggests that the NAALC's effects go beyond its procedural rules. Indeed, the NAALC's passage created an institutional arena in which the rules of regional economic integration could be contested. The NAALC provides a tangible institutional realm of influence. By engaging it, unions can use it to mobilize, organize, and act. The NAALC process helped to wipe away the Cold War residue and build trust among Mexican independent unions and what they had considered the "AFL-CIA" for decades.

Nonparticipants in the NAALC Process and Transnational Labor Rights Network

Not all unions engaged the NAALC or the transnational labor rights network. The ability of participants in the transnational trade-negotiating field to utilize their network after NAFTA's passage helps explain why unions that did not engage the field were less likely to file NAO submissions or to file them with few or no collaborators. Of the four submissions filed by unions that were not active in the transnational trade-negotiating field, two were filed with no collaborators, that is, by only one petitioner (DeCoster Egg Farm and Flight Attendants), one was filed by two petitioners (TAESA), and one was filed by four petitioners (Solec). All of these were filed after the submission with the largest number of co-petitioners (Echlin) was filed.

The DeCoster Egg submission, which alleged that the United States failed to protect the rights of Mexican migrant workers at the DeCoster Egg Farm in Maine, is particularly compelling because it was filed by the CTM – the only submission in which the federation has been involved to date. According to the CTM, the employer failed to adhere to minimum employment standards, engaged in racial discrimination and harassment, and subjected workers to unhealthy and unsafe working conditions. The CTM noted the historic nature of the submission: "In an unprecedented action, the Government of Mexico is participating as co-plaintiff in a class action suit to defend the employment and civil rights of Mexican farm workers.... The Confederation of Mexican Workers joins the Government of Mexico, taking advantage of the opportunity offered by the NAALC, to protect the employment rights of Mexican workers in the United States."[100] The Mexican NAO accepted the submission for review, and Ministerial Consultations were held. In response to the consultations, the U.S. Department of Labor organized outreach sessions and public forums on migrant agricultural workers, and the Secretariat published a guide on migrant workers' rights.

The submission would have been even more historic had it included the CTM's Cold War partner, the AFL-CIO. When asked if he had contact with U.S. or Canadian unions while working on the submission, however, the CTM's secretary of communications and member of its national committee, Netzahualcóyotl de la Vega García, replied: "Direct contact with the workers, nothing more. We didn't make any other contacts."[101] He then went on to laud his federation's relationship with the AFL-CIO:

We have a good relationship with the AFL-CIO.... We have maintained a good relationship with them, participating with them in the Inter-American Regional Workers' Organization, participating in the ILO. We have always had a good relation. So we worked with the workers and the AFL was pleased with this because they have agricultural workers affiliated with them and so logically they were interested in the situation."[102]

By failing to invite the AFL-CIO's participation in the submission, however, the CTM signaled that it did not wish to use the NAALC process as a vehicle for building transnational relationships.

---

[100] Public Communication submitted August 4, 1998 to the Mexican NAO by Netzahualcóyotl de la Vega García of the CTM.
[101] Personal interview with Netzahualcóyotl de la Vega García of the CTM, May 8, 2000.
[102] Ibid.

It is also not clear the AFL-CIO would have worked with the CTM on the submission had its participation been requested. The two federations viewed the NAALC and its potential quite differently; the AFL-CIO sought to expand labor protections, and the CTM was content with the agreement as written. As de la Vega García replied when asked if the NAALC should be expanded such that the violation of more of its labor principles (not just three) could result in trade sanctions: "No. We should enforce what we've got, not anything else, we don't need to expand on it.... We are opposed to a social clause in NAFTA. The agreement already has all the protections that we need."[103] In contrast to the laboralistas who used submissions to push the boundaries of the law with the intention of forcing the three governments to strengthen the NAALC, de la Vega García's vision of the DeCoster Egg submission was relatively narrow in scope. As he explained, his goal was to ensure that the law was enforced:

[M]ore than anything we supported Mexican workers in [the United States] whose rights were totally violated. We asked that the law be obeyed. We went very carefully. We were not asking that they reopen any situation that was already decided legally, only that they take into consideration that their rights had been violated, and that the American authorities know about the problem and take it into consideration, that's all. Nothing else.[104]

When asked his strategy to confront problems of enforcement, he replied, "We don't need specific strategies; the law provides adequately what we need."[105]

Among official Mexican union leaders, de la Vega García's opinion of the NAALC was not an anomaly. Indeed, almost all of the official union representatives I interviewed knew little or nothing about the NAALC process (in comparison, all of the leaders of independent unions knew a considerable amount about the process or had used it). When asked his opinion of the NAO process, the secretary general of one of Mexico's largest textile unions and a member of the CTM national executive committee did not appear to know what the NAALC was. Even after an explanation of the process, he seemed never to have heard of it and expressed skepticism of its existence: "No, I don't think this is possible. You have to file lawsuits in each country and deal with violations internally."[106]

---

[103] Personal interview with Netzahualcóyotl de la Vega García of the CTM, May 8, 2000.
[104] Ibid.
[105] Ibid.
[106] Personal interview with Adolfo Gott Trujillo of the CTM, May 2, 2000.

Fermín Lara Jiménez, secretary general of one of the CROC's largest textile unions and president of the National Textile Workers' Coalition, also knew nothing of the NAALC, declaring: "No, I don't know anything about it." After I explained the process and asked if he would ever consider participating in a submission, he replied: "I haven't heard of these cases. I totally don't know about this. If we have a problem, we fix it here. I wouldn't be interested in filing a submission. We have our own laws, and we have to respect them."[107]

Of the small number of official Mexican unionists who knew of the NAALC process, most professed little interest in it. The secretary general of one of the largest textile unions explained: "I don't know much about the process. I don't pay much attention. Each is going to defend its own."[108] Most leaders of official trucking and auto unions echoed these comments. And when asked if the CTM would use the NAALC process again, Salvador Medina, the CTM's subsecretary of relations, who had been involved in the DeCoster Egg submission, explained: "I don't think it will be necessary. We haven't had a problem we couldn't solve."[109]

Official Mexican unions' lack of interest in the NAALC process and the transnational labor rights network is largely explained by their support for NAFTA and opposition to strong labor protections in the NAALC. In general, however, unions that participated in the transnational trade-negotiating field were more likely to engage the NAALC process and recruit other unions to join them in filing submissions than those that did not. Even key U.S. and Canadian unions that did not develop transnational relationships with their official Mexican counterparts in response to NAFTA (such as the UAW, Teamsters, and UNITE) participated in NAO submissions with independent Mexican unions. They were able to do so because they made initial contact with representatives of independent unions in the transnational trade-negotiating field during NAFTA's negotiation.

NAALC under the Bush Administration (2001–2008)

The political winds that carried NAFTA across the continent shifted as the millennium came to a close. Voters in the United States and Mexico ushered in a conservative era. Mexicans broke the seventy-year domination

---

[107] Personal interview with Fermín Lara Jiménez of the CROC, May 11, 2000.
[108] Personal interview with David Tellez García of the CROM, May 5, 2000.
[109] Personal interview with Salvador Medina Torres of the CTM, May 15, 2000.

of the PRI to elect National Action Party (PAN) candidate and former
Coca-Cola executive Vicente Fox, who began his presidential term on
December 1, 2000. In a historic, contentious U.S. presidential election,
the Supreme Court became the final arbiter, and George W. Bush took
office on January 20, 2001. Some labor activists saw a silver lining to
the conservative political cloud that had settled across the continent –
Presidents Bush and Fox were open to considering immigration reform
policies.

On the evening of September 4, 2001, Fox arrived in Washington for
an official state visit to push for amnesty for Mexicans residing illegally
in the United States. Although such a plan faced stiff opposition from
President Bush and a Republican-dominated Congress, there seemed to be
room for compromise and reasons for optimism. The Bush administration
made strengthening ties with Mexico an international policy priority. At
the state dinner welcoming Fox, President Bush declared: "The United
States has no more important relationship in the world than the one
we have with Mexico."[110] The president and key members of Congress
expressed interest in a guest worker program that would allow Mexicans
living in the United States illegally to obtain permanent legal residency.

The hopes for an agreement on immigration reform were dashed only
days later when the attacks of September 11, 2001, threw the United
States into a state of turmoil. The political fallout affected a vast swath
of domestic and international policies and ultimately weakened the relationship between the United States and Mexico. Less than a year after
Fox's visit, talks on an immigration agreement were at a standstill.[111] The
relationship soured even more when Mexico – newly granted a nonper-
manent seat on the U.N. Security Council – threatened to vote against a
U.S. resolution to use military force in Iraq and when Fox vociferously
criticized the subsequent U.S. invasion of Iraq.

The U.S. labor movement viewed President Bush as one of the most
antilabor presidents in U.S. history. Whereas labor leaders resented President Clinton's benevolent neglect, they accused President Bush of blatant
hostility. They claimed he not only packed labor courts with judges less

---

[110] http://www.whitehouse.gov/news/releases/2002/05/20020504.html.
[111] As reported in November 2002 by the *San Diego Tribune*: "When the two leaders met
briefly last month at an international economic summit in Mexico, Fox tried again to
engage Bush on the undocumented immigrants Fox calls heroes and vows to protect.
Bush wasn't buying. He wanted to talk about the war on terrorism and the dangers of
Saddam Hussein. The confab was called a flop on both sides of the border." http://www.
signonsandiego.com/news/mexico/20021118-9999_1n17bushfox.html.

sympathetic to labor and promoted economic policies that threatened workers' security but also tried to undermine unions under the guise of national security. Bush allowed the newly formed Department of Homeland Security to quash the collective bargaining rights of airport security workers, and he invoked Taft-Hartley provisions against locked-out California dockworkers in 2002 – both in the name of national security. Moreover, the economic slowdown that began in 2000 and intensified after 9/11 had severe effects on workers as outsourcing increased and manufacturing declined across the continent.

In 2001, the AFL-CIO added a "BushWatch" feature to its Web site to report the president's attacks on labor. In 2004, the AFL-CIO magazine *America@Work* published "BushWatch: A Special Report on the Bush Record," which began:

Within a month of taking office in 2001, President Bush proposed a more than $2 trillion tax cut for the wealthy that consumed the nation's budget surplus he inherited when he took office. Next, he issued four antiworker, antiunion federal executive orders sought by corporate contributors, including one that ended job protections covering primarily low-income and female employees of service contractors in federal buildings. With those actions, Bush set the stage for the administration's priorities over the next three years: Provide massive tax breaks and payoffs to the richest individuals and corporate campaign contributors while rolling back the rights of working people and weakening their unions.[112]

The report went on to document in twenty-three pages the president's many antilabor policies and proposals on issues as diverse as privatization and social security reform.

The election of the more conservative, antilabor Bush administration further eroded unions' confidence in the NAALC's enforcement. The "BushWatch" report noted the president's stance on trade and labor rights: "Early in his administration President Bush called for the authority to negotiate trade agreements without including enforceable workers' rights or environmental protections. Speaking to business leaders at the White House in mid-June 2001, Bush said, 'We should not let legitimate environmental and labor concerns undermine the capacity of the president to make good free-trade agreements.'"[113] Bush also refused to fill the position of special representative for international labor affairs – a State Department office – during both his presidential terms.

---

[112] "BushWatch: A Special Report on the Bush Record." *America@Work*, May 2004, p. 2.
[113] Ibid., p. 7.

Labor activists believed many of President Clinton's labor appointees were sympathetic if not supportive of labor, including those responsible for administering the U.S. NAO. They had little confidence, however, in President Bush's secretary of labor, Elaine Chao, a former fellow at the conservative Heritage Foundation. At the end of her eight years leading the labor department, the AFL-CIO's director of government affairs provided the federation's definitive opinion on Chao, saying: "We don't think the secretary serves the interests of workers very effectively.... She seemed to take the side of employers more than workers when there were conflicts" (Greenhouse 2009, p. A12). The associate director of the AFL-CIO's International Department compared the NAO under the two administrations:

I think we saw that there was a real effort to make that office work, particularly under Irasema Garza. There was a real effort. But we found that in the Bush Administration...there was a real lack of engagement on the part of the office, and there was always a question as to whether it was effectively funded or effectively resourced.[114]

The Bush administration's antilabor policies further eroded labor activists' confidence in the already weak NAALC process.[115] Unwilling to devote the substantial time and resources to a process that yielded few concrete results (in terms of directly improving wages and working conditions under prolabor administrators), labor activists used the process less actively under the antilabor Bush administration. Whereas unions and labor organizations filed fourteen submissions with the U.S. NAO during the Clinton administration, they filed half that number during Bush's presidency, as Table 4.5 shows.

The evidence suggests labor activists' concerns with the administration's enforcement of the NAALC were well founded; of the fourteen submissions filed with the U.S. NAO during the Clinton administration, it recommended Ministerial Consultations for eight submissions and only denied two review. In contrast, of the seven NAO submissions filed under President Bush, the U.S. NAO recommended Ministerial Consultations for only one and did not accept four for review.

Unions' growing frustration with the NAALC process under the Bush administration is reflected in a letter UE President John Hovis wrote to Elaine Chao in July 2002 regarding a trinational seminar on Mexican

[114] Personal interview with Stan Gacek of the AFL-CIO, August 23, 2009.
[115] In 2006 a CLC official Chao appointed was forced to resign after being accused of misusing funds.

Table 4.5. *Union Participation in NAO Cases Filed during the Bush Administration (2001–2008)*

	Year	NAO	Submission	Issue/Principle	About	Outcome	Unions
1	2001	U.S.	Durobag (2001–01)	1, 2	Mexico	Declined for review	AFL-CIO, PACE
2	2001	Mexico	New York State (2001–01)	9, 10, 11	United States	Ministerial Consultations consultations recommended	
3	2003	U.S.	Puebla (2003–01)	1, 2, 6, 9	Mexico	Ministerial Consultations consultations recommended	(AFL-CIO, CLC, UNITE, UE)
4	2003	Canada	Puebla (2003–1)	1, 2, 6, 9	Mexico	Ministerial Consultations consultations recommended	(AFL-CIO, CLC, UNITE, UE)
5	2003	Mexico	North Carolina Farmworkers (2003–1)	1, 2, 3, 6, 7, 9, 10, 11	United States	Under consideration	
6	2004	U.S.	Yucatan (2004–01)	6, 9	Mexico	Submission withdrawn	UNITE
7	2005	U.S.	Labor Law Reform (2005–01)	1, 2, 3	Mexico	Declined for review	UE, UNT, CUSWA, CWA, CEP, AFL-CIO, CLC, UNITE, IBT, USW, UAW, CAW, and over eight other unions and organizations

(continued)

Table 4.5 (continued)

	Year	NAO	Submission	Issue/Principle	About	Outcome	Unions
8	2005	Mexico	H2-B Visa Workers (2005–1)	4, 6, 7, 8, 9, 10, 11	United States	Under consideration	
9	2005	U.S.	Mexican Pilots – ASPA (2005–02)	1, 2	Mexico	Declined for review	
10	2005	Canada	Mexican Pilots – ASPA (2005–01)	1, 2	Mexico	Declined for review	
11	2005	U.S.	Hidalgo (2005–03)	1, 2, 3, 4, 5, 6, 7, 9, 10	Mexico	Accepted for review	
12	2006	Mexico	North Carolina (2006–01)	1, 2, 6, 7, 8, 9, 10	United States	Accepted for review	FAT, UE, CLC, UNT, CAW, UAW, USW, CUSWA, UNITE HERE and over fifty other unions and organizations
13	2006	U.S.	Coahuila (2006–01)	1, 9	Mexico	Declined for review	USW
14	2008	Canada	North Carolina (2008–1)	1, 2, 6, 7, 8, 9, 10	United States	Declined for review	CALL (UE, FAT)

Note: The final column only includes unions/federations in my sample. Those in parentheses participated without officially signing as submitters (e.g., by donating funds, supporting the campaign, offering strategic advice, publicity, etc.). Data in columns 1–6 provided by the Commission on Labor Cooperation.

labor boards to take place as part of the action plan after Ministerial Consultations for the Echlin submission. Hovis expressed his disappointment that despite administration officials' assurances that unions would be consulted on the seminar location and agenda and be included at the event, their advice was ignored and their presence prohibited. He wrote:

We were subsequently assured by Mr. Karesh, Acting Secretary of the U.S. NAO, that the next seminar would be conducted in Mexico City, as we suggested, and that the principal focus would be on the issue of how the Labor Boards handle representation questions and specifically the question of secret ballot elections. We were also assured that he welcomed our suggestions regarding the agenda. We worked closely with organizations in the U.S., Mexico and Canada to prepare an agenda which was designed to take advantage of the experiences in each of our countries and to promote the active participation of workers and their legal representatives both as panelists and members of the audience. Mr. Karesh advised us that there was some discussion about including the TAESA case as well and asked our opinion. After consulting with our Mexican colleagues we informed him that we had no objection and worked that into the proposed agenda. . . . And then we waited . . . [a]nd waited. . . . [W]hen we inquired of the US NAO what was going on, we were finally faxed the Joint Declaration and press release which had been reached over a month earlier. We were told that the meeting would be held in Monterrey because the President of the Mexican labor board was from that area, that no part of the agenda we had proposed was being used, and that the only presenters would be government officials.[116]

Although Hovis's letter revealed that the NAALC process continued to serve as an arena for cross-border union collaboration – he described how unions worked on and approved decisions jointly – his final sentence seemed to seal the fate of the NAALC process for the UE: "Given this history, we believe that the NAO process has deteriorated into a farce, and under these circumstances we see no value in participating further."[117]

The Continued Relevance of the NAALC
The NAALC process was one of the key arenas of cross-border labor cooperation and a significant indicator of its persistence during the Clinton administration. Despite unions' reluctance to regularly engage the NAALC process under the Bush administration, however, they continued to utilize it as part of their strategic toolkit, particularly when faced with a problem for which they wanted to garner international support and attention. Many of the largest transnational labor campaigns

---

[116] Letter from UE President John Hovis to U.S. Secretary of Labor Elaine Chao, July 24, 2002.
[117] Ibid.

in North America during the Bush administration included NAO submissions. And although the Kukdong struggle, widely considered one
of the most successful transnational labor campaigns in North America
(Anner and Evans 2004; Ross 2004), did not include an NAO submission,
its leaders filed two related submissions repeatedly referencing Kukdong
to show a pattern of labor rights abuses in Puebla, Mexico. They also
received significant support and resources from labor unions, including
UNITE, the UE, the AFL-CIO, and the CLC – all active participants in
the transnational legal field and the NAALC process.

   In the post-NAFTA era, despite unions' disappointment and often dis-
gust with the NAALC process and conservative governments, the most
significant examples of transnationalism among labor unions across the
continent continued to involve the NAALC process in some way. In
2004, when the Mexican government threatened to change its labor laws
to undermine unions, U.S. and Canadian labor activists saw it as a collective threat. Never before had North American labor unions organized
a trinational campaign to target domestic labor law reform legislation.
Unlike previous submissions that targeted particular employers engaged
in labor rights violations or current government labor policies, the Labor
Law Reform submission in 2005 focused on a proposal that would have
changed Mexican labor laws by granting employers more flexibility in
hiring, firing, and dealing with unions. According to critics, the Abascal proposal (as it was known) presented to members of Congress in
December 2004 would have given employers tremendous flexibility in
the workplace while undermining workers' collective rights.[118]

   The Abascal proposal quickly became a lightning rod for unions across
the continent, and mobilization was intense. In Mexico, protesters organized marches, demonstrations, and a sit-in in the Mexican Congress.
The FAT requested assistance from the UE to launch an international
campaign. The FAT mobilized its networks to send letters of protest con-
cerning the Abascal proposal to President Fox and members of the Mexican Congress. On February 17, 2005, the Washington Office on Latin
America and over twenty U.S., Canadian, and Mexican labor unions –
including the UNT, UE, CEP, CWA, CLC, CAW, USW, IBT, UNITE
HERE, and UAW – filed an NAO public submission that claimed:

The labor law reform proposal would substantially weaken existing labor protections, thereby codifying systemic violations of the right of free association, the
right to organize and bargain collectively, the right to strike, and core labor rights

---

[118] The 2004 version was amended from a 2002 version. See Cook (2007) for details of
   the plan and the politics surrounding it.

protected by the Mexican Constitution, International Labor Organization (ILO) Conventions ratified by Mexico, and the North American Agreement on Labor Cooperation (NAALC).[119]

The submitters highlighted how the Abascal proposal violated not only international and Mexican law but also the terms of the NAALC, which committed the three countries to provide for high labor standards. As reported in the joint UE-FAT *Mexican Labor News and Analysis*:

Substantially weakening existing laws and failing to fix the numerous problems that already exist is clear evidence that Mexico is not striving to improve its standards. The obligations undertaken by the Parties under the NAALC would be rendered utterly meaningless if one were able to repeal those laws that protect workers and replace them with laws that violate the principles set forth in the NAALC.[120]

The petitioners worked with U.S. Congresswoman Marcy Kaptur, who wrote and circulated a congressional sign-on letter to Labor Secretary Elaine Chao requesting that she accept and review the submission quickly. Over a year after the submission was filed, the U.S. NAO declined to accept it for review in February 2006.[121] Despite the U.S. NAO's refusal to evaluate the Abascal proposal, labor activists – including Robin Alexander of the UE, whose president had vowed two years earlier to no longer participate in NAO submissions – saw the silver lining in the NAALC submission process. As Alexander explained:

The coming together of such an important group of labor organizations from various industries and sectors represented a new level of labor cooperation at the international level. Although most of the unions involved have little hope that the NAALC will be able to resolve these issues, or will even attempt to do so, the labor coalition that has developed represents an important step toward the strengthening of the North American labor movement. The petition to the NAALC in itself is an important political document, a scathing indictment of the lack of labor rights in Mexico.[122]

Four years later, in 2009, when I asked Alexander why the UE filed the submission given its leadership's prior assertion that it would no longer participate in the process, she reiterated her statement from our first interview (in 2000) that the process provides a platform. She reported that the submission was useful "because our audience was not the NAO, it

---

[119] U.S. NAO Submission No. 2005-01 (Labor Law Reform) filed February 17, 2005.

[120] *Mexican Labor News and Analysis*, February 2005, Vol. 10, No. 2.

[121] In 2004, the U.S. NAO was renamed Office of Trade Agreement Implementation (OTAI).

[122] LaBotz and Alexander (2005, p. 22).

was Mexico and the Mexican government and the Mexican press.... [I]t got major publicity, which had an impact – at least our friends tell us it did – on the Mexican government."[123] The trinational campaign around the Labor Law Reform submission showed that, a decade after the NAALC's passage, the new labor rights consciousness remained intact. It also reflects the NAALC's ability to help consolidate transnational actors and rights even in a conservative and hostile political environment.[124]

In 2005, the UE again incorporated the NAALC process into a large campaign targeting the state of North Carolina, which denies its public sector workers the right to bargain collectively (in General Statute 95–98). The campaign began after workers with UE Local 150 in North Carolina attended an exchange with FAT workers, first in North Carolina and then in Mexico. Inspired by the FAT's use of international legal mechanisms, the UE workers began a grassroots campaign – North Carolina International Worker Justice Campaign – to demand the repeal of General Statute 95–98. Transnational collective action lies at the heart of the campaign, with workers from Mexico and Canada regularly attending rallies and demonstrations and participating in yearly trinational meetings and exchanges.

The campaign led to the introduction of legislation in both houses of the North Carolina legislature to repeal the law. In December 2005, the UE filed a petition with the ILO, and in 2006 the FAT filed an NAO submission on behalf of UE workers in North Carolina, asserting that General Statute 95–98 violates the labor protections guaranteed by the NAALC. Over fifty labor organizations signed onto the submission, including the CAW, UNT, USW, UNITE HERE, and UAW. In 2008, the Canadian Association of Labour Lawyers filed a parallel submission with the Canadian NAO with the participation of forty organizations. Neither NAO has completed reviews of the submissions as of this writing. In 2009, Robin Alexander noted that although the submission "languished during the Bush administration," she expressed hope it would be "picked up and see some life and action now that there's a new administration in Washington."[125]

The Coahuila NAO submission, like the labor law submission, also generated North American labor solidarity during the Bush administration. After his 2002 election to lead the Mexican Miners and Metal

[123] Personal interview with Robin Alexander of the UE, August 21, 2009.
[124] It is important to emphasize the Ms. Alexander forcefully asserted during both interviews that she does not believe that the NAALC's ability to stimulate relationships justifies its many weaknesses and lack of strong enforcement mechanisms.
[125] Personal interview with Robin Alexander of the UE, August 21, 2009.

Workers Union (Sindicato Nacional de Trabajadores Mineros, Meta-
lúrgicos y Similares de la República Mexicana, or SNTMMSRM), the
brash and outspoken Napoleón Gómez Urrutia began a fledgling relationship with the USW, led by President Leo Gerard.[126] The two pledged
to engage in joint actions during disputes with common employers and
spearheaded efforts to create a coalition of metals and mining industry
unions in the western hemisphere with support from the International
Metalworkers Federation.[127] In April 2005, at the USW's constitutional
convention, the two unions signed a strategic alliance.

The issues on which the Coahuila NAO submission was filed began
to smolder in June 2005, when over 10,000 Mexican mine workers and
their supporters in the United States and Peru organized a simultaneous protest against Grupo Mexico – the third-largest copper producer in
the world – claiming the corporation exploited workers in unsafe mines,
repressed workers and their organizing efforts, and tried to undermine the
union by encouraging the formation of alternative and illegal company
unions. On February 19, 2006, sixty-five workers at Pasta de Conchos, a
Coahuila coal mine owned by a Grupo Mexico subsidiary, were killed in
an explosion after being forced to work despite the presence of explosive
methane gas in the shaft. Two days after the explosion, Gómez attacked
the government and Grupo Mexico by referring to the tragedy as "industrial homicide." Less than a week later, the Mexican government accused
Gómez of embezzling fifty-five million dollars, indicted him, and ultimately ousted him from his union position. Government officials then
froze his assets and those of the union and replaced him with someone
loyal to the company.[128]

---

[126] Gómez had been a thorn in the Fox administration's side since he took over the union
from his father in 2001 and then was elected secretary general in 2002. He negotiated
wage increases for his members that far exceeded the limits the government promulgated to attract foreign investment (Bacon 2008). Although his union belongs to the
CTM and the official labor movement, Gómez supports autonomous and authentic
labor organizations. He vociferously criticizes free trade and cites the many failures of
NAFTA, and roundly disparages the government's privatization efforts and the Abascal
proposal.

[127] International Metalworkers Federation is a Global Union – a federation of national
unions – formally referred to as an International Trade Secretariat.

[128] USW, International Metalworkers Federation, AFL-CIO, and SNTMMSRM officials
presented the results of an independent audit at a press conference in Mexico City that
showed no wrongdoing on Gómez's part. While leading his union in absentia from
Canada, Gomez was ultimately cleared of all federal charges against him. Charges in
various states, however, prevented him from returning to Mexico. As of this writing,
Gómez remains in Canada.

In early March 2006, Gómez's supporters – including the FAT, UNT, and STRM – organized a national strike to protest the government's handling of the Pasta de Conchos disaster. Leo Gerard also wrote a strong letter to President Fox, condemning the treatment of Gómez and his union as "naked aggression" and "a blatant attempt to stifle the voice of workers and all progressive unions in Mexico."[129] The violence continued. In April, police shot and killed two striking workers in Lázaro Cárdenas, Michoacán. Then the USW, fearing for Gómez's safety, helped him escape to Arizona and then Vancouver. The move infuriated the Mexican government, which requested that Canada extradite him. On November 9, 2006, the USW filed the Coahuila submission with the U.S. NAO based on the labor rights violations at the Pasta de Conchos mine, claiming that Mexico "repeatedly failed to fulfill its obligation to enforce labor regulations requiring employers to provide workers with satisfactory working conditions that are free of health and safety hazards."[130] The submission also highlighted violations of workers' organizing rights and the persistent interference of the government in the union's internal affairs. The USW sent a delegation to Mexico to meet with Gómez's supporters and organized rallies in six U.S. cities.

On August 31, 2007, the NAO declined to accept the submission for review. In November 2009, the USW's Gerald Fernandez confirmed that his union had almost completed a new NAO submission and intended to file it under the Obama administration, saying: "You have to have some forum to air your grievances. . . . You're not going to embarrass a country to death through the process . . . by saying they've been bad actors. That's not going to force them to change their ways. But that's what we have and it's a public relations game."[131] He expressed hope, however, that filing a submission under an administration more friendly to labor might produce a different outcome.

The mineworkers' struggle and the NAO submission it spawned helped solidify a relationship unprecedented between steel and mine industry unions across the continent. In April 2010, seventy-five members of the USW traveled to Michoacán, Mexico, to participate in a rally commemorating the four-year anniversary of the killing of two mineworkers during the 2006 strike. The historic alliance also reflects labor activists' continued

---

[129] "USW Condemns Fox Government's Suppression of Mexican Miners' Union as "Naked Aggression." USW Press Release, March 3, 2006.
[130] U.S. NAO Submission No. 2006-01 (Coahuila) filed November 9, 2006.
[131] Personal interview with Gerald Fernandez of the USW, November 19, 2009.

ability to identify transnational interests and build transnational goals, and to continue to invoke NAALC protections despite an unfavorable political climate. The signs USW members carried at U.S. rallies in support of Gómez and his union epitomize a shift to transnationalism among steelworkers. Their signs read: "North American Labor United."[132]

Measuring the NAALC's Effects

A key dimension of any international law or legal mechanism is its *redress effects*, or the ability to invoke legal protections and remedy grievances at the transnational level. The NAALC unequivocally has weak enforcement mechanisms, and therefore weak direct redress effects. It grants some labor rights violations less protection than others, prohibits all types of violations from reaching the highest level in the adjudicatory hierarchy, and provides insufficient penalties. Every labor activist I interviewed agreed that the NAALC is woefully inadequate as a tool for redressing labor rights violations across the continent. As former CLC President Bob White commented in the NAALC's four-year review: "Under the terms of the labor side agreement, even when the workers have proven their case satisfactorily, the remedies have been inconsequential and the abuses have continued.... Thus, a minimum condition for any expansion of NAFTA must be that it include enforceable labor and environmental standards in the agreement itself. The side-agreement approach has not worked."[133] The USW's Gerald Fernandez put it succinctly: "We all need to be [singing] out of the same hymnal: we all need to be singing sanctions. And we all have to force our governments to put sanctions into their trade agreements."[134]

The redress effects of the NAALC on the improvement in workers' lives are few; the transnational legal mechanism has done little, if anything, to improve the wages and working conditions of the continent's workers. However, respondents repeatedly stated that the NAALC has had one significant positive effect on workers' rights: it has helped decrease violence for organizing activities by independent Mexican unions, thereby opening political space for them and elevating their political significance. Although the NAALC's enforcement mechanisms are weak in all three countries, independent Mexican labor activists argue that the support of

---

[132] *USW@Work*, Spring 2006, p. 21.
[133] Comments of Bob White, Canadian Labour Congress, in NAFTA four-year review.
[134] Personal interview with Gerald Fernandez of the USW, November 19, 2009.

U.S. and Canadian unions and the utility of the NAALC process transcend the symbolic; these nascent legal mechanisms have helped undermine violence and government indifference. According to a FAT leader:

Through openings provided by these trade agreements . . . we've had the opportunity to denounce the Mexican government's antidemocratic practices: the repression of popular movements, systematic violation of human rights, and this has made [the government] care about its international image. For us international condemnation is very important because the eyes of NGOs and unions internationally can influence things.[135]

A Mexican labor lawyer suggested the NAALC process provided a disincentive for the Mexican government to tolerate violence during labor struggles. He explained:

We had another case where there was a recount in another workplace, and it began with a lot of violence. But physical violence didn't happen [here] because they knew that [there could be a case built around it]. Now the owners are not as obvious and violent, it's now more indirect coercion such as promising people things. But this is a benefit to workers. . . . Now voting isn't with rifles and pistols. So maybe we've obtained something. So it's worth it to use these processes through the NAO.[136]

Mexican activists also noted improved conditions in factories targeted by NAO submissions. As one Echlin worker revealed:

We had very bad working conditions, working with asbestos, for example. When all this happened and the firings started, then when the faxes started coming in saying to stop these firings, there was a period when they stopped [or at least to a certain degree]. And they stopped mistreating people as much.[137]

The Gender Discrimination submission (U.S. NAO 9701) also led to improved conditions and is therefore considered quite successful because some maquiladoras agreed to stop testing women workers for pregnancy, and the Mexican government eliminated pregnancy testing for women applicants to federal ministry jobs (Atleson et al. 2008).

Mexican independent unions find the NAALC process useful primarily because obstacles to organizing are frequently the result of state intervention and opposition. Thus, while U.S. and Canadian unions usually target companies in their labor rights struggles, independent Mexican unions usually target the state. During the Han Young struggle, for example, the

---

[135] Personal interview with Antonio Villalba Granados of the FAT, April 26, 2000.
[136] Personal interview with Eugenio Narcia Tovar of the ANAD, April 4, 2000.
[137] Personal interview with Maria Trinidad Delgado of the FAT, April 28, 2000.

Campaign for Labor Rights, on behalf of the FAT, argued: "The Mexican Government is the Issue: Although there are many players in the cast of the Han Young drama, one bad actor in particular has the role of villain. That player is the Mexican federal government" ("Mexican Government vs. Han Young Workers"). The NAALC process is therefore particularly useful to Mexican independent unions because they, like the side agreement, focus on the state's enforcement of its own domestic labor laws.

FAT leader Benedicto Martínez explained the importance of being able to engage an international venue and rally the support of U.S. and Canadian unions:

Now when we have a submission someone in the Mexican government will call and want to know why this, why that. They don't ignore it anymore, and this didn't exist before. We spoke but they didn't listen, we existed but they didn't see us. I think now that they listen, and they listen because what we do hurts them. And what we do is within the law.... I am confident that the government will have to change its labor policies. Not of their own volition, but because of the pressure we've been putting on them, because more and more the governments of the U.S. and Canada question the labor policies of the Mexican government.[138]

A U.S. labor lawyer concurred that the NAO process legitimized and helped strengthen independent Mexican unions:

And in Mexico I think it went a long way to overcome the isolation of the independent union forces. I mean they became real players because they had this. They were able to invoke this international mechanism. In the last year of the PRI government Bertha Luján [one of the FAT's national coordinators] was a regular visitor at the Secretary of Labor's Office. He would consult her because she was now a player.[139]

Smaller independent unions and federations such as the FAT use their international relationships to build status and significance that belie their smaller numbers. As an IBT official explained: "I think it was extremely important. I think it reduced their vulnerability. I think with the case of FAT in particular it greatly increased their credibility with other organizations in Mexico. I think that people began to look to them as a source if you want to make contacts."[140]

The AFL-CIO's support in particular increases independent unions' visibility and relevance at the national level. This is not lost on official

---

[138] Personal interview with Benedicto Martínez Orozco of the FAT, July 27, 1999.
[139] Personal interview with Lance Compa, U.S. labor lawyer, December 19, 2000.
[140] Personal interview with Matt Witt of the IBT, January 17, 2001.

Mexican unions, the government, or business. As Luis Medina, the Mexican expert on the NAALC four-year review committee of experts, wrote in his dissenting opinion:

The original goals of the NAALC run the risk of becoming adulterated by the perspective which nongovernmental United States trade unions have attempted to impose upon it. Although it has since allowed some of its unions to test the limits of the Agreement, especially those governing the freedom of trade union association, the AFL-CIO originally opposed and continues to formally express its opposition to the NAALC. This strategy has three main objectives: a) to focus attention on Mexico, which is considered an unfair competitor vis à vis the attraction of regional investment; b) to encourage a negative vision of judicial labor proceedings and the enforcement of labor law in Mexico; and c) to seek strategic alliances, especially with the so-called independent trade unions.[141]

SEMARNAP leader Roberto Tooms articulated a position shared by almost all independent Mexican labor activists interviewed for this book: "I think it is better to have trade agreements with labor protections, even if they are weak. If it's something or nothing, I prefer something."[142] The associate director of the AFL-CIO's International Department agreed with Tooms's assessment that a weak side agreement is preferable to none at all: "I will say, as opposed to not having any kind of labor dimension at all, it's absolutely . . . good to have this. It's comparatively better. It continues to be inadequate."[143] Labor lawyer Arturo Alcalde elaborated:

The side agreements are a result of the pressure U.S. unions put on President Clinton to reduce the ill effects of NAFTA. . . . The experience has been limited because the agreement is limited. And the agreement doesn't include labor freedom as one of its main tenets. So the side agreement was made not to work. But the labor problems are so significant that, even with the small spaces the side agreement provides, we have been able to show the world, above all else the U.S. and Canada, the harsh situation Mexican workers face. So we have taken advantage of the side agreement in order to use some pressure to open spaces for labor freedom. For this reason we take advantage of it even though cases don't get to the highest level, decisions are not complied with, etc., to create some pressure to create labor freedom.[144]

Mexican independent unionists' assertion that the NAALC is useful to them despite its weak enforcement mechanisms therefore suggests the importance of defining an international law's redress effects broadly to include its leverage potential.

---

[141] Medina (1998).
[142] Personal interview with Roberto Tooms of SEMARNAP, June 23, 1999.
[143] Personal interview with Stan Gacek of the AFL-CIO, August 23, 2009.
[144] Personal interview with Arturo Alcalde Justiniani of the FAT, March 29, 2000.

The experience of independent Mexican unionists also suggests that transnational laws with strong enforcement mechanisms are not only critical to improving workers' lives, welfare, and safety but are also important for transnational movement building. Strong enforcement mechanisms provide activists collective leverage with their targets (states, employers, corporations) and the possibility of forcing policy changes by imposing severe sanctions. Moreover, they justify the time and expense of utilizing legal mobilization strategies. The importance of an international law's redress effects for movement building is demonstrated by U.S. and Canadian unions' willingness to support independent Mexican unionists' use of the NAALC. At a 2001 meeting of laboralistas, Canadian participants expressed concern that their use of the NAALC process would encourage the Canadian government to incorporate similarly weak enforcement mechanisms in future trade agreements. They suggested that they may not participate in future cases. The FAT's Arturo Alcalde responded by explaining how Mexican activists benefited from NAALC cases:

It's an advantage, a strategic advantage. People ask us why we think it's important if nothing changes. We say things don't change overnight – we have an authoritarian system and we're looking at the possibility of change. We've discussed the Echlin case today, which raised the issue of voting rights in Mexican union elections. After the Echlin submission, for the first time we got a bill introduced on secret ballot elections so this case catapulted the issue into the public sphere.[145]

It was clear Canadian participants carefully and thoughtfully considered Alcalde's comments. As one responded: "We don't want to validate the NAALC so we must be careful the way we push. But the situation is not the same in Mexico, so we need to figure out how to push the Canadian government and still support our friends in Mexico."[146] When I later raised the issue with Gerry Barr of CUSWA, he emphatically stated that because the NAALC helps independent Mexican unions, it is worth using even if its direct remedies for U.S. and Canadian unions are minimal:

[The NAALC] has utility, absolutely. Well we thought [the FAT's] view was supremely authoritative. I mean it just was clear that it was useful for them. It's just as simple as that. And because it was useful for them it was interesting for us. This hasn't got anything to do with changing our perspective about the [NAALC]... which was and remains harshly critical of the mechanism. I mean

---

[145] The meeting was not tape-recorded; quotes are reconstructed from fieldnotes.
[146] The meeting was not tape-recorded; quotes are reconstructed from fieldnotes.

we think it just is a joke in so many ways . . . so there's just hardly a critique that you couldn't legitimately file against it. But it remained true that it was useful for the FAT. And it was useful not only for the FAT but for other people working around issues of independent trade unionism in Mexico. So it wasn't a hard choice at all; it just was obvious that it was valuable for them and we were prepared to be part of an initiative which supported them. That's it.[147]

Despite their concerns, Canadian unions and the CLC have continued to support and participate in NAO submissions. Some labor leaders contend that the support of U.S. and Canadian unions has been essential to the survival of independent Mexican unions, particularly in the last ten years. As the director of the Solidarity Center's office in Mexico, argued:

This may be a bit of hyperbole, but I actually think that had it not been for international solidarity, we basically would not have any democratic union movement in Mexico at this point. I think the miner's union would have been crushed. I think the grassroots campaigns would have been consigned to oblivion. The telephone workers might have held on this long, based on their international political strength, but they'd be increasingly isolated. . . . It's not like things are going great, but I actually do think that but for the [international relationships they would] be a lot worse, and there might not be anything at all at this point because the attack has been so savage.[148]

In 2010, Bertha Luján reaffirmed her belief that transnational relationships mattered for independent Mexican unions:

In general the theme of international solidarity continues to be important. Because it's obvious that if workers can't resolve their problems here they are going to look for other ways like international solidarity and international forums to denounce the Mexican government. And this continues to be damaging to the government – they consider it a problem. But that's the way it is, right? It's the price they have to pay because they continue on in the same way despite the fact that there's been – for example in the case of the miners and the electricians – a lot of international support. But they have to pay a huge price, which is being discredited internationally.[149]

In an ironic historical twist of fate, the most significant (and unforeseen) tool the NAALC provided North American labor activists was the ability to work toward improving labor rights protections in North

---

[147] Personal interview with Gerry Barr of the CUSWA, March 1, 2001.
[148] Personal interview with Benjamin Davis of the AFL-CIO Solidarity Center, April 23, 2010.
[149] Personal interview with Bertha Luján of the FAT, March 29, 2010.

America collectively. Bertha Luján captured the simultaneous irony and promise of the NAALC when she commented:

The labor side agreement was an achievement for unions and workers in the three countries. Unions in the three countries wanted NAFTA to include the protection of labor rights and wanted an agreement that would improve the conditions of workers. Transnational cooperation and collaboration began before NAFTA was passed to try to include these social clauses in the agreement. Unfortunately NAFTA was signed without these guarantees in the body of the agreement. . . . But the side agreements were passed in part due to the pressure of organizations in civil society. From the beginning we've seen the side agreements as a mechanism for defending the rights of workers against capital and the excesses of free trade. And from the beginning we've decided to use them in any way possible in our struggles and for those objectives.[150]

It is important to emphasize that the NAALC's stimulation of transnational labor relationships does not justify its inadequacies in redressing labor rights violations. But the analysis presented in this chapter suggests that it is quite important for nascent transnational movements to have transnational legal institutions to engage. Legal institutions can help overcome cultural, geographic, and political barriers that are less likely to stymie national social movements. By collaborating on submissions, unions solidify their common interests as North American unions. The flurry of collaborative activities in the transnational legal field demonstrates the importance of including even the most rudimentarily transparent and participatory mechanisms in governance institutions. These mechanisms not only enabled North American labor unions to strengthen their relationships in the transnational legal field but also allowed them to push beyond the confines of the NAALC process.

---

[150] Personal interview with Bertha Luján of the FAT, August 3, 1999.

5

Seizing the Opportunity NAFTA Provided

In the wake of the NAFTA defeat, North American labor unions that initiated transnational relationships during the struggle could have licked their wounds, ended their relationships, and allowed trinational networks to atrophy. Or they could have limited them to the confines of the NAALC process. Quite unexpectedly, however, key unions and labor federations actually renewed their commitment to a particular kind of international- ism – an internationalism based on equality, trust, and mutualism – and embarked on relationships that marked a dramatic shift in the history of North American union relations. The decision to nurture new rela- tionships catalyzed by the NAFTA struggle suggests that some unions achieved a critical amount of trust and confidence through initial inter- actions and saw significant benefits to continued collaboration. As these relationships developed, signatory and declarative contacts of old receded into the landscape of North American unionism.

Chapters 6 and 7 examine why some unions did not take advantage of the new institutional opportunities NAFTA provided to develop transna- tional relationships. This chapter, in contrast, explores why and how three sets of unions/federations – the UE, FAT, and CUSWA; the AFL- CIO, CLC, and FAT; and the CWA, CEP, and STRM – seized the oppor- tunity NAFTA initially provided to push their relationships beyond the constraints of anti-NAFTA coalitions and NAALC procedures in order to build more formal and collaborative transnational relationships. These cases show how newly constituted regional actors quickly extended the boundaries of NAFTA's fields to engage in more extensive labor rights advocacy and activism. In the expanded transnational legal field, unions that constantly made waves and those that only tested its waters worked to counteract collaboratively what they viewed as the negative effects of regional economic integration institutionalized by NAFTA. The process of engaging and expanding the legal field propelled North American labor unions and federations toward more developed transnational relationships based on trust and equity, and reinforced and solidified the constitution of regional actors and interests. As unions and their members engaged each other more regularly, racial stereotypes eroded further.

Through increased interaction in the expanded transnational legal field, all three sets of unions/federations formed transnational relationships and worked to address mutual needs and interests. The UE, FAT, and CUSWA are the only union triad that achieved a fully developed relationship with cooperative complementary identities or a shared recognition of mutual interest coupled with a commitment to joint action. For the three unions, the relationship was fully institutionalized and integrated into their union cultures. The AFL-CIO, CLC, and FAT and the CWA, CEP, and STRM achieved partially developed relationships. Although these unions did not achieve the level of institutionalization or identification of the former triad, their engagement with each other after NAFTA's passage was very significant.

Because fields are dynamic, the focus and strategies of actors within them change and develop. And as they do, identities and interests are institutionalized (Armstrong 2002). The cases presented in this chapter show that processes of expanding fields and institutionalizing identities and interests can be mutually reinforcing. Although union strategies changed in order to expand the transnational legal field, their goals remained the same: to defend workers' labor rights across the continent. In struggling for those rights, labor activists in these unions came to see themselves as uniquely connected.

A Fully Developed Relationship: The UE, FAT, and CUSWA

The relationship between the UE and FAT is the most celebrated example of labor transnationalism to emerge during the NAFTA era. Although the relationship began as an alliance to oppose NAFTA, it quite rapidly morphed into a strategic relationship with a bold and daunting goal: to jointly organize workers. Although the idea was not new, the decision to build a foundational relationship that could actually support the infrastructure of cross-border organizing was groundbreaking in North American union relations. Other U.S. and Mexican unions had talked about it, and a few had even provided mutual support for organizing drives. But during the Cold War era, when U.S. workers were reaping the benefits of U.S. industrial dominance and Mexican import substitution insulated many workers from poverty wages, the need to traverse the Rio Grande seemed minimal. NAFTA, however, threatened to drastically change the conditions of the North American economy and in so doing laid bare the collective vulnerability of workers. As NAFTA loomed, the benefits of collective action became apparent.

As described in Chapter 3, the UE and FAT's first discussion about the possibilities of a strategic organizing alliance occurred in 1991 when both unions descended on the trade ministers' meeting in Zacatecas. Their initial work together therefore began in the context of the transnational trade-negotiating field and focused on anti-NAFTA activities. After the NAALC's passage, it extended into the transnational legal field. But almost from the beginning of their relationship in 1991, the two unions expanded their work beyond the boundaries of NAFTA-related activities. Indeed, the UE and FAT were instrumental in expanding the legal field beyond the confines of NAFTA to create an arena in which North American unions could engage in broader labor advocacy and activism.

The UE-FAT alliance, in contrast to Cold War models, was built on a long-term strategy focused on mutual interest and equality. The UE's Bob Kingsley explained the unique vision of the alliance, the goal of which was not to keep jobs in the United States but rather to maintain decent labor rights and standards in *North America*:

The idea [was] that we could form an organizing alliance with the idea that rather than just publicly condemn what was going on we would try to fight it by identifying locations where our jobs had moved and targeting them for organization, and undertaking actual campaigns to improve wages and conditions in those locations, knowing that the result would not be that the work would return to the United States but trying to take the edge of exploitation out of what's going on here by raising wages and conditions for workers in the Mexican facilities.... And I left very hopeful actually, very excited after that discussion. Again we hadn't known one another very well. I didn't know they would be open to as detailed and concrete a program as we had in mind but they were more than open to it. They too were excited about it, and saw it again as a concrete form of fight[ing] back, a concrete form of international solidarity.[1]

Rather than run to the border for support at a moment of crisis, the UE and FAT decided to build a relationship that could provide ongoing support. FAT and UE leaders imagined that together they could potentially even avert crises by working toward upward harmonization of

---

[1] Personal interview with Bob Kingsley of the UE, January 23, 2001.

wages and working conditions in North America and by undermining the ability of companies to pit them against each other. The relationship would be strong enough to withstand differences of opinion and even conflicts. And, it would involve the membership in an active and meaningful way. Bob Kingsley described how UE leaders conceptualized the role of worker participation from the beginning:

We would want our people to be involved directly to the extent possible in the work by coming down and being an actual part of it because it would be a very important experience to bring back to our membership in the United States, to deepen their understanding of what's really going on here: What is the economic dynamic? What are the conditions? What are the issues? What are the companies doing to the workers in Mexico after they got done doing [it] to us here in the United States? ... [We chose GE as our first campaign because] we were thinking that this would be taking a practical piece of education about international trade union solidarity to a big group of our membership, in a way that we [could] more effectively involve members of UE in the work itself. Because there is such a big pool of members, because the example is so dramatic, because some of these locals have resources that some of our smaller locals in other companies might not have, this was a good place to do it.[2]

The two unions worked closely to develop a plan for organizing campaigns that would fulfill their vision of labor transnationalism. According to Kingsley:

In order to do this there would have to be organizers on the ground in Mexico that the FAT would identify and train, that they would have to get a paycheck somehow, that we would have to work together to identify appropriate targets, that we would have to assist with the financing of some of this work or at least raise money to support it in some way.[3]

The unions' first campaign at a General Electric (GE) plant in Juárez, Mexico, made manifest the ideological vision of the relationship. They chose GE because both unions would benefit from the organization of GE workers in Mexico. The company had relocated dozens of U.S. plants with UE membership to Mexico, where workers' rights were routinely violated. The campaign would enable the UE to help improve the conditions of its Mexican counterparts and send a strong message to the company that unions would collectively resist a corporate relocation strategy rooted in exploitation. As Bob Kingsley explained, the campaign would "fire a few shots across [GE CEO] Jack Welch's bow."[4] It would also allow the FAT to grow and gain some leverage in the maquiladora zone, where it had few

[2] Personal interview with Bob Kingsley of the UE, January 23, 2001.
[3] Ibid.
[4] Personal interview with Bob Kingsley of the UE, January 23, 2001.

resources and little infrastructure. The lack of resources, combined with the trenchant opposition of GE and the Mexican government, however, made success untenable. According to observers, it was too ambitious a plan for too powerful an employer.

Although the GE organizing campaign was not successful, the unions continued their work together. As Robin Alexander, the UE's director of international affairs, explained:

One of the reasons that I think that our relationship with the FAT has been so successful is that we don't look exclusively for major organizing victories as the sole measure of success. We saw it from the beginning as a long-term relationship. I think that there is a problem most unions sort of [have] – it's not solely related to international relationships, it's sort of how they do business – . . . a very short time frame. That's really not conducive to building relations, particularly international relationships, and particularly in a world where the U.S. labor movement is viewed somewhat skeptically to begin with.[5]

Alexander explained that because the unions had developed a sufficient amount of trust and commitment before the project began, the GE loss did not undermine the relationship. In fact, it was instrumental in strengthening the bonds between the FAT and the UE. She described an incident that reflected the strength of this trust and enabled it to deepen:

At this point I think there's the confidence that we're very straightforward with each other and we say what we think, and it may not always be pleasant, but ... there is enough trust there that there's a – I think – a total confidence that if there are criticisms to be made they're not personal and they're not with any malicious intent, but they're with the design of moving the work forward. . . . One thing I remember very clearly was after the campaign in Juárez was over and the FAT had lost – and it was the first time that Benedicto had ever lost a campaign and he was feeling really bad about it – and for some reason we were driving together from Pittsburgh to Washington, and so we were analyzing what had happened. And I said something about the lack of *capacidad*, really referring to resources, because I thought one of the problems was that we really hadn't put sufficient staff there. And he understood this as being lack of capability and was horribly offended and insulted. It sort of took a little while to sort out that we were really talking about two different things and that it was actually a linguistic problem. But if ever there [was] a point when our relationship came close to falling apart it was at that moment. And fortunately we knew each other well enough that he didn't just assume that I was out to insult him and make him feel bad, but maybe I was really trying to say something. It's a perfect example [where] something which was totally innocent and not intended could have had just disastrous results. And fortunately it didn't.[6]

---

[5] Personal interview with Robin Alexander of the UE, August 21, 2009.
[6] Personal interview with Robin Alexander of the UE, December 21, 2000.

Their commitment to a permanent relationship and the existence of a significant amount of respect and trust enabled Alexander and Martínez to remedy their misunderstanding and move forward. As Alexander suggests, without that trust, the relationship could have been jeopardized. With it, the relationship weathered its first significant storm.

The failure of the GE campaign provided activists from both unions an opportunity to reevaluate the project together, and ultimately to change their strategy. As Alexander explained, they realized that their failure stemmed, in part, from a lack of worker education and knowledge in northern Mexico. To remedy this problem, the two unions opened a workers' center in Ciudad Juárez in 1996, the Education Center and Labor Workshop (CETLAC by its Spanish acronym), and later two other centers in Monterrey and Chihuahua, Mexico. According to Alexander:

The response to that was that we needed to take a few steps back and do some of the basic education in a way that would begin to educate workers and prepare them for a different kind of struggle where they weren't just seeking some quick bucks and moving on but really seeking to gain some control within a plant.[7]

The failure of the GE campaign also led the two unions to file an NAO case together, as discussed previously.

Since NAFTA's implementation, the FAT and UE have been and continue to be in weekly, and often daily, contact. In 2009, Robin Alexander affirmed the continuing strength of the relationship: "I would say [it] has been maintained and gotten deeper, and also, it's really expanded in the sense that it served as a basis for us to relate to unions we didn't really relate to before, and the same thing for the FAT. It's sort of expanded that circle of solidarity."[8] The unions' ability to build a strong sense of identification and mutualism occurred relatively rapidly. Two years after the alliance formed, the work between the unions became so frequent and intense that a position was created to manage it. As Alexander, who was hired for the position, explained: "The position of [director of] international affairs was created really as a result of the relationship with the FAT. And initially it was a half-time position and then somewhat later it became a full-time position."[9] The unions institutionalized not only staff positions but also joint programs. The UE created an adopt-an-organizer program, which UE locals support through a voluntary supplementary

---

[7] Ibid.
[8] Personal interview with Robin Alexander of the UE, August 21, 2009.
[9] Personal interview with Robin Alexander of the UE, December 21, 2000.

dues check-off and monthly contributions. The UE and FAT also collaborate on an online bimonthly periodical, *Mexican Labor News and
Analysis*, initiated in January 1996. And the unions embarked on a mural
project; they commissioned a Mexican artist to paint a mural at the UE's
national office and a U.S. artist to do the same at the central offices of
the FAT in Mexico City celebrating the labor histories of workers in both
countries.

While the scope and intensity of the two unions' activities reflect a
strong commitment to mutual action, the nature of their interactions
suggests they have achieved a high level of identification. Unlike many
contacts between North American unions historically have been, the relationship between the UE and FAT is not one-sided (with northern unions
simply offering money and "expert" advice to Mexican unions). As Bob
Kingsley, the UE's director of organization, explained:

And let me note we search for that [vision] in a respectful way and I think that's an
important element in this work. We don't go down to Mexico and say hey, we're
going to do this and these guys are going to be our tool. We go down and have a
discussion with them about their goals and needs and where they want to go and
how we can work cooperatively to attain what would be mutual goals that are
good for both of our organizations. Or in cases where we've involved Canadians
and others, for everybody's. One of the consequences of the development of
the UE-FAT alliance has been the expansion of the FAT's relationships with
unions in several countries, and the base of financial and organizing support they
receive I think has been greatly enhanced by the direction [in which] this [has]
led.[10]

The FAT's Arturo Alcalde shared Kingsley's perception of labor transnationalism based on mutual respect and interest:

And international solidarity isn't just about the U.S. and Canada helping us, the
poorer less developed country, because the U.S. is not a haven of labor freedom.
There are many obstacles there. And here is the double-sidedness of international
solidarity, the old international solidarity which people criticized as being protectionist. We can't judge Americans in general; we committed many errors in
the past because we lacked information. The Americans also committed an error
because they assumed all Mexican unions were corrupt. They lacked information. So information is a central point in creating specific common programs and
collaborating; the exchanging of realities in a more simple manner is a good path
to follow.[11]

---

[10] Personal interview with Bob Kingsley of the UE, January 23, 2001.
[11] Personal interview with Arturo Alcalde Justiniani of the FAT, March 29, 2000.

In 1994, the unions' ideological commitment to mutualism was put into practice when the UE requested assistance from the FAT to organize Latino workers as part of its organizing drive in a Wisconsin plant. Chris Townsend, the UE's political action director, explained the reasons for the UE's decision to request a FAT organizer:

Well in that same conversation I was having with Kingsley about the need for Spanish speakers I said hey, we've got this . . . relationship with the FAT, obviously they're all Spanish speakers, let's get a busload of them. I mean that was my instant idea. . . . So Kingsley says I've already thought of that but I don't know if it will make sense or not. And I said, "Well that's not a brainstorm, we've got to do it, . . . what harm can it do?" So Kingsley's a pleasantly impulsive guy like that, and he's like yeah, the hell with it. So he gets a hold of Robin Alexander, and I think it was only in a week or two they had some guy from Mexico trucked in; it was only one. And I think in hindsight it was viewed as a useful thing.[12]

With the FAT's assistance, the UE won the election by twelve votes.[13] Townsend suggested that the collaborative strategy was more important than the victory itself because it reflected a historic shift in the direction of aid across the continent. His description illuminates the difference between the FAT–UE relationship and the transnational contacts that preceded it between other U.S. and Mexican unions: "But it is an interesting tactic. To me, it was a little bit of [a] turnabout. [In the past] U.S. labor people [were] running all over the planet giving out free advice and this was an example of where we had some turnabout and invite[d] somebody to come here. But it came out of a practical necessity."[14] A FAT national coordinator agreed that the strategy was significant because it marked a change in attitude and method for North American unions:

We need to create organizations that look beyond their borders and have respect for the idiosyncrasies of each country. I can't tell labor leaders in the U.S. what they need and they can't come here and teach me what I need. Labor leaders used to come here and try to teach us. . . . We need to give each other support and respect. We sent some organizers from here to go and help organize a plant in [Wisconsin] because they needed help organizing Latino workers; some were undocumented. This organizer went and they won the election. We need to say, "Where do you need our help and what kind of help do you need?"[15]

[12] Personal interview with Chris Townsend of the UE, December 18, 2000.
[13] Although ultimately the employer contested the results of the election and won.
[14] Personal interview with Chris Townsend of the UE, December 18, 2000.
[15] Personal interview with Benedicto Martínez Orozco of the FAT, July 27, 1999.

The mutualism of the FAT–UE relationship is also reflected in and strengthened by the involvement of rank-and-file workers. UE and FAT workers participate in yearly exchanges. The UE's Robin Alexander explained the importance of the exchanges for institutionalizing labor transnationalism within her union (echoing Arturo Alcalde's comment about the need to exchange realities):

I think the time and effort that we put into the worker-to-worker exchanges are really important, too. Part of the thinking behind them was we need to understand each other and each other's realities and it's not just a question of doing support for organizing work, but there has to be a deeper understanding within our organizations of what's going on and what the realities are because otherwise we're not really able to talk to each other.... But it's a wonderful thing to watch because you really visibly see peoples' mindsets shift within a ten day period, and it's pretty extraordinary. And it happens on both sides of the border.[16]

When asked the most significant lessons workers on both sides of the border learn from the exchanges, Alexander replied:

I think people...on both sides are just astounded by the similarities, that they expect things to be very different and yet they find that the details may be different, but in the broad strokes it's sort of the same. It's that organizing is hard in both places. I think people here tend to kind of assume that folks in Mexico probably don't really know what they're doing...and they get down there and it's like, ah, these people are really good, they work really hard, they're very dedicated...and they run into problems that are not all that dissimilar [from] what we confront, that workers are afraid to organize because they're afraid they're going to lose their jobs. That bosses are nasty. It's very familiar stuff, so I think our folks come back with a tremendous respect for the FAT that is much more focused. It's based on a much more real understanding of what's going on. And people who come here inevitably think it must be easy. And they are like blown away by the fact that it really isn't.[17]

Alexander's description suggests that the UE and FAT's joint participation in an expanded transnational legal field solidified the process of constituting regional actors and interests. It also helped undermine the foreign worker myth as rank-and-file workers in the United States and Mexico came to develop a more nuanced understanding of the living and working conditions of their "others" across the border. That UE workers are willing to support FAT workers with a voluntary dues check-off and FAT workers are willing to accept it suggests not only the success of leaders' efforts to educate workers about the value of transnationalism but also that rank-and-file participation is crucial to institutionalizing a

---

[16] Personal interview with Robin Alexander of the UE, December 21, 2000.
[17] Ibid.

culture of transnationalism. As Alexander explained in 2009, "People would think it was strange if the FAT wasn't at our convention, if we weren't doing international work. I think it's very much become part of who we are, more so now, probably, than ever."[18]

Like the UE, the Canadian Steelworkers also institutionalized its ties to the FAT by educating members about the value of labor transnationalism. In 1994, the FAT and CUSWA embarked on an innovative project to build a strike fund for the FAT, which previously had no access to emergency funds. CUSWA's David Mackenzie described the "Mutual Support and Solidarity Fund," known by its Spanish acronym FOSAM:

What's unique about our relationship with the FAT...is that we have built through the Humanity Fund a specific mutual support fund with them which they can access as a kind of emergency strike fund or emergency organizing relief fund in situations that are...well emergency situations basically or extremely stressful ones....They needed long-term support mechanisms to support people at strikes like [the one at] the Morelos print shop that's been going on for four years. So that's been a concrete way we can help them, and we've been working with them to build this assistance fund. And we've funded it up front, and we're funding it for a five-year period; it will end in a couple of years. And the FAT meanwhile have assigned people...to work full time getting the FAT locals and co-ops and other organizing members paying into the fund at their end so that after a while when we stop paying into it it will be self-sustaining; it will feel like part of joining the FAT is joining this mutual support fund.[19]

Whereas historically the money U.S. and Canadian unions gave to Latin American unions had long strings attached, CUSWA's support was not contingent on the FAT's compliance with any CUSWA directive. FOSAM's goal is to help make the FAT self-reliant and build its capacity. To that end, the Humanity Fund also contributed money to a project that supports the FAT's expansion and consolidation efforts. As the Steelworkers Humanity Fund Programme describes: "This is a two-year project meant to increase membership in iron, steel, metal-mechanic and textile sectors in the Valle de Mexico. It is carrying out organising campaigns and offering educational, legal and technical support for groups of workers in non-union workplaces or workplaces with 'official,' government-linked unions."[20] In addition to the FOSAM project, the collaborative work between CUSWA and the FAT includes regular meetings and exchanges. The two unions invest significant time and money

---

[18] Personal interview with Robin Alexander of the UE, August 21, 2009.
[19] Personal interview with David Mackenzie of CUSWA, February 16, 2001.
[20] "Steelworkers Humanity Fund's Programme." Canadian Steelworkers (n.d.).

for collaborations on health and safety issues. Many of these thematic exchanges include rank-and-file members.

CUSWA's David Mackenzie described how the success of Humanity Fund projects strengthens worker support for transnationalism and how, in turn, that support is channeled and reinforced through an innovative education program called "Thinking North-South":

> Over time, as people got increasingly proud of [the Humanity Fund], it compelled us to do a couple of things. One of the things was to ramp up our . . . international solidarity program education internally. We basically created a new one. We used to have a kind of half-assed course [where] we borrowed bits and pieces from other people, but we started using our Humanity Fund assisting our Education Department [in] developing a program we called "Thinking North-South," a week-long program that was very popular. And we find that it's very useful to have local union people in that who then go back to their locals all charged up, who want to bargain the Fund [i.e., include contributions to it in collective bargaining agreements] and get involved. So we've created a network through the Fund and through the Education Department, a network of international solidarity activists right in our local unions who are on top of these issues and extremely knowledgeable and constantly pressuring the union to do things. Like all unions have networks of health and safety activists, and we've got this really good group of international solidarity activists.[21]

As Mackenzie explained, the "Thinking North-South" program focuses on making connections between the plight of workers across the Americas. CUSWA, then, makes conscious efforts to undermine the foreign worker myth by providing the rank and file with a more nuanced understanding of how regional economic processes affect jobs and working conditions in North America. This understanding helps workers create an alternative script to that which, in knee-jerk fashion, blames foreign workers for job loss and factory relocation.

Creating Cooperative Complementary Identities

The most crucial step in forging a fully developed transnational relationship is the ability to develop a cooperative complementary identity, which I define as a shared recognition of mutual interest coupled with a commitment to joint action. The orientation must extend beyond key individuals and union leaders to become fully embedded within a union's culture. Taking significant steps to undermine the foreign worker myth within a union culture is a necessary, though not sufficient, condition

---

[21] Personal interview with David Mackenzie of CUSWA, February 16, 2001.

for unions to develop a cooperative complementary identity. Faced with employers and governments that often pit them against each other, North American unions find it extremely difficult to create cooperative complementary identities. Those that successfully develop this orientation are able to attribute a lack of jobs and labor rights to the economic policies and strategies of nation-states and transnational corporations, not to each other.

Forging a cooperative complementary identity does not require unions to eschew their unique and individual interests, which usually respond to and are shaped by national political and economic forces. Rather, it suggests that they are able to identify and develop mutual interests, and actively resist forces that would have them define their interests as antagonistic. Achieving a cooperative complementary identity, then, reflects the solidification of the process of being constituted as regional actors with regional interests.

Among the sets of unions/federations that developed transnational relationships, only the UE, FAT, and CUSWA achieved a fully developed transnational relationship and share a cooperative complementary identity. The consistency and quality of their relationship is unique in the North American labor movement. Members of the FAT, UE, and CUSWA see themselves as connected and have a strong sense of mutual interest. The FAT's Bertha Luján explained:

Ultimately counterparts are constructed through common processes, constructed through common interests, through common projects. The relationship of the FAT with the UE is a good relation, a strategic relationship because there are common projects. The kind of unionism that they push for in the United States is what we do here also.... We want a unionism that is democratic, autonomous, with participation from the base.[22]

Arturo Alcalde, one of the FAT's lawyers, was forceful in his defense of labor transnationalism based on mutual interest:

After this process of identification – which brings information and confidence, trust – it is very important to work on common agendas in which one helps the other, and I think union freedom is a very important area to work on. Here in Mexico there is practically no freedom of association. We have collective contracts with charro unions. So we need a common agenda, and for us Mexicans, international solidarity is very important because we have a government that intervenes in unions' international relations. We have seen that when a conflict generates international solidarity, the government attends to it. The few union

---

[22] Personal interview with Bertha Luján of the FAT, August 29, 2000.

registrations and collective contracts we have come through international solidarity. It's a proletarian strategy. It's a process of globalization of international solidarity.[23]

As Alcalde explains, areas of mutual interest must be identified and developed. Bertha Luján put it succinctly: "So I think there are differences and areas of convergence. And it is those areas of convergence which are common interests; there is where we must find and construct things in common."[24]

By definition, a cooperative complementary identity must permeate a union's culture. That is, it must be kept alive not by leaders and/or key staff but be accepted and supported by union members themselves. CUSWA's David Mackenzie explained the nature of the cultural shift toward transnationalism within his union:

Because of the history I've described and the relationships we've built, there is now an automatic expectation among our ordinary local officers and activists that every major conference – health, district – will have an international component. There will be an international speaker; somebody we've had a relationship with will be there. It's just sort of become an expected thing, and they would comment if it didn't happen now. Twenty years ago they wouldn't have [cared]. They would have seen it as something exotic or a waste of time. That's sort of the culture change in the organization. When you ask a lot of our activists what they are most proud of about their union, in the old days it might have been, oh that great strike at Inglis when we burned the boss's car, or the wonderful militant health and safety action, or this famous sit-down strike. As often as not, now they'll talk about the international work, the Humanity Fund, they're very proud of the Humanity Fund. You know, once they have the experience of actually giving in a selfless way to something and they see results or they hear international speakers come to a conference thanking the Steelworkers for their help, it is a cultural change. I don't know how else to describe it.[25]

The three unions have played a critical role in generating more contacts and engagement among other unions. By pulling other U.S., Canadian, and Mexican unions into the network of unions that engage the expanded transnational legal field, the UE, FAT, and CUSWA have helped catalyze and expand transnational relationships across the continent. Benedicto

---

[23] Personal interview with Arturo Alcalde Justiniani of the FAT, March 29, 2000.
[24] Personal interview with Bertha Luján of the FAT, August 29, 2000.
[25] Personal interview with David Mackenzie of CUSWA, February 16, 2001.

Martínez of the FAT described what he perceived as a post-NAFTA shift in the attitudes of North American unions:

With the passage of time and more exchanges among the U.S. and Mexico, there has developed a new and distinct attitude during the last five years. Of course there are still some with the protectionist attitude, but many have changed their position and are interested in working with unions in the other countries beyond their borders – and building relations that are respectful, have solidarity in the full meaning of the word. They realize what we've always realized, that multinationals move to wherever they obtain the most benefits; they don't care which country it is.... This they didn't see; now they see it with much clarity. And what do they do? They changed the relations between unions in Mexico and those in the U.S.[26]

A careful analysis of the data supports Martínez's assessment. Although no other unions have reached the level of mutual commitment of the UE, FAT, and CUSWA, key unions have changed not only their attitudes but also their practices to embrace a more expansive internationalism.

A Partially Developed Transnational Relationship: Telecommunications Unions

The emergence of a relationship among North America's telecommunications unions, when placed in the history of union relations across the continent, is quite unexpected. What is perhaps most surprising, however, is that it survived after NAFTA's passage. After inking a formal trinational alliance in 1992, North America's largest communications unions faced the daunting task of building trust where little had previously existed. As Chapter 4 revealed, their participation in NAO submissions helped the CWA, CEP, and STRM recognize and develop common goals. The CWA's former national director for international affairs explained how his union tried to build trust outside the boundaries of NAFTA activities by sharing valuable information and including the STRM in the CWA's networks:

It worked for the Mexicans as well because ... one of the best contracts that we have is with Southwestern Bell. So I was able to arrange for some meetings for Francisco [Hernández Juárez] and his regional people with our regional people, in Texas. And for the company in Mexico with the company in Texas, because the headquarters of Southwestern Bell is in Texas.... I invited them to almost

---

[26] Personal interview with Benedicto Martínez Orozco of the FAT, July 27, 1999.

every meeting that we could so that they would attend, and they would.... We
needed to eliminate fear and distrust, and build trust, and that's what we did.[27]

He described how information sharing and working through the PTTI
put the trinational commitment to cooperate into practice:

[We] brought them into PTTI, [we] made sure that they had a slot in the Advisory
Committee, [we] made sure that they attended all the meetings that were held
regionally, and they started to become part of it. And [we were] bombarding
them with information, you know everything that we would be doing. And as
you know we have a good research department, but we're doing things on trade,
doing things on technology, we're doing things on a number of fields. Everything
that we prepared in English or Spanish, I would send it to them. So they were
well fed, in a way that they would feel that it was not just talking, that we were
actually building something.[28]

Like the FAT, UE, and CUSWA, telecommunications unions built support for their trinational alliance by including their members in joint activities. And as trust grew, those activities multiplied. In 1995, Eduardo Diaz,
the North American director for PTTI, who in 1999 became the CWA's
international affairs director, organized a joint organizing school for bilin-
gual organizers in all three unions.[29] The STRM organizers learned about
CWA strategies to combat deregulation, and the CWA and CEP organizers learned about the political situation Mexican unionists faced. CWA
President Larry Cohen described the event:

It used some curriculum [on which] we collaborated with the AFL-CIO Organizing Institute [OI], but this was obviously in Spanish. It was one of the first
efforts to do it that way. The curriculum was very much based on being in
small groups ... about fifteen people from each union, frontline organizers, and
Eduardo was the main person who prepared that curriculum. It basically followed the model from the OI, which we promote very actively in terms of our
CWA members here doing these three-day sessions where they get a sense of
what it means to do organizing work by practicing a little bit, literally practicing
interaction.... So the good news was that that occurred and it led to things and
continues to lead to some things.[30]

After the exchange, two STRM organizers assisted for a week with
a CWA organizing campaign among Spanish-speaking workers in Los

---

[27] Personal interview with CWA official, 2001.
[28] Ibid.
[29] Eduardo Diaz passed away in 2000. To honor him, the CWA renamed a solidarity
program created in 1998 the Eduardo Diaz Union-to-Union Solidarity Program.
[30] Personal interview with Larry Cohen of the CWA, March 28, 2001.

Angeles. Larry Cohen argued that union activists from each country benefit by learning about each others' organizing styles and being poised to assist each other. According to Cohen, "While big business and government [have] *their* NAFTA, this is *our* North American Free Trade Agreement."[31]

In addition to engaging in joint organizing, the unions hashed out strategies to deal with a dynamic communications industry. Their goal – to strengthen their individual *and* collective positions with employers – reflected their commitment to action that addressed mutual interests. The STRM's Rafael Marino Roche explained how the transnational relationship enables the three unions to respond to the burgeoning and ever-changing global telecommunications industry:

> We have been having exchanges with the CWA, and learning about what is happening in other countries, technology changes, etc.... So our experiences have been much more rich because of these transformations. Now there is a community of interests and we can talk about our experiences and problems in this sector. We learned from the Americans and Canadians how to deal with technological change and how not to suffer the way they suffered when new technologies came. This process of economic integration and technological change has come to us at almost the same time and we can work to try to lessen the trauma of it.... This is very very useful. This allows us to take quick steps forward.[32]

The unions have not had difficulty finding ways to assist each other. Mateo Lejarza described how the alliance benefits all three unions and reflects a commitment to identify mutual interests:

> We have gotten more alliances with ... unions working for Southwestern Bell, vice presidents of CWA in California and Arizona. So we have concrete results. In the short term we send letters to the managers of the companies and they are signed by many of us, which looks good. We are looking to have a link with [AT&T] through Morton Bahr [CWA president at the time]. These are things we can't do alone. To talk with the directors of AT&T would be impossible without their help. The support of Morton has been great. Through his affiliation with the AFL, he has gotten us a few meetings with Sweeney.... This support is very useful. We supported Morton's election to the presidency of the Communications International and he won. We have supported each other mutually and it works and we have constant activities.[33]

---

[31] Cusick (1995, p. 11).
[32] Personal interview with Rafael Marino Roche of the STRM, May 15, 2000.
[33] Personal interview with Mateo Lejarza of the STRM, May 9, 2000.

As Marino and Lejarza's comments suggest, the purpose of information-sharing in either direction is not altruism; it supports the unions' individual and collective struggles. But it also supports another long-term goal: to enable the three unions to bargain collectively across North America. Although the idea is radical, and many would say untenable, the three unions are laying the groundwork so that they can one day achieve this goal. Mateo Lejarza explained these ambitions:

It is a cooperative alliance to improve our collective contracts and support our struggles over contract revisions, and local struggles, and to share experiences. We did a study together looking at our collective contracts to see what clauses could we use as examples as we worked toward getting similar contracts in the future. It also looked at Chile, Argentina, Venezuela, and Brazil, and from this we took on the idea of trying to work on getting similar contracts.... We will create a common protocol, and try to negotiate together [as] a group of unions with the same multinational.[34]

The three telecommunications unions built a solid relationship, and identification among them is strong. However, because a sense of identification does not fully permeate their union cultures, it has not coalesced into a cooperative complementary identity. To the extent that a sense of mutuality exists in these unions, it depends on key staffers and leaders whose tenure is not guaranteed.[35] For example, the STRM's Alicia Sepúlveda Nuñez was extremely successful in stimulating and nurturing transnational relationships on behalf of STRM workers. Sepúlveda explained the distinction between transnational relationships and transnational contacts: "My colleague one day told me I had so many contacts, implying that I was power hungry, because contacts imply power in Mexico. But I told him I'd been around two years, and he had been around twenty, and what I had made were relationships, not names in a book."[36]

Although identification among key leaders is strong, they have not regularly and actively engaged workers in transational activities and education programs. Telecommunications unions therefore have not completely institutionalized a culture of transnationalism. CWA President Larry Cohen agreed that their relationship has not fully developed, although

---

[34] Personal interview with Mateo Lejarza of the STRM, May 9, 2000.
[35] Fred Pomeroy of the CEP retired, Alicia Sepúlveda Nuñez left her STRM leadership position in October 2000, and the CWA's Eduardo Diaz died in 2000.
[36] Personal interview with Alicia Sepúlveda Nuñez of the STRM, February 16, 2000.

he conceded that it could in the future: "Those possibilities are still there for a deeper relationship."[37]

North American Labor Federations

If the emergence of labor transnationalism among North America's telecommunications unions was unexpected, that between North America's labor federations was quite shocking. The desire to kill NAFTA brought the AFL-CIO and CLC into close contact with a broad array of labor, environmental, and other advocacy organizations for the first time. It also brought them into contact with independent Mexican unions such as the STRM, the FAT, and its affiliates. As discussed in Chapter 4, the AFL-CIO and CLC increased their interactions with these unions in the transnational legal field by supporting and financing NAO submissions. Of course, most of these interactions were "unofficial." Their exclusivity with the CTM prevented the large powerful labor federations to the north from fully and openly engaging their struggling independent counterparts in the south.

A full and open shift toward labor transnationalism within the AFL-CIO did not come until 1998. The very public NAFTA defeat intensified internal conflicts within the organization. During the 1995 AFL-CIO Convention, an intense debate raged over international affairs. John Sweeney's "New Voice" slate proposed more progressive international policies. According to one AFL-CIO official: "People knew things [were] changing." The perception that the AFL-CIO leadership under Lane Kirkland handled NAFTA badly, or what this official referred to as its "failure to deal with NAFTA," plagued the organization.[38]

In addition, the AFL-CIO and its affiliates faced a membership crisis spurred in part by their failure to organize or recognize the needs of potential new members – Mexican Americans and Mexican immigrants among them. John Sweeney defeated Tom Donahue that year, as he called for an increase in organizing. His message stirred hopes for renewal, but his election victory also had significant implications for cross-border relations. Propelled by his cadre of new high-ranking staffers, particularly those in the International Department, Sweeney set out to change the federation's infamous anticommunist policies and improve its tarnished international image. The new focus, according to one AFL-CIO official, "was on

---

[37] Personal interview with Larry Cohen of the CWA, March 28, 2001.
[38] Personal interview with AFL-CIO official, 2000.

organizing, leaving the Cold War behind."[39] Another official concurred, explaining that the federation had ended its business of "importing Cold War ideology" into other countries.[40] A former director of the Solidarity Center's Mexico program provided an analysis:

A number of things happened at the same time; it's hard to say what was more important. Sweeney was elected to be the president, and the whole international policy of the AFL began to change then. And a generation of AFL officials, officers involved in international relations, retired or reached an age where they began to think about leaving, and I think that had an impact in the change of policy of the AFL. At the same time NAFTA was implemented, [and] that had an impact on the change in policy.[41]

In order to make manifest this change in policy, Sweeney's team closed the four AFL-CIO international institutes (one of which was AIFLD) and combined them into the American Center for International Labor Solidarity (Solidarity Center), which opened in 1997.[42] That year the Solidarity Center took over the AIFLD office in Mexico City, where the new director of the Solidarity Center's Mexico program would be based. Sweeney's administration also made the historic decision to openly work with independent Mexican unions and eschew exclusivity with the CTM. In 2010, as he explained his international policies, John Sweeney acknowledged that the historic link between the AFL and CIA was "exaggerated but accurate" and that his goal was to improve relations with official unions and build new ones with independent unions:

When I first came into office and I was at the ILO – I guess it was my first ILO as president – I sat down with the Mexicans and I said right from the start that I want to have a good relationship. And I want to talk about how we strengthen the relationship. And one of them said, "What's wrong with the way it is now?" And I wasn't about to get into specifics but I think that they understood what I wanted to accomplish. And that I wanted to have an open door with them and they to have an open door with me as well. And that's the way we started off. We also dealt with some of the independent unions. And we didn't really get into their internal fights, but we certainly gave them the kind of respect that I thought they deserved. And I wanted to have a dialogue with them. So the atmosphere changed slowly but surely.[43]

Bringing new blood into the organization was key to changing the atmosphere. Barbara Shailor, director of the International Department,

---

[39] Ibid.
[40] Personal interview with AFL-CIO official, 2000.
[41] Personal interview with Jeff Hermanson of the AFL-CIO'S Solidarity Center, August 24, 2000.
[42] This decision had been made under Lane Kirkland.
[43] Personal interview with John Sweeney of the AFL-CIO, April 30, 2010.

recommended Stan Gacek as assistant director for the Americas.[44] According to Gacek, Shailor told him: "I'm bringing you in and we're going to make revolution here."[45] After arriving in February 1997, Gacek recommended progressive labor activists to key positions in the International Department and the Solidarity Center. He explained his mission:

> Barbara expected that I set a new direction and policy for the AFL-CIO's relations with Latin America and the Caribbean that would maintain the best practices of the past, but also make for the many serious departures that were drastically needed for our federation to achieve improved credibility and capacity in the region. Following the retirements and attrition of AIFLD personnel in the field, I . . . decided to replace them by effectively recommending people with authentic experiences of trade union activism and a more progressive view on Latin America unionism.[46]

Even union leaders outside the AFL-CIO noted the significance of these changes. According to the UE's Bob Kingsley:

> There's been change in recent years that we've observed from our perspective on the outside within the AFL-CIO that's been very positive in our view. From the casting out of certain of the Cold Warriors from their international affairs operation and their replacement with some folks that have a little different, . . . broader view of the world, to what I think is more important, a much belated but greatly welcomed new focus on the pursuit of concrete international solidarity activities.[47]

The CTM's control over and monopolization of relationships with U.S. unions was further undermined by two critical events in 1997: the death of CTM leader Fidel Velázquez, which loosened the federation's grip on independent unionism, and the birth of the National Union of Workers (UNT), a progressive union federation created to oppose the CTM; the FAT and STRM were founding members. AFL-CIO representative Stan Gacek was invited to speak at the founding meeting of the UNT and at the FAT's annual congress in 1997 (the first time an AFL-CIO representative did so). In April 1999, the AFL-CIO signed a historic cooperative agreement with the UNT, marking the first time in AFL-CIO history that the federation had signed a formal agreement with an independent Mexican

---

[44] In 2006, Gacek became associate director of the AFL-CIO's International Department.
[45] Personal correspondence with Stan Gacek, September 23, 2007.
[46] Ibid.
[47] Personal interview with Bob Kingsley of the UE, January 23, 2001.

union federation. The CLC also began to work with the UNT. According to the FAT's Bertha Luján:

The FAT has also advanced in constructing relations with the AFL-CIO. This was possible because of the change of policies within the AFL-CIO with respect to Mexico. Before the AFL-CIO had a monopolistic relationship with the CTM. Beginning with NAFTA, the AFL-CIO changed its policy and strategy toward Mexico and today the AFL-CIO has developed relationships with independent unions like the FAT. This is a new relationship that we've been constructing in the last few years.[48]

For independent Mexican unions, the break in the AFL-CIO and CLC's exclusivity with the CTM not only signaled the federations' readiness to cooperate with independent forces in the Mexican labor movement but also remedied the long-standing contradiction inherent in the two federations' international policies: they promulgated the idea of democracy while supporting undemocratic official unions. As the STRM's Mateo Lejarza explained:

The CTM is very worried that the AFL-CIO has a relationship with us. The leaders went to Sweeney in D.C. and expressed their anger, but he didn't change. Sweeney is the first generation of change, not a complete change, but the first step; also in the CLC there are changes. If they change, and insist that we are in international forums, as part of Mexican unionism, it will help us a lot because they can't say they're democratic and have relations with undemocratic unions here. That is a political and ideological contradiction. Why is your relation with the CTM, which is undemocratic and against unions in many ways? We don't want to destroy the CTM, but we do want to be represented. They don't allow us to be there, and the CLC and AFL-CIO are helping us.[49]

The growth of confidence and trust between the AFL-CIO, CLC, and independent Mexican unions was facilitated by the northern federations' new ways of interacting and working with Mexican unionists. The CLC's Richard Martin explained:

I guess it would be fair to say about the mid-nineties we became much closer to some of the smaller organizations. In the main it started off with the FAT, and we had a lot of contact with FAT in Mexico, attended some of the conventions and conferences, and had their leadership up in Canada on a number of occasions both as guests of the CLC [and] as guests of the individual unions having conferences on

---

[48] Personal interview with Bertha Luján of the FAT, August 3, 1999.
[49] Personal interview with Mateo Lejarza of the STRM, May 9, 2000.

international affairs and in particular on issues such as NAFTA and the structure of the Mexican trade union movement.[50]

At an AFL-CIO mission to Mexico convened in January 1998 to discuss international policy, John Sweeney chose Tim Beaty to lead the Solidarity Center's Mexico program. According to Beaty, whose previous position was as inter-American secretary to the international trade secretariat Public Services International (PSI, now a Global Union Federation), the delegation's idea was to "better link what the AFL-CIO [was] doing internationally with domestic goals, and so Mexico [became] the highest priority." That same year, Sweeney visited Mexico and met with various union leaders, made speeches, and laid out the terms of what the AFL-CIO's activities and goals in Mexico would be. The AFL-CIO's mission in Mexico was threefold: to build sectoral relationships (e.g., among auto, textile, and agricultural unions) and to get affiliates connected and involved; to work on immigration issues; and to work on free trade issues, including joint efforts to amend NAFTA.

Jeff Hermanson, who became director of the Solidarity Center's Mexico program in 2000 when Tim Beaty was promoted to deputy director for international affairs, explained that the kind of international solidarity the AFL-CIO advocates differs profoundly from the policy in the AIFLD days:

It's a fundamental division between spontaneous struggles and improvising acts of solidarity as opposed to planning strategically to have a struggle that is ... in which you plan international solidarity. We are advocates of the latter approach, of strategic acts and long-term continuous relationships. And we see building that as our primary objective. ... I think up until Sweeney there was a different concept of international solidarity; the concept was more a diplomatic or representational conception rather than a strategic one of coordinating efforts.[51]

While the ideology of the AFL-CIO's Solidarity Center changed significantly, so have the actions in which it engages. The AFL-CIO continued to maintain contacts with official Mexican unions – including the CTM – after NAFTA's passage, but it also embarked on significant projects with the FAT and UNT. In addition to initiating the laboralistas network and supporting NAO submissions, the AFL-CIO provides funding and

---

[50] Personal interview with Richard Martin of the CLC, February 26, 2001.
[51] Personal interview with Jeff Hermanson of the AFL-CIO'S Solidarity Center, August 24, 2000.

support for many FAT projects, including women's programs, worker exchanges, meetings, and conferences.

The CLC is also actively engaged with the FAT. Sheila Katz of the CLC explained that her position was created to maintain relations that emerged during NAFTA's negotiation:

> They'd hired me to work on relations with NGOs and labor, to work on NAFTA sort of relations.... They got some money from the government to open a special position on NAFTA, and that was the focus they wanted. They wanted to build the CLC's participation in the coalition work. But prior to that the international relations in Mexico were uniquely through the Inter-American Regional Workers' Organization. In fact our international relations in the whole hemisphere were through the Inter-American Regional Workers' Organization.[52]

Katz described a joint NAFTA-related project she organized: "We did a joint monitoring project, held a conference in 1996. One of the first things I did in this job was organize this trinational; it was a hemispheric conference called 'Challenging Free Trade in the Americas.' And we did a report on that."[53] Katz also described a joint project the CLC has with the FAT:

> We're funding a development project with the FAT this year for the first time. It's a project to help support organizing in one particular sector, and it's the first time we're actually funding a development project with them. And so that's sort of the next step in the relationship. I personally have a great deal of respect for the FAT and feel that they're a very valuable partner – one of the few that you can work with in Mexico.[54]

The AFL-CIO, whose image in Latin America was arguably more tarnished than that of the CLC, built trust with independent Mexican unions through joint actions and a very conscious effort to change former modes of interaction that were not equitable or respectful. Tim Beaty explained that he was extremely careful to eschew old ways of doing things: "It was never how the AFL-CIO dealt with Europeans. I don't think that method is appropriate personally or as the AFL-CIO representative to tell Mexicans how to do things.... Now the AFL-CIO is making a better effort to understand Mexico and Mexican history and unions."[55] A former STRM official revealed what she told Beaty when he first arrived in Mexico: "I joke with him. I told him well, in Mexico everybody calls you the

---

[52] Personal interview with Sheila Katz of the CLC, February 26, 2001.
[53] Ibid.
[54] Ibid.
[55] Personal interview with Tim Beaty of the AFL-CIO, February 29, 2000.

AFL-CIA and everybody thinks you're spooks, so they won't think differently until you prove otherwise."[56] The AFL-CIO's Mark Anderson explained the importance of proving otherwise and earning the trust of Mexican unionists: "From our side I think there has to be a lot of confidence building vis-à-vis the Mexican labor movement that we can be trustworthy. And that's part of the process."[57] When asked in 2010 how his new hires in the international department quickly earned the trust of their Mexican counterparts, former AFL-CIO President John Sweeney explained: "Existing staff had to really adapt themselves to Sweeney's program. And it's my nature to be respectful, to want to work with people. And from the earliest days the staff got the message loud and clear. The people who we hired subsequently, when they were interviewed, and when they were trained, they got the message very clearly."[58]

Comments by independent Mexican labor activists such as Vicente Villamar suggest the effectiveness of Sweeney's program: "Tim Beaty of the AFL-CIO works well with Mexicans.... And Stan Gacek. They are a new generation of American unionists. They have a different attitude.... They are from a different perspective. They feel for the Mexicans and want them to have respect and worry about them, how they are treated.... I've seen a difference in the AFL-CIO."[59] Given how relatively recent the AFL-CIO's transformation on international issues has been, the ability of new AFL-CIO officials to engender such respect in such a short period of time, and to undermine old sentiments held by Mexican unionists about the AFL-CIO, is quite significant. Independent Mexican unionists' attitudes about U.S. unions in general and the AFL-CIO in particular suggest their more nuanced understanding of the AFL-CIO as a political institution. Many Mexican unionists' opinions of the AFL-CIO indicate that their conception of it as a monolithic institution is changing. As an activist explained: "We in Mexico realized that the AFL-CIO was an organization with many different positions, from conservative to progressive. We began to understand that not all U.S. unions follow the same position."[60]

Despite a recent and significant shift to a more egalitarian transnationalism, the AFL-CIO has not yet been able to fully incorporate a culture of transnationalism across the organization. This has inhibited the development of a strong cooperative complementary identity with its southern

---

[56] Personal interview with Alicia Sepúlveda Nuñez of the STRM, August 27, 2000.
[57] Personal interview with Mark Anderson of the AFL-CIO, January 8, 2001.
[58] Personal interview with John Sweeney of the AFL-CIO, April 30, 2010.
[59] Personal interview with Vicente Villamar, August 2, 1999.
[60] Personal interview with Alejandro Quiroz Soriano of SEMARNAP, June 23, 1999.

counterparts. One Mexican labor activist recognized that although the federation has made strides in leaps and bounds, its transformation is far from complete:

I think the majority of leadership of a lot of AFL-CIO affiliates is beginning to change. But it's not a change in one direction. Sometimes it advances depending on the leadership, and then it regresses. But I think in a pragmatic way there is a growing consciousness that if you want to defend American workers you can't just do it in the U.S. You have to open solidarity offices in Mexico and in other places. There's a pragmatic tendency to start creating an agenda which responds more to globalization, not to national politics.[61]

Explaining the Shift to Transnationalism

After NAFTA went into force, the nascent relationships catalyzed by the agreement did not atrophy. Rather, key North American unions continued to expand the transnational legal field beyond NAFTA. In doing so they transformed it into a more general labor rights field in which they framed issues, mobilized, and demanded that the economic processes unleashed by NAFTA be mediated by social protections. The expansion of an arena dedicated to labor advocacy pushed labor unions and federations toward more developed transnational relationships based on trust and mutual interest. Involving rank-and-file workers in relationships and educating them about the real source of the problems wrought by regional economic integration increased the likelihood that workers would support transnational activities in principle and in practice. It also helped solidify the process of constituting regional actors and interests and eroded racial stereotypes that in the past had stymied cross-border ties. As the FAT's international coordinator described the post-NAFTA state of union relations:

If we consider anything positive about NAFTA it would be opening up of relations with North American unions. At the beginning it was very difficult because the U.S. unions thought NAFTA would harm them, and that Mexican workers would benefit by gaining jobs. So they considered us scabs or thieves. This was the relation at the beginning; it was very tense because they accused us of being thieves. But with time and as the relations grew, we realized that we were the same – workers, just with different cultures. Ultimately we are not enemies; the principal enemy is the multinational that goes wherever labor is cheapest. And we have to struggle together to ensure that things don't get worse, which is what is happening with NAFTA.[62]

---

[61] Personal interview with Alejandro Villamar, February 29, 2000.
[62] Personal interview with Antonio Villalba Granados of the FAT, April 26, 2000.

Given the history of union relations prior to NAFTA, the emergence of labor transnationalism among unions that either had no former contact or had extremely negative experiences of each other is quite surprising. Despite the emergence of labor transnationalism in North America, however, only one set of unions – the UE, FAT, and CUSWA – has achieved a cooperative complementary identity. I now turn to an analysis of unions that, unlike those presented in this chapter, which constructed their interests to embrace transnationalism, constructed their interests to either fully or partially reject it.

PART TWO

VARIATIONS IN TRANSNATIONALISM

The first part of the NAFTA story centers on how the trade agreement's institutional structures created new transnational opportunities for labor unions that led to the *emergence* of labor transnationalism in North America in the early 1990s. Despite the strength of NAFTA's effect, however, not all unions developed transnational relationships in its wake. NAFTA's power to catalyze transnational labor relationships was significant, yet for some unions its effects were constrained by political and ideological factors that left the landscape of North American labor relationships significantly, though unevenly, transformed. In order to understand NAFTA's catalytic effect on North American unions, then, we must examine not only the nature of the transnational political opportunity structure it created but also the unique characteristics of unions poised to take advantage of it.

The NAFTA story, then, has a sequel. Whereas the first part of the story centers on structure, the second focuses on agency, specifically how unions responded differently to those opportunities. Part Two of the book therefore examines *variations* in unions' engagement in transnational activities in response to NAFTA. Chapter 6 examines the unions that did not take advantage of the opportunity provided by NAFTA, and Chapter 7 offers a more detailed analysis of the variation between unions that embraced and rejected transnationalism. A comparison of the positive and negative cases is essential because it highlights the predisposing characteristics that made some unions more susceptible to NAFTA's catalytic effect. It reveals that the most significant predictors of cross-border engagement are political rather than economic.

6

Missing the Opportunity NAFTA Provided

Although NAFTA stimulated transnational relationships among key union federations and industrial unions by providing a new transnational political opportunity structure that constituted North American actors and interests, not all industrial unions were transformed by its effects. The naysayers who predicted NAFTA would make cross-border collaboration impossible were not completely incorrect. Indeed, the trade agreement did little to generate transnational relationships among U.S. and Canadian unions in the auto, garment/apparel, and trucking industries and their counterparts in *official* Mexican unions. In addition, the free trade agreement created a rift in the uninspired though cordial relations among the AFL-CIO, CLC, and CTM, and generated significant contention between the Teamsters and CTM trucking unions. Rather than constitute them as regional actors, NAFTA actually underscored the national interests of unions in these industries and generated intense nationalistic sentiments and strategies. In NAFTA's wake, the majority of these unions had some contact and interaction. For most, contact was minimal and interaction intermittent. Labor leaders expressed little if any reluctance to admit poor relations with their counterparts. Ironically, their frankness in revealing this unflattering side of the history, and their unwillingness to paint a rosy picture of harmonious post-NAFTA relationships when they did not exist, strengthens the validity of the data in other chapters that demonstrate NAFTA's catalytic effect on labor relationships.

Despite U.S. and Canadian auto, garment/apparel, and trucking unions' inability to construct relationships with official unions, some did form moderately developed relationships with *independent* Mexican

199

unions. The Teamsters, UNITE, CAW, and UAW collaborated with the FAT, and the two auto unions also worked with SITIAVW, an independent Mexican union representing Volkswagen workers in Puebla. These relationships are much less developed than those among union federations, telecommunications unions, and the UE, FAT, and CUSWA. However, they are quite significant because they reveal that variation in transnationalism outcomes within unions is possible. The data labor leaders offered about their weak or strained transnational relations not only provide a more complete picture of the history of NAFTA's effects on labor transnationalism but also help illuminate the variables and mechanisms that led to different outcomes.

Differences in Union Structure across the Continent

The structure of Mexican unions actually limits the possibility of greater contact because Mexico does not have *national* auto, garment/apparel, or trucking unions. In general, individual unions are organized by plant and affiliated to a labor federation such as the CTM. Nothing comparable to the UAW, CAW, UNITE, or IBT exists in Mexico. Some official labor federations also organize multiple plants under larger umbrella unions (e.g., multiple garment factories under a larger CTM garment workers union). A CTM garment union, however, generally does not cover all workers in the industry, and competes with its counterpart unions in the CROC, CROM, and other federations.

Although many U.S. and Canadian industrial unions are organizing beyond their original sectors (e.g., the CAW and UAW in service), it is less common for Mexican unions to do so because they are generally granted a legal right, or registration from the government (called a registro), to organize in a particular industry. Moreover, key industries such as autos are organized by plant. As many Mexican unionists explained, this structure prevents even Mexican unions in these industries from being in regular contact with each other. However, it also has significant consequences for cross-border collaboration because the UAW and CAW, for example, do not have one national Mexican auto union with which to work. Whereas in the United States and Canada *national* unions wield power in key industries, in Mexico this power is concentrated within the largest official union federations. This structure renders Mexican unions outside primary industries less relevant as potential counterparts for U.S. and Canadian unions that want to collaborate in a given industry.

The independent Mexican unions in the auto, garment/apparel, and trucking industries with which U.S. and Canadian unions initiated relationships therefore represent few workers and wield little power within their respective industries. When asked why there is a lack of solidarity among auto unions, one Mexican unionist said:

Fragmentation, just plain fragmentation. It's very difficult to establish contact with twenty different unions, really difficult. Which union is the important one, who should you contact, what for? So I think that's what has made it much more difficult.... In Mexico we have many different unions; for example, in the Ford factories we don't have one union, we have many unions."[1]

The UAW's Steve Beckman agreed: "One [problem] is certainly the lack of an auto union in Mexico, the lack of a centralized place where auto workers in the U.S. and auto workers in Mexico can talk with each other."[2]

Relations in the Pre-NAFTA Period with Official Mexican Unions

In the years prior to NAFTA's passage, U.S. and Canadian auto, garment/apparel, and trucking industry unions had few contacts with *any* Mexican unions. The two primary U.S. garment/apparel unions, the International Ladies' Garment Workers' Union (ILGWU) and the Amalgamated Clothing and Textile Workers Union (ACTWU) (which merged to form UNITE in 1995, which then merged with HERE to form UNITE HERE in 2004), made little effort to work with CTM garment/apparel unions.[3] The pre-NAFTA transnational contacts among North American garment unions were usually brief interactions at International Trade Secretariat meetings.[4] As Adolfo Gott, secretary general of the CTM textile union (which includes garment/apparel workers) and member of the CTM national executive committee, reported: "We are part of the International Federation of Textile Workers.... We haven't had much contact, but it is a contact with U.S. and Canadian unions. We have been involved with the International for more than twenty years and participate in the annual meetings."[5] A former Teamsters official commented

---

[1] Personal interview with Alicia Sepúlveda Núñez of the STRM, August 27, 2000.
[2] Personal interview with Steve Beckman of the UAW, December 19, 2000.
[3] The majority of unionized Canadian garment industry workers belong to UNITE. Almost all of their international work occurs through UNITE's main New York office.
[4] UNITE and its predecessors had stronger relations with unions in Central America and the Caribbean.
[5] Personal interview with Adolfo Gott Trujillo of the CTM, May 2, 2000.

on his union's history of transnational relations: "Ron Carey took office in February 1992. As far as I know, there had been no real contact before that between the national union and unions of any kind in Mexico – neither the government-dominated federations nor the few independent organizations."[6]

Pre-NAFTA contact among the UAW, CAW, and CTM auto unions largely followed the same pattern. Interaction usually occurred in the context of joint participation in the International Metalworkers Federation (an ITS). Because ITS rules only allowed certain unions to join the federation, very few Mexican unions participated. Thus, the UAW and CAW had limited contact with the majority of Mexican auto unions. As Steve Beckman, the UAW's former assistant director of the Governmental and International Affairs Department, explained:

So we've had relations with the CTM and Mexican unions for a long time. They've participated – some of the unions in Mexico have participated – in various meetings of the International Metalworkers Federation, company councils. The Ford Workers Union in Mexico is an affiliate of the International Metalworkers Federation. It's the largest Mexican affiliate; there aren't very many. None of the other auto unions are affiliated. So we've come into contact with them reasonably frequently, but we don't have much of a relationship with them.[7]

According to Beckman, the UAW tried to work with the CTM to create a national Mexican auto union in order to facilitate more contact and collaboration: "In 1966, Walter Reuther went down to Mexico, had a meeting with the CTM, at which time the CTM committed to creating a national auto union. And of course it never happened. So we've had relations with the CTM and Mexican unions for a long time."[8] Relations, however, are quite distinct from relationships.

Although the UAW remained cautiously removed from labor relations in Mexico before NAFTA, some UAW locals did not. The events during one auto struggle caused a rift in the relationship between the UAW and CTM that had not been fully repaired at the time of this writing. The struggle involved a group of workers at the Ford Cuautitlán plant outside Mexico City who, in 1987, attempted to oust the CTM union and create their own independent union at the plant. By 1990, the struggle had escalated, with frequent work stoppages and demonstrations in Mexico

[6] Personal communication with Matt Witt of the IBT.
[7] Personal interview with Steve Beckman of the UAW, December 19, 2000.
[8] Ibid.

City. In January 1990, a worker was killed and nine wounded by two hundred armed CTM strikebreakers who attempted to regain the plant, which had been taken over by the workers.

Members from UAW Local 879 (St. Paul), UAW Region 1A (Michigan), and the CAW supported the dissidents and provided them with financial support. Indeed many UAW members considered themselves dissidents as members of "New Directions," a caucus within the UAW that opposed many of the union's policies and strategies. They believed that grassroots and cross-border organizing in Mexico could improve the wages of Mexican and American workers (Armbruster 1998). Although the UAW did not embrace the activities of these locals, it did not openly criticize them. Steve Beckman explained the reasons for the UAW's lack of support for the Ford Cuautitlán dissidents:

The union has a very strained institutional relationship with the CTM, and this prevents the UAW from intervening in local union matters. The CTM and the UAW distrust each other, but we cannot interfere in local disputes. Cross-border organizing requires a set of opportunities that do not currently exist in Mexico. The UAW has its own set of priorities right now and cross-border organizing is among them, but it competes with other issues as well.[9]

Héctor de la Cueva, one of the organizers of the Ford Cuautitlán struggle, confirmed that the dissidents received no support from the UAW:

When we stopped the plant for many months, we were the objects of violence on the part of the state, and then we began to develop relationships with auto workers in the U.S. and Canada, especially with a UAW local in St. Paul, Minnesota, and with the CAW. They displayed a lot of solidarity. We had meetings with auto workers. At that time there had not been many changes in the United States in terms of unions. . . . It was hard to obtain direct support from the UAW because of its official relationship with the CTM. Therefore most of the support we received was from locals. We had a more direct relationship with the CAW. We had many meetings, exchanges together.[10]

Beckman and de la Cueva's comments suggest that the UAW leadership was concerned with antagonizing the CTM, its only official partner at the time.

Although the evidence suggests the UAW did not support the Ford Cuautitlán dissidents, CTM leaders believed the powerful auto union had secretly done so. The comments of Juan José Sosa Arreola, who

[9] Quoted in Armbruster (1998, p. 34).
[10] Personal interview with Héctor de la Cueva of CILAS, July 22, 1999.

became secretary general of the CTM Ford union during the struggle, reveal a deep distrust of the UAW:

Before the [problems] Ford had the best contract in the auto industry. So the problem could not have been because of labor conditions. The reason was real; it was political. And there was support, financial support, from American unions. I was told they were American locals, but I understand that the locals had relations with the head of the whole union. So maybe they [got involved] in order to judge us, insult us, or try to manipulate us.[11]

The events at Ford Cuautitlán had significant implications for labor transnationalism among auto unions. According to one AFL-CIO official: "On the one hand I think . . . there was a failure, and I'm not really certain why that occurred several years ago at Ford Cuautitlán. And I know that the UAW was very put off by their experience. And the CTM also suspected UAW involvement in their internal affairs."[12] The problems generated by the Ford Cuautitlán struggle would reverberate for years to come.

NAFTA and Contention with the CTM and Its Unions

NAFTA most profoundly affected relations among the AFL-CIO, CLC, and CTM. As discussed previously, differences over NAFTA led the two northern federations to secretly seek out independent Mexican union counterparts during the agreement's negotiation. The AFL-CIO's decision to officially and publicly end exclusivity with the CTM in 1998, however, generated outrage even though the AFL-CIO remained committed to maintaining relations with the CTM. An AFL-CIO leader explained: "I mean I guess the metaphor might be . . . we've been dating for fifty years and we told them it was time that we both saw other people."[13] A high-ranking CTM official offered these sentiments when asked what kind of relationship the CTM has with the AFL-CIO:

Good, they have sometimes preferred other groups . . . such as with the UNT, with the FAT through Bertha Luján. They have been having a lot of influence; they are antagonistic toward us. [The AFL-CIO] has given them space and listened to them and have invited them to meetings. And this has been part of the objective of the CTM's protest, this attitude of the AFL. . . . In these pluralistic times you

[11] Personal interview with Juan José Sosa Arreola of the CTM, August 24, 2000.
[12] Personal interview with AFL-CIO official, 2000.
[13] Ibid.

have to look for everyone. We recognize this; the only thing is we feel injured because we were the only and suddenly they are looking for alliances with other people.[14]

With the end of exclusivity came the end of private criticism. In 1998, the crack in the foundation of the AFL-CIO–CTM relation became a deep fissure when John Sweeney visited Mexico. In a speech delivered at the National Autonomous University of Mexico, he indirectly criticized the CTM for its support of NAFTA and government privatization efforts. Four years after NAFTA went into force, AFL-CIO leaders still felt the sting of the CTM's pro-NAFTA blow.

NAFTA proved to be profoundly divisive not only for North America's largest union federations but also for the federations' affiliate unions in the garment/apparel, auto, and trucking industries. Most official Mexican garment/apparel union representatives viewed NAFTA as beneficial to their industry. As the CTM's national garment/apparel union leader argued:

NAFTA, from my point of view, came to open the market for the textile industry. If there hadn't been NAFTA, Mexico would be losing jobs in the industry. Twenty years ago about eighty percent of [what was produced in Mexico] was sold in Mexico, and fifteen percent was exported. Today eighty percent is exported and twenty percent is sold here. I therefore think NAFTA has benefited the national textile industry.[15]

Official Mexican auto unions also believed NAFTA would bring more jobs to Mexico. And because jobs in auto factories were some of the highest paid in Mexico, they unequivocally supported NAFTA's passage. This caused tensions to flare once again among the continent's largest auto unions. As the UAW's Steve Beckman described:

So the situation before NAFTA is [an] effort to establish common ground without finding much. The CTM wasn't particularly interested. They weren't very internationally oriented. Their major relationship was with the government, not with the international labor movement. And so we didn't have much going on. As NAFTA was being discussed, I'd say we were in meetings with some of the CTM unions; they took the government's position, there wasn't much basis for working together.[16]

---

[14] Personal interview with José Ramírez Gamero of the CTM, August 23, 2000.
[15] Personal interview with Adolfo Gott Trujillo of the CTM, May 2, 2000.
[16] Personal interview with Steve Beckman of the UAW, December 19, 2000.

Beckman described one contentious meeting with the CTM in 1992:

In 1992 there was a Latin American auto workers meeting in Brazil and there were general discussions but there was also a session where the regional groups got together. So the UAW and CAW and Mexican unions got together. And the Mexican representatives at that meeting were José Sosa from the Ford workers union [and] Juan Moisés Calleja, who's a lawyer for the CTM who I think is a CTM official now. He did all the talking. . . . And it was clear he had no time for us: "You are wasting our time sitting here, we disagree with you fundamentally with everything related to economic integration, so why don't you just leave us alone?" So that was the kind of interaction we would have with them. Not union-to-union on specific issues, but in any kind of arena in which we got thrown together. They just didn't have any interest in us; we didn't have any real basis for discussions with them, so there really wasn't much contact.[17]

Juan José Sosa Arreola, a UAW critic during the Ford Cuautitlán struggle, also remembered the meeting. As he explained how NAFTA became an additional source of tension between the two unions, it became apparent that his recollection was quite consistent with Beckman's:

They have always discussed NAFTA a lot. They want us to accept certain conditions that aren't good for our industry. I remember in 1992 . . . we were in São Paulo at a meeting of the International Federation of Metal Workers, and Steve Beckman of the UAW was there, and we discussed the situation with him. I said our worry here in Mexico is jobs, the need for jobs. And especially jobs like in the auto industry that are among the best there are. And they were looking for our support to go against NAFTA, and we said it was not possible, that our central [the CTM] had marked a very strict line about this. And don Fidel Velázquez said what we needed were jobs, and to assist in [creating conditions for jobs].[18]

The CAW also made overtures toward the CTM during the NAFTA struggle, but like the UAW, their efforts were not terribly well received. The CAW's Sam Gindin explained:

We had one really significant high-profile delegation that went soon after Buzz [Basil Hargrove] became president . . . in 1993 or '94. We were going to talk about the free trade agreements. We met with the CTM, we met with . . . don Fidel, and his second in command. And we met with . . . whoever we could. . . . They were incredibly suspicious about the Americans . . . the CTM particularly. . . . So Fidel was meeting with us I think partly because I think to him it was a way of a slap in the face to the Americans to meet with us. So I think he was using us, and I don't think he was very open to our arguments.[19]

[17] Personal interview with Steve Beckman of the UAW, December 19, 2000.
[18] Personal interview with Juan José Sosa Arreola of the CTM, August 24, 2000.
[19] Personal interview with Sam Gindin of the CAW, February 14, 2001.

The inability and reluctance of North America's auto unions to find common ground despite their differences in opinion over NAFTA only perpetuated the distrust that had characterized their relations for decades.

Constituting National Actors and Interests in NAFTA's Wake

During the NAFTA battle, relations among U.S. and Canadian unions and their official Mexican counterparts stagnated and their contacts and interactions were laced with suspicion rather than trust. NAFTA did little to inspire CTM union leaders to develop interests in common with northern unions. In its zeal to see NAFTA pass, the federation infused its strategic rhetoric with nationalistic overtones. And although the UAW and UNITE called for North American labor solidarity, their desperate efforts to preserve what they defined as "American" jobs often made their calls sound specious and ingenuine. One official Mexican union leader put it succinctly when asked how U.S. and Canadian unionists see their Mexican counterparts: "They view Latinos as enemies, as the ones who take their jobs."[20] Clearly, NAFTA's effects on catalyzing relationships were not consistent across the continent.

The Cold War legacy infused these relations with a tension palpable in the words of Juan José Sosa Arreola, who, when asked why his union does not have transnational relations with U.S. or Canadian auto unions, responded:

They judge our union to be antidemocratic, other things that people utilize when they don't like a circumstance. So with all respect I say to my compañeros in Canada and the United States, and the whole world, my country is my country. And the rules of my country are the rules of my country. . . . For many years I have seen the same leaders leading the CAW and UAW, so I ask where is democracy, or is it really effective? I can ask this. And I have the right to ask this. What I want from them is to be respectful of me, which is what I am giving them. If they look for alternatives that permit an interrelation as members of the same industry, interested in a labor all over the world, not just in North America, then we understand this and are willing to listen to ideas. To listen to ideas, not accept mandates. And many times they want to control and subject us to their conditions. This has been a problem that has prevented relations, both with Canadians and Americans.[21]

Sosa's attitude reflects a deeper mistrust of the UAW and CAW as a result of the events at Ford Cuautitlán, but other CTM officials offered

---

[20] Personal interview with David Téllez García, May 5, 2000.
[21] Personal interview with Juan José Sosa Arreola, August 24, 2000.

similar, though less strident, views. According to a leader of a national CTM textile union:

We want to continue our relations but national sovereignty must also be respected in each country because it would be bad if I were a conquistador of workers in the U.S. and very bad if unions in the U.S. came to Mexico without respecting our unions' sovereignty. If we respect each others' sovereignty we can have great alliances and play an important role in each of our countries.[22]

CTM leaders also perceive that their potential northern allies are simply concerned with keeping jobs in the United States. That is, many believe they are motivated by self-interest rather than mutual interest. CTM leader Juan José Sosa echoed the point:

Above all else I think what motivates them is the protection of their own labor conditions. What they look for, which I think is reasonable and a common desire, and I would do the same, is to protect their own market. . . . If they come and tell us we should earn so much because they do, the plant will close. And where will the work go? If I respect you, the only thing that I wish is that you respect me. And if I want my coffee hot, that's how I want it, even if you say, you're going to burn yourself. If I burn myself, I burn myself, let me! There are healthy concepts, universal ideas, and different interests, of Americans, Canadians, and Mexicans, and they defend their own interests.[23]

Clearly, Sosa does not construct his interests in common with those of his U.S. and Canadian counterparts. When asked if North American auto unions have common interests, he quipped: "Yes, but limited."[24] The FAT's Antonio Villalba revealed that official union leaders accuse him and the FAT of being puppets of the AFL-CIO. He recounts how, when he attends meetings and criticizes NAFTA, they tell him: "No, you are pro-yanqui, you're pro-AFL-CIO, you are gringo unions, because obviously the gringo unions are protecting their industries, they want the jobs to stay there, and so you are playing the gringos' game."[25] Jaime Lira, the secretary general of a CTM auto parts union, suggested that although North American auto unions have some common interests, they are a long way from identifying with each other in a meaningful way: "I don't think there is much international solidarity in the auto industry. There are intentions to, but really there are none. We see that there are

[22] Personal interview with Mario Alberto Sánchez Mondragón, July 7, 2000.
[23] Personal interview with Juan José Sosa Arreola, August 24, 2000.
[24] Ibid.
[25] Personal interview with Antonio Villalba Granados of the FAT, July 10, 2000.

different spaces through which we could identify but still there is not total identification."[26]

Instead of viewing transnational relationships as a way to forge common interests, many official Mexican unionists viewed them as utilitarian or instrumental (i.e., as a way for U.S. and Canadian unions to share valuable technology with Mexican unions). As the head of one official union answered when asked what his ideal vision for labor transnationalism would be:

To know about technology and new machines and training. We have two totally different worlds, and we need to reach their level. An exchange of experiences would be good; good for them, too. Each country is protecting its own, and that's obvious, so we want to know what is going on. We need understanding; more than help and collaboration we need information so that we are harmed as little as possible.[27]

An official with the CTM Nissan union reported that sharing technological information was the extent of his international contacts: "We still don't have contacts with U.S. and Canadian unions. We have some contact with Japanese unions. We went to look at new models."[28] Representatives of official Mexican auto unions often emphasized the limitations of labor transnationalism. Many balked at the idea of negotiating collective contracts across borders, and one official unionist emphatically responded when asked if he would support collective North American contracts: "No. We are too different. The economic situation is too different. We are not equal in our circumstances. We need to improve things in our country through our own laws, not create more problems."[29]

Although official Mexican unionists reveal a limited vision for transnational relationships, it is clear that U.S. and Canadian unions also lack a clear vision. A UNITE official admitted that his union's lack of sustained contact with Mexican unions is problematic:

I think probably on our side of the thing – I'll speak for UNITE now – I think we've been a bit erratic in the way we've tried to reach out and develop programs. I mean we're sort of crisis driven. We've got a plant that closes and it's got a subsidiary in Mexico, [and] we try to contact people there to find out what's going on there . . . so we need to be more proactive in how we relate to Mexico.[30]

---

[26] Personal interview with Jaime Lira of the CTM, July 27, 2000.
[27] Personal interview with David Téllez García, May 5, 2000.
[28] Personal interview with Agustín Salvat Moya, July 28, 2000.
[29] Personal interview with Fermín Lara Jiménez, May 11, 2000.
[30] Personal interview with Alan Howard of UNITE, December 15, 2000.

UNITE's tendency to run to the border when a problem emerges, instead of forging more permanent transnational relationships, alienates Mexican unions. According to Mexican labor educator and activist Carlos García, U.S. and Canadian garment/apparel unions have not pushed transnational relationships with official Mexican unions but rather ephemeral cross-border contacts:

I don't see big obstacles to international solidarity, I see difficulties that need to be resolved. It is a process that needs to be done step by step, and the first step is communication. Second, prepare an agenda. Third step, revise the agenda, and then try to create forms and strategies in common in order to improve the living conditions of all workers and eliminate social dumping. This is not happening now, this process. There are not possibilities of approaching each other now. U.S. unions come here to see what's going on, they visit some plants and unions, and then they leave. So they don't sit down for two or three days and talk about possibilities, create an agenda, and start to work on it. This isn't happening.[31]

The accuracy of García's evaluation of the state of labor transnationalism is demonstrated by a February 2000 UNITE delegation that met with Mexican labor leaders in Mexico City. A UNITE official described the meeting in quite positive terms:

And last February a UNITE delegation went to Mexico, met with the leadership with all the Labor Congress unions.... It was a cordial meeting; it was a constructive meeting in the sense that avenues of cooperation were opened with all these official unions. In other words, we have a policy of, wherever possible, we will work with these official unions in the interest of our members, their members, wherever that can work. We're involved in exchange of information programs in different levels, in different ways with several of these unions now, you know, sending newspapers and occasional correspondence and things like that.[32]

For Adolfo Gott, leader of the CTM garment union the UNITE delegation visited, the meeting did not appear to be extremely memorable. When I questioned him about the meeting three months after it occurred, he remembered that a U.S. union delegation had visited him recently but could not recall when or what union until he searched through the papers on his desk and found the meeting agenda. He then commented: "With UNITE. They came in February. We talked with them about the problems they have, about plants that close there and come here. And what we

---

[31] Personal interview with Carlos García Villanueva, coordinator of the Union Education Program, Friedrich Ebert Foundation, May 2, 2000.
[32] Personal interview with Alan Howard of UNITE, December 15, 2000.

demand is that there are good working conditions."³³ But when asked if relations with other North American unions would be useful, the CTM leader replied:

I don't think so. Only to talk and share impressions, friendly relations, because the U.S. has its own law, we have ours, so it would be really difficult to get together and do anything to help workers, since we are each under our own laws.... It's better to work through the International [Trade Secretariat], have a conversation and discuss conditions in the different countries.³⁴

Gott's vision of transnationalism resembles the pre-NAFTA model of labor diplomacy.

U.S. and Canadian auto unions did not expand the pre-NAFTA model with their official counterparts despite CAW leaders' more expansive vision of transnationalism. The CAW's Sam Gindin described his efforts to push an "ambitious initiative" to organize North American auto parts plants. As Gindin explained, the CAW's vision was not matched by its southern counterpart, the UAW:

What I suggested was that we have a Canada-U.S.-Mexico initiative to organize key parts plants. And the message we would send out was we're not going to try to organize them, we are *going* to organize them. Whether it takes ten years or not, we're going to create chaos until we organize them. So there's a message partly to the Big Three that there's going to be chaos unless you actually tell them they should stop fighting the union, and it was a message to the parts companies. And by doing it simultaneously, they couldn't play us off by saying we'll move jobs. And part of the analysis was that the market is really regional.... So Buzz [Hargrove, CAW president] proposed this to [UAW President Stephen] Yokich. And it took a long time to even get an answer back and it was one of those strained answers, I mean you know you think it'd be obvious and something to get excited about, and one of those answers of well thank you and we'll look into it but it raises a number of questions which we have to investigate. So it wasn't a no, but it was as good as a no, because if you're not enthusiastic you're not going to do anything.... We could have hosted a conference and just invited everybody, and if the CTM didn't come, they just would lose from it, we'd say we're going to work with whoever comes. And it wouldn't matter if the CTM wasn't in it; we'd organize with others. So there would be money involved. We'd be working with Mexicans, it wouldn't be imperialist and it would work. So we could have done it. We could have resolved any problems; in fact we could have used the [tactic] to get some of the Mexican locals and unions together. So that's one problem that the Americans have been in the way of.³⁵

³³ Personal interview with Adolfo Gott Trujillo of the CTM, May 2, 2000.
³⁴ Ibid.
³⁵ Personal interview with Sam Gindin of the CAW, February 14, 2001.

Whereas the CAW saw that trinational cooperation with independent and official Mexican unions was possible and could undermine corporations' ability to pit North American auto workers against each other, the UAW did not identify fully as a regional actor with North American interests. And the lack of support from the UAW – the most powerful auto union on the continent – stymied cooperative efforts across North America.

The Teamsters' Cross-Border Trucking Campaign

While the acrimony among U.S. and Canadian auto unions and their official Mexican counterparts smoldered, it exploded between unions in the trucking industry, and NAFTA provided the spark. The agreement caused a serious conflict between the IBT (which has U.S. and Canadian members) and CTM trucking unions, whose leaders did not see eye to eye on NAFTA's Chapter 12, which outlined an ambitious goal for North America: the free movement of surface transportation carriers across all borders. Although the majority of union leaders in the transnational trade-negotiating field eschewed racist responses to NAFTA, the Teamsters' campaign against Chapter 12 is widely regarded as the most notorious exception. The Teamsters case is also important, however, because it provides the most compelling example of collective censure in response to what were perceived as racist discursive strategies – and it is largely missing from the historiography.

Mexican trucking unions supported NAFTA and Chapter 12. As the CTM's secretary of transportation, Juan Carlos Velasco, argued: "We've got NAFTA, so the CTM's position is that NAFTA be respected."[36] The Teamsters vehemently opposed the agreement and did all it could to stop its passage and implementation. Union leaders feared Chapter 12's implementation would drive down labor, environmental, and safety standards across the continent. IBT President Ron Carey (who took over the Teamsters' leadership in February 1992 and remained until 1998) and his staff put together a comprehensive campaign to kill Chapter 12.[37] As Andy Banks, international representative of the Teamsters president, who was assigned to work out of the office of strategic campaigns, explained: "The Teamsters probably did more to fight NAFTA than any

---

[36] Personal interview with Juan Carlos Velasco of the CTM, August 30, 2000.
[37] Carey served as IBT president, winning reelection in 1996. In 1998, James P. Hoffa took over the presidency.

other union.... The fight against NAFTA was a core fight in the union. Early on it consolidated a lot of the strength and support of the Carey people. It became a major project of the union."[38] The IBT's Matt Witt confirmed that the union did not attempt to find common ground with the CTM or other official unions: "The Teamsters did not reach out to the government-dominated unions, simply not seeing it as a good use of time given their lack of independence from their corporate-controlled government and given that they were actively lobbying for the NAFTA that the corporations wanted."[39]

A resolution passed by the IBT General Executive Board on April 27, 1992, made it clear that it viewed NAFTA as a threat to workers in all three nations. It resolved to work with U.S. and Canadian progressive coalitions to oppose the free trade agreement and "arrange meetings between labor organizations in the affected countries in order to protect jobs in the U.S. and Canada, raise the living standard in Mexico and the Caribbean Basin, and defend the rights of workers in all nations."[40] In the resolution, the IBT also committed to "seek to develop contacts with labor unions and other organizations in Mexico which also oppose the North American Free Trade Agreement in order to coordinate lobbying efforts and to support organizing and collective bargaining by workers at the Mexican operations of U.S. and Canadian companies."[41] The campaign involved intense lobbying, public education, and grassroots organizing. The Teamsters also mobilized against Chapter 12 by filing a lawsuit to stymie the first stage of the implementation process, which would allow Mexican trucks to move freely among four U.S. border states. With support from highway safety and environmental organizations, the Teamsters convinced the Clinton administration to delay the implementation of Chapter 12.

The Teamsters relied on two key arguments against NAFTA and Chapter 12: the agreement would result in the loss of U.S. and Canadian jobs, and Mexican trucks threatened U.S. and Canadian health, safety, and environmental standards. Teamsters officials contend that the union made a conscious effort not to scapegoat Mexican workers and pushed

---

[38] Personal interview with Andy Banks of IBT, January 10, 2001.

[39] Personal communication with Matt Witt of the IBT.

[40] "Resolution of the General Executive Board: North American Free Trade Agreement," International Brotherhood of Teamsters, April 27, 1992.

[41] "Resolution of the General Executive Board: North American Free Trade Agreement," International Brotherhood of Teamsters, April 27, 1992.

an internationalist response to the agreement. As a former IBT official explained:

And the internationalist response, which was consistently taken by the Teamsters International union under Carey, is that we want trade policies that raise standards for everyone. You can find that internationalist response consistently throughout the Carey years in Teamster communications with the public, the union's members, and elected officials. Carey and the national union said over and over that Mexican workers were not the enemy, that the corporate vision of NAFTA wouldn't help workers on either side of the border, and that NAFTA should be renegotiated to raise standards for workers in all three countries.[42]

An examination of official Teamsters documents confirms these claims; union newspaper articles usually called for the need to improve wages and safety standards in Mexico. A 1992 article in *The New Teamster* proclaimed: "We have to help workers in Mexico improve their working conditions and living standards in order to protect our own."[43] An anti-NAFTA video titled "NAFTA: The Wrong Road for the Future" (1993b) featured President Carey explaining:

Our fight isn't with Mexican truck drivers; we both want the same thing – an agreement that raises wages and safety standards in Mexico instead of lowering them here. . . . We can do better than NAFTA; we can start over on a fair trade agreement that would raise labor and environmental standards and protect the rights of working people on both sides of the border. That's how you expand trade for everyone's benefit. That's the right road for the future.[44]

A more systematic examination of the Teamsters' anti-NAFTA rhetoric reveals that the vast majority of official IBT documents pushed an internationalist perspective (Borgers 1999). According to Borgers, who coded and analyzed IBT documents:

While causal attributions to Mexico dominate those to the U.S., the heavy emphasis on broad safety concerns and causal attributions to U.S. corporations compared to the relatively light references to U.S. job losses and causal attributions to Mexican drivers/workers indicate the creation of significant ideological breadth and political space for alliance building. . . . In many ways, the Teamsters campaign against NAFTA and the trucking provisions represents a very

---

[42] Personal communication with Matt Witt, formerly of the IBT.
[43] *The New Teamster*, December 1992b, p. 6.
[44] As quoted in Borgers (1999).

noteworthy, and in many ways ground-breaking, attempt to create an internationalist identity.[45]

As Borgers points out, despite union leaders' efforts to promote a trade agreement that would benefit North American workers, many NGO activists considered the Teamsters' rhetoric to be quite offensive. My data reveal that many U.S., Canadian, and Mexican unionists also found it problematic. They specifically interpreted two claims the Teamsters made as offensive or even racist: that Mexican truck drivers were potentially unsafe and that Chapter 12 would facilitate illegal drug smuggling into the United States. For example, an article that appeared in the December 1993 issue of *The New Teamster* titled "NAFTA: License to Kill" described how easy it was for unqualified truckers to obtain Mexican federal driver's licenses.[46] An IBT official explained the use of the rhetoric:

U.S. truckers had to meet strict requirements for a commercial driver's license, and yet U.S. companies would be free to now use drivers from Mexico who didn't. U.S. trucks had to have front brakes that Mexican trucks did not. Those were real threats to public safety, and the union said they should be dealt with by renegotiating the trucking part of NAFTA to raise standards for all instead of lowering them. The union was consistently explicit that this was not an attack on trucks or on drivers because they were Mexican but rather a call to use NAFTA to improve safety and environmental conditions, not undermine them. In the same way, the drug trafficking issue was real. Bringing 10,000 more trucks per day across the border, virtually none of which could possibly be inspected, would in fact make it easier for traffickers, something which would hardly benefit the public interest in either country. That didn't mean that Mexicans were all drug traffickers or somehow responsible for drug use in the U.S. But it would be hard to argue that it would be a good development for working people or good public policy.[47]

The official pointed out that these claims were usually coupled with a call to improve conditions throughout North America. Indeed, on the page opposite the "NAFTA: License to Kill" article appeared an article demanding fair trade that would raise wages and environmental and safety standards in Mexico.[48]

The data suggest, however, that the racially charged safety and drug trafficking rhetoric eclipsed the internationalist aspects of the message –

---

[45] Borgers (1999, p. 25).
[46] *The New Teamster*. 1993a. "NAFTA: License to Kill." December, p. 14.
[47] Personal communication with Matt Witt, formerly of the IBT.
[48] *The New Teamster*. 1993c. "NAFTA: Fair Trade is Our Alternative." December, p. 15.

even for labor activists who agreed that the Teamsters raised some legitimate safety concerns in the Mexican trucking industry. As one Mexican labor academic explained:

The truckers here don't have good working conditions. . . . It's true that the truckers here are not adequately trained. . . . Of course there's a problem that the agreement was signed, but the working conditions need to be condemned. I think they could reach an agreement with discussion. What I am against is racism just because they are Mexican. But I'm not against the Teamsters defending what they've worked so hard to get.[49]

Many independent *and* official Mexican labor leaders accused the Teamsters of relying on racial stereotypes to propel their campaign. When asked what he believed motivated the Teamsters' cross-border trucking position, one CTM official explained:

Besides racism it is fear that they will lose part of the economic control they have with the companies because they have such power that things are only moved that they authorize, and what they don't authorize doesn't get moved. No one else can enter. They feel they'll be displaced but we think there's enough work for everyone. Just like they enter our country and don't notice that they are displacing us.[50]

An official of an independent union expressed even greater disdain for the Teamsters' rhetoric:

If they demand open borders for American trucks to come into Mexico we should have reciprocity. And I didn't like the arguments. I thought that they were very racist and that's when I draw the line. I don't like racist arguments about Mexican truckers being drug dealers almost. And about Mexican trucks being dirty and unsafe and a hazard on the American highways. Because it isn't always true, it's a very racist picture and it just isn't correct. I understand the Teamsters wanting to protect their jobs. I respect that. But I didn't like the way they demanded concessions from the American government and the arguments they used. I find them deeply offending, very untrue in many cases, and I think I go back to what I have said before that I think that we can find ways to protect our jobs and to find ways that make both the Teamsters in the United States and Mexican truckers here in Mexico get better working conditions and advance their own demands without using [those kinds] of arguments and pressures against the governments.[51]

The interpretation of the Teamsters' rhetoric as racist was not limited to Mexican labor activists. Progressive U.S. and Canadian labor activists

---

[49] Personal interview with Graciela Bensusán, June 26, 2000.
[50] Personal interview with José Ramírez Gamero of the CTM, August 23, 2000.
[51] Personal interview with Alicia Sepúlveda Núñez of the STRM, August 27, 2000.

also saw the Teamsters' rhetoric as laced with racist overtones. An AFL-CIO official expressed his thoughts on the Teamsters' strategy:

Well I think certainly putting a picket line at the border[52] is not a good way to handle it because it's not going to elicit a positive response on [the Mexican] side of the border and it's going to be detrimental ultimately to the cause. So I would say, yeah, that they've made some mistakes tactically. And I think the way I would have liked to have seen it handled is by building a relationship between the Teamsters union and Mexican transport workers.[53]

The executive vice president of the CLC described a panel he participated on with an IBT representative:

And I remember him making the comment that if they had a free trade agreement it would mean Mexican truck drivers would start entering the U.S. And he said Mexican trucks don't even have front wheel brakes. And he said not only that; there's all kinds of drug problems in the U.S. And some very disparaging comments [were] made, and that was the essence of his presentation. It wasn't about what I believe the agreement was about, and really debate what this was about. And [I] felt obligated to take him on and I said I'm deeply disturbed and incensed by the comment that's been made here today that this [is] somehow about trucks having front wheel brakes and about drugs. And it's really ignorant to suggest it's anything about that. . . . It's not about front wheel brakes, and we're certainly not having a debate about NAFTA because of drugs. There's always been a drug problem; maybe we should debate the American desire to consume drugs. But it was very sad because the general state of debating in the U.S. I think at the time among some trade unionists was to say disparaging and racist things against Mexican workers rather than put the issue in its true context and say to the American people it's about the rights of our citizens versus the rights of corporations.[54]

When asked why he believed the Teamsters' anti-NAFTA rhetoric was perceived by so many as racist, an IBT official explained:

Clearly, some corporate interests and their PRI-CTM allies used it to fight the anti-NAFTA movement. Just as clearly, there were some Mexican allies of the Teamsters who found the highway safety and drug arguments offensive because of their legitimate feelings growing out of U.S.-Mexican history. While many

---

[52] Some local IBT members protested Chapter 12 by setting up pickets at the U.S.-Mexican border.

[53] Personal interview with AFL-CIO official, 2000.

[54] Personal interview with Hassan Yussuff of the CLC, February 28, 2001. Mr. Yussuff did not identify the IBT representative or specify whether he represented the International, a local affiliate, or was an IBT member.

progressives in the U.S. and Canada worked closely with the union, there were some who thought those arguments fed into anti-immigrant feeling.[55]

The Teamsters' Andy Banks had a similar explanation. He attributed the perception of the union's strategy as racist to its rhetorical focus on Mexican truckers, the actions of rogue affiliates, and Mexican corporate interests. He explained that although the intention of the Teamsters' campaign was not to promulgate a racist rhetoric, it was interpreted by many that way, and it did not help the Teamsters' cause:

I mean my God . . . there should be so much solidarity on this, but we set the tone badly. And so we didn't focus on the companies, and we focused on each other. . . . I mean you can't control rallies, right? You have rallies at the border that we organized, and you get one member saying one racist thing, even though it's not the policy; our ralliests would say don't do it. That is going to be front page headlines in the pro-business press in Mexico. Okay, . . . they have this sort of right wing anti-imperialist line that's pro-NAFTA there, the business press. We don't have alternative press like that, so you can use a very revolutionary rhetoric to be very right wing there . . . very pro-corporations. So they would do that brilliantly about the evil racist pig Teamsters, you know? So this was an issue.[56]

It could also be argued that the Teamsters' rhetoric changed after Carey and his staff left the union in 1998. Many official publications focused more heavily on highway safety and drug trafficking issues after Carey's departure. A 1999 issue of *Teamster* titled "The NAFTA Trucker: Crossing the Line" included four articles. One featured an "exclusive investigative report on Mexican truckers" and quoted a U.S. drug enforcement officer: "With Mexican truckers, we have a double whammy – not only are they screwing us by bringing in more dope, but there is the matter of truck safety. They fix things with bubble gum and tape."[57] The three other articles used the following alarmist titles: "Fighting the Mexican Truck Invasion"; "Report Says Mexican Trucks Unsafe"; and "Caution! Mexican Trucks To Enter U.S. Highways: The Real Y2K Problem."[58] The former began with the sentence: "January 1, 2000: The new century begins and a new plague awaits U.S. motorists."[59]

---

[55] Personal communication with Matt Witt, formerly of the IBT.
[56] Personal interview with Andy Banks of the IBT, January 10, 2001.
[57] Bowden (1999, p. 4).
[58] *Teamster*, 1999, pp. 6–8.
[59] Ibid.

According to an IBT official who worked in the union's Legislative Affairs Department, the decision to focus on these issues was instrumental, based on political efficacy and expediency: "But the urgency of the situation did not lend itself at the time to putting together the kind of solidarity campaign and organizing strategies, etc., that we think might be effective. We didn't have time. Maybe it was just we gotta get people to pay attention to us. What's the quickest and easiest way to do that?"[60] He explained that, in the United States, safety issues resonated with the public and in the halls of Congress:

To keep the border closed there had to be some evidence of highway safety issues. The Department of Transportation was not going to recommend to the President that we place this moratorium on cross border trucking because the Teamsters or anybody else were threatened by low-wage Mexican drivers. The threat to highway safety was the point that had to be made to have that happen.[61]

Although the IBT strategy forestalled the implementation of Chapter 12, it did little to build trust among Mexican trucking unions.

NAFTA and Relationship Building with Independent Mexican Unions

The Power of Transnational Fields: The Case of the Janus-Faced Teamsters

The case of the Teamsters' anti-NAFTA campaign does not end with Chapter 12. Indeed, what makes it so compelling is the Janus-faced nature of the union and its activities. While the union waged its battle against Chapter 12 and promulgated a rhetoric many found objectionable, it simultaneously engaged in concrete collaborative activities with Mexican unions through its participation in Mexico-U.S. Dialogos and subsequently with anti-NAFTA coalitions. The transnational trade-negotiating field therefore provided an opportunity for contact and interaction between the Teamsters and independent Mexican unions such as the FAT. The IBT's Andy Banks described why the FAT was identified as a potential partner:

I think they hired some staff people that already had relationships with the FAT before the Carey administration came in, and so those people brought those relationships. . . . I know one person, for example, a very good person, he actually spent a year working with the FAT in Mexico, like a year or two before he was hired. . . . At the time – let's say prior to '92, let's say '90 – the FAT was like the

---

[60] Personal interview with IBT official, 2001.
[61] Ibid.

only glimmer of even a hope . . . so if trade unionists were going to develop a relationship in Mexico, they were the ones you were going to develop a relationship with.[62]

Matt Witt described the union's efforts to build relationships with independent unions during the NAFTA struggle:

Under Carey, the union moved immediately to change [the lack of relationships], reaching out right away to independent unionists who had a common interest in fighting for a different kind of trade agreement that would benefit workers and not just corporations. . . . Eventually, FAT was able to identify trucking union leaders with whom there was some possibility of cooperation, and the Teamsters eagerly took advantage of that and met with them, together with Canadian truckers, to identify common interests.[63]

As the FAT and Teamsters participated in joint anti-NAFTA actions, their fledgling relationship developed. In August 1992, the Teamsters asked the FAT to send a representative to the United States to participate in a "California Caravan" to traverse the state and push the anti–free trade message. In September, the FAT's Raúl Márquez joined the three-week caravan. A December 1992 article in *The New Teamster* quoted the message Márquez gave to gathered crowds that met the caravan along its route: "We don't want to be used as international scabs. . . . We want to work with you to win good jobs for everyone."[64] According to the article: "Márquez told reporters at each caravan stop that his organization opposes the 'free trade' agreement and supports increased cooperation between unions in the U.S., Mexico, and Canada."[65]

The Teamsters' Matt Witt described the union's support for the FAT:

We started working whenever we could with FAT. Whenever they had people getting fired or other things, we would try to do publicity. A bunch of Teamsters went to an office of GE in Boston and held a fairly militant protest over the fact that someone who was trying [to form] a FAT union had been fired by GE.[66]

In NAFTA's wake, the Teamsters helped fund the UE and FAT's Education Center and Labor Workshop (CETLAC) in Ciudad Juárez and participated in various NAO cases.

By the time NAFTA went into effect in 1994, the Teamsters had developed a significant amount of trust with the FAT. The strength of the

---

[62] Personal interview with Andy Banks of the IBT, January 10, 2001.
[63] Personal communication with Matt Witt of the IBT.
[64] *The New Teamster*, December 1992b, p. 6.
[65] Ibid.
[66] Personal interview with Matt Witt of the IBT, January 17, 2001.

relationship between the two unions is perhaps best reflected by FAT leaders' honesty in criticizing certain elements of the Teamsters' campaign against Chapter 12 as racist. A FAT official explained:

There are racist elements in some of them. I couldn't say for sure that was the official position of the union.... But some of them are racist positions that are totally questionable. When we were in the struggle against NAFTA we criticized some of them: that the main reason the border should not be opened was that Mexican drivers were drunk and incompetent, that they were corrupt, that they obtained their licenses illegally, that they were not professional people. In the end these were their arguments. Obviously we were not in agreement with this. Not all Mexican workers are drunk, but also there are many U.S. workers with these problems.[67]

The FAT was not the only union to read the IBT the riot act over its Chapter 12 strategy. At a February 1996 trinational Mexico-U.S. Dialogos meeting convened in Cuernavaca, Mexico, participants criticized three IBT representatives for some of the union's cross-border trucking rhetoric. The UE's Robin Alexander recalled the meeting:

I remember very very clearly that there were some representatives of the Teamsters who came and were absolutely blown away by the fact that people whom they considered friends were very critical of their positions on the whole trucking question and how it was being presented. And I mean they were shocked. They had no idea that they were doing something offensive.... They were very harshly criticized at that meeting.[68]

IBT's Andy Banks described the experience of being on the receiving end of his colleagues' ire at the meeting:

I went over with two other Teamsters... and for about two of the three days we got the shit beaten out of us for what we were doing about Mexican drivers.... We sat and took the beating, and said this is not what we're about. We're going to make some changes when we go back. We were able to get some retractions done, and stuff like that.[69]

The events in Cuernavaca that Banks described are extraordinary for three reasons. First, that labor activists from all three NAFTA countries continued to meet and cooperate after the agreement went into effect reflects the strength of the connections they made during its negotiation. Second, labor activists' criticism of certain aspects of the Teamsters'

---

[67] Personal interview with Bertha Luján of the FAT, August 29, 2000.
[68] Personal interview with Robin Alexander of the UE, December 21, 2000.
[69] Personal interview with Andy Banks of the IBT, January 10, 2001.

campaign suggests a shift toward transnationalism; newly constituted North American actors identified new ground rules for cooperation that eschewed the use of racist stereotypes. In the transnational fields that emerged in response to NAFTA, racial scapegoating was unacceptable. When the Teamsters appeared to be violating the rules, the union faced collective trinational censure.

Finally, and perhaps most unexpectedly, the Teamsters changed aspects of their strategy and rhetoric as a result of international criticism. After the Cuernavaca meeting, the union took out an ad in the large progressive daily Mexican newspaper *La Jornada* to clarify its position on Chapter 12 and reiterate its internationalist perspective. And in an effort to build allies and find common ground with Mexican trucking unions on Chapter 12, the Teamsters held a trinational "NAFTA Truckers' Summit" in Chicago a month after the Cuernavaca meeting. Mexican participants included the FAT and two small independent trucking unions.

The STRM's Alicia Sepúlveda Nuñez described the meeting: "They had an international conference and invited people from Mexico. And they were open-minded to discussing problems that NAFTA was going to create for both countries."[70] According to the UE's Robin Alexander, the meeting helped smooth relations after the meeting in Cuernavaca:

And as a result [of the Dialogos meeting] there was sort of an effort to do things differently and they put together a trinational conference – I think in Chicago – with truckers from the U.S., Mexico and Canada, and sort of the rhetoric really changed. They started talking about safety for all trucks and whatever. And again it's not everybody and even if you've got good rhetoric coming out of the national office, it's not going to prevent whoever is stopped by a reporter from saying whatever he or she may actually think about Mexican workers. But at least the official position improved markedly after that. I mean that was a very clear example, ... probably the clearest one that I could think of, of how relationships in Mexico changed how a U.S. union dealt with an issue. And clearly the more contact you have, the more that's going to happen.[71]

As Alexander suggests, the Teamsters' participation in transnational fields made their use of racialized rhetoric untenable. The Teamsters' press release from the Chicago Summit included calls for solidarity from union leaders in all three countries:

"NAFTA threatens jobs and highway safety in all three countries. It's time for truckers to unite," said Ron Carey, President of the Teamsters Union and convener

[70] Personal interview with Alicia Sepúlveda Nuñez of the STRM, August 27, 2000.
[71] Personal interview with Robin Alexander of the UE, December 21, 2000.

of today's meeting. "Our fight is not with each other. Our fight is against corporate greed that is destroying jobs and wages on both sides of the border," Carey added.

Teamsters Canada President Louis Lacroix said, "Canadian Teamsters are committed to working with their brothers and sisters in the US and Mexico to defeat the corporate agenda. International solidarity is the most powerful weapon that working people have to resist attacks by transnational employers."

"We all need to work together to face the challenges of NAFTA," said Alfredo Dominguez of the [FAT] and also speaking on behalf of the participating Mexican trade unionists.[72]

North American labor unions that engaged in transnational fields could not rely on tactics that grew out of isolationist perspectives and experiences. The repercussions of the Teamsters' anti-NAFTA campaign demonstrated that the days of the foreign worker myth were over. Indeed, anything that could be interpreted as racist rhetoric would not only be ineffective in dealing with new economic realities but also destructive to the development of transnational relationships and international cooperation. Unions that wished to engage in labor transnationalism, as the Teamsters did, would have to change their rhetoric or risk undermining cross-border relationships.[73]

Auto and Garment/Apparel Unions
Like the Teamsters, U.S. and Canadian garment/apparel and auto unions also initiated moderately developed relationships with independent Mexican unions. Many of the initial contacts among these unions occurred through trinational anti-NAFTA coalitions. Both the UAW's Steve Beckman and ACTWU's Ron Blackwell regularly helped organize Mexico-U.S. Dialogos meetings. It was in this venue that ACTWU (later UNITE) developed ties with the FAT.[74] UNITE's Alan Howard characterized his union's relationship with the FAT: "It's much easier to collaborate with

---

[72] "New Allies Join Campaign to Delay NAFTA Trucking Provisions," Teamsters press release, March 13, 1996.

[73] As of this writing, the IBT continues its campaign to prevent the implementation of Chapter 12. The Bush administration began a program to allow some Mexican trucks into the United States in accordance with NAFTA, which the Obama administration suspended in March 2009.

[74] In the mid-1980s, The ILGWU worked with the independent "Nineteenth of September" Garment Workers Union, which struggled for the right to represent its workers, but the relationship with the Mexican union was fraught with problems and did not produce a strong transnational relationship. For a detailed account of the struggle, see Carrillo (1990).

them and we have, usually around very specific cases that come up. We call them or get in touch with them, and vice versa. It's a good relationship, not [a] particularly intense close working relationship, but it's close."[75] The FAT's Antonio Villalba concurred:

We have worked with UNITE. We have good relations with them. They are in Canada also [Canadian unions are part of the International]. . . . Delegations have come to visit our plants, and we're working with them, but we need much more unity. . . . We are pushing to get international unions created by sector so that we can work together. So that if a plant wants to violate workers' rights, they can't go to Guatemala or Honduras because there will be a union there that will fight for their rights.[76]

Because the FAT represents few workers in the garment/apparel industry, however, the two unions have engaged in very few concrete activities.

It was also through Mexico-U.S. Dialogos that UAW officials first met FAT leaders, as Steve Beckman explained:

Somebody who had worked with the FAT was at early meetings. Bertha Luján was at several meetings. So there was a relationship there that started and we talked with the FAT about their auto parts membership. Again it's very small, but we tried to work on that relationship as a foundation for our common work because we had our political and social perspectives in common, which was not the case with the CTM, the vast bulk of the union membership in Mexico. So trying to figure out how to do things in Mexico through this other avenue was certainly desirable and dealing with those people was fun; they're great people. We had done a few things over the years, nothing terribly dramatic and nothing all that successful I'm afraid, but we have had long ongoing contacts with Benedicto Martínez and the other FAT leaders who are involved in the auto industry and on trade issues in general.[77]

Sam Gindin also recalled that the CAW's first contact with the FAT occurred in the context of NAFTA:

During the free trade fight a lot of our work, you also have to realize, started to be done through people who actually had some expertise in Mexico, because of language and context and the free trade fight. So we were really working with Common Frontiers. So in terms of international work we contributed a lot to these organizations. . . . It would have been done through Common Frontiers, and Common Frontiers would have been working through FAT, so we were supportive, but we were basically trying to be nonsectarian. We didn't honestly

[75] Personal interview with Alan Howard of UNITE, December 15, 2000.
[76] Personal interview with Antonio Villalba Granados of the FAT, July 10, 2000.
[77] Personal interview with Steve Beckman of the UAW, December 19, 2000.

know how to assess anything, supported whatever seemed to be working, established some informal contacts with FAT, met them when we went down there and toured some of their plants.[78]

Héctor de la Cueva of the Labor Research and Union Assistance Center (CILAS), which has strong ties to the FAT, described his organization's attempts to facilitate labor transnationalism among auto unions during NAFTA's negotiation:

CILAS organized two meetings of auto workers from the three countries, held in Mexico. It was organized to discuss problems and issues in common and an agenda of solidarity. So before NAFTA we began to work very hard to build relationships among workers in the three countries.... Before NAFTA's passage a large wave of exchange and knowledge among workers in the three countries began to grow to fight NAFTA. In these trinational meetings we discussed plans for campaigns to affect the negotiation of NAFTA. Specifically among auto workers [and] telecommunications workers, they compared wages and conditions, etc., and discussed common strategies.[79]

The UAW and CAW's primary contact is with STIMAHCS, a FAT-affiliated auto and metalworkers' union led by Benedicto Martínez. The CAW and UAW have also worked with and supported the UNT-affiliated Volkswagen union (SITIAVW) in Puebla, Mexico. These unions have organized exchanges and conferences, but their primary actions have involved filing NAO cases together. According to the FAT's Bertha Luján:

There have been various exchanges among workers in the auto industry, promoted by various universities here like the University of Puebla, in which there is an important group of investigators researching the auto industry.... I think unlike other industries like food and furniture, in this industry – both auto and auto parts – is where we see more examples during various years of support and mutual solidarity. In the case of STIMAHCS you know about the experience of [Echlin], that the UAW has gotten closer to STIMAHCS, as well as the Canadian Auto Workers.[80]

As the UAW's Steve Beckman explained, working together in anti-NAFTA coalitions also helped improve what had been an icy relationship between the UAW and CAW after the latter broke from the UAW:

NAFTA certainly created lots of contacts and cooperative work with the Canadian unions. Between us and the CAW we did talk about specific strategies for proposals to make. We did work with them on proposals we made to the U.S.

[78] Personal interview with Sam Gindin of the CAW, February 14, 2001.
[79] Personal interview with Héctor de la Cueva of CILAS, July 22, 1999.
[80] Personal interview with Bertha Luján of the FAT, August 29, 2000.

government. It created another opportunity to demonstrate that we really do have common interests and we can work together; it's no big deal. So I think it reconfirmed, at the staff [level] at least, decent relationships.[81]

NAFTA's ability to help build more substantive interactions among U.S., Canadian, and independent Mexican unions – and to mend fences between the UAW and CAW – stands in stark contrast to its role as instigator of ill feelings among North America's largest auto, garment/apparel, and trucking unions.

U.S. and Canadian Unions: A Mixed Record of Transnationalism

As economic integration proceeded, North American unions were differentially constituted as transnational actors. NAFTA drove a wedge between U.S. and Canadian auto, garment/apparel, and trucking unions and their official Mexican counterparts. The former were among the most ardent opponents of NAFTA. They spearheaded grassroots organizing and education campaigns, participated in anti-NAFTA coalitions, and initiated intense lobbying efforts. Their official Mexican counterparts, in contrast, saw the free trade agreement as a panacea for Mexico's economic troubles and a welcome inducement for foreign investment. The largest unions in these industries were not able to bridge the ideological and political divide that separated them, and their contact remained sporadic or nonexistent.

The UAW, CAW, UNITE, and Teamsters' inability to find common ground with official Mexican unions belies their more complex and varied engagement with independent Mexican unions. All four unions were active participants in the transnational trade-negotiating field and through their work in this arena encountered independent Mexican unions that shared their perspective on regional economic integration. Key among them was the FAT, whose leaders believe that North American labor unions share common interests and nurture this sentiment among their members. The difference between official and independent union leaders' evaluation of and vision for transnationalism is quite striking, as the FAT's Bertha Luján revealed:

I think the principal motivation is the recognition that alone we will not be able to achieve anything. That the force of companies has gone beyond individual nations, that the corporations will pay much less in other places than here. So

---

[81] Personal interview with Steve Beckman of the UAW, December 19, 2000.

we always have the risk that they will leave or that they just decrease our wages here. So the struggle to elevate wages and improve conditions for all workers is a common struggle. So we have to force the companies to respect minimum international standards and codes of conduct. The struggles of the future are going to be international struggles and the unionism of the future is going to be at this level.... I think there are common interests. One of those interests is that common standards increase, that salaries increase, that conditions improve, that there are better collective contracts, that they don't give Ford workers in the United States forty dollars an hour and one dollar here. Mexican worker don't want this. So this is a common interest. Everyone wants to earn more and to earn better.[82]

The majority of collaborative work with independent unions was centered in the transnational legal field through the NAALC process. Of the thirty-five NAO submissions unions and labor organizations filed from 1994 to 2008, the Teamsters participated in nine, UNITE in seven, the UAW in six, and the CAW in five. Only the UE and FAT participated in more: ten and twelve, respectively. Some of these cases, such as Han Young and Echlin, involved large transnational campaigns with rank-and-file participation. Ironically, the UAW's Steve Beckman, who dismissed the viability of cross-border organizing and getting involved in local affairs in Mexico during the Ford Cuautitlán struggle, served on the U.S. NAO's advisory committee and provided testimony at the Han Young NAO hearing in 1998.

Although U.S. and Canadian auto, garment/apparel, and trucking unions found a reliable ally in the FAT and engaged in significant collaborative activities with the union, their relationships remained only moderately developed. A sense of mutualism does not fully permeate these unions' cultures. As the UAW's Steve Beckman argued, auto unions are far from developing complementary cooperative identities: "So the optimal union solidarity is one that's based entirely on respect and trust of well-meaning goals of your partners. And sort of common interests and objectives that you then make progress in achieving. But you can't assume those common interests from the beginning. They aren't necessarily there, and the differences in structure make every relationship different."[83] Benedicto Martínez, secretary general of STIMAHCS, explained how the actions of UAW leaders during a 1998 General Motors (GM) strike alienated Mexican workers because the strike shut down Mexican plants.

---

[82] Personal interview with Bertha Luján of the FAT, August 29, 2000.
[83] Personal interview with Steve Beckman of the UAW, December 19, 2000.

His story demonstrates that a culture of transnationalism has not fully penetrated the largest North American auto union:

I spoke to the president of the UAW and he told me the GM strike was successful and I told him it created resentment in Mexico, and it would have been beneficial to come and explain things to Mexican labor leaders and workers so that they would see the benefits of the strike and incorporate their own needs into the struggle so it could be better. He said he hadn't thought of that. Mexican workers felt the U.S. strikers got what they needed and the Mexicans paid the consequences. In the future we must look for mechanisms so that this doesn't happen, so that a struggle strengthens alliances of solidarity and unity among workers. And then a GM or Ford is going to think beforehand, and negotiate because it will get hit from both sides.[84]

Martínez suggests that the UAW's inability to see its struggle as inextricably linked to those of Mexican workers not only caused resentment but weakened North American labor movements and processes of transnationalism. In Martínez's vision, labor struggles would be consciously and strategically waged to benefit all North American workers. The FAT similarly critiqued the Teamsters' cross-border trucking campaign for not addressing the interests of North American workers. As Bertha Luján explained: "Well we criticized the decision as being a unilateral one made by the United States because these are symptoms of protectionism. Instead of looking for an agreement that would not affect workers from here or there, what they did was to protect their own interests, and the situation of workers in Mexico didn't matter to them."[85]

NAFTA: Necessary but Not Sufficient

Although all North American unions were exposed to NAFTA as a potential catalyst of labor transnationalism, only certain unions actually developed transnational relationships in NAFTA's wake. This suggests that NAFTA was a necessary but not sufficient condition for the development of labor transnationalism in the early 1990s. While the majority of industrial unions followed the example of garment/apparel, auto, and trucking unions and did not fully embrace transnationalism, key industrial unions created a sense of mutualism that permeates their institutional cultures and captures the imaginations of rank-and-file members. A comparison of these negative and positive cases of transnationalism in response to

---

[84] Personal interview with Benedicto Martínez Orozco of STIMAHCS, July 27, 1999.
[85] Personal interview with Bertha Luján of the FAT, August 29, 2000.

NAFTA in Chapters 5 and 6 therefore presents a striking and compelling contrast. But the question remains – what explains the variation in the emergence of labor transnationalism in North America? Why were some unions able to embrace the transnational opportunity NAFTA provided to undermine the foreign worker myth and create a union culture that values relationships? The answer lies less in the objective external threat of regional economic integration and more in the internal effects of union leadership on constructing union interests in relationship to integration and transnationalism. Progressive leadership fostered consistent inter-actions and joint projects that solidified mutual interests among North American unions and allowed a long-cherished but utopian vision of international solidarity to escape its rhetorical constraints and develop into practice.

7

Explaining Variation in the Emergence of Labor Transnationalism

All North American unions were exposed to NAFTA as a potential catalyst for labor transnationalism. Only certain unions, however, developed transnational relationships in NAFTA's wake. The degree to which unions embraced labor transnationalism varied significantly. Although the majority recognized some common interests with their counterparts across the continent, not all unions adopted strategies that furthered mutual interests through concrete action. The trade agreement's power to catalyze transnational labor relationships, though significant, was therefore not absolute. It is clear from the data in previous chapters that economic factors alone – including the perception of NAFTA as a threat – do not adequately explain the emergence of labor transnationalism. Explaining variation in NAFTA's effect therefore requires examining the politics rather than simply the economics of globalization.

Four industrial and institutional variables emerged from interview data as the most crucial to the emergence of and variation in labor transnationalism: (1) a progressive U.S. union; (2) a progressive Canadian union; (3) a progressive Mexican union; and (4) industry vulnerability to foreign trade (defined as industries vulnerable to job movement and/or foreign competition, including factory or work relocation, work reorganization, and import competition). Although there is no scholarly consensus on whether unions vulnerable to foreign trade are more or less likely to cooperate transnationally (see Bhagwati 2000), data from previous chapters suggest that many of the largest U.S. and Canadian industrial unions in the most vulnerable industries responded to NAFTA's threat by joining transnational coalitions and seeking out potential partners in Mexico. It is clear, however, that vulnerability to foreign trade *alone* does not seem

230

to be predictive for either outcome; some unions in the same industries responded differently to NAFTA. Unions in the electronics assembly, steel, auto, and garment/apparel industries are extremely vulnerable to work relocation and foreign competition. Those in the trucking industry are vulnerable to competition through linked shipping routes, and those in the communications industry are less vulnerable to job relocation.[1]

Although there are other causal conditions that could reasonably be hypothesized to affect outcomes, their effects seem to be minor. Variables such as a union's financial resources, membership losses, size, and sector, for example, played a negligible role in the emergence of relationships. Because international travel and communication are expensive, one hypothesis is that unions with few financial resources would be less inclined to engage in labor transnationalism. The UE and FAT are the most resource-poor unions in the sample, yet they have the strongest relationship. Nor do data support the inverse hypothesis (i.e., that unions with few financial resources are more likely to engage in labor transnationalism as a way to bolster their position). The CWA and STRM are among the most financially sound in their respective countries and yet prioritize transnationalism. Although the weakness of Mexican unions is also a potential explanatory variable, the evidence suggests that it is not robust. One of the unions with the strongest transnational relationship, the independent STRM, is also one of the strongest domestically. And few of the many weak Mexican unions have developed transnational relationships.

It is also plausible that unions that experienced significant job losses would be *less* likely to engage in transnationalism. The data, however, show that the variable does not accurately predict either a positive or negative outcome: unions with similar net membership losses between 1991 and 1993 (the period of NAFTA's negotiation) responded very differently to the agreement (see Appendix Table A.1 for union membership data). For example, whereas the UAW led anti-NAFTA coalitions and forged moderately developed relationships with independent Mexican unions, the USW was a more marginal player in anti-NAFTA coalitions and did not build significant relationships with Mexican unions until after 2001.[2] Each union lost 8.3 percent of its membership during that period.

---

[1] Some unions historically less vulnerable to foreign trade, such as telecommunications unions, have increased their vulnerability by expanding beyond their core sectors to various manufacturing sectors. The CWA, for example, merged with the IUE in 2000.

[2] The USW did, however, spearhead efforts to develop and file a lawsuit to overturn NAFTA, claiming it violated the U.S. Constitution because it was a treaty and therefore required approval by a two-thirds vote of the Senate.

Size and sector are also potentially relevant explanatory variables. Larger unions such as the UAW lack large independent counterparts in their core sectors with which to form strong relationships. Moreover, large unions may be more reluctant than small unions to engage independent Mexican unions for fear of antagonizing their official union counterparts – as evidenced by the UAW leadership's refusal to support the Ford Cuautitlán dissident struggle. Although the paucity of large independent unions in key sectors such as autos creates limitations for relationship building, if size and sector alone affect unions' willingness to engage in transnationalism, then we would expect to see no variation in relationship building between the UAW and the CAW. However, as the previous chapter shows, the CAW engages in transnationalism more actively than its southern counterpart; its leadership openly supported the Ford Cuautitlán dissidents and developed a plan to trinationally organize auto parts plants (which was not implemented because the UAW failed to participate). Another argument against size and sector as explanatory variables is internal variation within large unions themselves. The UAW's former reluctance to antagonize official auto unions changed over time; both the CAW and UAW formed moderately developed relationships with STIMAHCS and the UNT-affiliated Volkswagen union (SITIAVW) in Puebla and criticized official Mexican unions in NAO submissions such as Han Young and Echlin.

Interview data suggest that a union's ideological orientation – specifically progressive leadership – is an important predictor of its participation in transnational relationships. There are different indicators of progressive unionism. They include a union's affiliation with progressive organizations such as the CIO (see Stepan-Norris and Zeitlin 2002), levels of democracy and member participation, or the emergence of internal democratic opposition groups (e.g., Teamsters for a Democratic Union in the IBT and New Directions in the UAW). Progressive unionism can also be measured by autonomy or distance from the government or the mainstream labor movement. In Mexico, for example, progressive unions tend to be politically independent from the government or ruling party (although this is not always the case). Unions' policy positions on key issues (e.g., civil and women's rights, immigration, etc.) can constitute another indicator. And shifts from business unionism to social movement unionism (see Voss and Sherman 2000) and increased organizing (see Bronfenbrenner and Hickey 2004) can also be used as proxies for progressivism. None of these indicators, however, is completely adequate as a measure across each of the countries.

The definition of progressive leadership used here captures both its ideological and strategic dimensions: high-level union officials (either primary or secondary leaders) who embrace a broader social agenda of progressive reform and militant action.[3] Although a union's social agenda may vary by country, progressive leaders generally support policies to undermine poverty and inequality and often work across sectors with NGOs and community organizations on campaigns for economic and social justice. Progressive leaders also tend to promote organizing marginalized workers – such as immigrants and women – within their unions. Because leaders can have a significant influence on a union's ideological orientation and strategy, progressive leadership often reflects the adoption of progressive policy positions and democratic practices. And conversely, a union with a long progressive history is more likely to elect progressive leaders. During the 1980s and 1990s, the UE, FAT, CUSWA, STRM, CEP, CWA, and CAW had consistent progressive leadership, and the IBT, USW, UAW, UNITE, and CTM did not.[4]

Pathways to Transnationalism

A modified qualitative comparative approach (Ragin 1987) allows us to analyze how different industrial and institutional variables interact to create positive or negative outcomes (i.e., the presence or absence of a transnational relationship), and to isolate the multiple pathways to these outcomes.[5] Table 7.1 summarizes the presence or absence of the four variables and two outcomes for each of ten possible union triads.

Table 7.1 reveals which variables are most crucial to the emergence of transnational relationships and the combinations of conditions that are necessary and sufficient for their attainment. It shows that progressive

---

[3] My coding of progressive unions is relatively consistent with Herzenberg (2000), Scher (1997) and Fantasia and Voss's (2004) categorization of left unions (broadly defined). The only two industrial unions Fantasia and Voss (2004) categorize differently are UNITE and the UAW's higher education division (which does not reflect the union as a whole). Scher categorizes the IBT under Carey as progressive.

[4] Because the period under study includes the Hoffa administration (IBT) and the Becker administration (USW), I do not code the IBT and USW as progressive unions. UNITE is a debatable case, because ACTWU had progressive leadership under Jack Sheinkman, while the ILGWU'S leaders Sol C. Chaiken and Jay Mazur were less progressive (despite pressure from more progressive regional and local leaders and staffers). Dana Frank (1999) illuminates the less progressive tendencies of the ILGWU.

[5] Qualitative comparative analysis (QCA) uses Boolean algebra to test how certain variables, or conditions, affect outcomes.

Table 7.1. *Presence or Absence of Causal Conditions and Outcomes for North American Labor Unions*

	Progressive U.S. Union	Progressive Canadian Union	Progressive Mexican Union	Vulnerability to Foreign Trade	Transnational Relationship
1 UE, CUSWA, FAT (electrical manufacturing)	Y	Y	Y	Y	Y
2 CWA, CEP, STRM (telecommunications)	Y	Y	Y	N	Y
3 UAW, CAW, STIMAHCS (auto)	N	Y	Y	Y	Y
4 UNITE, UNITE (Can), FAT (garment/apparel)	N	N	Y	Y	Y
5 IBT, IBT (Can), FAT (trucking)	N	N	Y	Y	Y
6 UAW, CAW, CTM (auto)	N	Y	N	Y	N
7 UNITE, UNITE (Can), CTM (garment/apparel)	N	N	N	Y	N
8 UE, CUSWA, CTM (electrical manufacturing)	Y	Y	N	Y	N
9 IBT, IBT (Can), CTM (trucking)	N	N	N	Y	N
10 USW, CUSWA, CTM (steel)	N	Y	N	Y	N

Notes: With the exception of the FAT – which in the Mexican context resembles and acts like a national union in the United States or Canada – I exclude union federations. The CTM does not refer to the labor federation but rather to a CTM union that would potentially participate in a transnational relationship in a given industry. Because there are no national Mexican auto, garment/apparel, or trucking industry unions, I use this nomenclature for simplicity.

"Y" indicates the presence of a condition or outcome; "N" indicates its absence.

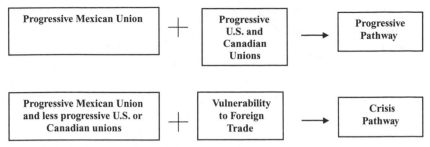

Figure 7.1. Pathways to Labor Transnationalism

unions are more likely to develop transnational relationships even if they are not vulnerable to foreign trade. It also shows that even less progressive U.S. and Canadian unions can develop transnational relationships if they are vulnerable to foreign trade and have a progressive Mexican union counterpart. The analysis, however, does not suggest that all will; only that the likelihood of a relationship developing is greater with more progressive participants.

An analysis of the data in Table 7.1 therefore reveals two pathways to labor transnationalism. In the first, the "progressive" pathway, a transnational labor relationship is possible with the presence of an independent Mexican union and progressive U.S. and Canadian unions. In the second, the "crisis" pathway, a transnational labor relationship is possible with the presence of an independent Mexican union and vulnerability to foreign trade. Figure 7.1 provides a visual distinction between the two pathways.

The progressive pathway to labor transnationalism suggests that U.S. and Canadian unions are motivated to participate in transnational relationships by progressive ideologies that support labor transnationalism. The crisis pathway suggests that even if a U.S. or Canadian union lacks progressive leadership, it can still be motivated to participate in a transnational relationship if it is vulnerable to foreign trade and has a progressive Mexican union partner. This is the case with the UAW (which collaborates with the CAW and STIMAHCS but not with CTM unions), UNITE, and the IBT.

Explaining Transnationalism: Vulnerability to Foreign Trade

My analysis sheds more light on the relationship between a union's vulnerability to foreign trade and its participation in transnational relationships. It shows that relationships do not necessarily emerge among unions that are vulnerable to foreign trade or integrated along common production chains; vulnerability must be accompanied by progressive leadership in at least one of the unions in the relationship. The paucity of transnational relationships among unions vulnerable to foreign trade, it could be argued, is actually quite surprising. It is plausible that unions in vulnerable industries would be more likely to collaborate in order to mitigate actual or potential competition. By cooperating in collective bargaining and sharing information about contracts and health and safety issues, North American unions could try to forestall or prevent the downward harmonization of wages, benefits, and conditions as manufacturing relocates to Mexico, where workers are usually paid less than their U.S. and Canadian counterparts. Similarly it could be argued that cross-border cooperation would increase as a result of integrated production (or, in the case of trucking, linked shipping routes). That is, as transnational companies open factories in Mexico, North American workers are more likely to work for the same company or for companies that interact (e.g., an auto parts and an auto manufacturer) and to see themselves as uniquely connected with the same or similar interests.

If vulnerability to factory relocation, foreign competition, and integrated production generate labor transnationalism, auto unions that began to experience the effects of regional economic integration long before NAFTA's passage should have been among the first to collaborate transnationally.[6] Beginning with Mexico's introduction of an export-oriented assembly industry program in 1965, U.S. companies could assemble goods in Mexico with U.S. components and import them back into the United States, paying duties only on the value added (Sklair 1993). In the 1970s and 1980s, faced with increasing competition from Japanese automakers, U.S. auto manufacturers began to close factories, lay off workers, and move production outside the United States and Canada. By the mid-1980s, almost all of the major U.S. auto manufacturers had opened plants in Mexico. The combination of maquiladoras and automobiles was responsible for the rapid growth of Mexico's export industry in the 1980s (Shaiken 1990). The numbers were staggering: "Export growth in the auto industry has been equally impressive. Exports climbed from $366 million in 1980 to over $3 billion in the first nine months of 1989,

---

[6] Electronics industry unions also experienced these effects, and some unions with workers in the industry did develop relationships in NAFTA's wake, such as the UE, FAT, and CUSWA.

with much of the increase coming from new capital-intensive plants" (Shaiken 1990, p. 2).

As a result, the motor vehicle sector went from a $1.5 billion trade deficit in 1980 to a $1.4 billion trade surplus for Mexico in the first nine months of 1989 alone (Shaiken 1990, p. 2). Many of the auto parts and assembly factories built in Mexico received substantial capital investment and utilized the most advanced technology and equipment for production. Mexican high-tech auto manufacturing plants could therefore compete with their U.S. and Japanese counterparts (Shaiken 1990). By the early 1990s, Mexico had developed a strong and stable infrastructure for automobile production. In 2002, the trade deficit in U.S. automotive parts totaled over $19 billion, compared with a $4 billion deficit in 1997. Mexican auto parts imports accounted for over $8.7 billion of the 2002 deficit.[7]

Although high levels of integrated production would make the auto industry ideal for transnational union collaboration, leaders in these industries did not move beyond mere transnational contacts with their official CTM counterparts. A similar story is true for garment/apparel, trucking, and the majority of electronics industry unions. Labor unions do not simply respond to the crisis of free trade by creating transnational relationships that could potentially give them more bargaining power and leverage with employers. Although some unions that are quite vulnerable to work relocation and foreign competition developed relationships, most did not. And one of the strongest relationships emerged among telecommunications industry unions, which are less vulnerable to job relocation in their core sectors than other unions in the sample. As the data demonstrate, vulnerability to foreign competition alone does not reliably predict the emergence of labor transnationalism.

Explaining Transnationalism: Progressive Leadership

The two pathways to labor transnationalism show that whereas external economic variables cannot fully explain variations in labor transnationalism, a union's institutional capacity and culture hold tremendous explanatory power. Of the transnational relationships that emerged in NAFTA's wake, all included at least one union with progressive leadership. Leaders or high-level union officials altered the calculus of support for transnationalism by seeking out and nurturing relationships and educating and

---

[7] "U.S. Automotive Parts Industry Annual Assessment." 2009. Office of Transportation and Machinery, United States Department of Commerce, Table 13.

including the rank and file. The consistency of transnationalism with a progressive agenda helps explain its emergence among progressive unions. Ideologically left-of-center unions are more likely to value solidarity in theory and in practice and to have key staff people that prioritize cooperation and manage relationship building. Moreover, unions that aggressively try to purge racism at home are less likely to tolerate it as part of their international policy. Analysis of interview data in conjunction with information on union history and leaders' backgrounds helps flesh out why progressive unions were more likely to construct their interests to embrace transnationalism than unions that lacked progressive leadership.

Progressive Mexican Unions

All transnational relationships that emerged in NAFTA's wake have one key variable in common: the presence of a progressive Mexican union. Among the progressive unions in this sample – the FAT and its affiliates, the STRM, and the Volkswagen union (SITIAVW) – all are also politically independent of the government. They participated in the El Foro group (The Forum – Unions Face the Nation), which demanded democratic reforms within the Labor Congress (Congreso del Trabajo, CT) and subsequently helped found the UNT in 1997 as a progressive union federation in opposition to the official Mexican labor federations.

The FAT was formed in 1960 by progressive factions of the Catholic Church as an independent federation of Mexican labor unions and worker organizations (Hathaway 2000). Although subjected to government repression, the FAT survived and is among Mexico's most ideologically intransigent independent union federations. The FAT promulgates union democracy and independence. Its founding constitution states:

The principles that will guide our course at all times will be (a) union liberty, (b) union democracy, (c) independence from all political parties, (d) autonomy from government and employers, and (e) the constant struggle for the material and spiritual elevation of the working-class.[8]

To translate its ideology into action, the FAT holds democratic elections and reorganized its national structure in 1990 to provide more representation in its national council (Hathaway 2000). The FAT is also committed to gender equality. Since 1990 it has focused considerable attention on women's issues. Official policy dictates that one of the FAT's three national coordinators must be a woman.

---

[8] Hathaway (2000, p. 54).

The STRM's Francisco Hernández Juárez was also at the center of leftist union activity in the 1970s, ultimately severing his union's relationship with the CTM to form an independent union in 1976. The STRM is usually hailed as one of Mexico's most democratic unions, and its leadership among the most progressive. Although some STRM insiders and critics claim that Hernández Juárez's efforts to remain in power have compromised his leftist ideals, secondary leaders around him in the 1990s pushed a progressive agenda, particularly three key members of the STRM's executive committee: Mateo Lejarza, Rafael Marino Roche, and Alicia Sepúlveda Nuñez.[9] The 1996 election of Alicia Sepúlveda Nuñez to the position of foreign and recording secretary for a four-year term was arguably the most salient for the union's international relations. Sepúlveda came out of the Mexican women's movement (through which she developed extensive ties in the United States and Canada) and speaks four languages.

When she began her term, Sepúlveda recognized that her predecessor had done very little to support the efforts of Lejarza and Marino Roche. As she explained: "Well there was an infrastructure because Mateo and Marino had been working on creating international relations for some years. But... they were the only ones who really knew what was going on."[10] Sepúlveda described her predecessor as ineffectual, and explained how she sought to extend the STRM's international work and make it more active:

I found it very academic. It was sort of let's discuss, then let's create an agenda and then let's write down a paper.... Then we signed these agreements and I saw these agreements not as a paper that you frame and say look I have this agreement.... I saw it as a basis for working jointly on campaigns because I think that what brings people together are actions; things to do, not things to discuss. Because you can be discussing something for fifty years and it just sort of never comes to fruition.[11]

During her term, which began after NAFTA's passage, Sepúlveda strengthened the union's relationship with the CWA and CEP and forged a

---

[9] By Mexican standards, the STRM is relatively democratic: elections are held, contracts are readily available, and internal dissention is permitted. The STRM's statutes that prohibit two consecutive terms for any executive committee position, however, are routinely ignored for Hernández Juárez. This and other antidemocratic practices inspired a strong opposition movement within the STRM, which offered an alternative slate of candidates in the 2000 executive committee elections. The slate lost, but the opposition group maintains its own newsletter and is quite vocal about its dissent.

[10] Personal interview with Alicia Sepúlveda Nuñez of the STRM, August 27, 2000.

[11] Ibid.

new relationship with the Service Employees International Union (SEIU). After meeting a leader of the SEIU at a Mexico-U.S. Dialogos meeting in Cuernavaca, Mexico, in 1996, Sepúlveda worked for two years to develop a relationship between STRM Local 87 and SEIU Local 1877 in California. She revealed how she convinced her colleagues to sign a formal agreement with SEIU, which they did in 1998:

I proposed that we sign an agreement with SEIU and that we help with the Justice for Janitors campaign because we have a very big local that has janitors in it, it's called Local 87, it's about 5,000 strong, and it's only natural to sign an agreement between Local 87 and Local 1877.... I explained that SEIU had been led by Sweeney, has a migrant worker strategy, a strategy for women, and is progressive in its policies.[12]

Sepúlveda chose to pursue a relationship with SEIU not simply because her union shared a common workforce but because it shared a similarly progressive agenda. She made manifest her vision of solidarity as action by supporting the SEIU's struggle against Hewlett-Packard:

We decided that we were going to organize a multinational protest against Hewlett-Packard. We had our friends from the Unified Workers' Central in Brazil.... And some brothers from Great Britain were also trying to organize something. And I was here in Mexico and Héctor [Figueroa of SEIU] was organizing in several cities in the United States, and it was a great success. It was on the "Justice for Janitors" day, which is June fifteenth. We held a demonstration outside the Hewlett-Packard plant here in Mexico City and they were absolutely flabbergasted because they never expected a multinational protest.... This was a great success. To me it was a great triumph because salaries were increased and working conditions were improved.[13]

The case of the CWA, CEP, and STRM demonstrates that differences of opinion over NAFTA did not sabotage every potential transnational relationship. Although the STRM supported the free trade agreement, the union was still able to work productively with the CWA and CEP on a variety of other issues of common concern regarding the North American telecommunications industry. According to CWA President Larry Cohen, the STRM's independence was a key factor in the CWA's decision to work with the union: "But it's definitely the case that [STRM's] relative independence from the PRI was a factor and their relative willingness to think through strategies without the strategies being determined by

---

[12] Personal interviews with Alicia Sepúlveda Nuñez of the STRM, August 27, 2000.
[13] Ibid.

some other organization like the CTM or the PRI or anybody else."[14] Perhaps part of the problem in solidifying transnational relationships prior to NAFTA was the CWA's choice of counterparts. In 1991, when CWA activists visited an AT&T plant in Matamoros, Mexico, the CTM "phantom" union created to represent workers was not interested in joint activities with the CWA.

The emergence of labor transnationalism is profoundly constrained by official Mexican unions' ties to their national government, which prioritizes attracting and maintaining foreign trade and investment. Official union leaders generally believe that increased trade and investment will improve the position of Mexican workers. But even if they see value in creating transnational relationships, they find it difficult to nurture what the government views as a potential threat to its economic development strategy. Given that official Mexican unions prioritize their relationship with the nation-state, it is unlikely that they would work with U.S. and Canadian unions in any significant way unless, as our model predicts, they perceive severe economic vulnerability *and* find progressive partners.

It is also possible, however, that progressive official locals or sections could forge relationships if they could achieve some autonomy from the official union hierarchy. Although most official unions are often extremely authoritarian, some locals and sections can be quite democratic and autonomous.[15] Gaining the autonomy to be able to develop relationships, however, would be quite difficult. Some progressive CTM leaders and workers secretly opposed NAFTA, but during its negotiation, they found it difficult to contest the government's policies. Opposing NAFTA and working with northern unions to kill it would have been seen as a betrayal, and quite likely would have resulted in severe sanctions. In contrast to leaders of official garment/apparel unions who years after NAFTA's passage continue to extol its virtues, representatives of progressive sections contend that NAFTA has hurt their industries. As the leader of one CTM garment union section, who spoke on condition of anonymity, argued: "I think NAFTA has had a very negative impact in our country. I think only the most dynamic industries have gained anything, like telecommunications, auto, petrochemical. We were less prepared for NAFTA."[16]

---

[14] Personal interview with Larry Cohen of the CWA, March 28, 2001.

[15] This point was first made firmly and unequivocally by Carlos García, who argued that CTM unions often have progressive sections.

[16] Interview with anonymous Mexican CTM leader, June 14, 2000.

Leaders of progressive CTM sections, unlike their less progressive counterparts, articulated a clear sense of common interest with U.S. and Canadian unions. As one progressive leader explained when asked why U.S. and Canadian unions look for alliances with Mexican unions:

To create common actions over labor and work questions. I think these alliances could ultimately defend workers' common interests. No matter where you're from, your interests are the same. Your reason for being is the same, to defend your interests. . . . We want workers' lives to be better, and our advantage is cheap labor, but we want to make them better. And if there are alliances they should be to help workers in all three countries.[17]

Although he claimed not to know much about the NAALC process, he knew more than many of the leaders of large CTM unions I interviewed, and seemed to be more supportive of the process: "I know there is a submission process. I heard about it and would like to use the process. At this moment tools like that are necessary, imperative." When asked if the CTM would permit him to file an NAO submission, he replied: "I don't think they would like it. They would not take the initiative to use it themselves. It's an advantage for CTM leaders if the workers don't know about the process and use it."[18] Although progressive CTM section leaders nurture a vision of transnationalism based on common interest, their ability to engage in transnational relationships is severely constrained by the CTM hierarchy.

Progressive official sections and their leaders are not permitted to develop their own international contacts; nor are they encouraged to openly oppose the policies of the national leadership. The progressive CTM leader explained the political internal dynamics that limit locals' ability to create alliances with U.S. and Canadian unions:

I have no relations with unions in the U.S. and Canada. . . . We as sections don't have access to these relations. . . . My opinion is that [national leaders] hoard them for themselves. It's a form of control. I don't know if we could look for them if we wanted them. It would be difficult. The leaders wouldn't allow it or like it. But I would like it. I would like to know the experiences and points of view that they have. These relations should be democratized so that rank-and-file workers can participate.[19]

When asked if he could simply go to the Solidarity Center office in Mexico City and make his own contacts, he replied that he could not: "Because

[17] Interview with anonymous Mexican CTM leader, June 14, 2000.
[18] Ibid.
[19] Interview with anonymous official Mexican auto union leader, June 14, 2000.

of control. It would be looked badly upon; they may bother me about it."[20]

He was also quite skeptical about national CTM leaders' true feelings about transnational relationships. Although he viewed collective bargaining across national borders as positive, he argued that it was not realistic to expect national leaders to accept this idea in the near future:

It would be good, the ideal, but are the leaders going to permit it? The collective contracts belong to the leaders; they make them rich. So I don't think they will be interested. They do what gives them power, so this would affect alliances. I am not sure if the national leaders really want them because . . . their interests, political and economic, . . . are not always the same as the workers'.[21]

Another progressive leader of a CTM section, when asked if he believes the national leadership fosters international contacts, explained: "They are at the top, they manage them, and don't share them with us. I'm sure they have contacts, but I have no idea how they manage them. I would like it if they shared them with us."[22]

When asked why his union doesn't leave the CTM, he replied: "It's more advantageous to stay with the CTM. We could get hurt if we left the CTM. People can get fired. They're hitting independent unions hard now. So for convenience we stay with the CTM because we would have more protection, and we can maintain our independence at the local level."[23]

Progressive U.S. and Canadian Unions

A Mexican union's progressiveness is critical to the development of a transnational relationship, but the absence of relationships among U.S. and Canadian unions that engaged independent Mexican unions in the transnational trade-negotiating field suggests that the nature of the former also matters. The United Steelworkers of America (USW), for example, did not develop a relationship with the FAT even though its Canadian counterpart did. Similarly, the International Union of Electronic, Electrical, Salaried, Machine and Furniture Workers (IUE), whose president, William Bywater, was a vociferous and engaged NAFTA opponent, did not emerge from the NAFTA struggle with close ties to Mexican unions.

[20] Ibid.
[21] Ibid.
[22] Personal interview with anonymous official Mexican auto union leader, June 7, 2000.
[23] Ibid.

An analysis of the U.S. and Canadian unions that engage in partially and fully developed relationships suggest they share one key variable in common: progressive leadership. Among unions that have formed relationships with Mexican unions, the UE and CWA are currently among the most progressive industrial unions in the United States, and the CAW, CUSWA, and CEP are among the most progressive in Canada. By any indicator, the UE is one of the most democratic and progressive in the United States. The UE's three national officers are elected annually at its national convention, and their salaries are capped by the UE Constitution at the highest wage paid in the industry. UE policy is determined by locally elected rank-and-file delegates at the annual national conventions and includes commitments to organize immigrants. The UE proudly describes its left-of-center positions:

UE gained an early reputation as a fighter for the rights of women workers and as an opponent of racial discrimination. In the 1950s, UE mounted public campaigns to force major electrical manufacturing corporations to agree to non-discrimination clauses. UE was among the first to organize undocumented workers and speak out on behalf of immigrants. As an early critic of the Vietnam War, the union campaigned for redirecting the federal budget toward job-creating, socially-useful production.[24]

In the 1990s, UE President John H. Hovis, Jr and a progressive cadre of secondary leaders worked to keep the union on its left-leaning course. The UE helped found the Labor Party in 1996 and endorsed Green Party presidential candidate Ralph Nader in 2000. It also maintains its reputation for militancy by engaging in strikes and organizing drives and refusing to participate in worker–management cooperation programs such as quality circles.

Although few if any U.S. unions can match the consistency of the UE's progressive agenda, the CWA has also embraced progressive leadership and labor militancy, with major strikes each decade since its birth in 1947.[25] Morton Bahr, elected president in 1985, continued the union's militancy by encouraging rank-and-file mobilization during 1989 negotiations with AT&T and leading the union to victory in the NYNEX strike the same year. One of the union's secondary leaders, Larry Cohen, was

---

[24] http://www.ranknfile-ue.org/uewho3.html.
[25] The National Federation of Telephone Workers (NFTW) was formed in 1938. In 1947, at the first CWA convention, delegates chose to merge the autonomous organizations of the NFTW into the CWA. Although the CWA has historically not always been among the nation's most progressive unions, since the mid-1980s its leadership has put the union on a more progressive course.

extremely influential in promoting progressive policies. Cohen served as assistant to the CWA president and director of organizing until 1998, when he was elected executive vice president. In 2001, former CEP President Fred Pomeroy described Cohen's role in the union:

Morty is the front person who gives the union a substantial logical face, and Larry is the aggressive visionary of the organization, thinking about where does it have to go, how does it have to change, thinking about how do you revitalize the labor movement in the U.S. and everything. I mean, he just about chokes himself talking so fast because he's got all these ideas coming out of him.[26]

In 1987, during his tenure under Bahr, Cohen founded Jobs with Justice, an organization dedicated to supporting workers' rights struggles through "long-term multi-issue coalition building, grassroots base-building and organizing and strategic militant action."[27] In 2005, Cohen was elected president of the CWA.

Although the Canadian labor movement was inspired by the militancy and progressivism of U.S. unions in the 1930s and 1940s, Canadian unions today are generally more progressive than their U.S. counterparts. One of the explanations given for the longevity of progressive Canadian unionism is the existence of a viable party that represents labor interests, the New Democratic Party (NDP).[28] The CLC was one of the founders of the social-democratic NDP in 1961 and maintains strong ties to and influence within the party. Canadian labor leaders are routinely elected as NDP representatives to the federal and provincial governments, serving as members of parliament, members of the provincial parliament, and members of the legislative assembly. Moreover, labor is given twenty-five percent of all votes in the party's conventions. Progressive Canadian unions share and often shape the NDP's positions on poverty reduction, environmental protection, human rights, and industrial policy.

The CAW, CUSWA, and CEP have all supported the left-of-center NDP, and their primary and secondary leaders are known for their commitment to economic and social justice and militant social movement

---

[26] Personal interview with Fred Pomeroy of the CEP, February 28, 2001.
[27] http://www.jwj.org/about.html.
[28] The NDP emerged out of the Cooperative Commonwealth Federation, which was founded in 1932 and initially developed the close relationship with labor. (See Lipset and Meltz 2004; Robinson 1993; Bruce 1989; Adams 1989.)

unionism.[29] Leadership supported and often led struggles for affirmative action, pay equity for women, and immigrant rights. As Canadian director of the UAW (a post he took in 1978), Robert White opposed the international's concession bargaining and urged his membership to form an autonomous Canadian auto union. He then led the newly formed CAW for three terms before becoming CLC president in 1992. White also served as vice president of the federal NDP.

During his tenure with the CAW, White was surrounded by a close group of colleagues who helped set the union's militant and progressive path, including Basil "Buzz" Hargrove, who succeeded him in 1992 as CAW president. Their refusal to accept concessions is legendary. They built a "culture of resistance" members embraced, and that led to successful strikes against Chrysler in 1982 and GM in 1984 among many others during the CAW's first two decades.[30]

CUSWA also has a history of progressive leadership. Leo Gerard led CUSWA as the USW's national director for Canada during NAFTA's negotiation from 1991 to 1994. During this his time Gerard led a ninety-five–day strike against Stelco, one of Canada's largest steel producers, and initiated CUSWA's relationship with the FAT. Gerard was elected USW president in November 2001 – the second Canadian to hold the office. The importance of progressive leadership for transnationalism is reflected in the USW's shift to transnationalism under Gerard. Whereas the USW only had transnational contacts with Mexican unions prior to 2001, under Gerard's leadership the USW developed a strong relationship with a Mexican mineworkers union and created Workers Uniting, which will join the USW and Unite the Union (the largest labor organization in the United Kingdom and Ireland) as the first global union.

In the mid-1970s, Fred Pomeroy led the CWC's effort to successfully organize Bell workers in Ontario and Quebec and to gain better contracts through legal and wildcat strikes (in 1979 and 1980). Under his leadership, the CWC prioritized pay equity in bargaining and antidiscrimination policies. In November 1992, Pomeroy became the executive vice president of the new CEP, then president, serving until his retirement in 2000. Although the CEP (like the CWA and STRM) has, at times, cooperated with management on workplace reorganization decisions, the union has

---

[29] CAW President Bob White and USW National Director for Canada Leo Gerard criticized the NDP for its handling of free trade. In recent years, CAW leadership assailed the NDP for what they feel is a move to the center, failed to endorse the party in key elections, and even urged a split with the NDP.

[30] Gindin (1995, pp. 199–228).

maintained its militancy.[31] CEP officials estimate that "during the five years from 1996 to 2001, almost 35,000 CEP members were on strike at some point, costing the union more than $100 million in strike pay, special strike funds, and appeals."[32]

Canadian unions' progressivism is reflected in and reinforced by humanity/social justice funds that support progressive international solidarity and development work. CUSWA created the first Humanity Fund in 1985 to contribute to international relief efforts and later to international solidarity projects. The CAW followed suit in 1990 and the CWC in 1992. Although the funds' administration varies by union, they usually combine employee and employer contributions and are negotiated as part of collective agreements. To be viable, the funds must have rank-and-file support – workers contribute to the funds directly through their wages. Willingness to contribute directly to the funds therefore reflects rank-and-file commitment to progressive international work.

How Does Progressivism Matter?

The data suggest that North American unions with progressive leadership are more likely to engage in transnationalism. But why are progressive leaders more likely to construct their interests to embrace transnational cooperation? And why are union leaders in industries vulnerable to foreign trade not always transnationalism's biggest proponents? The answer is both ideological and strategic/organizational. Most salient is how progressive leaders construct the problem of globalization or regionalization, and how they conceptualize the possible solutions to these economic and socio-political changes. At the domestic level, progressive leaders embrace a broader social agenda of progressive reform and militant action – a social unionism.

At the international level, progressive leaders view globalization and trade as not inherently inimical to workers' interests. But because they see the interests of workers and capital as intrinsically opposed, they insist that nation-states should mediate the negative aspects of globalization through progressive policies that protect workers. Workers should not rely solely on the state, however, but should actively struggle to protect their rights and collective interests. The CLC's secretary-treasurer, Hassan Yussuff, articulated the progressive internationalist position:

[31] Dubb (1999).
[32] Swift (2003, p. 7).

For all our history we've had a trading relationship with the U.S. and other countries. I mean it would be naïve for Canadians to think that we couldn't or wouldn't continue along those lines. Our fundamental difference in regard to the struggle was that we didn't think the free flow of commerce was in our interest. We think that we should have commerce, but there should be rules that govern investment, technology – in relation to jobs and the economy – and there should be some rules that the government should play [by]. And we saw the free trade agreement as really eroding the sovereignty of our parliament to intervene on behalf of workers. And once you start that trend, you're going to be forever stuck in that model of saying you can't do anything different, you have to keep building on these trade agreements. And we saw it further eroding any ability of working people, whether [they] be in the U.S. or Canada, having direct control.[33]

Progressive leaders' solution to domestic problems is to build a working-class movement that involves broad coalitional support and participation. Their solution to the problems of regionalization/globalization is to build stronger ties transnationally in order to more effectively combat globalization's effects. Leaders therefore construct transnationalism as consistent with the political ideology and strategies of social unionism. The UE's Robin Alexander succinctly captured the progressive labor response to globalization: "In a globalized world, it doesn't take tremendous intelligence to realize that if we're going to have a future, we really need to figure out how to establish relations with unions in other countries."[34] Progressive leaders tend to look forward to new innovative strategies of equitable transnational cooperation rather than backward to nationalist inward-looking strategies. The CAW's Sam Gindin argued that the primary obstacle to labor transnationalism – the competition for jobs across the continent – can be mitigated with creative strategies and education:

There really [are] some questions about how ... you have some solidaristic relationships that aren't competitive. These are the basic questions. I mean if you're going to sit around and just blame each [other] and try to undercut each other for jobs, then getting together every couple of years at a conference and making speeches about solidarity is completely irrelevant. So the question is, is there any way to get together to talk [so] that you can come up with something that is progressive, solidaristic, addresses each of our problems, takes on the companies,

---

[33] Personal interview with Hassan Yussuff of the CLC, February 28, 2001.
[34] Personal interview with Robin Alexander of the UE, December 21, 2000.

has a political program, addresses human rights – and there is. So we've been thinking through some creative stuff.[35]

The CAW distinguished itself among U.S. and Canadian industrial unions by promulgating a quite unique and developed vision of labor transnationalism based on North American mutualism. While it vociferously opposed NAFTA, the union also argued that new jobs in the auto sector should be created in Mexico. Gindin explained how the union attempted to translate its vision of labor transnationalism into North American economic policy:

During the free trade discussions, we tried to push an argument of a North American Auto Pact.[36] And we tried to argue that . . . we supported the development of the Mexican auto industry; they had as much of a right to jobs as we did. And assuming that their market would grow fastest, we thought that their production should grow in line with their market. So we wanted to make that kind of an argument, that that's how the industry should grow. And that in the long term, rather than a strategy based on low wages and disciplining workers and keeping them unorganized as a way of attracting American investment it would be attracting it as a right, the same way we did with the Auto Pact.[37]

What makes progressive leaders unique is not only their ideological framing of globalization but also their strategic and organizational response to it. Unions that fostered transnationalism in response to NAFTA took steps to institutionalize transnationalism and an organizational culture in which it could flourish. They were more likely to hire and support staff who valued relationships and devoted significant time to building them. Although progressive leadership can set a course toward embracing transnationalism, it will likely fail in the long term if it is not institutionalized. Primary and secondary leaders therefore need to build a constituency for maintaining transnational relationships. Unions that constructed fully and partially developed transnational relationships that survived NAFTA's passage educated rank-and-file workers about the benefits of cross-border cooperation and included them in transnational activities. This work helped build support for transnationalism among

[35] Personal interview with Sam Gindin of the CAW, February 14, 2001.
[36] The Auto Pact, as mentioned in Chapter 2, eliminated trade tariffs on auto parts and stated that one car had to be built in Canada for every car sold in Canada. In addition, each vehicle built in Canada had to be produced with sixty percent Canadian parts and labor content.
[37] Personal interview with Sam Gindin of the CAW, February 14, 2001.

workers, who ultimately had to be convinced that its time and expense were justified.

The importance of progressive leadership is reflected in the case of the Janus-faced Teamsters, whose inconsistent support of transnationalism can be explained, in part, by leadership changes. The IBT has historically been considered a militant, though less progressive and less democratic, union.[38] Under the leadership of a more progressive president, the union embraced cross-border cooperation. Ron Carey hired Matt Witt and Andy Banks, who developed fledgling relationships with the FAT and devoted considerable time to NAO submissions. When less progressive James Hoffa assumed the presidency of the IBT, however, he devoted fewer resources to building relationships with Mexican unions, and the fledgling relationship with the FAT stagnated. The case of the Teamsters suggests that building an organizational culture around transnationalism is difficult, if not impossible, without progressive leadership. The cases of the UAW and USW reinforce the point; while committed key staffers such as Steve Beckman and Dan Kovalik initiated fledgling relationships with independent Mexican unions, the ambivalence of less progressive presidents Owen Bieber, Stephen Yokich, and George Becker severely constrained them.

This examination demonstrates that processes that lead to the emergence of labor transnationalism are quite complex. NAFTA's power to catalyze transnational labor relationships was constrained by ideological and organizational factors that limited the breadth and depth of transnational collaboration. Suggesting that political rather than economic factors more adequately explain the variation in the emergence of labor transnationalism in North America challenges the Polanyian assumption that transnational labor movements will spontaneously emerge out of a reconfiguration of the global economy – that trade and globalization alone will stimulate protective transnational countermovements.[39]

---

[38] The IBT supported Republican presidential candidates Ronald Reagan and George H.W. Bush. Rank-and-file union members could not vote for IBT president until 1996. Of course, the union has always had progressive locals, and recent changes suggest the Hoffa administration is moving toward more progressive policies. The union, for example, endorsed Democratic candidate Barack Obama for president in 2008.

[39] Karl Polanyi argues in *The Great Transformation: The Political and Economic Origins of Our Time* (1944, 2001) that unregulated markets are not viable; society will not tolerate the vagaries of a pure free market economy and will form counter-movements to preserve social relations.

Although NAFTA's institutional fields created a new transnational political opportunity structure that helped constitute transnational interests and actors, only some unions were poised to take advantage of it. The experience of North American labor unions suggests that political factors will continue to propel unions toward, or away, from transnational cooperation and simultaneously limit the character and scope of their relationships.

PART THREE

CONCLUSIONS

8

Global Governance and Labor Transnationalism

Between 1985 and 2001, the terrain on which labor unions in North America struggled changed significantly. Prior to 1990, unions across the continent generally waged independent and isolated battles against transnational corporations and unresponsive or hostile national governments. Rarely did they cooperate across national borders. In the exceptional instances in which unions did attempt to collaborate transnationally, their exchanges were usually not driven by mutual interests and had few long-term results. Moreover, they were generally reactive rather than proactive, amounting to little more than obligatory though empty gestures of support and solidarity. In the pre-NAFTA era, not one national industrial union in North America participated in a transnational relationship based on long-term strategic action and mutual interest. The solidification of processes of regional economic integration in the form of a North American free trade agreement, however, sent a shock across the continent that forced unions to respond in new and creative ways.

Unions in North America responded to NAFTA's threat by forming broad coalitions to defeat its passage. NAFTA helped union leaders recognize that processes of regional economic integration inextricably entwined the economic fates of North American workers. To combat the forces of multinational corporations and neoliberal governments alone would be futile. Only through cooperation would it be possible to counter the neoliberal economic project in North America. But cooperation required slaying the "foreign worker" myth and the notion that only workers north of the Rio Grande were entitled to the benefits and protections of decent jobs.

For the first time, unions in all three North American nations worked collaboratively on a concrete goal for an extended period of time. Although participants in anti-NAFTA coalitions faced defeat when the free trade agreement passed in 1993, key unions carried on in the collaborative spirit that marked the historic anti-NAFTA battle. NAFTA, then, had the unintended consequence of catalyzing labor transnationalism in North America. The much despised free trade agreement had this effect by helping key labor federations and industrial unions in North America expand their identities and their strategic repertoires. That is, they began to conceptualize themselves *not only* as national unions but also as North American unions. And they began to incorporate transnationally collaborative and cooperative activities into their strategic toolkits.

The emergence of labor transnationalism in North America confounded the naysayers who predicted that NAFTA would only intensify animosity among North America's unions and generate even more isolationism and racism. But while the anti–free traders bemoaned the giant sucking sound, North American labor unions fashioned a different response to the potential havoc NAFTA would wreak on jobs, wages, and working conditions. With few exceptions, the call from the upper echelons of North America's labor unions and federations was for cross-border unity (even among leaders who did not forge relationships). The threat of free trade led union leaders and their constituencies to cross the physical borders of North America to witness how their supposed "competitors" lived. The realization that workers across the continent actually faced many of the same problems led many union leaders in all three countries to redraw the ideological borders within their unions.

The message was clear: unions would resist continental whipsawing and no longer participate in or tolerate the scapegoating of foreign workers for the problems created by transnational corporations and governments. Unions that did not conform could face collective censure, as the Teamsters did when their colleagues deemed that some elements of their campaign against cross-border trucking relied on and reinforced racialized stereotypes. Labor activists in the United States began to see Mexican workers not only as similar but also as potential allies. The trope of the Mexican "wetback" was quickly replaced by the Mexican compañero.

Global Governance Institutions and Transnational Fields

That NAFTA stimulated unions to identify and develop mutual interests presents a compelling empirical and theoretical puzzle. How did this neoliberal free trade agreement scorned by the vast majority of North

America's labor unions actually facilitate their continued collaboration and cooperation? How did it stimulate transnational relationships among unions, some of whose leaders would not be photographed together a mere five years before? The answer lies not simply in the threat NAFTA embodied but rather in the institutional fields it created. NAFTA, an emergent global governance institution, catalyzed labor transnationalism by creating two new fields – transnational trade-negotiating and legal fields – through which North American labor activists could engage each other. These new fields were essential to transnational coalition-building among a broad array of unions and civil society organizations that opposed free trade because they provided a space to mobilize collective action.

These new institutional fields were also critical to the process of developing transnational labor relationships because they helped constitute the activists that engaged that space as transnational actors with transnational interests and rights. In the course of mobilizing and adjudicating collectively in NAFTA-generated fields, activists built trust and began to chip away at racism and ethnocentrism within their ranks. They also enjoyed significant successes. Their collective activities in the transnational trade-negotiating field helped ensure the linkage of labor protections and free trade, which ultimately became embodied in the NAALC itself. And their collective action in the transnational legal field helped build networks and support broader labor rights campaigns. The unions that engaged these fields – among them the largest and most powerful labor unions and federations in North America – created a new strategic and antiracist rhetorical repertoire that had significant implications for all North American unions. Although not all industrial unions participated in NAFTA fields, even those at its margins did not remain immune from their effects.

The two institutional fields NAFTA created also propelled key unions from mere contacts toward equitable ongoing interactions. A few even institutionalized their relationships through joint programs and permanent staff positions. One set of unions – the FAT, UE, and CUSWA – developed a cooperative complementary identity. Through support and participation among leaders and the rank and file, they infused their unions with a culture of transnationalism characterized by action and identification. Trust was essential to this process, as one AFL-CIO official emphasized: "You need to build a sort of personal and institutional trust structure with folks which is a very time consuming kind of circumstance and is very difficult."[1]

---

[1] Personal interview with Mark Anderson of the AFL-CIO, January 8, 2001.

Many unions that came together in the transnational trade-negotiating field quickly extended their collaborative work beyond the purview of NAFTA toward more general labor activism and advocacy. They engaged in joint actions and campaigns and built new institutions (such as the FAT's strike fund). Unions' collaborative activities simultaneously solidified the process of constituting regional actors and interests and undermined the use of racialized rhetoric that, prior to NAFTA's negotiation, had limited the possibilities for labor transnationalism.

Transnational Institutional Fields and Political Opportunities

These unanticipated consequences of regional economic integration in North America not only beg empirical analysis but also offer a unique opportunity to expand our theoretical understanding of the relationship between global governance institutions and transnational social movements. An analysis of NAFTA as a case of a new global governance institution is intriguing because it illuminates the *process* by which global governance institutions can create new transnational opportunity structures for movements. Specifically, it unearths the links between transnational institutional fields and opportunity structures, reconceptualizes the dimensions of political opportunity structures as mechanisms with constitutive functions, and explores the constitutive effects of international laws and legal mechanisms on social movements.

In this book, I suggest that transnational political opportunity structures emerge from transnational institutional fields that create spaces where activists come together, mobilize, and develop their interests and identities in relationship to each other. In order for fields to be catalysts, they must promote or facilitate the constitution of transnational actors and interests and the definition, recognition, and adjudication of transnational rights. These constitutive mechanisms of transnational institutional fields underscore the differences in how power is constituted at the national and transnational levels.

The first mechanism highlights the importance of constituting regional or North American actors with North American interests (as opposed to national actors with national interests). Actors in the transnational arena often have opposing interests that stem from varied geographical, cultural, economic, and political experiences and positionings. Some scholars insist that these differences are particularly difficult for labor movements to overcome because the interests of labor unions in developed and developing countries are antagonistic. That is, the global economy forces workers in different countries to compete for jobs. But, as Chapter 3 shows, through their common struggle to define and defeat the threat of regional economic integration, unions in North America came to identify and organize around their common interests as *North American unions*.

The second mechanism underscores the importance of legal rights for movement building. Whereas nation-states have the power to define and grant the rights of national "citizens," global governance institutions define and recognize the rights of transnational or regional social actors and their organizations. That is, global governance institutions constitute them as "citizens of standing" in transnational adjudicative arenas. The transnational legal field defined and recognized transnational rights and granted legitimacy to transnational actors and their claims.

Finally, global governance institutions provide a formal political-institutional structure that makes rules and provides mechanisms for expressing and adjudicating grievances when rules are violated at the transnational level. As Chapter 4 shows, NAFTA constituted a transnational labor rights regime that strengthened existing transnational relationships and catalyzed others. Although the NAALC's enforcement mechanisms are weak, the creation of transnational standards and norms is useful to labor activists whose grievances are legitimized at the transnational level. Moreover, by engaging the NAALC process and collaborating on NAO submissions, North American labor unions solidify their common interests.

Theoretically, the NAFTA case reveals the difficulty that political process theory – which developed almost exclusively in relationship to nation-states and national political processes and institutions – has in accounting for the nature and nuances of transnational political opportunity structures. Examining transnational institutional fields helps illuminate how power is constituted at the transnational level. Whereas some social movement scholars contend that social movements lack power in the transnational arena, my analysis suggests that power is not absent but rather is constituted differently than on the national level, where electoral politics is a primary determinant of social movement strategies and options.

In the transnational realm, power is constituted in the interstices between national governments and global governance institutions. As Keck and Sikkink (1998) and Tarrow (2005) demonstrate, transnational social movement networks engage power by exploiting the relationship between national and transnational political institutions. Thus, just as the nation-state constitutes a national power structure that provides political opportunities for national social movements, global governance institutions (such as NAFTA and the NAALC) constitute transnational power structures that provide new political opportunities for emergent transnational social movements. The case of NAFTA suggests that state-like entities in the international arena *can* play a crucial role in the emergence of transnational social movements, as nation-states do in the emergence of national social movements (Tilly 1984). Indeed, the lack of statelike global governance regimes could explain the paucity of transnational social movements in an era of globalization. If we look at the universe of cases of transnationalism and global governance, however, we are currently at an intermediate stage. We have some transnational governance institutions that stimulate and provide a target for transnational movements. But they have not developed to the extent that theories of transnational institutional fields and opportunities will allow us to explain the variation in their effects.

The dimensions of transnational fields, political opportunity structures, and global governance institutions I identify as being the most salient to labor transnationalism are useful yardsticks by which to measure other global governance institutions and their potential to serve as catalysts for different kinds of transnational social movements. Given the uncertainty of how future governance institutions and mechanisms will emerge and be structured, further research is necessary to build on and test my model. I believe, however, that the value of a theory of transnational institutional fields in relationship to transnational social movement building is its ability to explain strategies and outcomes in a variety of different cases and contexts. My assumption is *not* that the same set of forces that gave rise to NAFTA will necessarily exist in the future but that different sets of forces will prevail at different historical moments and during different struggles. If sufficiently robust, my theoretical framework will be able to account for these differences while still providing explanatory power.

My analysis of the NAFTA case illuminates the potential effects of other new international governance structures on different kinds of social movements, from environmental movements seeking climate change regulation to investors lobbying for corporate governance reform. Indeed, international climate change coalitions began to emerge and coalesce in response to the United Nations Kyoto Protocol process and contestation over the measurement, abatement, and enforcement mechanisms the treaty would have. Although the conditions under which the international climate change movement are forming are very different from those that gave birth to NAFTA, the role of global goverance institutions and institutional fields that facilitate the creation of transnational interests, actors, and rights remains central to the process.

The Local versus the Transnational

The story of labor transnationalism in North America is colored by the relationship between national labor movements and their respective nation-states. One of NAFTA's most enduring lessons is that, in an era of globalization, drawing sharp distinctions between the local and the global becomes increasingly anachronistic. The model of transnational institutional fields I offer here suggests that constructing the local and global in opposition to each other is misguided because transnational fields almost always connect domestic *and* transnational arenas. Movements that have an institutionalized relationship to the state, such as the labor movement, cannot completely disengage from national arenas. Theorizing transnational fields therefore helps reconcile the local–global dichotomy.

Although they exploit transnational political opportunity structures and engage transnational fields, national labor movements' *primary* focus is still the state. And this orientation presents significant obstacles to labor transnationalism. Although almost all industrial unions engaged NAFTA's transnational fields in some way, the majority of them did not create transnational relationships. The most significant predictor of the emergence of labor transnationalism is the presence of a progressive Mexican union – which almost always refers to a union not tied to its nation-state. Official Mexican unions' pact with the Mexican government or ruling party severely limited their ability to oppose government economic development strategics and neoliberal economic policies. Official unions' hierarchical structures, designed in part to limit contention, therefore prevented progressive sections from making transnational contacts and participating in transnational fields with other North American unions that opposed free trade.

U.S. and Canadian unions' tendency to privilege their relationship with the nation-state also affects the possibilities for labor transnationalism. Some leaders of Canadian unions express reluctance to engage the NAALC process for fear that it will signal to the Canadian government that the NAALC is an acceptable mechanism on which to model future trade agreements. Canadians' refusal to engage the NAALC process would undermine the ability of labor activists to push the NAALC process to be more effective and responsive to labor rights violations through trinational collective action.

An analysis of the Teamsters' cross-border trucking campaign reveals that strategic decision makers crafted certain elements of their rhetoric (related to unsafe trucks and drugs) to persuade members of Congress to keep U.S. borders closed. Although the strategy succeeded in garnering congressional support, it did little to endear the IBT to progressive unions and NGOs across the continent. U.S. unions' historic ties to the Democratic Party also undermined transnationalism during the NAFTA struggle. Some argue that the AFL-CIO's reluctance to oppose newly elected President Clinton's free trade agreement early on actually facilitated its passage (see Evans and Kay 2008). The federation supported Clinton's election and yet, on this key issue, AFL-CIO leaders and their members found themselves head-to-head with the president they helped elect. Hoping to influence the administration and key democrats behind closed doors, the AFL-CIO hedged its bets and restrained its public assault.

The Clinton administration offered the labor side agreement as an enticement for labor's support of NAFTA. The AFL-CIO balked at the toothless side agreement but remained at the table. Finally, just months before NAFTA was signed, the AFL-CIO recognized the folly of negotiating with the administration and publicly announced its opposition to NAFTA. But the administration's efforts had gained momentum, and the AFL-CIO lost the battle. The AFL-CIO's strategy prevented it from fully and openly engaging with independent Mexican unions and progressive NGOs in the transnational trade-negotiating and legal fields.

Because the relationship between labor movements and nation-states is unique, future work that focuses on how transnational movements with different relationships to nation-states emerge and mobilize (e.g., human and women's rights, environmental movements, etc.) would be invaluable to our understanding of transnationalism.

Labor Transnationalism and the Primacy of Political Catalysts

While national politics shape the boundaries of labor transnationalism, so does a union's ideological orientation. The existence of global governance institutions therefore does not guarantee movement building. What makes NAFTA particularly useful as a case is that unions responded differently to its effects, revealing the importance of leadership, strategy, and education to changing organizational cultures. Not all unions developed relationships, but those that did participated in

NAFTA's transnational fields. NAFTA was therefore a necessary but not sufficient condition for the development of labor transnationalism in the early 1990s. Only unions that had certain predisposing characteristics were susceptible to NAFTA's catalyzing effect. The analysis in Chapter 7 suggests that NAFTA's power to catalyze transnational labor relationships was constrained by political and ideological factors that limited the breadth and depth of transnational collaboration. Unions with progressive leaders were more likely to engage in transnational relationships than those with less progressive leadership. These leaders helped build their unions' ideological and organizational culture to support transnationalism and provided alternative analyses and rhetorical frameworks that did not rely on scapegoating foreign workers to explain regional economic integration. Leaders therefore had a tremendous effect on the emergence of labor transnationalism.

Economic factors, in contrast, had less effect on unions' participation in transnational relationships. As we saw in Chapter 1, processes of regional economic integration per se (such as increased trade and investment) do not adequately account for the emergence of transnational labor relationships. Nor do relationships necessarily develop among unions that are vulnerable to foreign trade or integrated along common production chains. This analysis therefore challenges scholars' assumption that transnational labor movements will spontaneously emerge out of a reconfiguration of the global economy – that labor unions will respond to the crisis of free trade by creating transnational relationships that could potentially give them more bargaining power and leverage with employers. To the extent that transnational relationships emerged in North America, they did so in response to NAFTA's nascent transnational fields, which had *political* effects by constituting transnational actors and interests.

The Consequences of NAFTA and Labor Transnationalism

At the same time that NAFTA catalyzed labor transnationalism in North America, it also generated changes within national labor movements across the continent. To deal with the free trade threat, North American labor unions reevaluated key domestic policies and made significant changes in their internal structures. For example, the AFL-CIO created the Task Force on Trade, restructured its international and public policy departments, and hired economists and lawyers to focus on trade issues. Similarly, the Canadian Labour Congress created a special position on NAFTA in its international department in response to the free trade agreement. These organizational changes suggest that NAFTA presented a crisis for the continent's labor unions that required a reassessment of trade policies and a reorientation of internal structures. Some AFL-CIO activists even explained John Sweeney's election as the result of his predecessor's failure to successfully deal with the changes wrought by globalization, as embodied primarily in the NAFTA defeat.

In Mexico, processes of regional economic integration had debilitating effects on the government-controlled labor movement, and NAFTA helped propel the trend forward. In the 1980s, after years of producing largely for a domestic market, economic crises led the Mexican government to court foreign investors and multinational companies with promises of cheap, controlled labor and economic incentives. The PRI's inability to maintain a stranglehold on state and local government positions provided a political opening for independent labor unions and federations that, in the past, were severely constrained by the government. As free trade loomed, official unions stagnated and toed the government line, whereas their enterprising independent counterparts actively joined the NAFTA debate and formed trinational networks with U.S. and Canadian unions.

International contacts provided independent unions with much-needed legitimacy, while their international acumen gave them new support both within Mexico and across the continent. Mexican labor activists contend that processes of regional economic integration culminating in NAFTA provided new space for independent Mexican unions, and thus for a more democratic Mexican labor movement. As one Mexican activist said: "The independent labor movement is stronger here after NAFTA. The signing of NAFTA coincided with a big fracturing of Salinas's neoliberal model, and the independent movement grew.... The UNT represented a fracture in the corporatist structure."[2]

Immigration

In NAFTA's aftermath, U.S. labor unions were also forced to reevaluate their stance on key domestic issues, particularly immigration. Historically the AFL-CIO and most U.S. unions supported the enforcement of immigration laws that prevented Mexican immigrants from entering the U.S. labor market, including the Immigration Reform and Control Act

[2] Personal interview with Antonio Almazán of the SME, July 27, 1999.

of 1986 (IRCA), which required employers to verify that employees were not "illegal" immigrants. Although critics argued that employer sanctions resulted in the discrimination and intimidation of immigrants, the AFL-CIO backed the law.

In the years after NAFTA's passage, however, the AFL-CIO began to reevaluate its position on immigration. In 1995, the AFL-CIO Executive Council issued a statement on immigration that definitively outlined the federation's position on racial scapegoating and immigration:

The facts are these: immigrants are not the cause of America's declining wages and the export of good jobs overseas. Immigrants are not responsible for the "downsizing" that is sweeping through many U.S. industries and throwing millions of Americans out of work. And immigrants cannot be blamed for the fraying of the country's social fabric that so many Americans perceive with uneasiness and alarm.[3]

In stark contrast to its 1968 Executive Council Report on U.S.-Mexican Border Problems, a 1999 AFL-CIO resolution on immigration placed the blame for economic dislocation squarely on employers rather than on foreign workers: "Far too many employers have sought to exploit the H-2B (other skilled worker) and H-2A (agricultural guest worker) programs in order to depress the wages and working conditions of U.S. workers."[4]

The final nail in the coffin for draconian U.S. union immigration policy came in 2000 when the AFL-CIO reversed its previous support for IRCA. The federation called for the repeal of major parts of the legislation. The language used by the Central Labor Council of Alameda County in a 1999 resolution speaks volumes about the change in the U.S. labor movement's position on immigration: "Thousands of immigrant workers, both with and without documents, have mounted large and effective campaigns to organize unions in California in the last decade. These efforts have created new unions and strengthened and revived many others, benefiting all labor, immigrant and native-born alike."[5]

Although the AFL-CIO's historic new stance on immigration policy is a result of a variety of factors – including pressure from progressive affiliates and individual local leaders, declining union density, and the influx of immigrants into certain jobs and industries – many labor activists

---

[3] "Statement by the AFL-CIO Executive Council on Immigration and the American Dream," February 23, 1995.
[4] Resolution of the 23rd AFL-CIO Biennial Convention (1999).
[5] Ibid.

assert that NAFTA was among the constellation of forces that led to a change in the policy. As the UAW's Steve Beckman explained:

By putting so much focus on Mexico, the immigration issues obviously changed. The way the labor movement deals with immigration has changed.... So that broader social issue has become more prominent for the labor movement because of the ways in which NAFTA demonstrated the increasing integration of product markets and labor markets in a way that was unavoidable. So there's some reassessment on domestic economic policy in that way.[6]

In 2010, the Solidarity Center's Benjamin Davis stated emphatically: "I don't think you would have had the shifts in the AFL immigration policy without the cross-border work around NAFTA."[7] Years earlier, he had explained:

I think [NAFTA] started a process and a debate that has really gone a very long way in the past eight years. And not to overplay it, but I think certainly Seattle demonstrates and some of the other changes in AFL-CIO policies, for example on immigration, demonstrate that that political debate has really [borne fruit] in terms of a consciousness that workers in other countries are not our enemies.[8]

The IBT's Matt Witt was even more specific. When asked if NAFTA had an impact on labor solidarity, he responded: "Yeah, I think it had a lot of impact. And in a lot of ways it had impact on how the Teamsters and other unions relate to immigrant workers in this country." When asked in what way, he continued:

I think there's a definite connection there [between NAFTA and immigration policy]. [In 2001] the new president of the Teamsters [Ron Carey] went to California and gave a speech about how the union stands with immigrant workers and we need to change the immigration laws and immigrants can't continue to be exploited and so on. It was just an unthinkable speech to have been given in 1991; it would never [have] happened. A president of the Teamsters in 1991 wouldn't have thought of giving that speech, but if they did it would have taken about ten seconds to make a political judgment that their members wouldn't like it if they said it. But I think the whole evolution of groups working together across the border and people coming to an understanding that the global economy means us – it's not just the companies moving their money around but it's workers becoming more integrated – is something that has affected everybody's thinking....[9]

---

[6] Personal interview with Steve Beckman of the UAW, December 19, 2000.
[7] Personal interview with Benjamin Davis of the AFL-CIO's Solidarity Center, April 23, 2010.
[8] Personal interview with Benjamin Davis of the AFL-CIO's Solidarity Center, December 6, 2000.
[9] Personal interview with Matt Witt of the IBT, January 17, 2001.

NAFTA also had a more subtle effect on immigration policy by stimulating contacts among U.S. and Mexican unions. Given Mexican unionists' concern for immigrant workers, they looked favorably on U.S. unions' support of immigrants and progressive immigration policy. A UNITE activist explained how contacts with Mexican unionists affected UNITE's decision to fight for new immigration policies:

Definitely contact with Mexican unions was a contributing factor to the change in policy. I think that that's true.... You sit down with Mexican unionists and you start figuring out what you can do together. Like, in our case, we've been doing this immigrants' rights stuff for [years]... and you see how they respond. They think that's great. And it makes them very responsive and receptive to other things. So in our case it's this mutual reinforcing that's going on. So we see oh, they like this. So we'll try to do more of it.[10]

As Hassan Yussuff, the vice president of the CLC, explained, free trade also helped push the Canadian labor movement to reevaluate its policies and programs on immigration and antiracism:

During the free trade debate you were dealing with people from the south and they understood the consequences.... The fact that the trade agreement created so much pressure on the labor movement to recreate itself [that] allowed this space to start happening because if they didn't create space for these people, these groups, the labor movement wouldn't [have] the numbers it [has] today and it certainly wouldn't be the kind of labor movement it's becoming.... But it was... the trade agreements, I think, that put real tremendous pressure on the labor movement to do that.[11]

Influenced in part by NAFTA, the CLC launched an antiracism campaign in 1998 and made efforts to organize and create space in the Canadian labor movement for immigrant and minority workers.

The emergence of anti-immigrant militias and calls for a border fence between Mexico and the United States (though not between the United States and Canada) also generated almost unanimous criticism from unions across the continent, including official Mexican unions. After 9/11, bolstered in part by the AFL-CIO's shift in immigration policy, many of its affiliates promoted immigrant worker rights. Unions organized immigrants, engaged in marches and protests, and supported workers displaced by immigration raids. In the fall of 2003, unions helped spearhead the immigrant workers freedom ride modeled after the 1960s civil rights freedom rides. Over one thousand immigrant riders and their supporters

---

[10] Personal interview with Alan Howard of UNITE, December 15, 2000.
[11] Personal interview with Hassan Yussuff of the CLC, February 28, 2001.

boarded buses in nine U.S. cities and traveled for twelve days across the country to converge in Washington, D.C., on October 1. There they met with members of the U.S. Congress and ultimately converged in New York for a rally attended by over 125,000 people. Of the twenty-seven members of the freedom ride's national sponsoring committee, twelve were labor unions or labor-related organizations, including the AFL-CIO and UNITE.

In the spring of 2006, the issue of immigration reform exploded after the U.S. House of Representatives passed legislation that would have imposed severe penalties on illegal immigrants, classifying them and anyone who helped them enter or stay in the United States as felons. Unions again were among those at the forefront, organizing marches and protests across the country. Between February and May 2006, millions of people protested in cities all over the country and around the world. On April 10, marches were held in 102 cities. On May 1– Labor Day in many parts of the world – nationwide strikes of U.S. schools and businesses drew enormous crowds into the streets, the largest estimated at up to 700,000 people in Chicago. Among protesters' demands were legalization, amnesty, and respect for immigrants' rights. U.S. unions also condemned immigrant raids by Immigration and Customs Enforcement and advocated and provided services and legal representation for workers displaced by raids. And even as I write, the introduction of Arizona's draconian immigration law (SB 1070) is generating a groundswell of opposition and legal wrangling, much of it led by labor unions.

The tragedy of 9/11 could have reversed North American unions' general embrace of more progressive immigration policies after NAFTA. Indeed, unions could have retrenched in response to the anti-immigrant sentiment that spread across the country, focusing solely on members' needs and tempering rhetoric on immigrant workers' rights. Although union decline and an increase in immigrant workers were critical to unions' continued support of progressive immigration reform legislation after 9/11, so was the ascendency of a new cadre of progressive leaders – many of them first- or second-generation immigrants themselves – who had helped construct an antiracist response to NAFTA less than ten years earlier. In the early 1990s, they were not able to convince the AFL-CIO's top brass, however, to push for the inclusion of migration as part of NAFTA's negotiations. Because official *and* independent Mexican unions supported its inclusion, the AFL-CIO squandered an opportunity to build transnationalism around immigration reform during NAFTA negotiations. North American unions' ideological convergence on progressive immigration reform post-9/11 had the unintended consequence of creating new opportunities for transnationalism. It remains to be seen, however, whether the continent's largest union federations will fully take advantage of them.

Trade Agreements

For many unions and labor activists, NAFTA symbolized the first "shot heard round the world" in the trade wars. It galvanized a broader antiglobalization movement that has arguably been the most active and sustained international social movement of the last thirty-five years – surpassing even the antiwar movement. The coalitions that became trinational during NAFTA's negotiation regrouped and broadened as new free trade agreements emerged on the political horizon. One of the most compelling effects of NAFTA is the stimulation of trinational social movement coalitions that include labor and other civil society NGOs and organizations. Many of these connections endured and broadened as new trade agreements emerged. The Hemispheric Social Alliance (HSA) organized in 1997 to oppose the Free Trade Agreement of the Americas (FTAA). Seasoned anti-NAFTA activists formed its core. As one of the participating NGOs noted on its Web site:

The HSA is a historic coalition of citizens' networks representing some 50 million people in the Americas. It has evolved out of more than a decade of cross-border cooperation among civil-society organizations, beginning with the development of a strong trinational network during the NAFTA debate during the early 1990s. As the official talks began to extend that model throughout the region, multisectoral coalitions on trade emerged in many countries. In 1997, the Brazilian CUT labor federation hosted a major summit of labor unions and NGOs held parallel to the FTAA trade ministers' meeting in Belo Horizonte, Brazil. The event involved the North American networks, as well as activists from several other Latin American countries. The final declaration of this gathering served as a framework for future collaboration to help build a movement in support of an alternative approach to the FTAA.[12]

Activists in all three countries argue that networks such as HSA are unique because they are based on a long-term commitment to broaden labor struggles to include civil society actors and to strategize in more comprehensive ways. As one participant explained: "In building the Hemispheric Social Alliance we are creating space, opportunity and capacity for progressive civil society organizations of the Americas to come together as

12 Alliance for Responsible Trade. http://www.art-us.org/HSA.html.

equals to define new strategies and common targets. It is the new face for solidarity for the millennium."[13] Labor activists, in the face of regional economic integration, saw the benefits of building permanent pan-social movement coalitions for long-term struggles. The plethora of progressive civil society organizations that now exists as a powerful voice for fair trade in the Americas is extremely significant and reflects one of the most positive and unintended outcomes of processes of regional economic integration.

Although most activists believe they have done little to thwart processes of globalization, they have actually had significant successes. Activists killed fast-track authorizations in the United States in 1997 and 1998. In 1998, negotiations over the Multilateral Agreement on Investment (MAI) among OECD countries failed after worldwide criticism from a broad coalition of civil society organizations and developing countries. The MAI was being negotiated in secret between 1995 and 1997 until an OECD insider leaked a copy to a Canadian NGO. The draft copy revealed that the agreement sought to create international investment rules that would supersede national laws. As reported in a Canadian newspaper: "The Director General of the WTO, Renato Ruggiero, described the undertaking bluntly: 'We are writing the constitution of a single global economy.'"[14] The draft even allowed corporations to sue governments if laws protecting the environment, health, or labor constrained their profit-making.

North American unions condemned the MAI and highlighted its relevance in the broader globalization debate. An AFL-CIO statement explained:

We are at an important historic turning point. The expert wisdom of a few years ago – that a deregulated world market would create prosperity for all – is now discredited. We have an opportunity to rethink and reshape the rules of the global economy. We should ensure that the global economy of the future is one built on a solid foundation of democratic, sustainable, and egalitarian growth, not unlimited profit for a few corporate giants.[15]

In 1998, the negotiations failed, largely as a result of pressure from labor, environmental, and other civil society organizations – many of which participated in anti-NAFTA coalitions. An effort to introduce an MAI in

[13] Quote by Patty C. Barrera of Common Frontiers-Canada, as reported at http://www.web.net/comfront/cfhems.htm.
[14] Harvey (1997).
[15] AFL-CIO Executive Council, "AFL-CIO Statement on the MAI," October 14, 1998.

September 2003 at the WTO Ministerial in Cancun also failed after these organizations and developing countries pushed back yet again.

Labor and other activists' greatest success came in November 2005, when the FTAA died in Mar del Plata, Argentina, after over a decade of negotiations. In December 1994, less than a year after NAFTA went into force, leaders across the Americas introduced this extension of NAFTA at the Summit of the Americas in Miami. Just months before 9/11, the April 2001 Summit meeting in Quebec City drew an unprecedented number of protesters, who clashed with police and kept a rapt international public glued to the news. Protesters converged again two years later at the 2003 Summit in Miami. By 2005, the ceaseless pressure from large labor federations, groups such as the Hemispheric Social Alliance, and disgruntled governments stalled the negotiations indefinitely.

Although labor and its allies did not kill every trade agreement that emerged after NAFTA, few if any agreements failed to meet stiff opposition and resistance. In 2007, for example, Costa Rica's labor federations and unions launched a massive campaign along with other civil society organizations against the referendum vote on the Dominican Republic-Central American Free Trade Agreement (DR-CAFTA). Costa Rica's decision to have the electorate vote yes or no on the agreement was quite historic; it was the first time citizens in any nation directly voted on a trade agreement. On September 30, just a week before the vote, anti–DR-CAFTA activists staged one of the largest protests in the nation's history, with crowds estimated at over 100,000 converging on the capital. The AFL-CIO, CLC, and the International Trade Union Confederation supported Costa Rica's opposition movement. Costa Rican government and business launched their own campaign for the agreement's passage, however, and ultimately it passed with fifty-two percent of voters in favor. That free trade continues to be a lightning rod, and that North American unions persistently reconvene and mobilize in broad-based coalitions to fight against new agreements as they emerge, attests to the strength of NAFTA as a catalyst both of protest and transnational cooperation.

Implications for Transnational Social Movements

An analysis of NAFTA and labor transnationalism has several implications for the study of transnational social movements. First, it suggests that social movement scholars should focus more analytical attention on how global governance institutions create shifts in national and transnational political opportunity structures by creating institutional fields. As this analysis demonstrates, it was not economic changes or changes in existing national political systems and institutions that stimulated tri-national alliances and created a shift in the North American political opportunity structure. Rather, changes in the transnational arena and the introduction of new global governance institutions and institutional fields – NAFTA, the NAALC, the NAOs – stimulated new political strategies in the transnational sphere.[16]

Second, a case analysis of NAFTA offers much-needed insight into the obstacles to labor transnationalism. Excavating the mechanisms by which NAFTA and the NAALC stimulated labor transnationalism suggests that global governance institutions that grant legitimacy and provide mechanisms for expressing and redressing grievances when rules are violated are critical to the development of transnational social movements. Unions' experience with the NAALC suggests that it is not only the existence of legal institutions that matters but the range of issues and the remedies they provide.

NAFTA generates resistance to globalization in different ways than global governance institutions that lack adjudicative functions. Labor and other activists flock to large transnational demonstrations – such as the 1999 "battle of Seattle" – to protest the policies of the WTO, World Bank, and other organizations. However, activists' strategic options are limited because these institutions have no public adjudicative processes or legal rights mechanisms that activists can engage. Activists themselves point to the limitations of most global governance institutions and call for them to incorporate and promote more transparency and democratic participatory processes. Global governance institutions that are intimately connected to nation-states, it could be argued, are better positioned to serve these functions than those that are not accountable to nation-states.

NAFTA was unique because both the transnational trade-negotiating and legal fields allowed public participation, however limited. The former mandated labor union participation in the negotiation process, and the latter allows it in its adjudicatory process. The NAALC's endorsement of public hearings is quite rare among transnational labor rights mechanisms and fosters not only transnational collaboration among unions but also media coverage of and broader public interest in labor rights struggles. Indeed, under the Bush administration, when unions began to use

---

[16] It is plausible that labor transnationalism could also emerge as a result of significant policy or procedural changes in existing global governance institutions.

the NAALC process less frequently, they also engaged in fewer large-scale continental campaigns (such as Echlin and Han Young) and generated less mainstream media attention. Having concrete transnational political institutions to engage in the ephemeral transnational arena is critically important to social movements. The story of NAFTA, then, is a story of institutional relevance.

Although an analysis of NAFTA shows that many unions came to the new institutional arena NAFTA built, it is critical to examine whether or not they were willing to stay. Although NAFTA is more responsive than global governance institutions such as the International Monetary Fund and World Bank that lack adjudicative functions, the NAALC's failure to provide meaningful redress on core labor rights undermines its ability to help generate labor transnationalism. It is therefore critical that transnational actors remain proactively engaged in the process of shaping and strengthening trade agreements to ensure that they provide more political opportunities and democratic mechanisms, not fewer. Few social movements are as well positioned to serve as ballast against the vagaries of an ever-expanding global economy as a transnational labor movement, with its established membership, political clout, and financial resources. If labor unions refuse to engage global governance institutions such as the NAALC and demand that they have not simply teeth but fangs, then their ability not only to protect workers' rights but also serve as a mechanism to build labor transnationalism will be diminished. *How* new legal mechanisms and governance institutions are built is therefore critically important to transnational social movement development.

Legal mechanisms that require transnational contact and collaboration through procedural rules can help generate transnational relationships. The lack of similar rules in other governance mechanisms such as the ILO, IACHR, and labor clause of the GSP could help explain why they did not stimulate transnational relationships among North American unions prior to NAFTA. The failure of NAFTA's environmental side agreement (NAAEC) process to generate transnational relationships among environmental organizations, however, provides the strongest evidence that the structure of transnational governance institutions can have significant effects on transnational movement building. Few if any trinational relationships or large continental campaigns emerged in response to the NAAEC process. Of the sixty-five NAAEC submissions filed between 1994 and 2008, forty-eight were filed by individual citizens or organizations and only two included submitters from all three NAFTA countries. Moreover, neither of these two submissions *directly* involved issues related to human health (e.g., pollution, contamination, etc.) and/or specific communities but rather involved the protection of continental species and resources: migratory birds and forests.[17]

The very different effects of the two side agreements on transnationalism underscore the importance of institutional structures and mechanisms. The key difference between the NAALC and NAAEC is an adjudicatory procedure – one facilitates collective submissions and the other privileges individual submissions. A seemingly small institutional peculiarity that provides incentives for collective action, it turns out, has significant effects on transnational movement building.

My analysis suggests that the ability of transnational social movements to mitigate the inequalities created by globalization processes could be improved by stronger – meaning more responsive, transparent, and participatory – global governance institutions. But because so few trade agreements, global governance institution instruments, or international laws have strong enforcement mechanisms for violations of labor and human rights, scholars and movement actors should also be attentive to how their structures and mechanisms undermine or optimize movement building. As the NAFTA case shows, even institutions with weak enforcement and policy outcomes can have strong movement outcomes.

The analysis also demonstrates that processes of regional economic integration need not undermine labor movements. Their embodiment in free trade agreements such as NAFTA provides new challenges *and* new transnational political opportunity structures for the continent's labor movements. More than a decade and a half after its passage, labor activists in all three NAFTA countries agree unequivocally that the NAALC *has not met* their expectations or workers' needs. NAFTA has not materially improved the lives of workers. In its review of the NAALC after four years, the Canadian Association of Labour Lawyers wrote that although the promise of the NAALC is substantial: "the agreement is seriously flawed, and has achieved little of its original promise."[18] The AFL-CIO's assessment echoed these comments: "[The NAALC] has failed to bring about substantial improvement in worker rights and standards in the three NAFTA countries."[19]

---

[17] The Migratory Birds (1999) and Logging Rider (1995) submissions.

[18] Review of the North American Agreement on Labor Cooperation 1994–1997, Public Comments, Annex 5. Available at http://www.naalc.org/english/review_annex5_can .shtml.

[19] Review of the North American Agreement on Labor Cooperation 1994–1997, Public Comments, Annex 5. http://www.naalc.org/english/review_annex5_usa.shtml.

A provision within the agreement that allows for NAFTA's renegotiation offers a rallying point and a glimmer of hope for labor activists. Many of the labor unions involved in the anti–free trade struggle continue to push for a social clause to be added to NAFTA or for NAFTA to be renegotiated. Under the Bush administration their efforts did not bear fruit, but many remain optimistic about the possibility of strengthening NAFTA during the Obama presidency. Although labor activists wish to retain the social and legal protections that their nation-states provide (for example, Canadians demand the maintenance of uniquely Canadian social policies and labor laws), they argue for upward harmonization in the form of enforceable North American labor standards, protections, and rights. This perspective is not nationalistic but rather regional in nature. As one Mexican activist explained:

Economic integration was the source of the change from a nationalistic perspective to a more global one. Globalization opened the door. It ruptured those nationalistic perspectives and forced [all of us] to adopt a policy of cooperation and find out who the workers in the other country were.... I think NAFTA helped break the barriers of a nationalistic attitude. NAFTA opened our eyes a little, obligated us to see that the process of economic integration was occurring from above.[20]

Although all of the labor leaders I interviewed criticized the NAALC for failing to provide sufficient remedies for labor rights violations in North America, they also agreed that the new transnational political arena the NAALC provides has value. They do not see the NAALC as an effective mechanism to eliminate labor abuses, but they do see it as useful insofar as it gives them standing and legitimacy in a transnational arena and facilitates their continued cooperation.

Labor transnationalism in North America is in its initial stages. Even unions that have formed trinational labor relationships find it extremely difficult to maximize their potential. As the transnational political opportunity structure develops, labor activists will have to build their capacity to take advantage of it, amend their strategic repertoires, and continue to demand that they help determine the rules governing the regional economy. This possibility would not exist were it not for the initial contacts and relationships stimulated by NAFTA. The case of NAFTA suggests that agency can be found even in toothless neoliberal trade agreements. The extent to which labor movements can find and exploit nascent transnational political opportunity structures, undermine internal barriers to labor transnationalism (such as racism and ethnocentrism), and

[20] Personal interview with Alejandro Quiroz Soriano of SEMARNAP, June 23, 1999.

simultaneously leverage nation-states and global governance institutions will determine not only their survival transnationally but also their relevance within the national contexts in which they are embedded.

NAFTA's Enduring Legacy

Sixteen years after its implementation, NAFTA continues to be a lightning rod of controversy and contention across the continent. Its proponents claim the agreement has helped stimulate trade, investment, and new jobs, whereas its critics contend it has increased poverty and inequality, intensified migration, and killed jobs, particularly in manufacturing. NAFTA's relevance is best reflected by its continued reference; over a decade and a half after its passage, NGOs and think tanks continue to mark its anniversaries with reports (e.g., "NAFTA at Ten"), and activists still take to the streets to protest its effects. On January 1, 2008, when all tariffs on corn and beans were finally eliminated under the trade deal, protesters marched on both sides of the U.S.-Mexican border.

Moreover, NAFTA still serves as a political litmus test: a political candidate's position on NAFTA often makes front-page news. In 2008, during the Democratic primary race, NAFTA's potential renegotiation was a key policy issue; candidates regularly weighed in on the topic during speeches and formal debates. A minor brouhaha ensued when critics accused then-Senator Barack Obama of "flip flopping" on NAFTA. The story of discrepancies between his statements and those of his economic adviser generated a spate of media attention.

One of the most widely reported missteps of Obama's Democratic primary campaign also involved NAFTA. At a San Francisco fundraiser in April 2008, Obama tried to explain the reactions of workers to job losses across the Rust Belt: "They get bitter, they cling to guns or religion or antipathy to people who aren't like them or anti-immigrant sentiment or anti-trade sentiment as a way to explain their frustrations" (Pallasch 2008). When the quote appeared on a political blog a few days later, the media exploded. The guns and religion aspect of Obama's quote largely eclipsed the antitrade point. Nevertheless, at a labor event, Obama quickly tried to clarify his remarks:

I know that there's been a lot of fuss over the last couple of days because I said that people were bitter. People seemed to misunderstand what that means. Yes, people are angry. If you've been filling up your gas tank you're angry. If you've watched your entire community decimated because a steel plant is closed, that will make you mad. You've got to feel some frustration.[21]

---

[21] Zeleny (2008).

Sixteen years after its passage, NAFTA has hardly faded into the collective memory of the continent's population. To the contrary, the agreement that catalyzed the fair trade and antiglobalization movements continues to incite controversy and remains firmly rooted in the political terra firma of North America. The story of labor transnationalism that unfolds in this book is one of the most important legacies of NAFTA and the labor activists who used its nascent transnational legal mechanisms to fight for labor rights across the continent. To measure their success solely by victories and campaigns won misses their most significant and historic achievement – creating models of equitable and respectful collaboration that others, inspired, sought to emulate. The endurance of labor relationships in a hostile and conservative post-9/11 political climate is therefore a testament to the vision of progressive leaders and rank-and-file workers who changed the landscape of labor relations in North America by changing the way they saw and treated each other.

Appendix

Data and Methods

Selecting a sample of unions to study proved to be quite challenging because there exist no aggregate data on transnational labor relationships. Unions do not maintain records of every contact and interaction they have with unions in other countries, and only large events and campaigns appear in union publications and documents. Moreover, because many unions do not have departments dedicated to managing international work, the reporting of that work in formal archived sources is not routinized and tends to be sporadic. Finally, international work is usually conducted by key actors in unions through informal mechanisms – there is little institutional memory regarding how relations emerged and developed. Determining the universe of unions involved in transnational relationships is therefore extremely problematic.

To mitigate these challenges, I employed a three-prong strategy to identify industrial unions involved in transnational relationships. I began by selecting an initial sample of the ten largest U.S. industrial unions in 1991, prior to NAFTA's negotiation.[1] Table A.1 presents them from largest to smallest. It also provides membership data for 1993 – before NAFTA went into effect – and net and percentage losses in membership between 1991 and 1993.

Because the UPIU, OCAW, URW, and IUE merged with other unions after 1991, I included in the sample the unions into which each merged: the USW for the first three and the CWA for the fourth.[2] The ACTWU

---

[1] I did not include the Graphic Communications International Union (GCIU) and Bakery, Confectionery and Tobacco Workers (BCTW).

[2] In 1999, the UPIU merged with OCAW to form the Paper, Allied-Industrial, Chemical and Energy Workers International Union (PACE). PACE merged with the USW in 2005. The URW merged with the USW in 1999. The IUE merged with the CWA in 2000.

Table A.1. *Ten Largest U.S. Industrial Unions and Membership Change between 1991 and 1993*

Union	Industry	Membership		Net Loss	Percentage Loss
		1991	1993		
International Brotherhood of Teamsters (IBT)	Trucking	1,379,000	1,316,000	−63,000	−4.6
United Automobile, Aerospace & Agricultural Implement Workers of America International Union (UAW)	Auto	840,000	771,000	−70,000	−8.2
International Association of Machinists and Aerospace Workers (IAM)	Airline and auto	534,000	474,000	−60,000	−11.2
United Steelworkers of America (USW)	Steel	459,000	421,000	−38,000	−8.3
United Paperworkers International Union (UPIU)	Paper manufacturing	202,000	188,000	−14,000	−6.9
International Union of Electronic, Electrical, Salaried, Machine and Furniture Workers (IUE)	Electronics	160,000	143,000	−17,000	−10.6
Amalgamated Clothing and Textile Workers Union (ACTWU)	Garment/apparel	154,000	143,000	−11,000	−7.1
International Ladies' Garment Workers' Union (ILGWU)	Garment/apparel	143,000	133,000	−10,000	−7.0
Oil, Chemical, and Atomic Workers International Union (OCAW)	Oil, chemical	90,000	86,000	−4,000	−4.4
United Rubber Workers (URW)	Rubber	89,000	81,000	−8,000	−9.0

Note: Bold refers to unions in the sample. AFL-CIO data.

and ILGWU merged with each other in 1995 to form the Union of Needle-trades, Industrial and Textile Employees (UNITE), which I included. Because the UAW and IAM cover similar industries, I included the larger union, the UAW. This left five unions in the sample: IBT, UAW, USW, UNITE, and CWA.

It was crucial that I have positive cases in my sample. A random sample of all industrial unions would not necessarily have yielded the positive cases. I tackled the problem of identifying positive cases by isolating the population of U.S. and Canadian industrial unions that were engaged in transnational relationships with Mexican unions between 1985 and 1999. I searched the newspapers and magazines of the AFL-CIO and Canadian Labour Congress (CLC) during a fifteen-year period (1985–1999) for articles that discussed labor transnationalism in North America.[3] I also examined the union newspapers and magazines of the five unions in my initial sample (and/or their predecessor unions) and their Canadian counterparts. Among these twenty-four publications, there were no articles prior to 1991 that mentioned transnational relationships. The articles that appeared only mentioned transnational contacts, usually meetings of high-level union leaders through international trade secretariats or other international bodies.[4] Articles also discussed various unions' support for Polish Solidarity workers and the anti-Apartheid movement in South Africa.

After 1991, published articles appeared that discussed eight unions or federations that had relationships: UE, FAT, CUSWA, CWA, CEP, STRM, AFL-CIO, and CLC. To ensure that I had not missed any positive cases, I compared my sample to the population of unions that participated in Mexico-U.S. Dialogos. Compared with the larger universe of North American unions, the unions that participated in Mexico-U.S. Dialogos meetings were directly affected by trade.[5] Meetings were held annually, from 1988 until 1992. I consulted the roster of participants of all Mexico-U.S. Dialogos meetings and then compiled a list of industrial unions (international and national, not local) and federations that participated

---

[3] This included twenty-four publications (due to changes in publication names over time, union mergers, and distinct series published in Canada). The publications were collected at Princeton University; the University of California, Berkeley; the University of Toronto; and the archives of various unions and federations. Although some individual issues were missing, the collections were relatively complete.

[4] Such as the ILO, ICFTU, and others.

[5] Although industrial unions comprised the majority of union participants, unions representing public employees and service workers attended.

Table A.2. *Union Participation in Mexico-U.S. Dialogos Meetings*

Union	Meetings Attended
UE	6, 7
FAT	4, 5, 6, 7
CUSWA	7
CWA	2, 3, 4, 6, 7
CEP	6
STRM	4, 6, 7
UAW	1, 2, 3, 4, 5, 6, 7
CLC	4, 6, 7
AFL-CIO	2, 3, 4, 5, 6, 7
CTM	4, 5, 7
ACTWU	2, 3, 4, 5, 6, 7
ILGWU	1, 3, 4, 7
IBT	7
CTM	

Note: Numbers represent the following meetings:
(1) 1988 Chicago; (2) 1989 Washington; (3) 1990
Austin; (4) 1991 Chicago; (5) 1992 San Diego;
(6) 1994 Austin; (7) 1996 Cuernevaca, Mexico. The
IUE also participated, but because it merged with
the CWA in 2000 I did not include it in this list.

in each meeting (see Table A.1, column 2). All were represented in my initial sample except the CTM (a negative case).[6] These data are presented in Table A.2.

To further test this population for its validity, I consulted a variety of labor activists to identify unions that were engaged in transnational relationships after 1991. I also spent the summer of 1999 conducting pilot interviews in Mexico to ensure I had not missed any positive cases. A small population emerged, and it matched the group that I developed by culling from union newspapers and rosters of Mexico-U.S. Dialogos meetings. It also included partially developed transnational relationships among the AFL-CIO, CLC, and UNT and moderately developed transnational relationships among the UAW, CAW, and STIMAHCS, a FAT-affiliated auto union), between the IBT and FAT, and between UNITE (in the United States and Canada) and a FAT-affiliated garment union.

---

[6] David Brooks confirmed CTM participation, but national level CTM leaders rarely attended, and did not always appear on official rosters.

Table 1.2 (Unions, Industries, and Transnational Relationship Outcomes) in Chapter 1 lays out both the positive cases and the negative cases.

Because the study measures a shift in the nature of the relations among unions, it required a qualitative and comparative approach. I conducted in-depth interviews with key informants in each union. In-depth interviews were essential because archival materials were incomplete and key individuals in each union usually managed international relations. Due to the lack of recordkeeping on this issue, a survey would have generated innumerable blank responses. Memories needed to be gently prodded and documents locked away in files needed to be consulted to verify dates and places. Determining the key players was not difficult – they were inevitably labor leaders or union elites. I conducted over 140 interviews with Mexican, Canadian, and U.S. labor leaders and union staff, government officials, NAALC officials, labor activists in NGOs, and labor lawyers between 1999 and 2001.[7] Interviews lasted between one and four hours and were tape recorded and transcribed.[8] Interview transcripts generated over 3,000 single-spaced pages of text.

I completed interviews with Mexican officials in Mexico City and Puebla between June 1999 and August 2000. All interviews were conducted in Spanish. Respondents included national leaders of major Mexican unions and union federations (including secretaries general, directors of international relations, etc.), directors and national presidents of nongovernmental organizations, prominent labor lawyers, lead organizers, and government officials (including a trade negotiator and Mexican congressional members). I conducted interviews with U.S. and Canadian respondents between May 2000 and March 2001 in New York; Washington, D.C.; Pittsburgh; Berkeley, California; Toronto; and Ottawa. Respondents included national leaders of key U.S. and Canadian unions and union federations (including presidents and vice presidents and directors of international departments), government officials (including NAALC and Labor Department officials and trade negotiators), national directors and coordinators of nongovernmental organizations, and prominent labor lawyers. In 2009 and 2010, I conducted a small set of follow-up interviews with key labor leaders to gauge whether the landscape of labor transnationalism had changed significantly since my initial interviews.

---

[7] See the bibliography for a list of interview respondents. Eight interviews were conducted by research assistants.

[8] With only three exceptions.

In addition to conducting in-depth interviews, I examined Mexican, Canadian, and U.S. union newspapers and magazines during a fifteen-year period (1985–2000)[9] and union documents culled from archival collections of major North American labor unions. Archived documents included press releases, internal memoranda, educational materials, newsletters, position papers and policy statements, and correspondence. Finally, I reviewed legal documents and the twenty-three NAO public submissions filed between 1994 and May 2001. Examining available documentation helped ensure that the data gathered from respondents were valid.

[9] *AFL-CIO News* (AFL-CIO) (1984–1996); *America At Work* (AFL-CIO) (1997–2000); *Canadian Labour* (CLC) (1985–1989); *CEP Journal* (CEP) (1993–1996); *CLC Today* (CLC) (1990–1993); *Connections* (CWC) (1986–1991); *CWA News* (CWA) (1985–1999); *International Teamster* (IBT) (1985–1992); *Justice* (ILGWU) (1985–1992); *Labor Unity* (ACTWU) (1985–1995); *The Machinist* (IAM) (1985–1992); *National Union Magazine* (CAW) (1987–1988); *Out Front* (CLC) (1997–1999); *Resistencia Obrera* (FAT) (1978–2000); *Solidarity* (UAW Canada) (1985–1987); *Steelabor* (USWA) (1985–1990); *Steelabor* (Canadian version) (1986–1999); *Teamster* (IBT) (1995–1999); *New Teamster* (IBT) (1992–1995); *UAW Solidarity* (UAW) (1984–1999); *The Union* (CAW) (1988–1993); *UE News* (UE) (1987–1999); *UNITE!* (UNITE) (1995–1999); *UNITE In Action* (Canadian version) (1997–1999). See the bibliography for references to specific issues of these publications.

Bibliography

Printed and Online Sources

Adams, Roy. 1989. "North American Industrial Relations: Divergent Trends in Canada and the United States." *International Labour Review* 128 (1): 47–64.

AFL-CIO. 1968. "Report of the Subcommittee of Executive Council on U.S.-Mexican Border Problems." August 5. RG1-038, Office of the President-George Meany Files, 1940–1980, The George Meany Memorial Archives.

1985. *AFL-CIO News*. August 31, p. 8.

1985. *AFL-CIO News*. "Failed Trade Policy Hit for Raising Risk of More Job Losses." Volume 30, No. 47, November 23, p. 1.

1985. *AFL-CIO News*. "Who Says Imports Cost Less?" Volume 30, No. 47, November 23, p. 1.

1985. *AFL-CIO News*. Volume 30, No. 51, December 21, p. 1.

1986. *AFL-CIO News*. "Economic Realities." Volume 31, No. 24, June 14, p. 7.

1986. *AFL-CIO News*. "Label Week." August 30.

1987. *AFL-CIO News*. "House Junks Import Flatware." Volume 32, No. 5, January 31, p. 1.

1987. *AFL-CIO News*. "Poverty and Profiteers Fuel Maquiladora System: Jobs of American Workers Wiped Out as Multinational Firms Search for Lowest Wages." December 19.

1994. *AFL-CIO News*. Photo by Jack Miller. May 16.

1994. *AFL-CIO News*. "Worker Rights Link to Trade Gains Supporters." July 11.

1995. "Statement by the AFL-CIO Executive Council on Immigration and the American Dream." February 23.

1999. "Resolution of the 23rd AFL-CIO Biennial Convention."

AFL-CIO Executive Council. 1998. "AFL-CIO Statement on the MAI." October 14.

Alexander, Robin. 1999. "Experience and Reflections on the Use of the NAALC." In *Memorias: Encuentro Trinacional de Laboralistas Democráticos*, pp. 139–66. México: Universidad Nacional Autónoma de México.

America@Work. 2004. "Bush Watch: A Special Report on the Bush Record." May, pp. 2, 7.

Aminzade, Ronald. 1979. "The Transformation of Social Solidarities in Nineteenth-Century Toulouse." In *Consciousness and Class Experience in Nineteenth-Century Europe*, ed. John Merriman, pp. 85–106. New York: Holmes and Meier.

Andersen, E. A. 2005. *Out of the Closets and into the Courts*. Ann Arbor: University of Michigan Press.

Anner, Mark S. 2002. "Local and Transnational Campaigns to End Sweatshop Practices." In *Transnational Cooperation among Labor Unions*, ed. Michael E. Gordon and Lowell Turner, pp. 238–55. Ithaca, NY: Cornell University Press.

Anner, Mark and Peter Evans. 2004. "Building Bridges across a Double Divide: Alliances between US and Latin American Labour and NGOs." *Development in Practice* 14 (1): 34–47.

Armbruster, Ralph. 1995. "Cross National Labor Organizing Strategies." *Critical Sociology* 21 (2): 75–89.

    1998. "Cross Border Labor Organizing in the Garment and Automobile Industries: The Phillips Van Heusen and Ford Cuautitlán Cases." *Journal of World Systems Research* 4 (1): 20–51.

Armstrong, Elizabeth A. 2002. *Forging Gay Identities: Organizing Sexuality in San Francisco, 1950–1994*. Chicago: University of Chicago Press.

Atleson, James, Lance Compa, Kerry Rittich, Calvin William Sharpe, and Marley S. Weiss. 2008. *International Labor Law: Cases and Materials on Workers' Rights in the Global Economy*. Eagan, MN: Thomson West.

Auerbach, Stuart. 1991. "Factions Dig in Positions against Mexico Trade Pact; Opposition Fears Loss of Jobs, Factories." *Washington Post*, February 8, p. F1.

Ayres, Jeffrey M. 1998. *Defying Conventional Wisdom: Political Movements and Popular Contention against North American Free Trade*. Toronto: University of Toronto Press.

Bacon, David. 1998. "Han Young: Free Trade's Nightmare." *San Francisco Bay Guardian*, April 1, p. 27.

    2008. "Right to Strike Imperiled in Cananea." *Nation*, January 25.

Bardacke, Frank. 1993. "Cesar's Ghost: Decline and Fall of the U.F.W." *Nation*, July 26, p. 132.

Berejikian, Jeffrey. 1992. "Revolutionary Collective Action and the Agent-Structure Problem." *American Political Science Review* 86: 647–57.

Bhagwati, Jagdish. 2000. "Why Nike Is on the Right Track." *Financial Times*, May 1.

Borgers, Frank. 1999. "Rhetoric and Power: An Analysis of the United Brotherhood of Teamsters NAFTA Trucking Campaign." Paper presented at the UCLEA Conference.

Boswell, Terry, and Dimitris Stevis. 1997. "Globalization and International Labor Organizing: A World-System Perspective." *Work and Occupations* 24 (3): 288–308.

Bowden, Charles. 1999. "The NAFTA Trucker: Crossing the Line: An Exclusive Investigative Report on Mexican Truckers." *Teamster* (Special NAFTA Trucking Edition), November, pp. 1–7.

Brecher, Jeremy, and Tim Costello. 1994. *Global Village or Global Pillage: Economic Restructuring from the Bottom Up*. Boston: South End Press.

Bronfenbrenner, Kate. 1997. "Final Report: The Effects of Plant Closing or Threat of Plant Closing on the Right of Workers to Organize." Dallas: Secretariat of the Commission for Labor Cooperation.

Bronfenbrenner, Kate, and Robert Hickey. 2004. "Changing to Organize: A National Assessment of Union Strategies." In *Rebuilding Labor: Organizing and Organizers in the New Labor Movement*, ed. Ruth Milkman and Kim Voss, pp. 17–61. Ithaca, NY: Cornell University Press.

Brooks, David. 1992. "Proposed Draft Agenda for Trinational Exchange, Mexico 1996." Memo to "Trinational Conveners." April 16.

Browne, Harry, and Beth Sims. 1993. "Global Capitalism, Global Unionism." *Resource Center Bulletin*, Winter. Resource Center: Albuquerque.

Bruce, Peter. 1989. "Political Parties and Labor Legislation in Canada and the US." *Industrial Relations: A Journal of Economy and Society* 28 (2): 115–41.

Cameron, Maxwell, and Brian Tomlin. 2000. *The Making of NAFTA: How the Deal Was Done*. Ithaca, NY: Cornell University Press.

Campaign for Labor Rights. 1998, March 6.

Campbell, Bruce, Carlos Salas, and Robert E. Scott. 2001. "NAFTA at Seven : Its Impact on Workers in All Three Nations." Briefing paper. Washington, DC: Economic Policy Institute. http://www.epi.org/publications/entry/briefingpapers_nafta01_index/.

Canadian Labour. 1986. December.

Canadian Steelworkers. n. d. "Steelworkers Humanity Fund's Programme."

Cantor, Daniel, and Juliet Schor. 1987. *Tunnel Vision: Labor, the World Economy and Central America*. Boston: South End Press.

Carr, Barry. 1999. "Globalization from Below: Labour Internationalism under NAFTA." *International Social Science Journal* 51 (159): 49–59.

Carrillo, Teresa. 1990. *Women, Trade Unions, and New Social Movements in Mexico: The Case of the 'Nineteenth of September' Garment Workers Union*. Ph.D. dissertation, Department of Political Science, Stanford University.

Citizens Trade Campaign. 1993. November 12.

CLC Today. 1990. "Trade Vultures Gather for Easy Pickings." October.

CLC Today. 1991. "The Trade Deal Stand-Off." May, p. 6.

Clemens, Elisabeth S. 1993. "Organizational Repertoires and Institutional Change: Women's Groups and the Transformation of U.S. Politics, 1890–1920." *American Journal of Sociology* 98:755–98.

Clinton, Bill. 1992. "Expanding Trade and Creating American Jobs." Speech delivered at North Carolina State University, Raleigh, North Carolina

(text available at: http://www.ibiblio.org/pub/academic/political-science/
speeches/clinton.dir/c151.txt).

Cohen, Larry, and Steve Early. 1998. "Defending Workers' Rights in the New
Global Economy: The CWA Experience." In *Which Direction for Organized
Labor? Essays on Organizing, Outreach, and Internal Transformations*, ed.
Bruce Nissen, pp. 143–66. Detroit: Wayne State University Press.

Commission for Labor Cooperation. 2000. *Labor Relations Law in North America*. Secretariat of the Commission for Labor Cooperation.

Communication Workers of America. 1996. "Communication Workers of America Files NAFTA Complaint Charging Failure by Mexico to Enforce Labor
Laws." Press release. October 11.

Communication Workers of Canada. 1991. "Words Simply Cannot Describe
What I Saw and How I Felt." Winter: 4–5.

Compa, Lance. 1999. "The North American Agreement on Labor Cooperation
and International Labor Solidarity." In *Memorias: Encuentro Trînacional
de Laboralistas Democráticos*, pp. 185–211. México: Universidad Nacional
Autónoma de México.

Cook, Maria Lorena. 1997. "Regional Integration and Transnational Politics:
Popular Sector Strategies in the NAFTA Era." In *The New Politics of Inequal-
ity in Latin America*, ed. Douglas A. Chalmers, Carlos M. Vilas, Katherine
Hile, Scott B. Martin, Kerianne Piester, and Monique Segarra, pp. 516–40.
Oxford: Oxford University Press.

  2007. *The Politics of Labor Reform in Latin America: Between Flexibility and
Rights*. University Park, PA: Penn State University Press.

Cusick, John. 1995. "Response to NAFTA: U.S. and Mexican Telecom Unions
Build North American Labor Solidarity." *CWA News*, November/December,
p. 10.

Damgaard, Bodil. 1999a. "Cooperación Laboral Transnacional en América del
Norte a Finales de los Noventa." *El Cotidiano* 94 (March–April): 23–37.

  1999b. "ACLAN: Experiencias y Tendencias Después de Cinco Años." In
Memorias: Encuentro Trinacional de Laboralistas Democráticos, pp. 95–
122. México: Universidad Nacional Autónoma de México.

Davis, Henry L. 1993. "Jackson Leads Protest March against Free-Trade Agreement." *Buffalo News*, October 3.

de Buen, Néstor. 1999. "El Acuerdo de Cooperación Laboral de América del
Norte." *El Cotidiano* 94 (March–April): 5–12.

de la Vega Garcia, Netzahualcóyotl. 1998. Public communication to the Mexican
NAO from the CTM. August 4.

DiMaggio, Paul, and Walter Powell. 1991. *The New Institutionalism in Organizational Analysis*. Chicago: University of Chicago Press.

Donahue, Tom. 1993. Letter to USTR Mickey Kantor, June 17.

Dubb, Steve. 1999. *Logics of Resistance: Globalization and Telephone Unionism
in Mexico and British Columbia*. New York: Garland Publishers.

Dubro, Alec. 2001. "Otto Reich's Dirty Laundry." *Foreign Policy in Focus*, April
1. http://www.fpif.org/articles/otto_reichs_dirty_laundry.

Dunne, Nancy. 1991. "Fears Over US-Mexico Free Trade Pact." *Financial Times*
(London), January 30, p. 4.

Evans, Rhonda. 2002. *The Rise of Ethical Trade Advocacy: NAFTA and the New Politics of Trade.* Unpublished Ph.D. dissertation, University of California, Berkeley.

Evans, Rhonda, and Tamara Kay. 2008. "How Environmentalists 'Greened' Trade Policy: Strategic Action and the Architecture of Field Overlap." *American Sociological Review* 73 (6): 970–91.

Ewick, Patricia, and Susan S. Silbey. 1998. *The Common Place of Law: Stories from Everyday Life, Language and Legal Discourse.* Chicago: University of Chicago Press.

Fantasia, Rick. 1988. *Cultures of Solidarity: Consciousness, Action, and Contemporary American Workers.* Berkeley: University of California Press.

Fantasia, Rick, and Kim Voss. 2004. *Hard Work: Remaking the American Labor Movement.* Berkeley: University of California Press.

Farrell, John Aloysius, and Michael Putzel. 1993. "House Gives Clinton NAFTA Win; Decisive 234–200 Vote Comes after a Day of Horse-Trading." *The Boston Globe*, November 18, p. 1.

Fligstein, Neil. 1985. "The Spread of the Multidivisional Form among Large Firms, 1919–1979." *American Sociological Review* 50:377–91.

2001. *The Architecture of Markets: An Economic Sociology of Twenty-First-Century Capitalist Societies.* Princeton, NJ: Princeton University Press.

Frank, Dana. 1999. *Buy American: The Untold Story of Economic Nationalism.* Boston: Beacon Press.

Gindin, Sam. *The Canadian Auto Workers: The Birth and Transformation of a Union.* Toronto: James Lorimer & Company Ltd., Publishers.

Goldstone, Jack A., and Charles Tilly. 2001. "Threat (and Opportunity)." In *Silence and Voice in the Study of Contentious Politics*, ed. Ronald Aminzade, Jack Goldstone, Doug McAdam, Elizabeth Perry, William Sewell, Sidney Tarrow, and Charles Tilly, pp. 179–94. Cambridge: Cambridge University Press.

Graubart, Jonathan. 2008. *Legalizing Transnational Activism: The Struggle to Gain Social Change from NAFTA's Citizen Petitions.* University Park, PA: Penn State University Press.

Greenhouse, Steven. 2009. "Departing Secretary of Labor Fends off Critics." *New York Times*, January 10, p. A12.

Harvey, Janice A. 1997. "M.A.I. is M.I.A." *Telegraph-Journal*, New Brunswick, Canada. April 30.

Hathaway, Dale. 2000. *Allies across the Border: Mexico's "Authentic Labor Front" and Global Solidarity.* Cambridge: South End Press.

Hattam, Victoria. 1992. "Institutions and Political Change: Working-Class Formation in England and the United States." *Politics and Society* 20 (2): 133–66.

Herod, Andrew, 1997. "Labor as an Agent of Globalization and as a Global Agent." In *Spaces of Globalization: Reasserting the Power of the Local*, ed. Kevin R Cox. New York: Guilford Press.

Herzenberg, Steve. 2000. "Reinventing the US Labour Movement, Inventing Postindustrial Prosperity: A Progress Report." Geneva: International Labor Organization.

Hill, Herbert. 1985. *Black Labor and the American Legal System: Race, Work, and the Law*. Madison: The University of Wisconsin Press.

Hovis, John H., Jr. 1994. Letter to Jorge F. Perez-Lopez, Acting Secretary, United States National Administrative Office, February 10.

2002. Letter to U.S. Secretary of Labor Elaine Chao, July 24.

Howard, Andrew. 1995. "Global Capital and Labor Internationalism in Comparative Historical Perspective: A Marxist Analysis." *Sociological Inquiry* 65 (3/4): 365–94.

Inside U.S. Trade. 1991a. January 11.

1991b. "House Members Tie Fast-Track Support to Inclusion of Environment in FTA." *Inside U.S. Trade*, February 22, p. 5.

1993a. *Inside U.S. Trade*, August 13, p. 10.

1993b. *Inside U.S. Trade*, August 13, p. 18.

International Brotherhood of Teamsters. 1992a. "Resolution of the General Executive Board: North American Free Trade Agreement." April 27.

1992b. "Mexican Labor Leader Joins Teamster Caravan." *The New Teamster*, December, p. 6.

1993a. "NAFTA: License to Kill." *The New Teamster*, December, p. 14.

1993b. "NAFTA: The Wrong Road for the Future." Video.

1993c. "NAFTA: Fair Trade Is Our Alternative." *The New Teamster*, December, p. 15.

1996. "New Allies Join Campaign to Delay NAFTA Trucking Provisions." Press release. March 13.

1999. *Teamster*, pp. 6–8.

Jenkins, J. Craig, David Jacobs, and Jon Agnone. 2003. "Political Opportunities and African-American Protest, 1948–1997." *American Journal of Sociology* 109:277–303.

Jessup, David, and Michael E. Gordon. 2002. "Organizing in Export Processing Zones: The Bibong Experience in the Dominican Republic." In *Transnational Cooperation among Labor Unions*, ed. Michael E. Gordon and Lowell Turner, pp. 179–201. Ithaca, NY: Cornell University Press.

Katznelson, Ira. 1985. "Working-Class Formation and the State: Nineteenth-Century England in American Perspective." In *Bringing the State Back in*, ed. Peter Evans, Dietrich Rueschemeyer, and Theda Skocpol, pp. 257–84. Cambridge: Cambridge University Press.

Kay, Tamara. 2005. "Labor Transnationalism and Global Governance: The Impact of NAFTA on Transnational Labor Relationships in North America." *American Journal of Sociology* 11(3): 715–56.

Kay, Tamara, and Rhonda Evans. (unpublished ms.) "Trading Alliances and State Preferences: How Environmental and Labor Movements Shaped NAFTA."

Keck, Margaret, and Kathryn Sikkink. 1998. *Activists Beyond Borders: Advocacy Networks in International Politics*. Ithaca, NY: Cornell University Press.

Kelber, Harry. 2001. "Solidarity Center Still Relies on Federal Funds and Secrecy to Conduct Labor's Global Struggle." *Inside the AFL-CIO*, column in *The Labor Educator*, May 15. http://www.laboreducator.org/inside9.htm.

Khagram, Sanjeev, James V. Riker, and Kathryn Sikkink. 2002. "From Santiago to Seattle: Transnational Advocacy Groups Restructuring World Politics." In

Restructuring World Politics: Transnational Social Movements, Networks, and Norms, ed. Sanjeev Khagram, James V. Riker, and Kathryn Sikkink, pp. 3–23. Minneapolis: University of Minnesota Press.

Kidder, Thalia G. 2002. "Networks in Transnational Labor Organizing." In *Restructuring World Politics: Transnational Social Movements, Networks, and Norms*, ed. Sanjeev Khagram, James V. Riker, and Kathryn Sikkink, pp. 269–93. Minneapolis: University of Minnesota Press.

Kiser, George C., and Martha Woody Kiser. 1979. *Mexican Workers in the United States: Historical and Political Perspectives*. Albuquerque: University of New Mexico Press.

Klare, Karl. 1978. "Judicial Deradicalization of the Wagner Act and the Origins of Modern Legal Consciousness, 1937–1941" *Minnesota Law Review* 62:265–339.

Krasner, Stephen. 1983. *International Regimes*. Ithaca, NY: Cornell University Press.

Kriesi, Hanspeter, Ruud Koopmans, Jan Willem Duyvendak, and Marco G. Giugni. 1995. *New Social Movements in Western Europe: A Comparative Analysis*. Minneapolis: University of Minnesota Press.

LaBotz, Dan, and Robin Alexander. 2005. "The Escalating Struggles over Mexico's Labor Law." *NACLA Report on the Americas* (July/August), p. 22.

Lewis, Charles. 1993. "The NAFTA-Math; Clinton Got His Trade Deal, but How Many Millions Did It Cost the Nation?" *Washington Post*, December 26.

Lipset, Seymour Martin, and Noah M. Meltz. 2004. The Paradox of American Unionism: Why Americans Like Unions More Than Canadians Do, But Join Much Less. Ithaca, NY: Cornell University Press.

Lounsbury, Michael. 2007. "A Tale of Two Cities: Competing Logics and Practice Variation in the Professionalizing of Mutual Funds." *Academy of Management Journal* 50:289–307.

Luján, Bertha E. 1999. "Estándares Laborales y Globalización: El Caso del ACLAN." *El Cotidiano* 94 (March–April): 13–22.

Maggs, John. 1991. "US Labor Fights Mexico Trade Pact." *Journal of Commerce*, February 6, p. 1A.

McAdam, Doug. 1996. "Conceptual Origins, Current Problems, Future Directions." In *Comparative Perspectives on Social Movements: Political Opportunities, Mobilizing Structures, and Cultural Framings*, ed. Doug McAdam, John D. McCarthy, and Mayer N. Zald, pp. 23–40. Cambridge: Cambridge University Press.

McAdam, Doug, and W. Richard Scott. 2005. "Organizations and Social Movements." In *Social Movements and Organization Theory*, ed. Gerald F. Davis, Doug McAdam, W. Richard Scott, and Mayer N. Zald, pp. 4–40. Cambridge: Cambridge University Press.

McCann, Michael W. 1994. *Rights at Work: Pay Equity Reform and the Politics of Legal Mobilization*. Chicago: University of Chicago Press.

——— 1998. "How Does Law Matter for Social Movements?" In *How Does Law Matter?* ed. B. Garth and A. Sarat, pp. 76–108. Evanston, IL: Northwestern University Press.

McQueen, Rod. 1991. "Mexico Scares U.S. Senators: Carla Hills Gets a Grilling about New Trade Negotiations." *The Financial Post* (Toronto), February 7, section 1, p. 3.

Medina, Luis. 1998. "A Dissenting Opinion." Review of the North American Agreement on Labor Cooperation 1994–1997. http://new.naalc.org/index .cfm?page=240.

Melucci, A. 1985. "The Symbolic Challenge of Contemporary Movements." *Social Research* 52 (4): 789–816.

Merry, Sally Engle. 1990. *Getting Justice and Getting Even: Legal Consciousness among Working-Class Americans*. Chicago: University of Chicago Press.

Mexican Labor News and Analysis. 2005. Vol. 10, No. 2 (February).

Middlebrook, Kevin J. 1995. *The Paradox of Revolution: Labor, the State, and Authoritarianism in Mexico*. Baltimore: The Johns Hopkins University Press.

Minow, Martha. 1990. *Making All the Difference: Inclusion, Exclusion, and American Law*. Ithaca, NY: Cornell University Press.

Morris, George. 1967. *The CIA, the AFL-CIO, and American Foreign Policy*. New York: International Publishers.

Neal, Steve. 1993. "Jackson Takes Lead vs. NAFTA." *Chicago Sun-Times*, September 5, p. 41.

Nobles, Melissa. 2000. *Shades of Citizenship: Race and the Census in Modern Politics*. Stanford, CA: Stanford University Press.

"North American Agreement on Labor Cooperation." 1993. Text of the Agreement. September 13. http://www.naalc.org/english/agreement.shtml.

O'Brien, Robert. 1998. "Shallow Foundations: Labour and the Selective Regulation of Free Trade." In *The Economics and Politics of International Trade: Freedom and Trade: Volume II*, ed. G. Cook, pp. 105–24. London: Routledge.

O'Brien, Robert, Anne Marie Goetz, Jan Aart Scholte, and Marc Williams. 2000. *Contesting Global Governance: Multilateral Economic Institutions and Global Social Movements*. Cambridge, Cambridge University Press.

Pallasch, Abdon M. 2008. "Obama: God, Guns Are only Refuge of Bitter Pennsylvanians." *Chicago Sun-Times*, April 12, p. 2.

Piore, Michael J., and Andrew Schrank. 2008. "Toward Managed Flexibility: The Revival of Labour Inspection in the Latin World." *International Labour Review* 147 (1): 1–23.

Polanyi, Karl. 2001. *The Great Transformation: The Political and Economic Origins of Our Time*. Boston: Beacon Press. (Originally published in 1944.)

Ragin, Charles. 1987. *The Comparative Method: Moving Beyond Qualitative and Quantitative Strategies*. Berkeley: University of California Press.

Reagan, Ronald. 1988. "State of the Union Address," as printed in *New York Times*, January 26.

Reisler, Mark. 1976. *By the Sweat of Their Brow: Mexican Immigrant Labor in the United States, 1900–1940*. Westport, CT: Greenwood Press.

Resistencia Obrera. 1979. "En el D.F. Se organizan los trabajadores para recibir a Carter." No. 13, January, p. 5.

Review of the North American Agreement on Labor Cooperation 1994–1997, Annex 5: Public Comments. http://www.naalc.org/naalc/4year-review.htm.

Robinson, Ian. 1993. "Economistic Unionism in Crisis: The Origins, Consequences, and Prospects of Canada-U.S. Labour Movement Character Divergence." In *The Challenge of restructuring: North American Labor Movements Respond*, ed. Jane Jenson and Rianne Mahon. Philadelphia: Temple University Press.

Rogers, Joel. 1990. "Divide and Conquer: Further Reflections on the Distinctive Character of American Labor Laws." *Wisconsin Law Review* 1990:1–147.

Ross, Robert J.S. 2004. *Slaves to Fashion: Poverty and Abuse in the New Sweatshops*. Ann Arbor: University of Michigan Press.

Ruggie, John. 1993. "Multilateralism: The Anatomy of an Institution." In *Multilateralism Matters: The Theory and Praxis of an Institutional Form*, ed. John Ruggie. New York: Columbia University Press.

Rupert, M. 1995. "(Re) Politicizing the Global Economy: Liberal Common Sense and Ideological Struggle in the US NAFTA Debate." *Review of International Political Economy* 2:658–92.

San Diego Tribune. 2002. November 18. (http://www.signonsandiego.com/news/mexico/20021118–999_1in17bushfox.html (site now discontinued).

Sarat, Austin. 1990. "'. . . The Law Is All Over': Power, Resistance and the Legal Consciousness of the Welfare Poor." *Yale Journal of Law and the Humanities* 2 (2): 343–80.

Scher, Abby. 1997. "Coming in from the Cold in the Struggle for Solidarity." *Dollars and Sense* No. 213 (September): 24–28.

Schneiberg, Marc, and Sarah Soule. 2005. "Institutionalization as a Contested, Multilevel Process: The Case of Rate Regulation in American Fire Insurance." In *Social Movements and Organization Theory*, ed. Gerald F. Davis, Doug McAdam, W. Richard Scott, and Mayer N. Zald, pp. 122–60. Cambridge: Cambridge University Press.

Schneider, Elizabeth M. 1986. "The Dialectic of Rights and Politics: Perspectives from the Women's Movement." *New York University Law Review* 61:554.

Schrank, Andrew, and M. Victoria Murillo. 2005. "With a Little Help from My Friends: Partisan Politics, Transnational Alliances, and Labor Rights in Latin America." *Comparative Political Studies* 38 (8): 971–99.

Shaiken, Harley, 1990. *Mexico in the Global Economy: High Technology and Work Organization in Export Industries*. San Diego: Center for U.S.-Mexican Studies, University of California.

——— 1994. "Advanced Manufacturing and Mexico: A New International Division of Labor?" *Latin American Research Review* 29 (2): 39–71.

Sikkink, Kathryn, and Jackie Smith. 2002. "Infrastructures for Change: Transnational Organizations, 1953–93." In *Restructuring World Politics: Transnational Social Movements, Networks, and Norms*, ed. Sanjeev Khagram, James V. Riker, and Kathryn Sikkink, pp. 24–44. Minneapolis: University of Minnesota Press.

Silbey, Susan. 1992. "Making a Place for Cultural Analyses of Law." *Law and Social Inquiry* 17:39.

Sklair, Leslie. 1993. *Assembling for Development: The Maquila Industry in Mexico and the United States*. Berkeley: Center for U.S.-Mexican Studies, University of California.

Smith, Jackie, and Ellen Reese, eds. 2008. "Special Issue on the World Social Forum Process." *Mobilization: An International Quarterly* 13 (4): 373–94.

Spalding, Hobart. 1992. "The Two Latin American Foreign Policies of the U.S. Labor Movement." *Science and Society* 56 (4): 421–39.

Stepan-Norris, Judith, and Maurice Zeitlin. 2002. *Left Out: Reds and America's Industrial Unions*. Cambridge: Cambridge University Press.

Stevis, Dimitris. 1998. "International Labor Organizations, 1864–1997: The Weight of History and the Challenges of the Present." *Journal of World-Systems Research* 4:52–75.

Stone, Katherine Van Wezel. 1981. "The Post-War Paradigm in American Labor Law." *Yale Law Journal* 90 (7): 1509–80.

Sweeney, John J. 1996. Letter to Irasema Garza, Secretary of the U.S. NAO. October 21.

Swift, Jamie. 2003. *Walking the Union Walk: Stories from the CEP's First Ten Years*.

Tarrow, Sidney. 1994. *Power in Movement: Social Movements and Contentious Politics*. Cambridge: Cambridge University Press.

  1996. "States and Opportunities: The Political Structuring of Social Movements." In *Comparative Perspectives on Social Movements: Political Opportunities, Mobilizing Structures, and Cultural Framings*, ed. Doug McAdam, John D. McCarthy, and Mayer N. Zald, pp. 41–61. Cambridge: Cambridge University Press.

  1998. "Fishnets, Internets, and Catnets: Globalization and Transnational Collective Action." In *Challenging Authority: The Historical Study of Contentious Politics*, ed. Michael Hanagan, Leslie Page Moch, and Wayne Ph. Te Brake, pp. 228–44. Minneapolis: University of Minnesota Press.

  2005. *The New Transnational Activism*. Cambridge: Cambridge University Press.

Thorup, Cathryn. 1993. "Redefining Governance in North America: Citizen Diplomacy and Cross-Border Coalitions." *Enfoque* (spring). Center for U.S.-Mexican Studies, University of California, San Diego.

Tilly, Charles. 1984. "Social Movements and National Politics." In *Statemaking and Social Movements: Essays in History and Theory*, ed. C. Bright and S. Harding, pp. 297–317. Ann Arbor: University of Michigan Press.

UE News. 1994. November 18.

United States Department of Commerce. 2009. "U.S. Automotive Parts Industry Annual Assessment." Office of Transportation and Machinery.

United States National Administrative Office Submission No. 2005-01. Filed February 17, 2005.

United States National Administrative Office Submission No. 2006-01. Filed November 9, 2006.

United Steelworkers. 2008. "USW Condemns Fox Government's Suppression of Mexican Miners' Union as 'Naked Aggression.'" Press release, March 3.

  2006. *USW@Work*. Spring, p. 21.

Voss, Kim. 1993. *The Making of American Exceptionalism: The Knights of Labor and Class Formation in the Nineteenth Century*. Ithaca, NY: Cornell University Press.

Voss, Kim, and Rachel Sherman. 2000. "Breaking the Iron Law of Oligarchy: Union Revitalization in the American Labor Movement." *American Journal of Sociology* 106:303–49.

White, Robert. 1990. Letter to Shirley Carr. CAW archives. September 4.

Williams, Heather L. 2003. "Of Labor Tragedy and Legal Farce: The Han Young Factory Struggle in Tijuana, Mexico." *Social Science History* 27 (4): 525–50.

Wilson, Jim. 2002. "From 'Solidarity' to Convergence: International Trade Union Cooperation in the Media Sector." In *Transnational Cooperation among Labor Unions*, ed. Michael E. Gordon and Lowell Turner, pp. 153–78. Ithaca, NY: Cornell University Press.

Wines, Michael. 1993. "The Free Trade Accord; A 'Bazaar' Way of Rounding Up Votes." *New York Times*, November 11, p. A23.

Zack, Gene. 1986a. "Reagan Job-Export Scheme Draws Fire: Runaways Spell Misery for American and Mexican Workers." *AFL-CIO News*, Volume 30, No. 48, November 29, pp. 1–2.

1986b. "Runaways to Mexico Spread Economic Woe." *AFL-CIO News*, Volume 31, No. 47, November 22, pp. 1, 6.

1987. "Huge Tariff Breaks Aid Runaway Firms: Growth of U.S.-Owned Plants in Mexico Jeopardizes Economy." *AFL-CIO News*, Volume 32, No. 35, August 29, pp. 1, 5.

Zeleny, Jeff. 2008. "In Labor Speech, Obama Revisits Bitterness." *New York Times*, April 15.

Zinn, Kenneth. 2002. "Solidarity across Borders: The UMWA's Corporate Campaign against Peabody and Hanson PLC." In *Transnational Cooperation among Labor Unions*, ed. Michael E. Gordon and Lowell Turner, pp. 223–37. Ithaca, NY: Cornell University Press.

List of Interviews

Respondents' organizational affiliations and titles current as of date of interview. All interviews conducted by author in person unless otherwise noted. For acronyms, please see the list in the front of the book.

Acuña Soto, Víctor. 2000. Member of RMALC. Personal interview on May 9 in Mexico City.

Alcalde Justiniani, Arturo. 2000. Labor lawyer for the FAT. Member of ANAD. Personal interview on March 29 in Mexico City.

2010. Personal interview on March 29 by phone.

Alexander, Robin. 1999. Director of International Labor Affairs, UE. Personal interview on July 6 in Mexico City.

2000. Personal interview on December 21 in Pittsburgh, PA.

2009. Personal interview on August 21 and 22 by phone.

Almazán, Antonio. 1999. Pro-Secretario de Escalafones, SME. Personal interview on July 27 in Mexico City.

Alvarez, Angel. 2000. Representative of CILAS. Personal interview on May 8 in Mexico City.

Alzaga S., Oscar. 2000. Director, Consejería Jurídica y de Servicios Legales, Dirección de Defensoría de Oficio, Ciudad de México. Personal interview on June 9 in Mexico City.

Anderson, Mark. 2001. President, Food & Allied Service Trades. Former Director, International Economic Affairs, AFL-CIO. Former Director, Task Force on Trade, AFL-CIO. Personal interview on January 8 in Washington, DC.

Anderson Nevarez, Hilda. 2000. Comité Ejecutivo, CTM. Former Member of the Mexican Congress. Personal interview on August 17 in Mexico City.

Anonymous. 2000. CTM. Personal interview on June 14 in Mexico City.

Aranda Vollmer, Rafael. 2000. Director General, Coordinación General de Asuntos Internacionales, NAO, Mexico. Personal interview on June 15 in Mexico City.

Bahena Lóme, Benito. 2000. Secretary General, Alianza de Tranviarios de México and Comite Central Ejecutivo, CT. Personal interview on August 31 in Mexico City.

Bakvis, Peter. 2001. Director, International Confederation of Free Trade Unions Washington Office. Former Director, National Union Confederation (CSN, Canada). Personal interview on January 17 in Washington, DC.

Banks, Andy. 2001. George Meany Center for Labor Studies. Formerly International Representative of the President, IBT. Personal interview on January 10 in Silver Spring, MD.

Barba García, Héctor. 2000. Apoderado General del Sindicato, SITIAVW. Labor lawyer for STRM. Personal interview on May 8 in Mexico City.

Barr, Gerry. 2001. President-CEO, Canadian Council for International Co-operation. Founding Director of the Steelworkers Humanity Fund. Personal interview on March 1 in Ottawa.

Bastida Marín, Rodolfo. 2000. Secretary General, Sindicato Nacional de Trabajadores de Autotransportes, Similares y Conexos de la República Mexicana, CROC. Comité Ejecutivo Nacional, CROC. Personal interview on August 24 in Mexico City.

Beaty, Tim. 2000a. Deputy Director of International Affairs, AFL-CIO. Former Representative, Mexico City Office, Solidarity Center. Personal interview on February 29 in Mexico City.

2000b. Personal interview on December 8 in Washington, DC.

Beckman, Steve. 2000. Assistant Director, Governmental and International Affairs, UAW. Personal interview on December 19 in Washington, DC.

Bensusán, Graciela. 2000. Facultad Latinoamericana de Ciencias Sociales (FLACSO). Personal interview on June 26 in Mexico City.

Biggs-Adams, Carrie. 2001. International Affairs Representative, CWA. Personal interview on January 22 in Washington, DC.

Blackstaffe, Trish. 2001. Executive Assistant to the President, CLC. Personal interview on February 27 in Ottawa.

Bouzas Ortíz, José Alfonso. 2000. Labor lawyer and professor, the National Autonomous University of Mexico. Personal interview on February 29 in Mexico City.

Brooks, David. 2001. Writer, *La Jornada*, and Director of Mexico-U.S. Dialogos. Personal interview on January 4 in Washington, DC.

Brown, David. 2001. President, Canadian Association of Labour Lawyers. Personal interview on February 2 in Toronto.

de Buen Lozano, Dr. Néstor. 2000. Bufete de Buen, S.C. Labor lawyer and Mexican trade negotiator for NAFTA. Personal interview on June 19 in Mexico City.

Campos Linas, Jesus. 2000. Labor lawyer for DINA. Member of ANAD. Former labor lawyer for STRM. Personal interview on June 29 in Mexico City.

Carrillo Alejandro, Patricia. 2000. Secretaria de Relaciones y Solidaridad, SEMARNAP. Personal interview on April 7 in Mexico City.

Cohen, Larry. 2001. Executive Vice President, CWA. Personal interview on March 28 in Washington, DC.

Compa, Lance. 2000. Cornell University and Consultant, Human Rights Watch. Former Director of Labor Law and Economic Research, Commission for Labor Cooperation. Personal interview on December 19 in Washington, DC.

Contreras Marina, Gerardo. 2000. Secretary General, Sindicato Planta de Motores y Transmisiones, Coahuila. Interviewed by research assistant in July in Mexico.

Cruz Aguilar, Jovita. 2000. Comité de Huelga Morales and Worker of Imprenta Morales, FAT. Personal interview on June 24 in Mexico City.

Dagg, Alexandra. 2001. Co-Director, UNITE. Ontario Council. Personal interview on February 20 in Toronto.

Davis, Benjamin. 2000. Coordinator, Americas, Solidarity Center, AFL-CIO. Personal interview on December 6 in Mexico City.

   2010. Mexico Country Program Director, Solidarity Center, AFL-CIO. Personal interview on April 23 by phone.

De la Cueva, Héctor. 1999. Representative of CILAS. Personal interview on July 22 in Mexico City.

De La Vega García, Netzahualcoyotl. 2000. Secretary of Public Communication and Member of National Committee, CTM. Personal interview on May 8 in Mexico City.

Delgado, María Trinidad. 2000. FAT organizer and Itapsa worker. CILAS organizer. Personal interview on April 28 in Mexico City.

Díaz Reguera, Eduardo. 2000. Labor lawyer, former counsel for the FAT. Personal interview on March 10 in Mexico City.

Dip Rame, Elías. 2000. National President, Confederación Nacional de Transportistas Mexicanos, A.C. Personal interview on August 23 in Mexico City.

Domínguez, Alfredo. 2000. National Coordinator, FAT. National Coordinating Committee member and member of the Commission on Economic, Political and Social Affairs, UNT. Personal interview on April 3 in Mexico City.

Drake, Elizabeth. 2000. International Financial Analyst, Public Policy Department, AFL-CIO. Personal interview on December 7.

Easterling, Barbara. 2001. Secretary-Treasurer, CWA. Personal interview on January 9 in Washington, DC.

Eaton, Jonathan. 2001. Assistant to the Canadian Director, UNITE. Personal interview on February 13 in Toronto.

Feigen, Edward. 2001. Strategic Projects Coordinator, Department of Field Mobilization, AFL-CIO. Personal interview on January 12 in Washington, DC.

Fernández Arras, Dr. Arturo. 2000. Lawyer at Consultoría Jurídica Obrera. Personal interview on March 6 in Mexico City.

Fernandez, Gerald. 2009. Director of International Affairs, USW. Personal interview on November 19 by phone.

Floxes, Gloria. 2000. Imprenta Morales, FAT. Personal interview on June 24 in Mexico City.

Friedman, Sheldon. 2000. Economist, Public Policy Department, AFL-CIO. Personal interview on December 18 in Washington, DC.

Gacek, Stanley. 2001. Assistant Director, International Affairs Department, AFL-CIO. Personal interview on January 12 in Washington, DC.
  2009. Associate Director, International Affairs Department, AFL-CIO. Personal interview on August 23 by phone.

Gallardo Oropeza, Adán. 2000. Director, Centro de Estudios y Estadística, Asociación Sindical de Pilotos Aviadores de México. Personal interview on April 27 in Mexico City.

García Pichado, Arnulfo. 2000. Auto union representative. Interviewed by research assistant in July in Mexico.

García Villanueva, Carlos. 2000. Coordinator of the Union Education Program, Friedrich Ebert Foundation (Mexico City office). Personal interview on May 2 in Mexico City.

Garza, Irasema. 2001. Director, U.S. Department of Labor, Women's Bureau. Former Director, U.S. NAO. Personal interview on January 5 in Washington, DC.

Gindin, Sam. 2001. Former Director of Research and Assistant to the President, CAW. Personal interview on February 14 in Toronto.

Gott Trujillo, Adolfo. 2000. Secretary General, Sindicato de Trabajadores de la Industria Textil, de la Confección Similares y Conexos de la República Mexicana, CTM. Member of Comité Ejecutivo Nacional, CTM. Personal interview on May 2 in Mexico City.

Harvey, Pharis. 2000. Executive Director, International Labor Rights Fund. Personal interview on December 7 in Washington, DC.

Hermanson, Jeff. 2000. Representative, Mexico City Office, Solidarity Center. Personal interview on August 24 in Mexico City.

Herrera Ireta, Jorge. 1999. Pro-Secretario de Sucursales, SME. Personal interview on August 2 in Mexico City.

Herzenberg, Steve. 2002. U.S. Department of Labor. Personal interview on September 27 in Berkeley, CA.

Hoffman, Ann. 2001. Legislative Director, UNITE. Personal interview on January 16 in Washington, DC.

Howard, Alan. 2000. Assistant to the President, UNITE. Personal interview on December 15 in New York.

Jackson, Andrew. 2001. Director of Research, Canadian Council on Social Development. Former Economist, CLC. Personal interview on March 2 in Ottawa.

Juárez Núñez, Huberto. 2000. Economist, Universidad Autonoma de Puebla. Personal interview on June 23 in Puebla, Mexico.

Katz, Sheila. 2001. International Department, CLC. Personal interview on February 26 in Ottawa.

Kingsley, Bob. 2001. Director of Organization, UE. Personal interview on January 23 in Alexandria, VA.

Kinkaid, James. 2001. National Representative (Regulatory Affairs), CEP. Personal interview on February 23 in Ottawa.

Kovalik, Dan. 2000. Assistant General Counsel, USW. Personal interview on December 21 in Pittsburgh, PA.

Lara Jiménez, Fermín. 2000. Secretary General, Sindicato Nacional Mártires de San Angel del la Industria Textil Similares y Conexos (CROC). President, Coalición Nacional Obrera de la Industria Textil. Personal interview on May 11 in Mexico City.

Lee, Thea. 2000. Assistant Director for International Economics, AFL-CIO. Personal interview on December 8 in Washington, DC.

Lejarza, Mateo. 2000. National Executive Committee, STRM. Personal interview on May 9 in Mexico City.

Lira, Jaime. 2000. Secretary General and Executive Committee, Tremec (auto-parts). Interviewed by research assistant on July 27 in Mexico.

Littlehale, Scott. 2000. International Trade and Sourcing Specialist, UNITE. Personal interview on December 13 in New York.

López Guizar, Guillermo. 2000. Director of ILO Mexico Office. Personal interview on August 24 in Mexico City.

Luce, Frank. 2001. Associate Counsel, CAW. Personal interview on February 5 in Toronto.

Luján, Bertha. 1999. National Coordinator, FAT. National Coordinating Committee and member of the Commission on Economic, Political, and Social Affairs, UNT. Personal interview on August 3 in Mexico City.

——— 2000. Personal interview on August 29 in Mexico City.

——— 2010. Personal interview on March 29 by phone.

Mackenzie, David. 2001. Executive Director, Steelworkers Humanity Fund, and former Organizing Coordinator, United Steelworkers of America, Canadian National Office. Personal interview on February 16 in Toronto.

Marino Roche, Rafael. 2000. Political Action Commission and National Executive Committee, STRM. Personal interview on May 15 in Mexico City.

Martin, Richard. 2001. President, Inter-American Regional Workers' Organization, and Former Secretary-Treasurer, CLC. Personal interview on February 26 in Ottawa.

Martínez González, Porfirio. 2000. Secretary of Finance, Partido de la Revolución Democrática (PRD), in Mexico City. Labor lawyer and Executive Committee member, PRD, in Mexico City. Personal interview on March 13 in Mexico City.

Martínez Orozco, Benedicto. 1999. National Coordinator, FAT. Secretary General, STIMAHCS. Vice President, Communications, UNT. Personal interview on July 27 in Mexico City.
    2010. Personal interview on April 18 by phone.
McLuckie, Fred. 2001. Legislative Coordinator, IBT. Personal interview on January 26 in Washington, DC.
Medina Torres, Salvador. 2000. Undersecretary of Relations and National Committee, CTM. Personal interview on May 15 in Mexico City.
Mejía, Remedios. 2000. Imprenta Morales, FAT. Personal interview on June 24 in Mexico City.
Melançon, Claude. 2001. Canadian Association of Labor Lawyers. Melançon, Marceau, Grenier & Sciortino. Personal interview on February 3 in Toronto.
Monguia Sánchez, Ignacio. 2000. President of the Strike Committee, Imprenta Morales, FAT. Personal interview on June 24 in Mexico City.
Monroy Mejía, Lázaro. 2000. Secretary General, Sección 170 del Sindicato Nacional Textil Fabrica Texlamex, CTM. Personal interview on June 7 in Mexico City.
Moore, Lou. 2001. Former National Director for International Affairs, CWA. Personal interview on January 13 in Washington, DC.
Mora Amador, Alejandro. 2000. Education Coordinator, CTM. Personal interview on August 17 in Mexico City.
Moreno Martínez, Oscar. 2000. Director of International Affairs, Cámara Nacional del Autotransporte de Carga. Personal interview on August 28 in Mexico City.
Muñoz Lopez, José Refugio. 2000. Director General, Cámara Nacional del Autotransporte de Carga. Personal interview on August 28 in Mexico City.
Narcia Tovar, Eugenio. 2000. Labor lawyer and member of ANAD. Personal interview on April 4 in Mexico City.
Newman, Keith. 2001. Research Director, CEP. Personal interview on March 2 in Ottawa.
Nicolá de Jesús, Teresce. 2000. Strike Committee, Imprenta Morales, FAT. Personal interview on June 24 in Mexico City.
Ortíz, Julio. 1999. Representative of Centro de Reflexion y Acción Laboral. Personal interview in Mexico City.
Pérez Arce Ibarra, Francisco. 1999. Director, Subsecretaría de Trabajo y Previsión Social, Dirección Ejecutiva de Estudios del Trabajo Ciudad de México. Personal interview on July 30 in Mexico City.
Phillips, Carol. 2001. Director of International Department, and Director, Social Justice Fund, CAW. Personal interview on February 12 in Toronto.
Pomeroy, Fred. 2001. Former President, CEP. Personal interview on February 28 in Ottawa.
Quezada, Adrián. 2000. Secretary General, Imprenta Morales, FAT. Personal interview on June 24 in Mexico City.
Quiroz Soriano, Alejandro. 1999. Secretary of Exterior Relations, SEMARNAP. Founding member, RMALC. Personal interview on June 23 in Mexico City.
    2000. Personal interview on July 6 in Mexico City.

Ramírez Fuentes, Agustín. 1999. Secretary General of Sindicato de Trabajadores de la Universidad Nacional Autónoma de México (STUNAM) and UNT. Personal interview on August 3 in Mexico City.

Ramírez Gamero, José. 2000. Secretary General, Sindicato de Trabajadores de la Industria del Auto-Transporte, Similares y Conexos de la República Mexicana and Comité Nacional, CTM. Personal interview on August 23 in Mexico City.

Ríos, María Estela. 1999. Former President of ANAD. Personal interview on July 13 in Mexico City.

Ritchie, John. 2000. Labor Information Officer, U.S. Embassy. Personal interview on May 2 in Mexico City.

Ritchie, Laurell. 2001. Work Organization and Training Department, CAW. Personal interview on Feburary 12 in Toronto.

Rivera, Francisco. 2000. Asesor, General Motors plant. Interviewed by research assistant in July in Mexico.

Rodríguez Salazar, José Luis. 2000. Secretary General, SITIAVW. Personal interview on June 23 in Puebla, Mexico.

Rosenfeld, Herman. 2001. National Representative, Education and International Affairs, CAW. Personal interview on February 12 in Toronto.

Rowlinson, Mark. 2001. Counsel, United Steelworkers of America, Canadian National Office. Personal interview on February 15 in Toronto.

Rubio González, Oscar. 2000. Labor lawyer and member of ANAD. Personal interview on May 3 in Mexico City.

Ruiz Rubio, Ruben. 2000. FAT organizer and former Itapsa worker and organizer. Personal interview on April 13 in Mexico City.

Ruiz Vázquez, Miguel. 2000. Ford, Cuautitlán Delegado Departamental. Interviewed by research assistant on July 26 in Mexico.

Salvat Moya, Agustín. 2000. Secretaría de Organización y Propaganda, Sindicato de Nissan, Mexicano, planta Aguascalientes. Interviewed by research assistant in Mexico on July 28.

Sánchez, Victor M. 2000. Asesor, Secretarios General y Exterior de SME. Personal interview on June 14 in Mexico City.

Sánchez Mondragón, Mario Alberto. 2000. Secretary General, Sindicato Nacional "Francisco Villa" de la Industria Textil y de la Confección Similares y Conexos de La R.M., CTM. Personal interview on July 7 in Mexico City.

Sandoval, Juan Manuel. 2000. Coordinador General Seminario Permanente de Estudios Chicanos y de Frontera DEAS-INAH, and RMALC. Personal interview on May 9 in Mexico City.

Schenk, Chris. 2001. Research Director, Ontario Federation of Labour (CLC). Personal interview on February 13 in Toronto.

Sepúlveda Nuñez, Alicia. 1999. Secretaria de Relaciones y Actas, STRM. Personal interview on June 24 in Mexico City.

2000a. Personal interviews on February 9 and 16 in Mexico City.

2000b. Personal interview on August 27 in Mexico City.

Servidores, Agustín. 2000. Auto union representative. Interviewed by research assistant in July in Mexico.

Sol Orea, Lauro Jonathan. 2000. Lawyer at Sol, Anguiano, y Asociados, Abogados. Member of ANAD. Personal interview on March 22 in Mexico City.

Solano Pérez, Feliciano. 2000. Asesor Sindical, BMW. Interviewed by research assistant on July 28 in Mexico.

Sosa Arreola, Juan José. 2000. Secretary General, Sindicato Nacional de Trabajadores de Ford Motor Company CTM, Comité Ejecutivo Nacional. Personal interview on August 24 in Mexico City.

Sweeney, John J. 2010. President Emeritus, AFL-CIO. Personal interview on April 30 in Cambridge, Massachusetts.

Téllez García, David. 2000. Secretary General, Asociaciones Sindicales Agustín L. Téllez (CROM). Personal interview on May 5 in Mexico City.

Tooms, Roberto. 1999. Representative of SEMARNAP. Personal interview on June 23 in Mexico City.

2000. Personal interview on April 5 in Mexico City.

Torres Arroyo, Eduardo. 1999. Director, Public Communication, STRM. Personal interview on July 12 in Mexico City.

Townsend, Chris. 2000. Political Action Director, UE. Personal interview on December 18 in Alexandria, VA.

Vázquez, Lorenzo. 2000. Representative of Nissan, Toluca. Interviewed by research assistant in July in Mexico.

Vega Nuñez, José Luis. 1999. President and Coordinador of Consejo Nacional de los Trabajadores. Personal interview on July 30 in Mexico City.

Vega Solano, Javier. 2000. Union delegate, Sindicato "Independencia" UNT. Personal interview on June 7 in Mexico City.

Velasco, Juan Carlos. 2000. Secretary of Transportation, CTM. Member of National Committee, CTM. Personal interview on August 30 in Mexico City.

Villalba Granados, Antonio. 2000a. Coordinator of International Relations, FAT. Personal interview on April 26 in Mexico City.

2000b. Personal interview on July 10 in Mexico City.

Villamar, Alejandro. 2000. Member of RMALC. Member of Mexican Congress. Personal interview February 29 in Mexico City.

Villamar, Vicente. 1999. Representative of Sindicato de Bancos. Personal interview on August 2 in Mexico City.

Wilson, Charity. 2001. Senior Policy Analyst, Public Policy Department, AFL-CIO. Personal interview on January 12 in Washington, DC.

Witt, Matt. 2001. Former Communications Director, IBT. Personal interview on January 17 in Washington, DC.

Yussuff, Hassan. 2001. Executive Vice President, CLC. Personal interview on February 28 in Ottawa.

Zarco, Salvador. 1999. Former Secretary General, Ferrocarriles Nacionales de México. Personal interview on August 4 in Mexico City.

Zelenko, Carin. 2001. Director, Office of Corporate and Strategic Initiatives, IBT. Personal interview on January 24 in Washington, DC.

Index

303